THE DARKNESS

ACCURSED VOLUME 2

WRITTEN BY:

PHIL HESTER

THE DARKNESS CREATED BY:
MARC SILVESTRI, GARTH ENNIS
AND DAVID WOHL

published by
Top Cow Productions, Inc.
Los Angeles

D0841289

THE DARKNESS
ACCURSED
VOLUME 2

written by: **Phil Hester**

"La Bruja En Las Paredes" volume 3 issue #7

lineart by: **Jorge Lucas**

colors by: **Lee Loughridge**

"Crooked part 1" volume 3 issue #8

lineart by: **Jorge Lucas**

colors by: **Lee Loughridge**

"Crooked part 2: The Road to Hell" volume 3 issue #9

lineart by: **Jorge Lucas**

colors by: **Lee Loughridge**

"Crooked part 3: Black Teeth" volume 3 iss

lineart by: **Jorge Lucas**

colors by: **Felix Serrano**

letters: **Troy Peteri**

Jackie's caption font by: **Dave Lanphear**

•

credits for *The Darkness* issue #75 on page 94

M MATURE AUDIENCE
GRAPHIC CONTENT
SOME MATERIAL MAY NOT
BE SUITABLE FOR CHILDREN

For Top Cow Productions, Inc.:
Marc Silvestri - Chief Executive Officer
Matt Hawkins - President and Chief Operating Officer
Filip Sablik - Publisher
Phil Smith - Managing Editor
Adrian Nicita - Webmaster
Bryan Rountree - Assistant to the Publisher
Rob Levin - Consulting Editor

for **image** comics
publisher:
Eric Stephenson

COMIC SHOP LOCATOR SERVICE
888-COMIC-BOOK

to find the comic shop
nearest you call:
1-888-COMICBOOK

Want more info? check out:
www.topcow.com and **www.topcowstore.com**
for news and exclusive Top Cow merchandise!

For this edition Cover art by:
Michael Broussard,
Steve Firchow

For this edition
Book Design and Layout by:
Phil Smith

The Darkness: Accursed volume 2 Trade Paperback
September 2009. FIRST PRINTING. ISBN: 978-1-60706-044-4
Published by Image Comics Inc. Office of Publication: 2134 Allston Way, Second Floor Berkeley,
CA 94704. $9.99 U.S.D. Originally published in single magazine form as The Darkness
volume 3 issues #7-10 and #75. © 2009 Top Cow Productions, Inc. All rights reserved. "The
Darkness,""Top Cow," the Top Cow logo and the Darkness logos are registered trademarks of
Top Cow Productions, Inc.. The likeness of all characters (human or otherwise) featured herein
are trademarks of Top Cow Productions, Inc. Image Comics and the Image Comics logo are
trademarks of Image Comics, Inc. The characters, events, and stories in this publication are
entirely fictional. Any resemblance to actual persons (living or dead), events, institutions, or
locales, without satiric intent, is coincidental. No portion of this publication may be reproduced
or transmitted, in any form or by any means, without the express written permission of Top Cow
Productions, Inc.

editor's note: Starting with *The Dark
volume 3 issue #11 *The Darkness* s
issues are numbered in a "Le
numbering system. The Legacy nu
denotes the total number of is
published regardless of volume num

TABLE OF CONTENTS

INTRODUCTION
BY: B. CLAY MOORE   PAGE   4

"LA BRUJA EN LAS PAREDES"   PAGE   7

"CROOKED"
PART 1   PAGE   29

"CROOKED"
PART 2: THE ROAD TO HELL   PAGE   51

"CROOKED"
PART 3: BLACK TEETH   PAGE   73

"ABSOLUTE DARKNESS"   PAGE   95

COVER GALLERY   PAGE   132

BONUS MATERIALS   PAGE   148

INTRODUCTION

While fully understanding what a terrific artist Phil Hester is, I've long whined to anyone who would listen that Phil is also one of the best writers working in comics today. That doesn't mean it didn't surprise me when I heard that Phil was signing on to handle a big, fat chunk of THE DARKNESS. If you know Phil, you know he's one of the most well-adjusted, decent guys in comics. I've seen Phil give detailed feedback to neophyte artists trying to find their way in the world, and I've seen Phil assist pals by suggesting the perfect entrée at fine restaurants (a running joke amongst Phil's friends is that his mutant superpower is the ability to remember exactly what his dining companions ordered the last time they ate somewhere). So hearing he was leaping into a concept as inherently twisted and – well – dark as THE DARKNESS came as something of a surprise. And then I remembered that Phil is also the guy who jumped into comics with his own brilliantly dark creation, THE WRETCH. He's the guy who routinely works the black arts into his own creator-owned work, somehow inspired by the placid Iowa landscape that surrounds his house to lead readers down sinister walkways of the imagination. So, yeah. Forget Phil the good fella. Phil the writer was actually a brilliant choice to shepherd THE DARKNESS into new arenas of sin and horror. And kudos to Top Cow for having the balls to lock him up for a nice, long run. It's rare to see a writer afforded the time to really develop an existing character, and so far with what Phil's done on this book, it's clear that the Cow made the correct decision in handing him the well-worn keys. They've also paired him with a couple of up and coming stars in Michael Broussard and now Jorge Lucas, and it's a testament to the power of Phil's vision that these two guys have turned out some of their best work to date on THE DARKNESS.

With his first major arc, Phil went big, pushing Jackie Estacado, our compelling yet severely flawed protagonist, into the seat of a Central

This volume finds Jackie struggling to stay ahead of his many demons, his power diminished, his future in question. And then Phil plunges Jackie into a gothic road movie from hell. As a warm-up, we meet a pair of witches who don't quite understand what they've bargained for in Jackie. Before too long Aphrodite IV shows up on a pig farm as Jackie attempts to gun down an entire street gang. And then, you know…stuff gets really weird. And also really interesting. Phil takes the old tropes: deals with the devil, the risk of eternal damnation, and spins them on their head, finding inventive and unexpected ways to challenge both Jackie and the reader. It's frightening stuff. Violent, dark stuff. But it's also very smart stuff. And the whole thing culminates in grand fashion, as Lucas shares the stage with a bevy of the best artists in comics in a tale of Jackie Estacado's personal apocalypse.

I honestly think, when all is said and done, that Phil Hester's run on THE DARKNESS will go down as one of those seminal chunks of comic book history. Once of those moments when the right creator found new corners of an existing world to explore, and helped breathe fantastic new life into a character we already thought we knew.

So, yeah. Turns out Phil's your guy for friendly career advice, impeccable dinner recommendations…and gut-wrenching horror. Dig in.

--B. Clay Moore
March 2009

B. Clay Moore is the writer and co-creator of *Hawaiian Dick*, *Battle Hymn*, *The Expatriate*, and *The Leading Man*. He has also written for numerous comic publishers including Marvel Comics, DC Comics, and Image Comics.

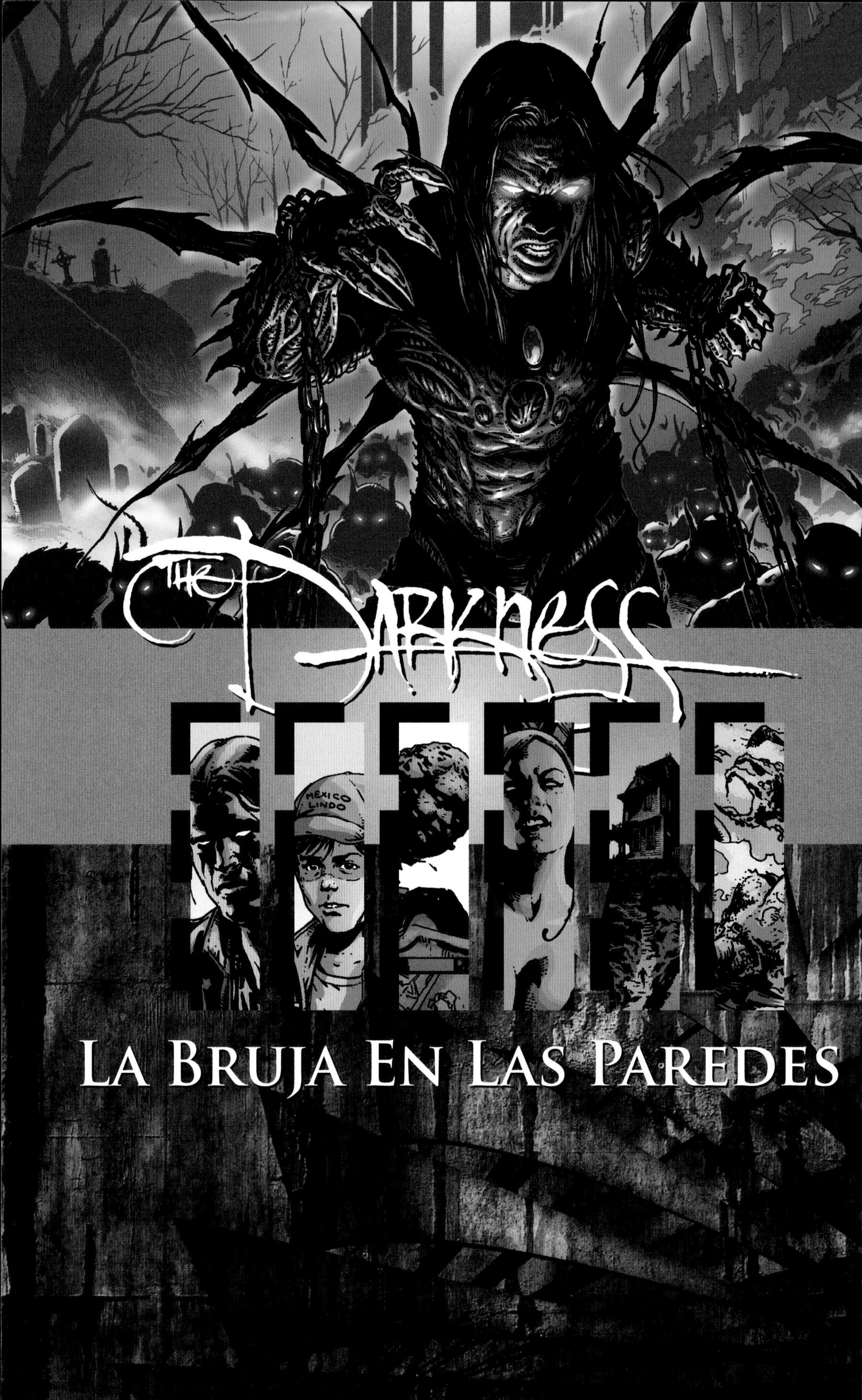
The Darkness®
MEXICO
LINDO

La Bruja En Las Paredes

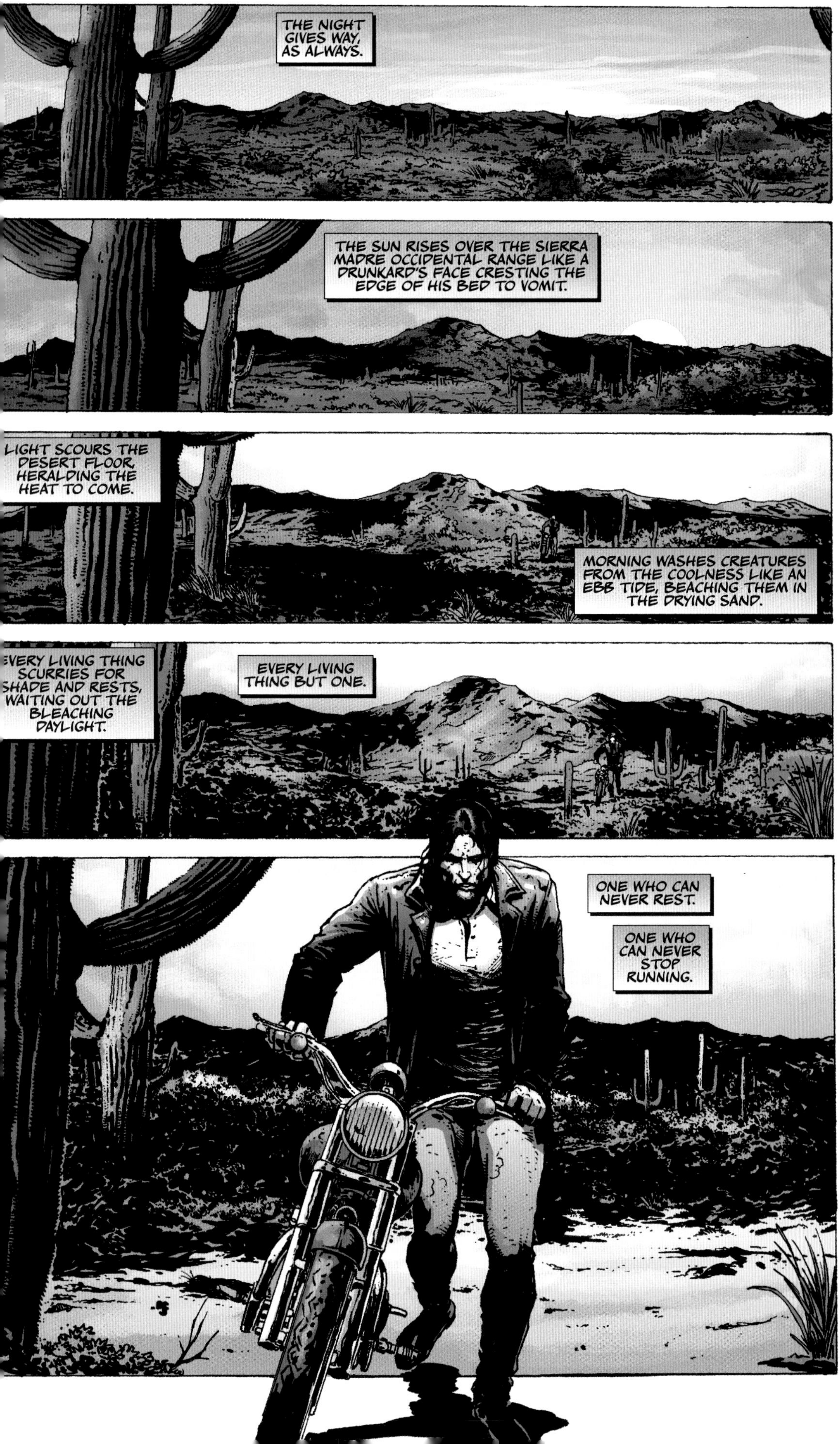
THE NIGHT GIVES WAY, AS ALWAYS.
THE SUN RISES OVER THE SIERRA MADRE OCCIDENTAL RANGE LIKE A DRUNKARD'S FACE CRESTING THE EDGE OF HIS BED TO VOMIT.
LIGHT SCOURS THE DESERT FLOOR, HERALDING THE HEAT TO COME.
MORNING WASHES CREATURES FROM THE COOLNESS LIKE AN EBB TIDE, BEACHING THEM IN THE DRYING SAND.
EVERY LIVING THING SCURRIES FOR SHADE AND RESTS, WAITING OUT THE BLEACHING DAYLIGHT.
EVERY LIVING THING BUT ONE.
ONE WHO CAN NEVER REST.
ONE WHO CAN NEVER STOP RUNNING.

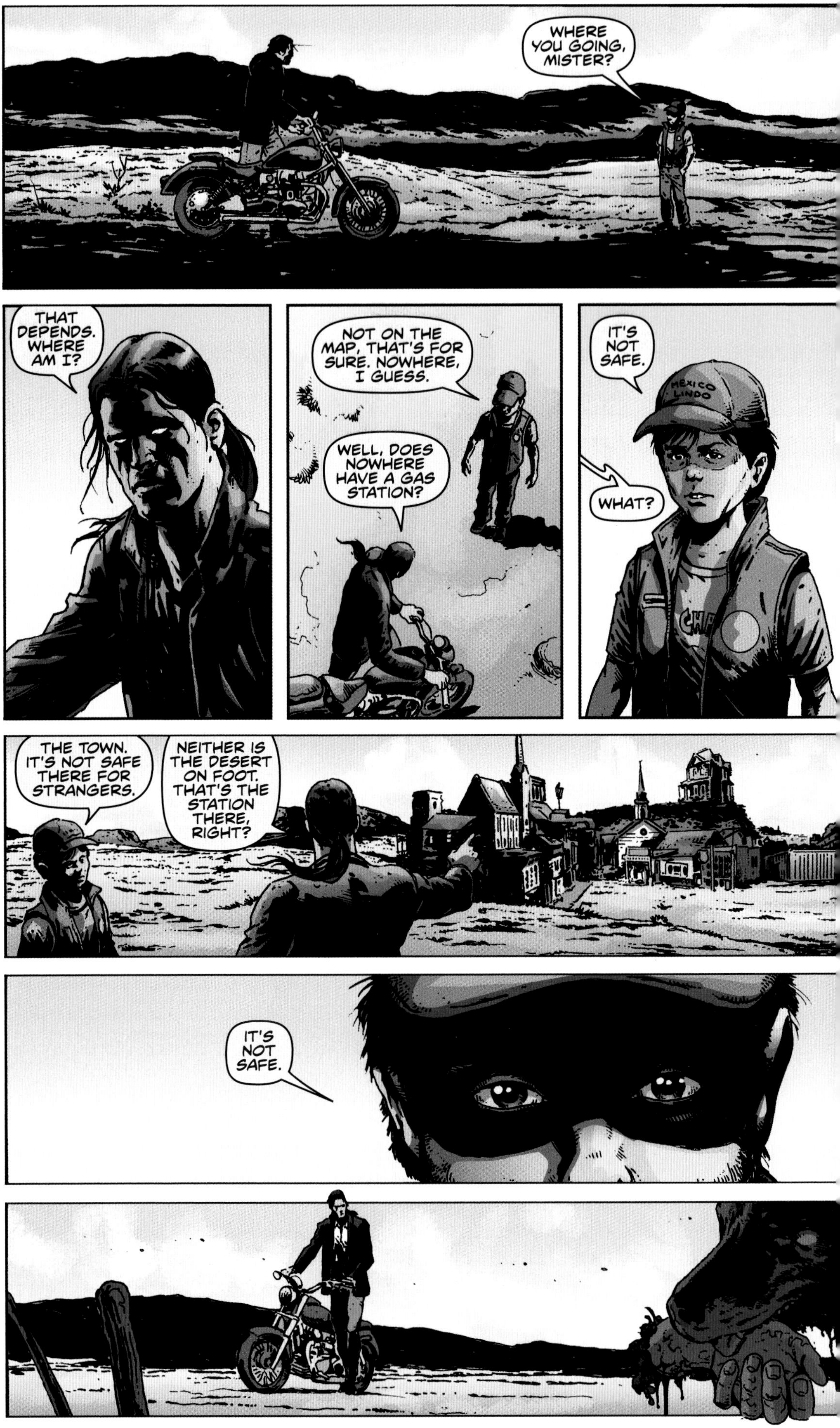
WHERE YOU GOING, MISTER?
THAT DEPENDS. WHERE AM I?
NOT ON THE MAP, THAT'S FOR SURE. NOWHERE, I GUESS.
WELL, DOES NOWHERE HAVE A GAS STATION?
IT'S NOT SAFE.
MEXICO LINDO
WHAT?
THE TOWN. IT'S NOT SAFE THERE FOR STRANGERS.
NEITHER IS THE DESERT ON FOOT. THAT'S THE STATION THERE, RIGHT?
IT'S NOT SAFE.

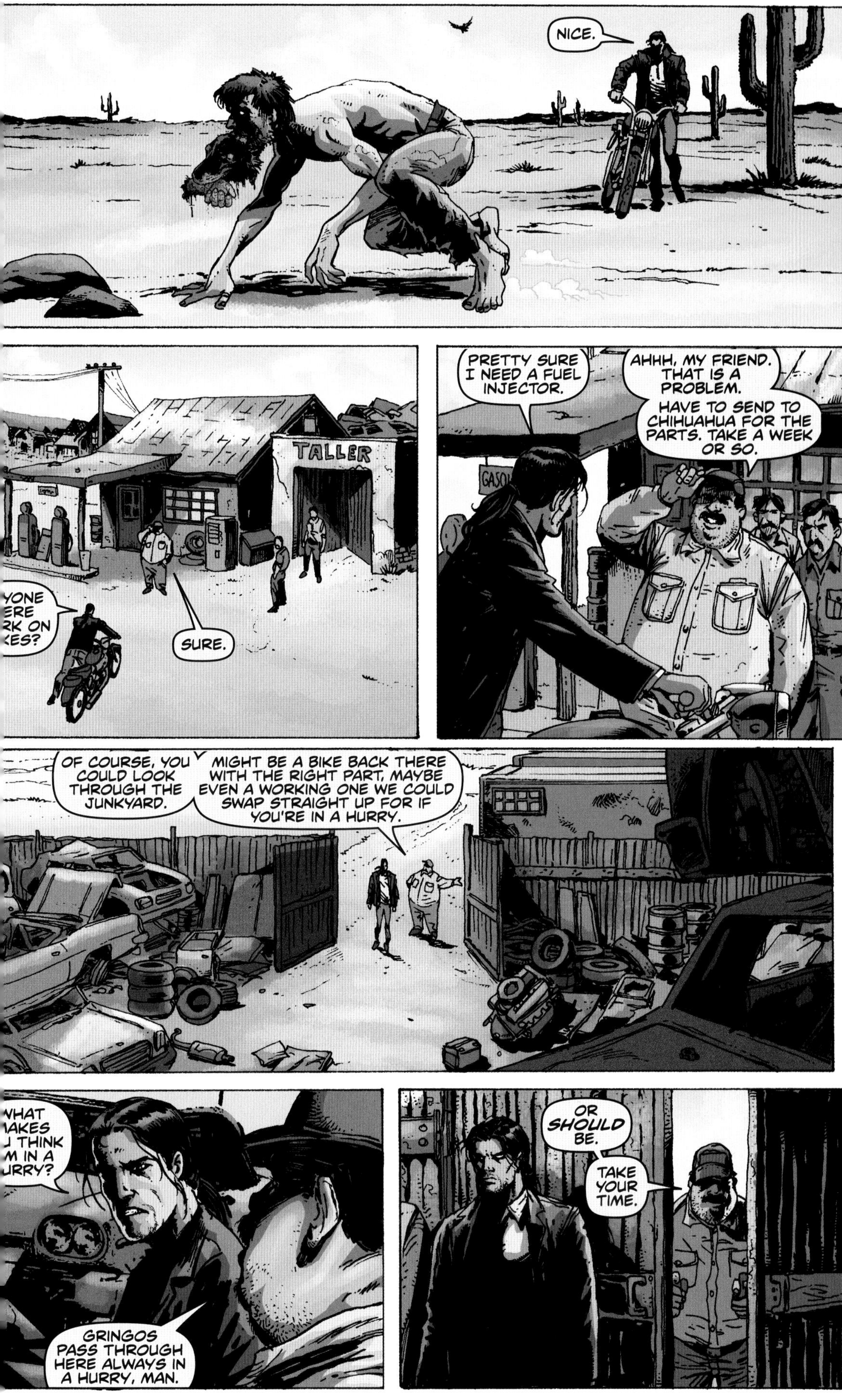
NICE.
TALLER
YONE
ERE
RK ON
KES?
SURE.
PRETTY SURE I NEED A FUEL INJECTOR.
AHHH, MY FRIEND. THAT IS A PROBLEM.
HAVE TO SEND TO CHIHUAHUA FOR THE PARTS. TAKE A WEEK OR SO.
GASO
OF COURSE, YOU COULD LOOK THROUGH THE JUNKYARD.
MIGHT BE A BIKE BACK THERE WITH THE RIGHT PART, MAYBE EVEN A WORKING ONE WE COULD SWAP STRAIGHT UP FOR IF YOU'RE IN A HURRY.
WHAT
AKES
J THINK
M IN A
URRY?
GRINGOS PASS THROUGH HERE ALWAYS IN A HURRY, MAN.
OR *SHOULD* BE.
TAKE YOUR TIME.

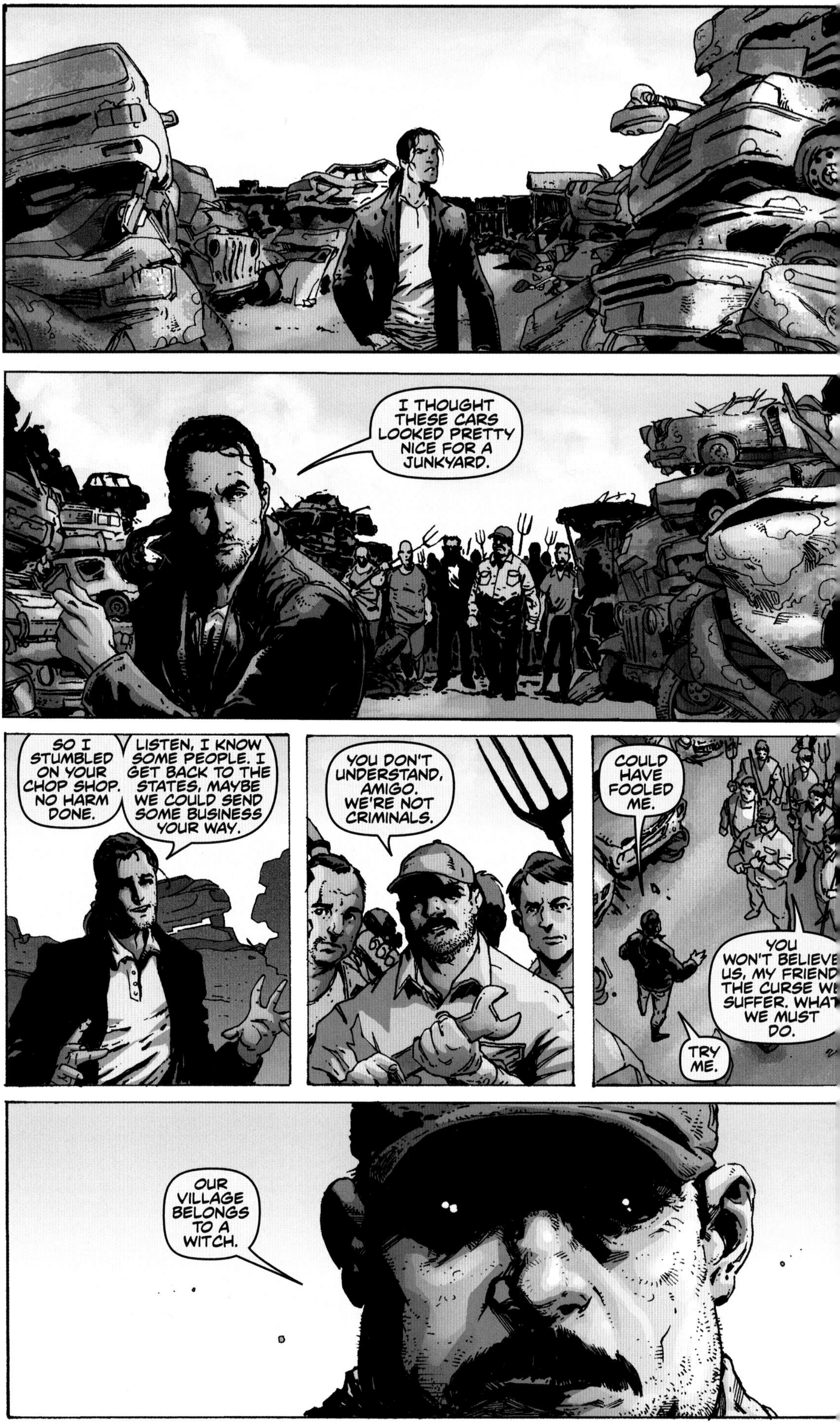
I THOUGHT THESE CARS LOOKED PRETTY NICE FOR A JUNKYARD.
SO I STUMBLED ON YOUR CHOP SHOP. NO HARM DONE.
LISTEN, I KNOW SOME PEOPLE. I GET BACK TO THE STATES, MAYBE WE COULD SEND SOME BUSINESS YOUR WAY.
YOU DON'T UNDERSTAND, AMIGO. WE'RE NOT CRIMINALS.
COULD HAVE FOOLED ME.
YOU WON'T BELIEVE US, MY FRIEND THE CURSE WE SUFFER. WHAT WE MUST DO.
TRY ME.
OUR VILLAGE BELONGS TO A WITCH.

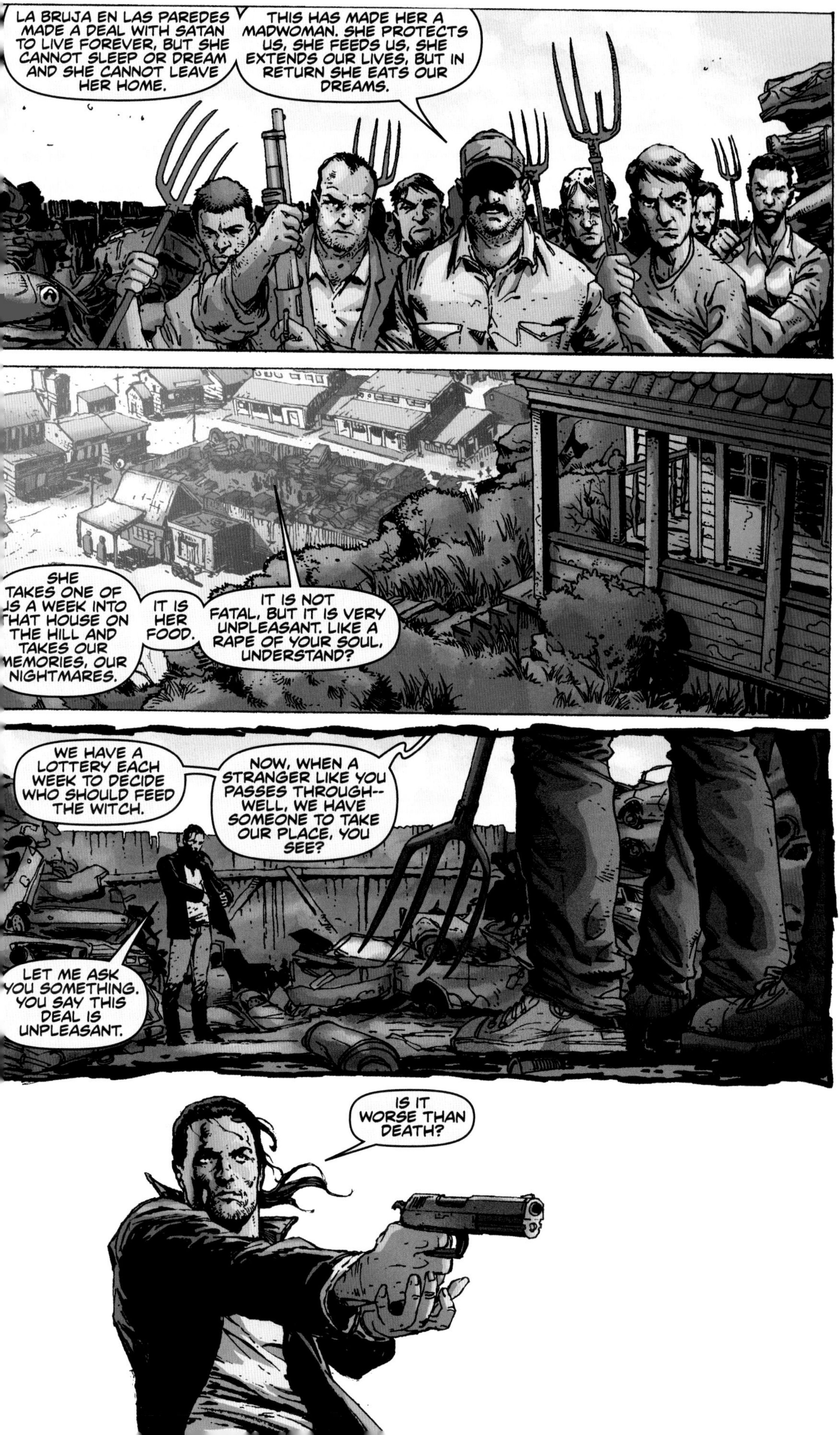
LA BRUJA EN LAS PAREDES MADE A DEAL WITH SATAN TO LIVE FOREVER, BUT SHE CANNOT SLEEP OR DREAM AND SHE CANNOT LEAVE HER HOME.
THIS HAS MADE HER A MADWOMAN. SHE PROTECTS US, SHE FEEDS US, SHE EXTENDS OUR LIVES, BUT IN RETURN SHE EATS OUR DREAMS.
SHE TAKES ONE OF US A WEEK INTO THAT HOUSE ON THE HILL AND TAKES OUR MEMORIES, OUR NIGHTMARES.
IT IS HER FOOD.
IT IS NOT FATAL, BUT IT IS VERY UNPLEASANT. LIKE A RAPE OF YOUR SOUL, UNDERSTAND?
WE HAVE A LOTTERY EACH WEEK TO DECIDE WHO SHOULD FEED THE WITCH.
NOW, WHEN A STRANGER LIKE YOU PASSES THROUGH-- WELL, WE HAVE SOMEONE TO TAKE OUR PLACE, YOU SEE?
LET ME ASK YOU SOMETHING. YOU SAY THIS DEAL IS UNPLEASANT.
IS IT WORSE THAN DEATH?

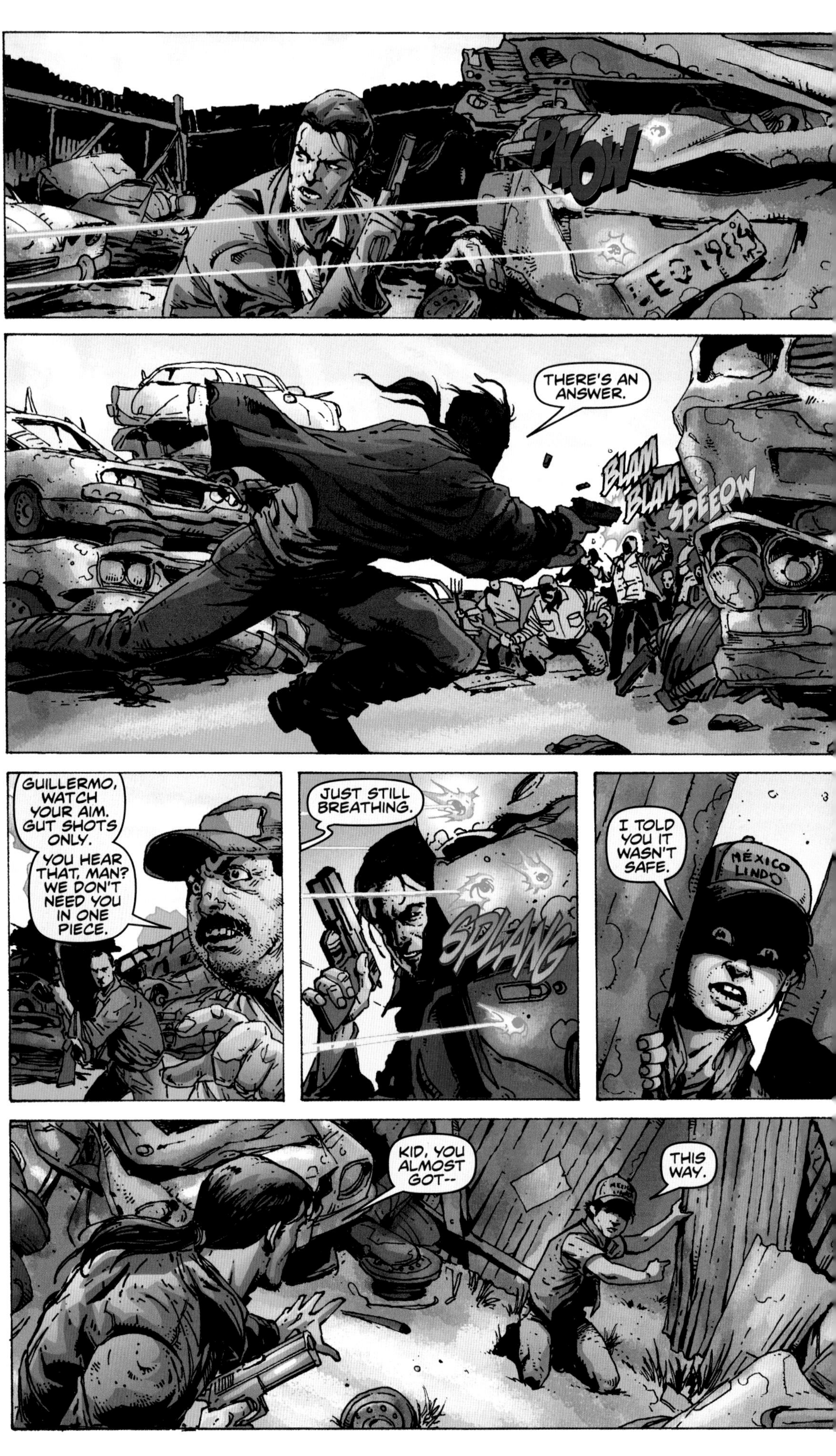

PKOW
THERE'S AN ANSWER.
BLAM
BLAM
SPEEOW
GUILLERMO, WATCH YOUR AIM. GUT SHOTS ONLY.
YOU HEAR THAT, MAN? WE DON'T NEED YOU IN ONE PIECE.
JUST STILL BREATHING.
SPLANG
I TOLD YOU IT WASN'T SAFE.
MÉXICO LINDO
KID, YOU ALMOST GOT--
THIS WAY.

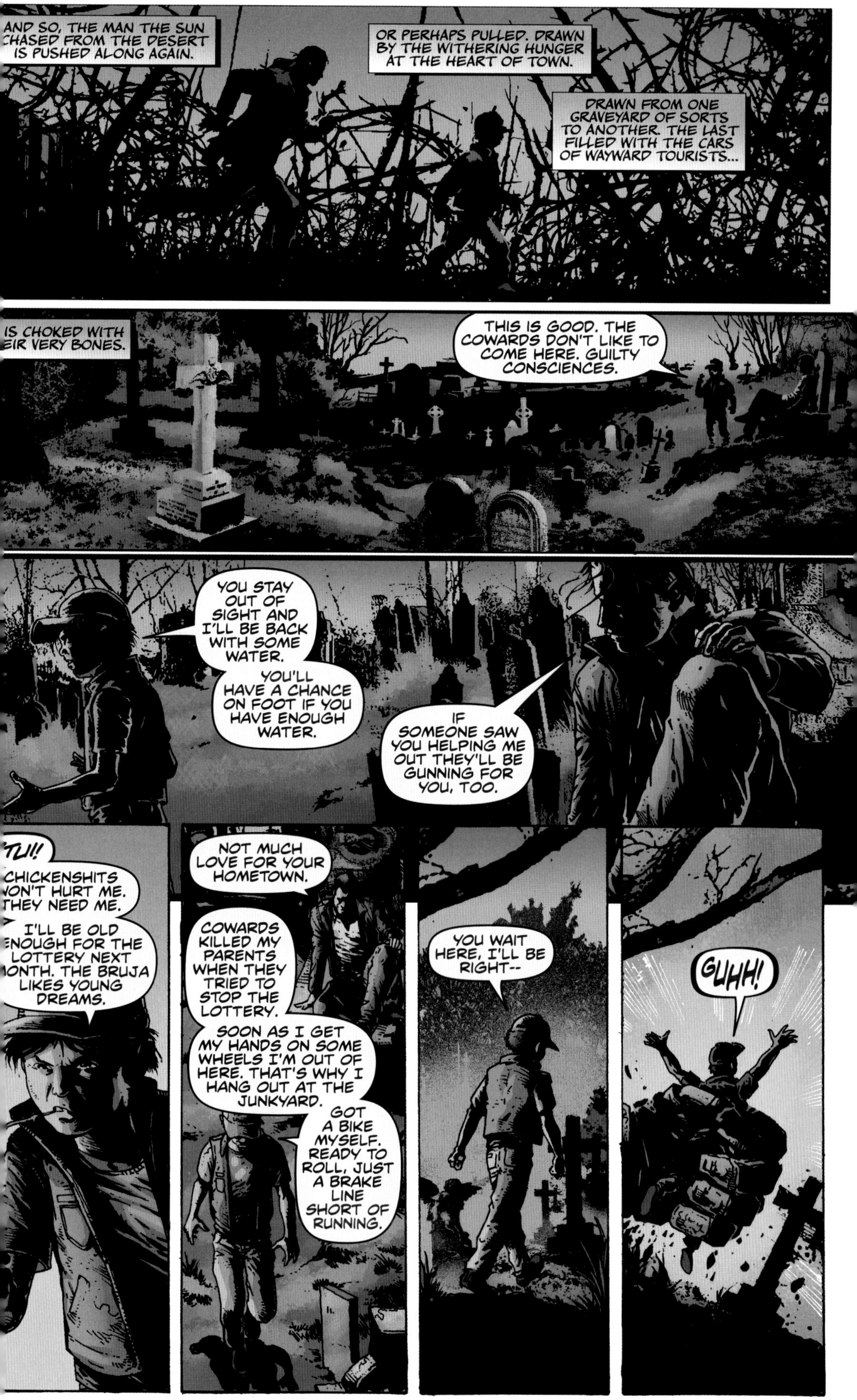
AND SO, THE MAN THE SUN CHASED FROM THE DESERT IS PUSHED ALONG AGAIN.
OR PERHAPS PULLED. DRAWN BY THE WITHERING HUNGER AT THE HEART OF TOWN.
DRAWN FROM ONE GRAVEYARD OF SORTS TO ANOTHER. THE LAST FILLED WITH THE CARS OF WAYWARD TOURISTS...
IS CHOKED WITH EIR VERY BONES.
THIS IS GOOD. THE COWARDS DON'T LIKE TO COME HERE. GUILTY CONSCIENCES.
YOU STAY OUT OF SIGHT AND I'LL BE BACK WITH SOME WATER.
YOU'LL HAVE A CHANCE ON FOOT IF YOU HAVE ENOUGH WATER.
IF SOMEONE SAW YOU HELPING ME OUT THEY'LL BE GUNNING FOR YOU, TOO.
TUI!!
CHICKENSHITS WON'T HURT ME. THEY NEED ME.
I'LL BE OLD ENOUGH FOR THE LOTTERY NEXT MONTH. THE BRUJA LIKES YOUNG DREAMS.
NOT MUCH LOVE FOR YOUR HOMETOWN.
COWARDS KILLED MY PARENTS WHEN THEY TRIED TO STOP THE LOTTERY.
SOON AS I GET MY HANDS ON SOME WHEELS I'M OUT OF HERE. THAT'S WHY I HANG OUT AT THE JUNKYARD.
GOT A BIKE MYSELF. READY TO ROLL, JUST A BRAKE LINE SHORT OF RUNNING.
YOU WAIT HERE, I'LL BE RIGHT--
GUHH!

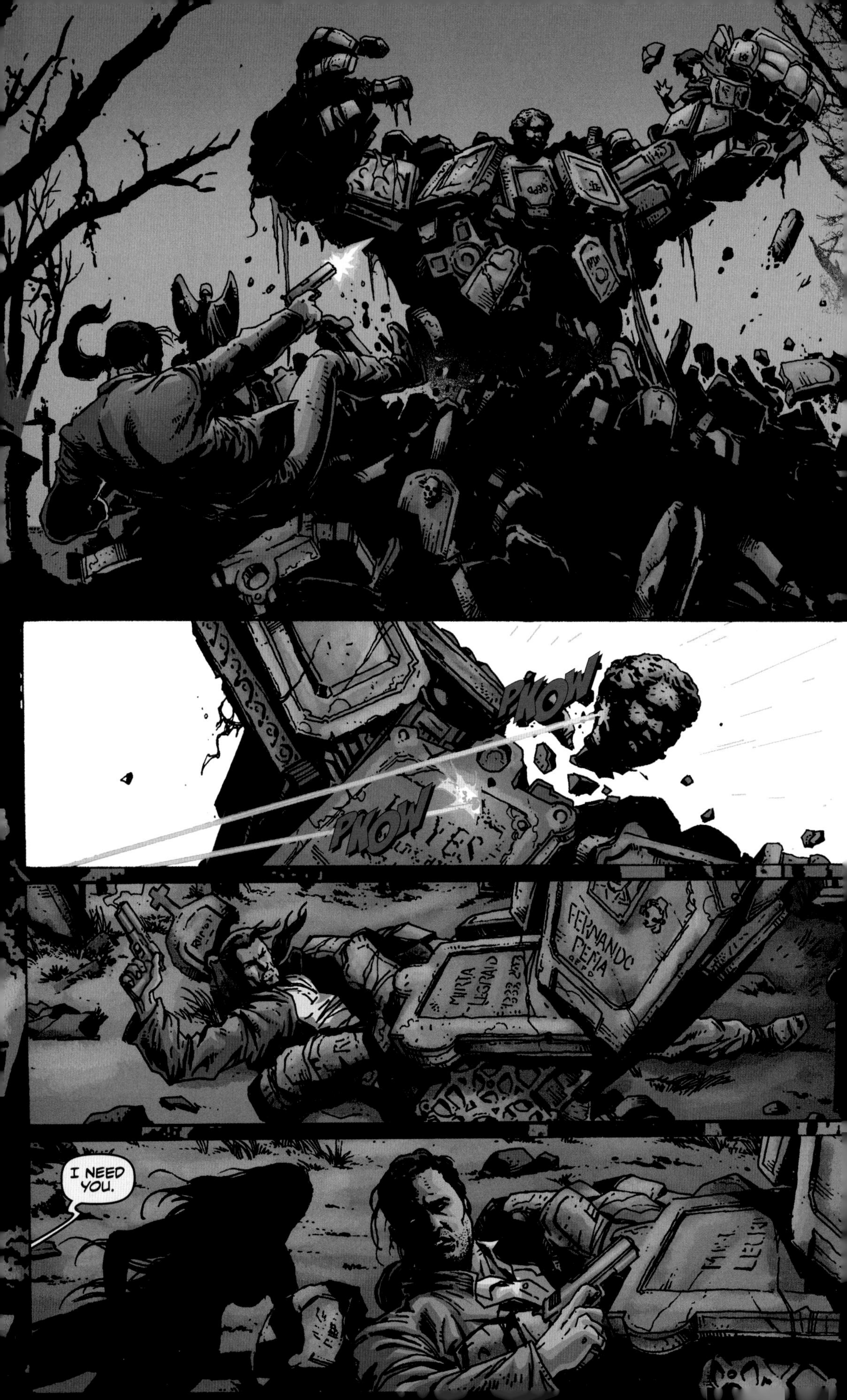

PKOW
PKOW
FERNANDO PEÑA
I NEED YOU.

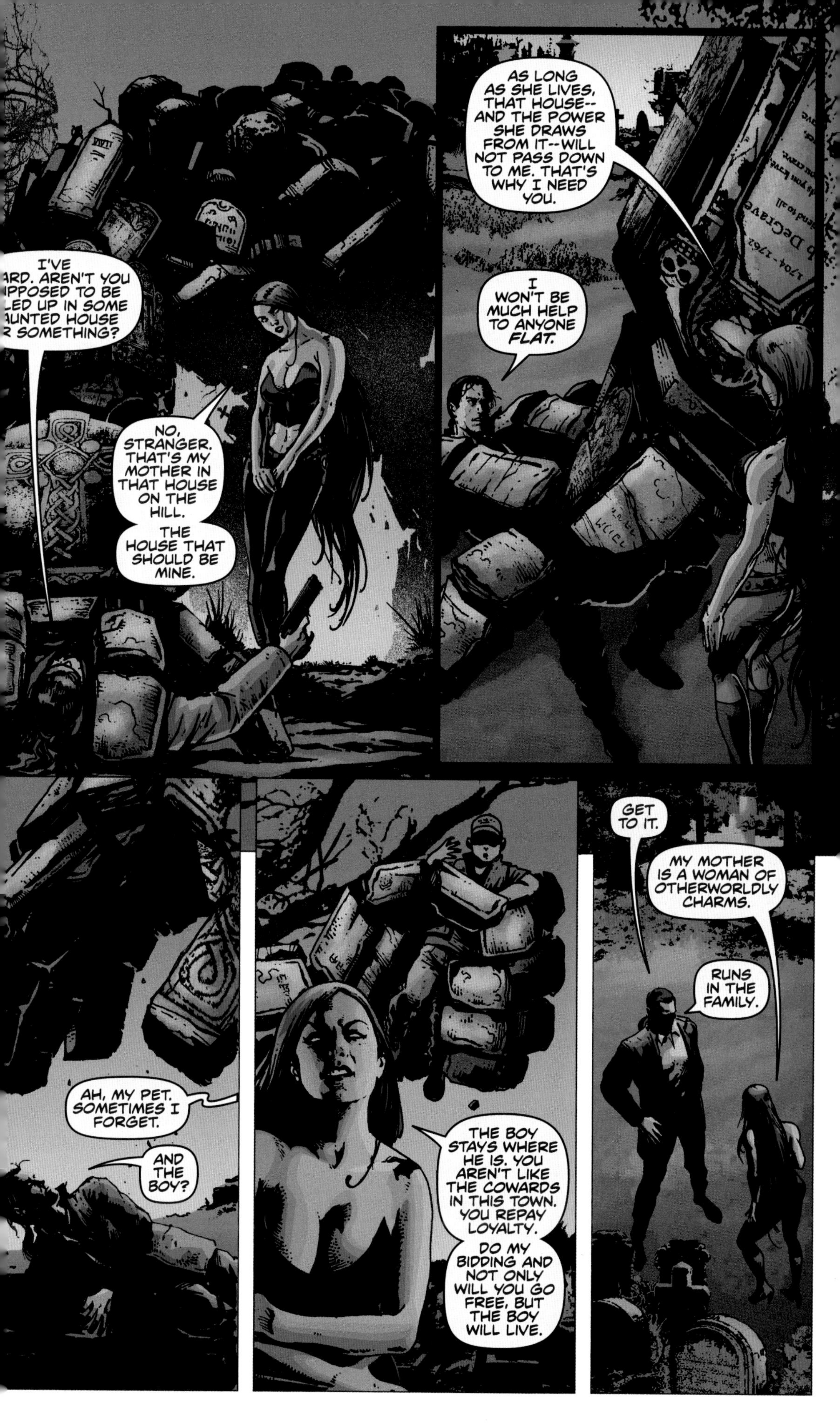

I'VE
ARD. AREN'T YOU
PPOSED TO BE
LED UP IN SOME
AUNTED HOUSE
R SOMETHING?
NO, STRANGER. THAT'S MY MOTHER IN THAT HOUSE ON THE HILL.
THE HOUSE THAT SHOULD BE MINE.
AS LONG AS SHE LIVES, THAT HOUSE-- AND THE POWER SHE DRAWS FROM IT--WILL NOT PASS DOWN TO ME. THAT'S WHY I NEED YOU.
I WON'T BE MUCH HELP TO ANYONE *FLAT.*
AH, MY PET. SOMETIMES I FORGET.
AND THE BOY?
THE BOY STAYS WHERE HE IS. YOU AREN'T LIKE THE COWARDS IN THIS TOWN. YOU REPAY LOYALTY.
DO MY BIDDING AND NOT ONLY WILL YOU GO FREE, BUT THE BOY WILL LIVE.
GET TO IT.
MY MOTHER IS A WOMAN OF OTHERWORLDLY CHARMS.
RUNS IN THE FAMILY.

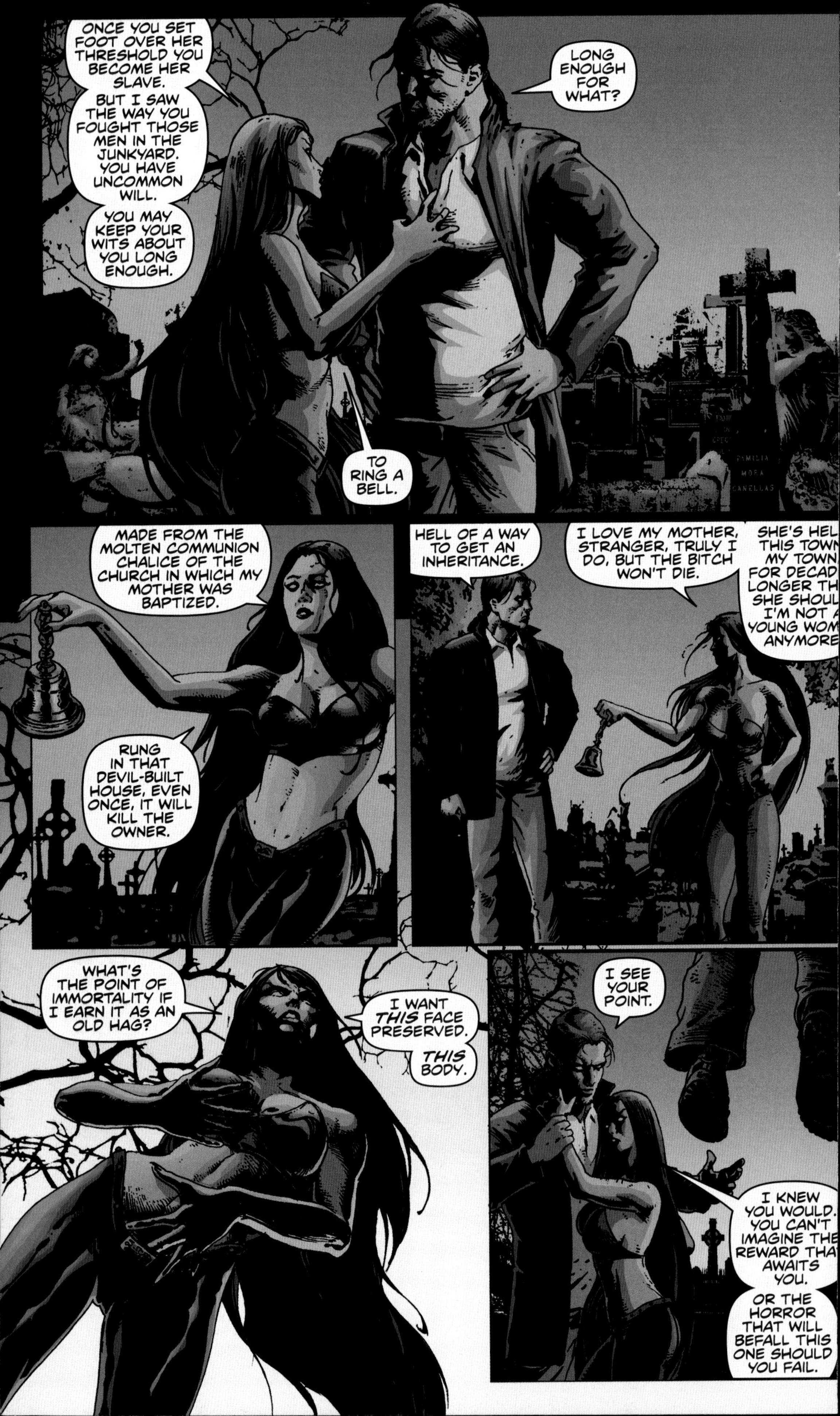
ONCE YOU SET FOOT OVER HER THRESHOLD YOU BECOME HER SLAVE.
BUT I SAW THE WAY YOU FOUGHT THOSE MEN IN THE JUNKYARD. YOU HAVE UNCOMMON WILL.
YOU MAY KEEP YOUR WITS ABOUT YOU LONG ENOUGH.
LONG ENOUGH FOR WHAT?
TO RING A BELL.
FAMILIA MORA CANELLAS
MADE FROM THE MOLTEN COMMUNION CHALICE OF THE CHURCH IN WHICH MY MOTHER WAS BAPTIZED.
RUNG IN THAT DEVIL-BUILT HOUSE, EVEN ONCE, IT WILL KILL THE OWNER.
HELL OF A WAY TO GET AN INHERITANCE.
I LOVE MY MOTHER, STRANGER, TRULY I DO, BUT THE BITCH WON'T DIE.
SHE'S HEL THIS TOWN MY TOWN FOR DECAD LONGER TH SHE SHOUL I'M NOT A YOUNG WOM ANYMORE
WHAT'S THE POINT OF IMMORTALITY IF I EARN IT AS AN OLD HAG?
I WANT *THIS* FACE PRESERVED.
THIS BODY.
I SEE YOUR POINT.
I KNEW YOU WOULD. YOU CAN'T IMAGINE THE REWARD THA AWAITS YOU.
OR THE HORROR THAT WILL BEFALL THIS ONE SHOULD YOU FAIL.

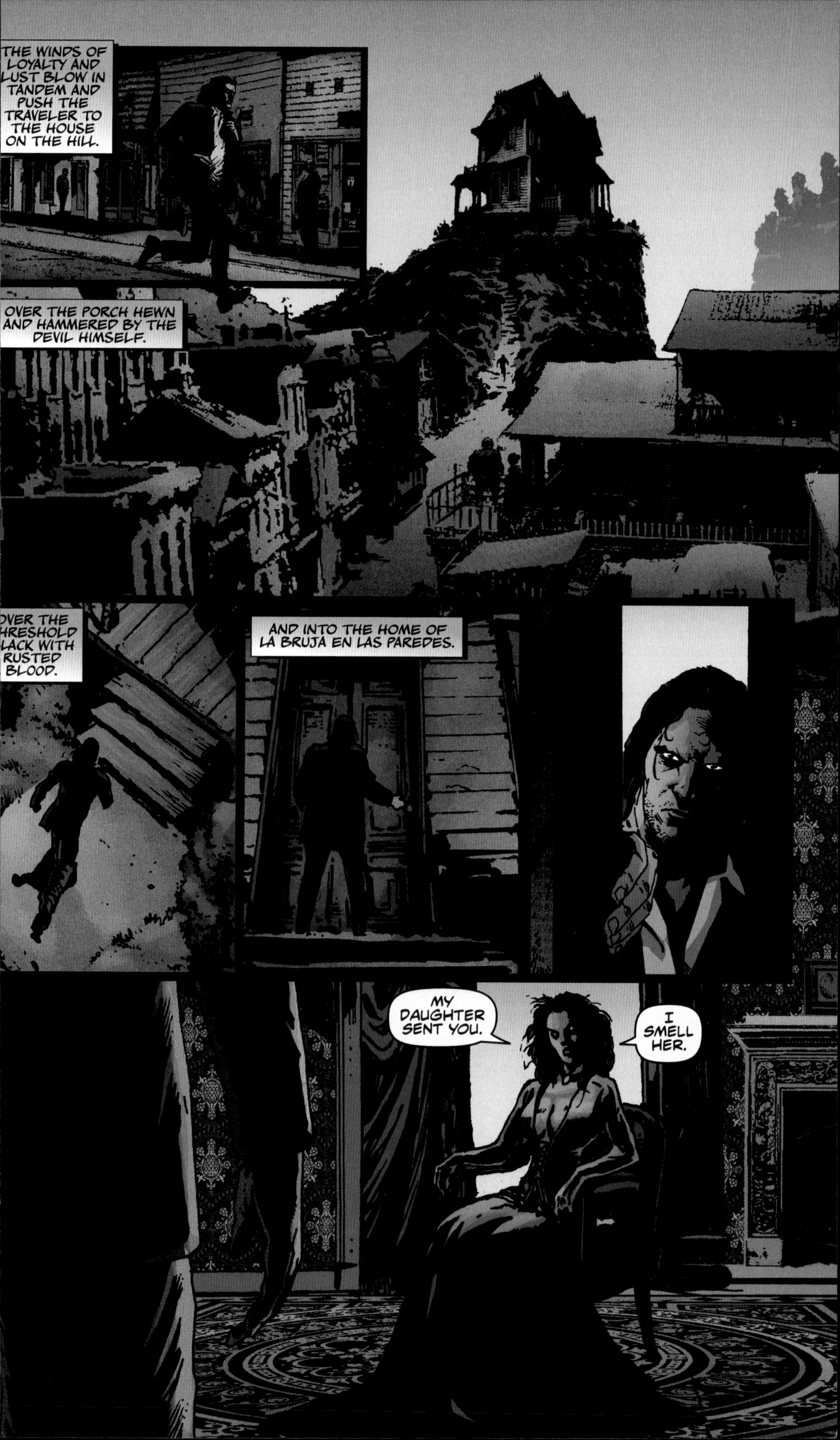
THE WINDS OF LOYALTY AND LUST BLOW IN TANDEM AND PUSH THE TRAVELER TO THE HOUSE ON THE HILL.
OVER THE PORCH HEWN AND HAMMERED BY THE DEVIL HIMSELF.
OVER THE THRESHOLD BLACK WITH RUSTED BLOOD.
AND INTO THE HOME OF LA BRUJA EN LAS PAREDES.
MY DAUGHTER SENT YOU.
I SMELL HER.

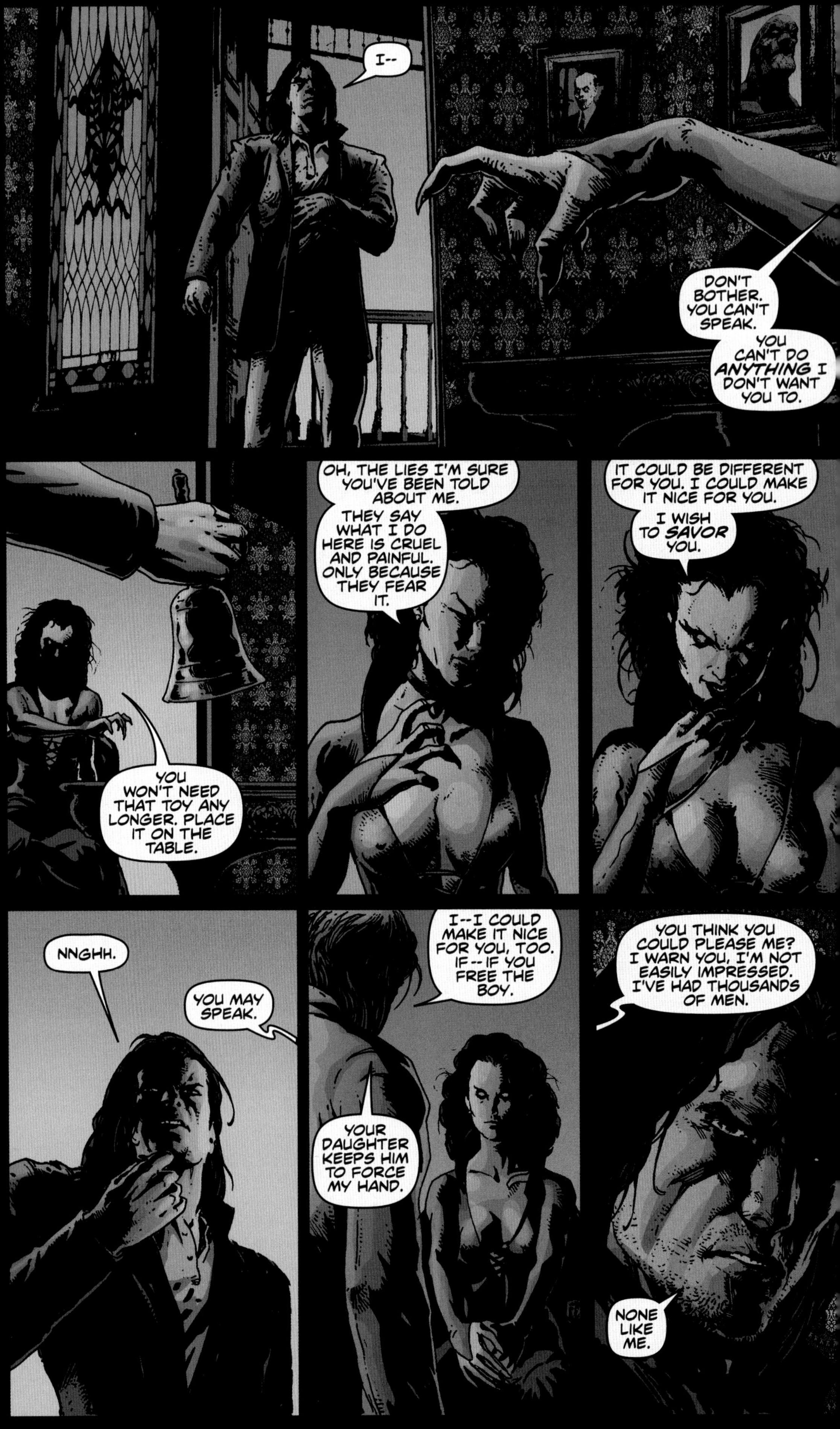
I--
DON'T BOTHER. YOU CAN'T SPEAK.
YOU CAN'T DO ANYTHING I DON'T WANT YOU TO.
YOU WON'T NEED THAT TOY ANY LONGER. PLACE IT ON THE TABLE.
OH, THE LIES I'M SURE YOU'VE BEEN TOLD ABOUT ME.
THEY SAY WHAT I DO HERE IS CRUEL AND PAINFUL. ONLY BECAUSE THEY FEAR IT.
IT COULD BE DIFFERENT FOR YOU. I COULD MAKE IT NICE FOR YOU.
I WISH TO SAVOR YOU.
NNGHH.
YOU MAY SPEAK.
I--I COULD MAKE IT NICE FOR YOU, TOO. IF--IF YOU FREE THE BOY.
YOUR DAUGHTER KEEPS HIM TO FORCE MY HAND.
YOU THINK YOU COULD PLEASE ME? I WARN YOU, I'M NOT EASILY IMPRESSED. I'VE HAD THOUSANDS OF MEN.
NONE LIKE ME.

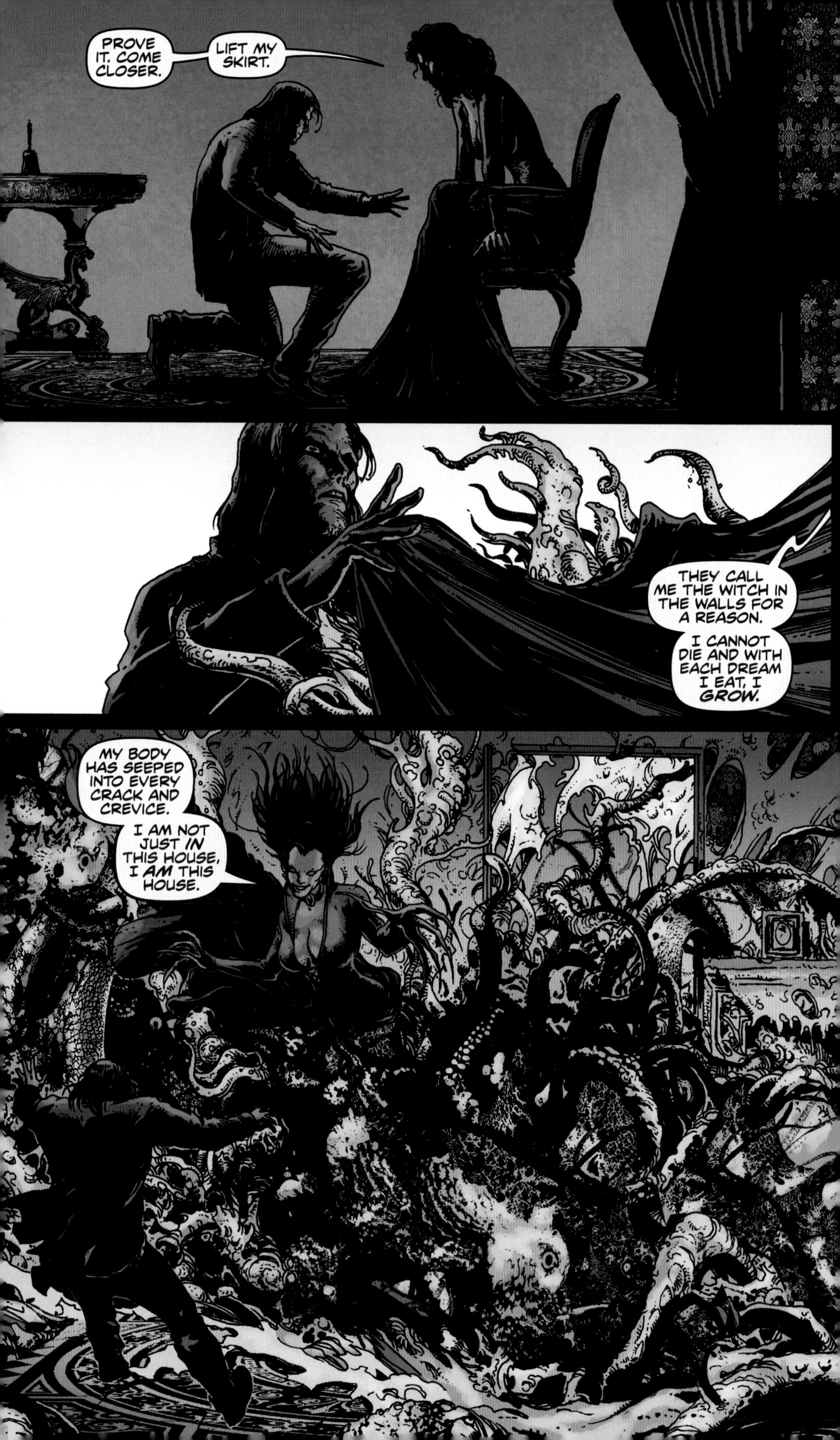
PROVE IT. COME CLOSER.
LIFT MY SKIRT.
THEY CALL ME THE WITCH IN THE WALLS FOR A REASON.
I CANNOT DIE AND WITH EACH DREAM I EAT, I GROW.
MY BODY HAS SEEPED INTO EVERY CRACK AND CREVICE.
I AM NOT JUST IN THIS HOUSE, I AM THIS HOUSE.

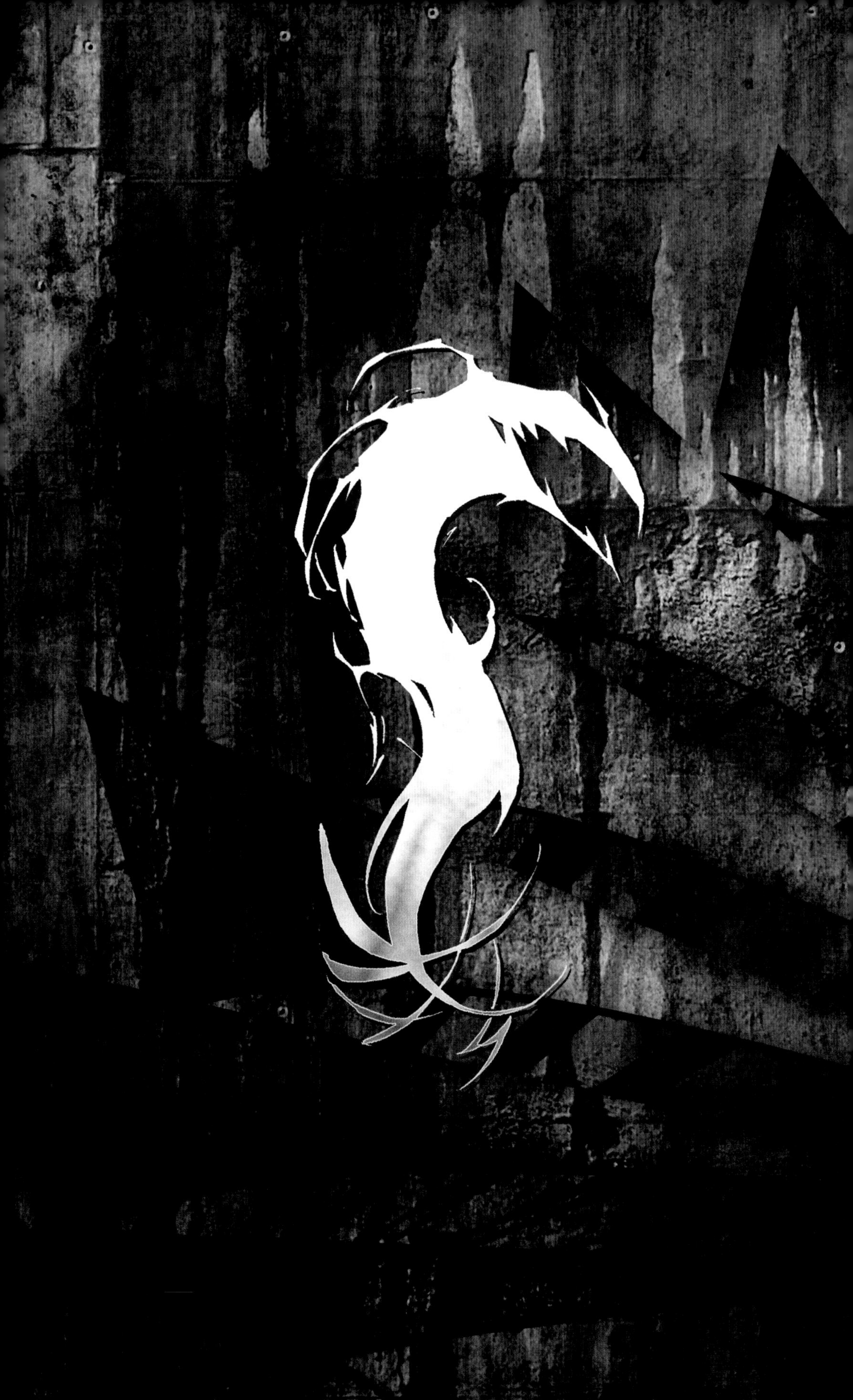

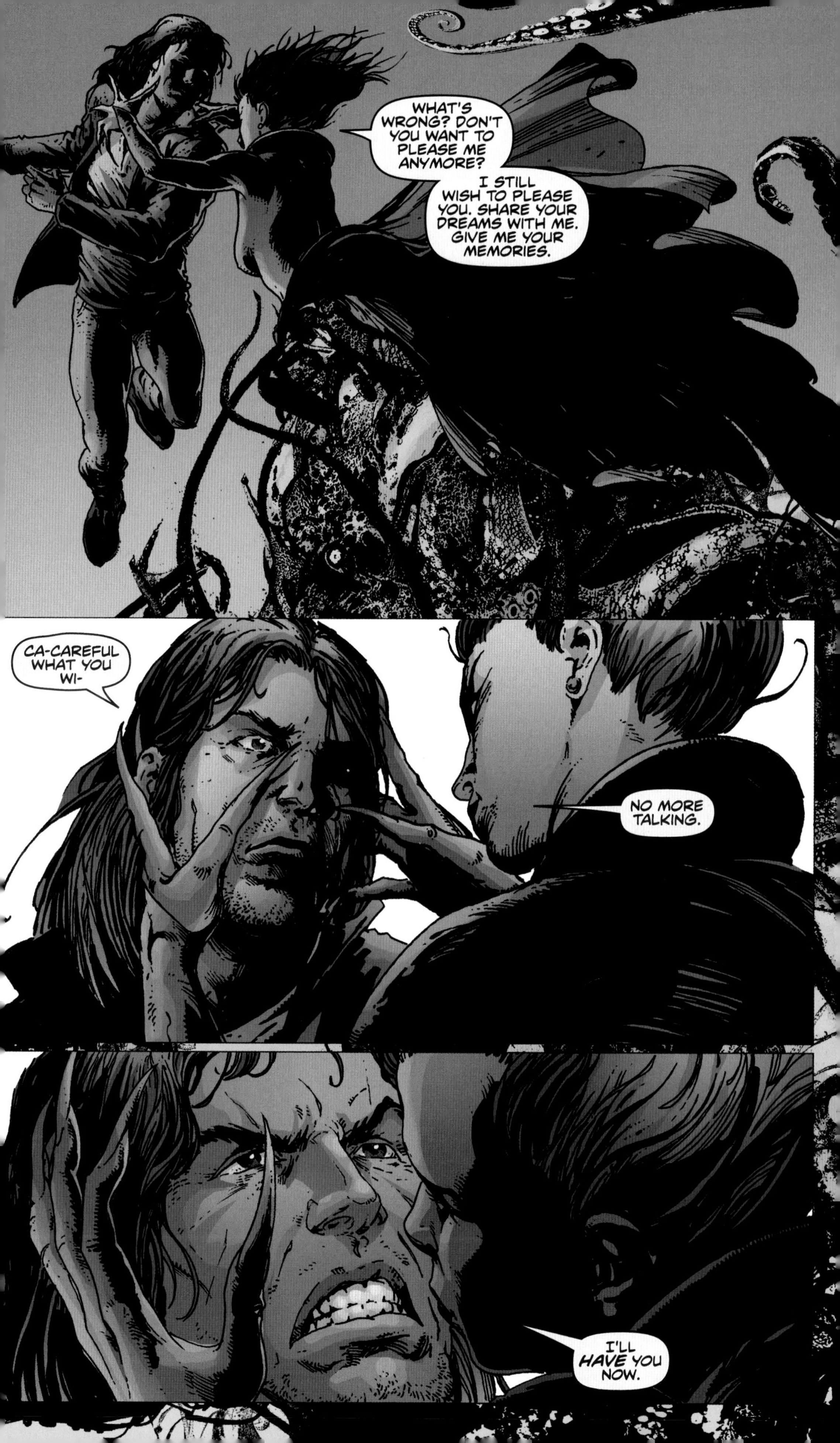
WHAT'S WRONG? DON'T YOU WANT TO PLEASE ME ANYMORE?
I STILL WISH TO PLEASE YOU. SHARE YOUR DREAMS WITH ME. GIVE ME YOUR MEMORIES.
CA-CAREFUL WHAT YOU WI-
NO MORE TALKING.
I'LL *HAVE* YOU NOW.

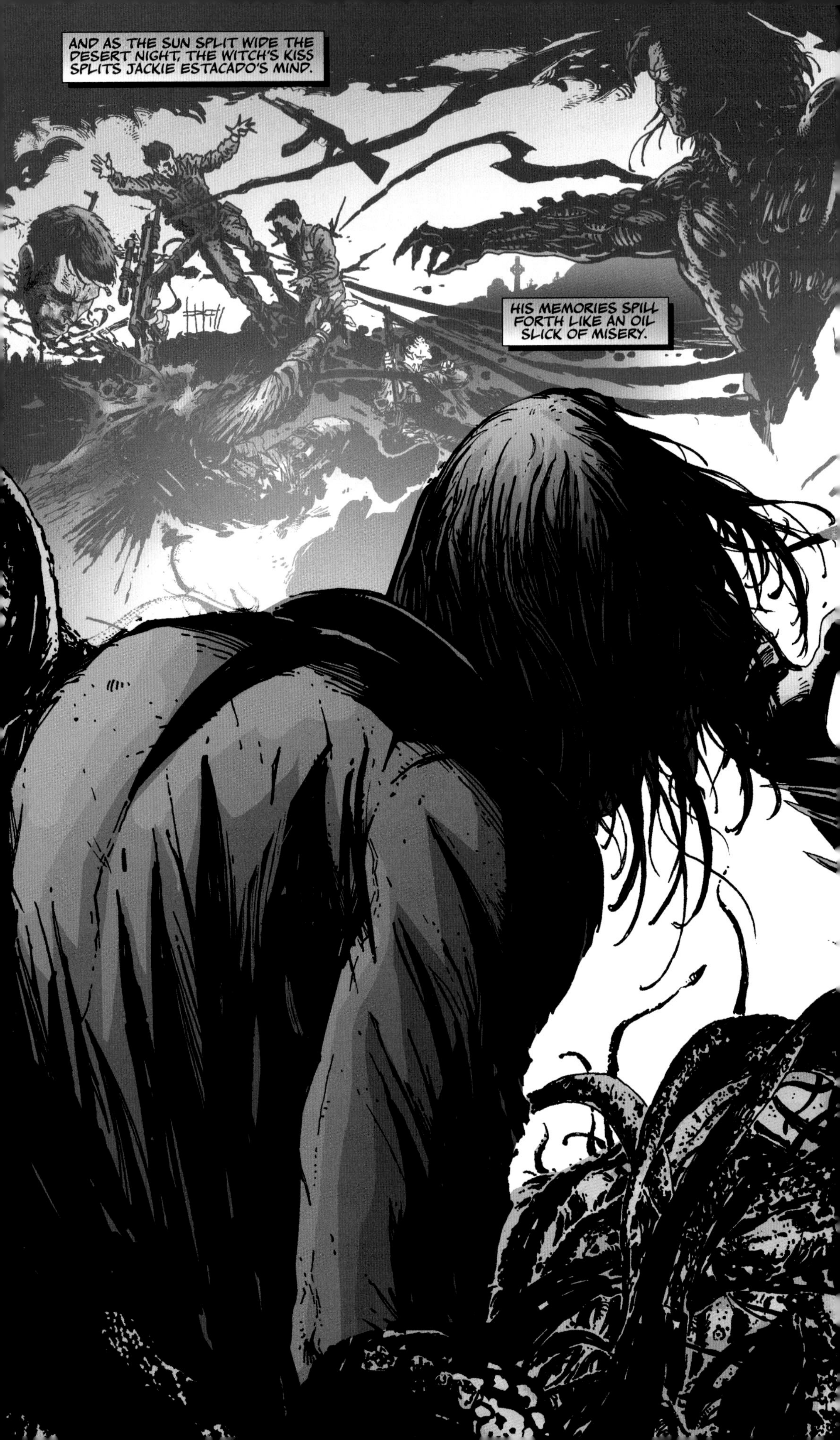
AND AS THE SUN SPLIT WIDE THE DESERT NIGHT, THE WITCH'S KISS SPLITS JACKIE ESTACADO'S MIND.
HIS MEMORIES SPILL FORTH LIKE AN OIL SLICK OF MISERY.

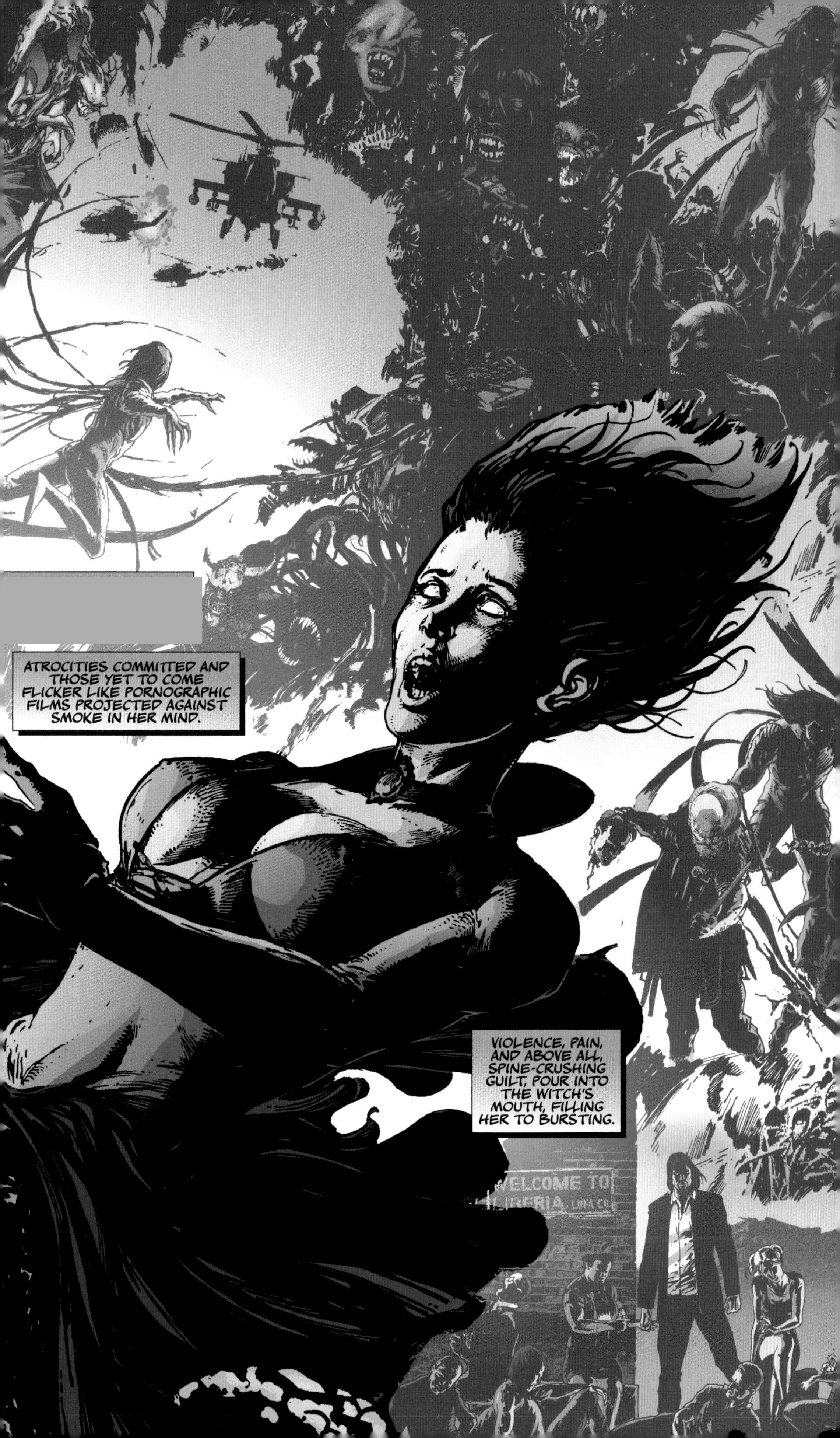
ATROCITIES COMMITTED AND THOSE YET TO COME FLICKER LIKE PORNOGRAPHIC FILMS PROJECTED AGAINST SMOKE IN HER MIND.
VIOLENCE, PAIN, AND ABOVE ALL, SPINE-CRUSHING GUILT, POUR INTO THE WITCH'S MOUTH, FILLING HER TO BURSTING.
WELCOME TO
LOFA CO.

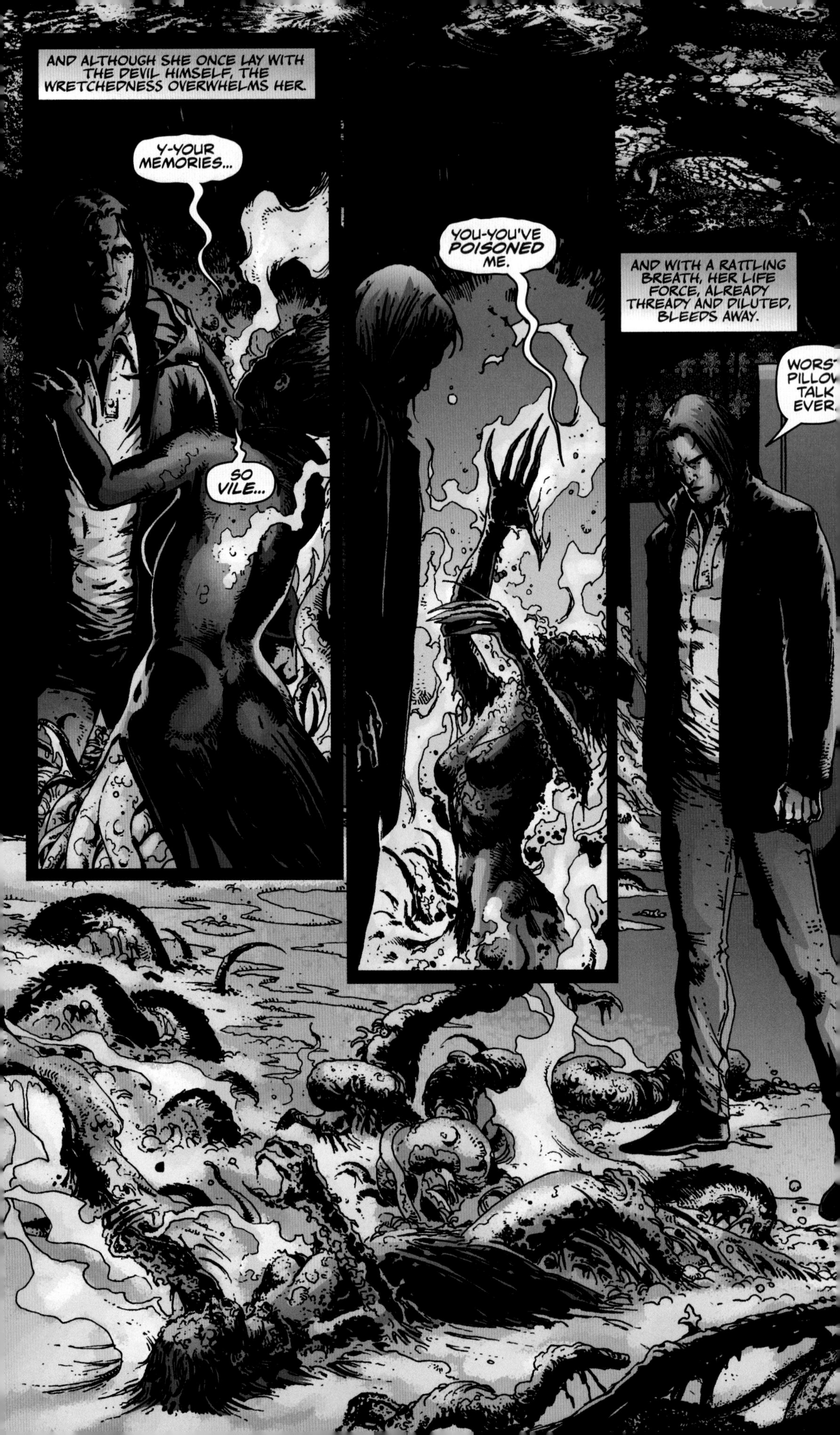
AND ALTHOUGH SHE ONCE LAY WITH THE DEVIL HIMSELF, THE WRETCHEDNESS OVERWHELMS HER.
Y-YOUR MEMORIES...
SO VILE...
YOU-YOU'VE POISONED ME.
AND WITH A RATTLING BREATH, HER LIFE FORCE, ALREADY THREADY AND DILUTED, BLEEDS AWAY.
WORST PILLOW TALK EVER.

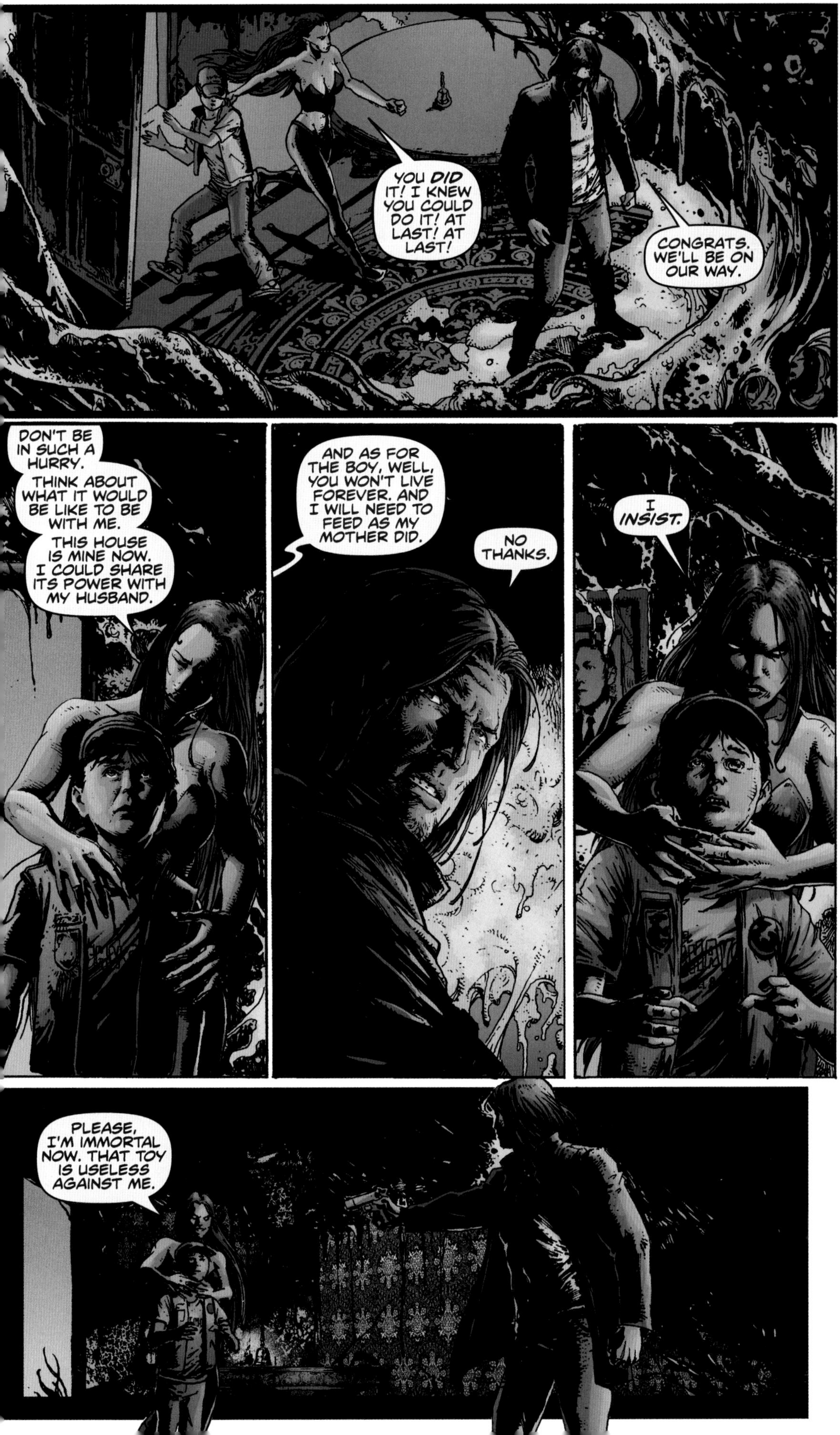
YOU *DID* IT! I KNEW YOU COULD DO IT! AT LAST! AT LAST!
CONGRATS. WE'LL BE ON OUR WAY.
DON'T BE IN SUCH A HURRY.
THINK ABOUT WHAT IT WOULD BE LIKE TO BE WITH ME.
THIS HOUSE IS MINE NOW. I COULD SHARE ITS POWER WITH MY HUSBAND.
AND AS FOR THE BOY, WELL, YOU WON'T LIVE FOREVER. AND I WILL NEED TO FEED AS MY MOTHER DID.
NO THANKS.
I *INSIST.*
PLEASE, I'M IMMORTAL NOW. THAT TOY IS USELESS AGAINST ME.

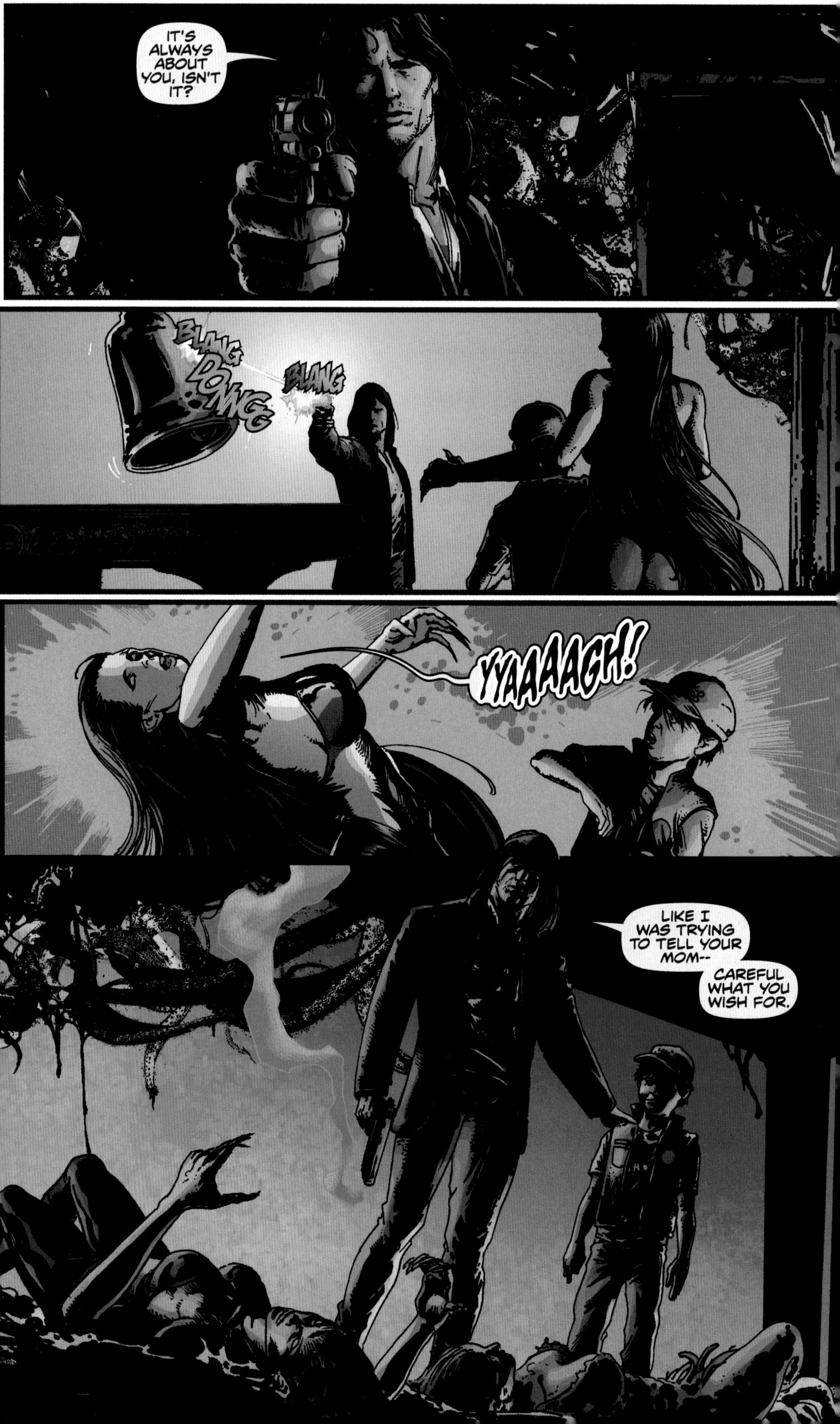
IT'S ALWAYS ABOUT YOU, ISN'T IT?
BLANG
DONNGG
BLANG
YYAAAAGH!
LIKE I WAS TRYING TO TELL YOUR MOM--
CAREFUL WHAT YOU WISH FOR.

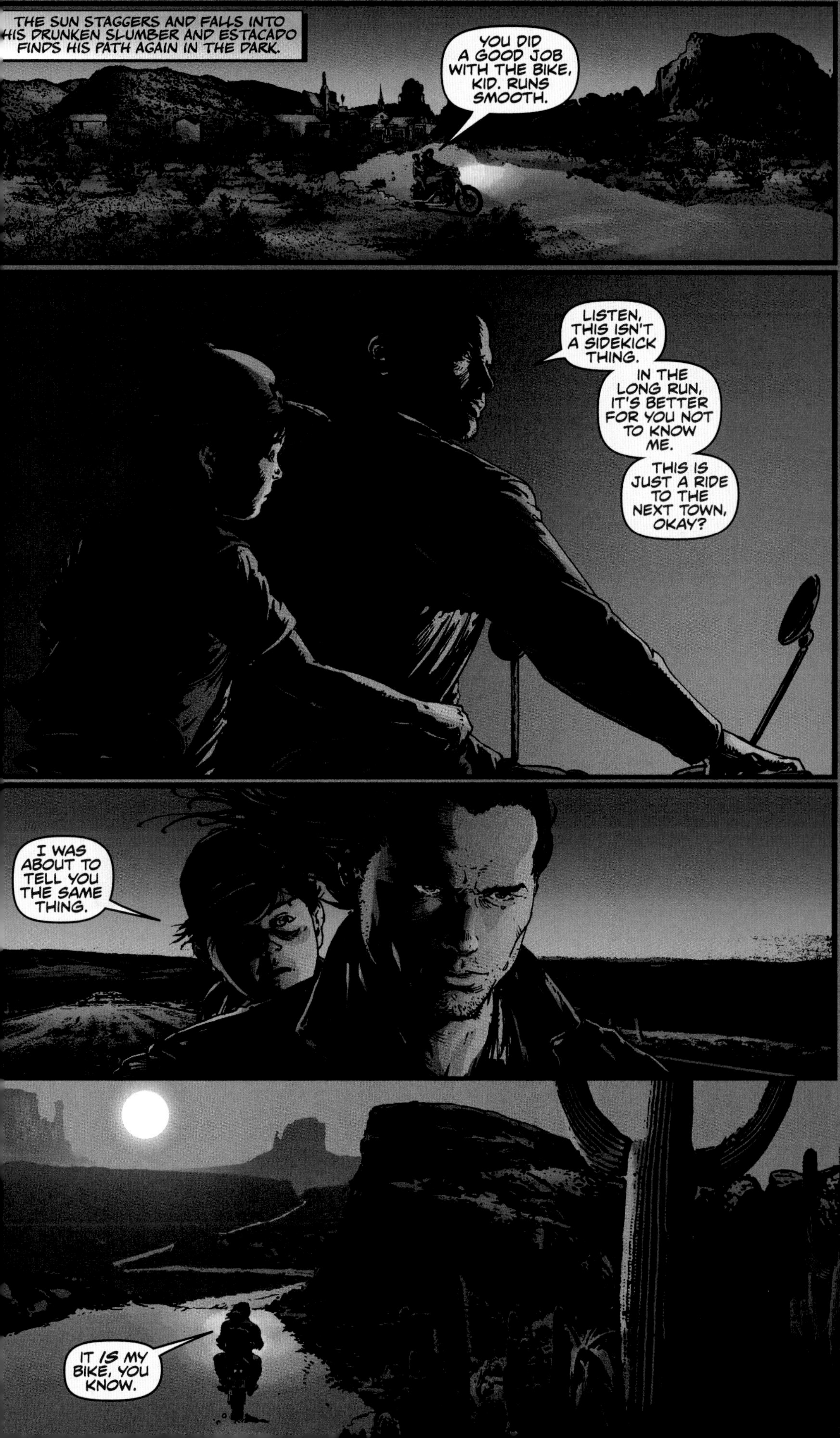
THE SUN STAGGERS AND FALLS INTO HIS DRUNKEN SLUMBER AND ESTACADO FINDS HIS PATH AGAIN IN THE DARK.
YOU DID A GOOD JOB WITH THE BIKE, KID. RUNS SMOOTH.
LISTEN, THIS ISN'T A SIDEKICK THING.
IN THE LONG RUN, IT'S BETTER FOR YOU NOT TO KNOW ME.
THIS IS JUST A RIDE TO THE NEXT TOWN, OKAY?
I WAS ABOUT TO TELL YOU THE SAME THING.
IT IS MY BIKE, YOU KNOW.

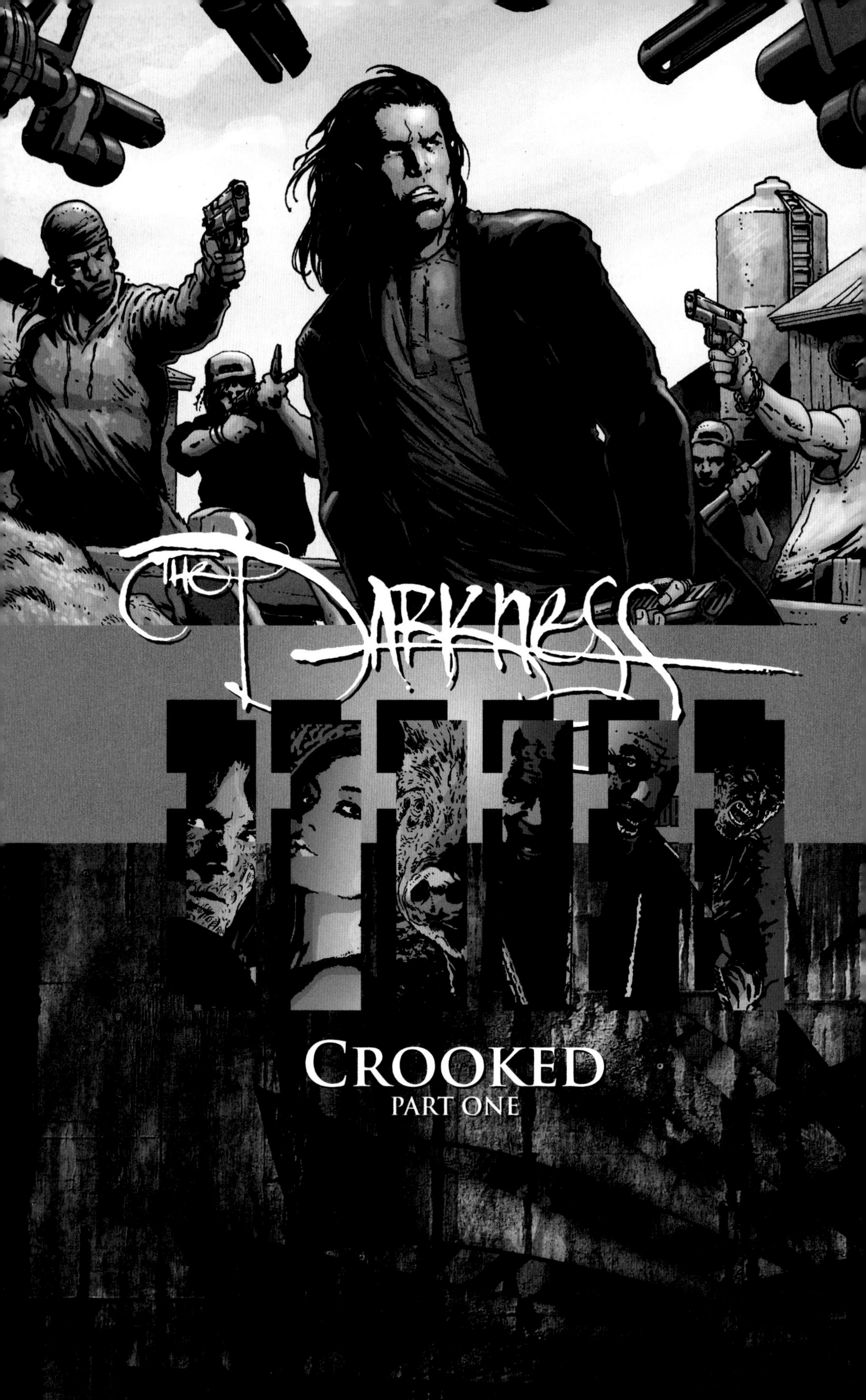
THE DARKNESS
CROOKED
PART ONE

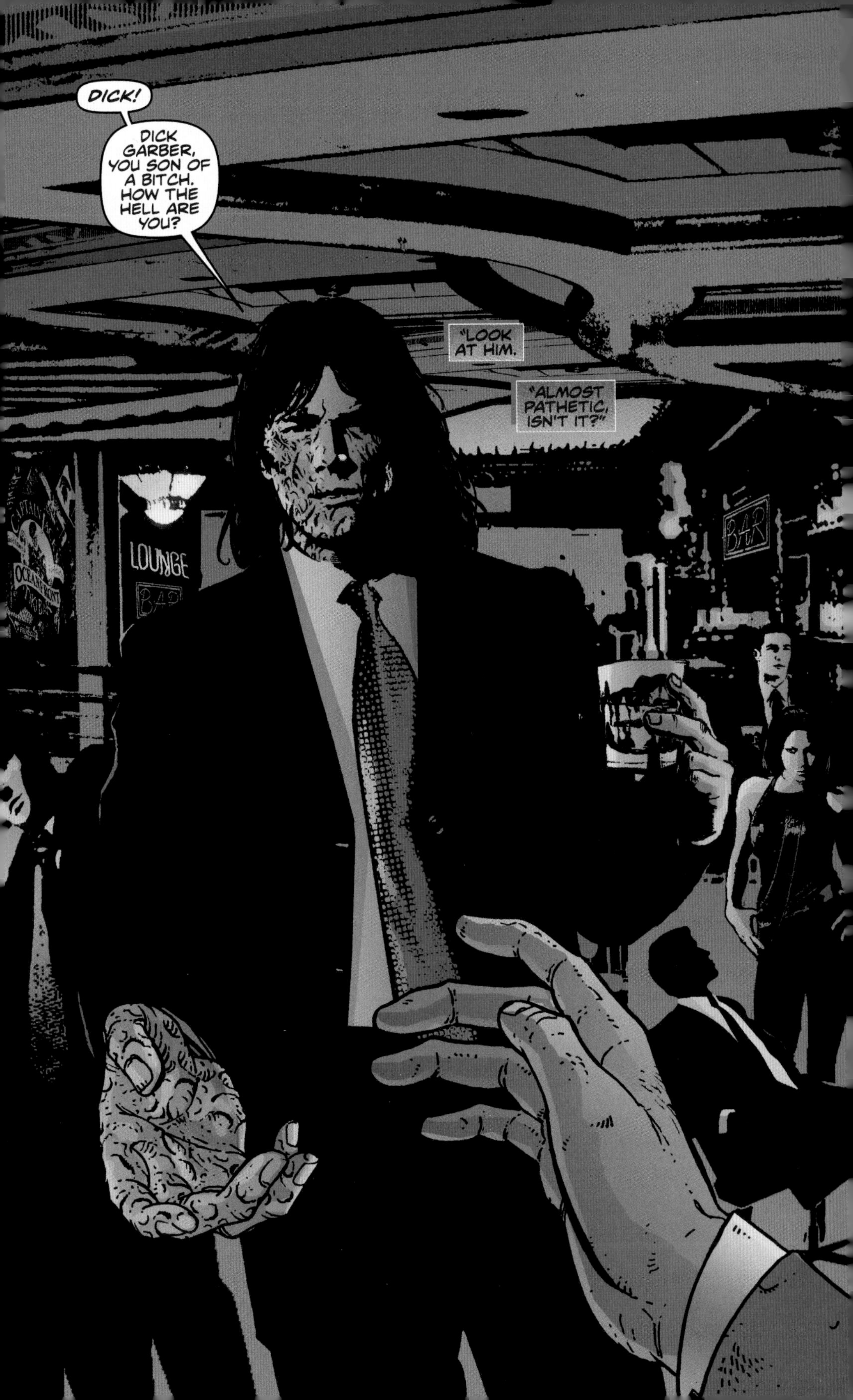
DICK!
DICK GARBER, YOU SON OF A BITCH. HOW THE HELL ARE YOU?
"LOOK AT HIM.
"ALMOST PATHETIC, ISN'T IT?"
LOUNGE
BAR
OCEANFRONT

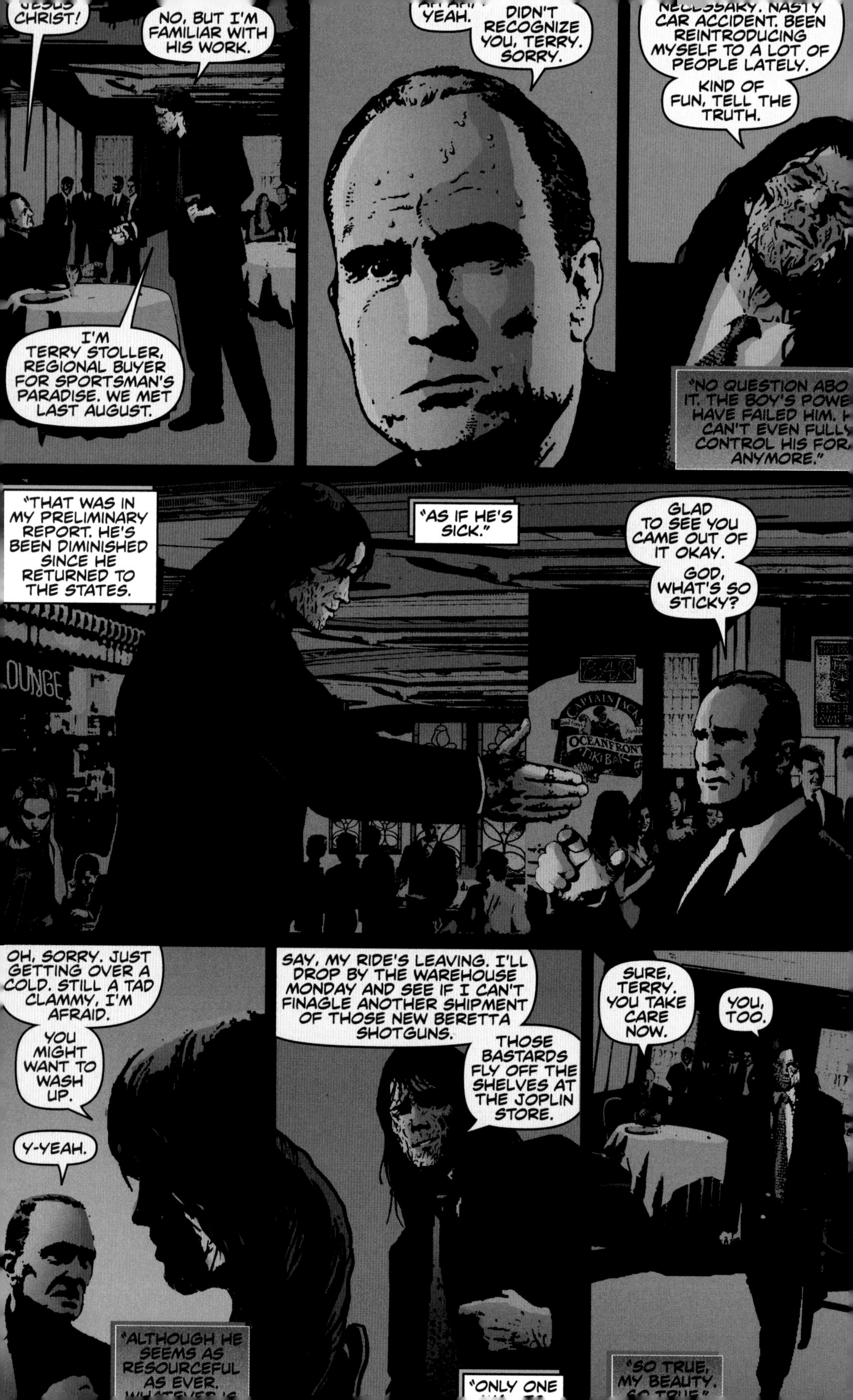
CHRIST!
NO, BUT I'M FAMILIAR WITH HIS WORK.
I'M TERRY STOLLER, REGIONAL BUYER FOR SPORTSMAN'S PARADISE. WE MET LAST AUGUST.
YEAH.
DIDN'T RECOGNIZE YOU, TERRY. SORRY.
CAR ACCIDENT. BEEN REINTRODUCING MYSELF TO A LOT OF PEOPLE LATELY.
KIND OF FUN, TELL THE TRUTH.
"NO QUESTION ABO
IT. THE BOY'S POWE
HAVE FAILED HIM.
CAN'T EVEN FULL
CONTROL HIS FOR
ANYMORE."
"THAT WAS IN MY PRELIMINARY REPORT. HE'S BEEN DIMINISHED SINCE HE RETURNED TO THE STATES.
"AS IF HE'S SICK."
GLAD TO SEE YOU CAME OUT OF IT OKAY.
GOD, WHAT'S SO STICKY?
LOUNGE
BAR
OCEANFRONT TIKI BAR
OH, SORRY. JUST GETTING OVER A COLD. STILL A TAD CLAMMY, I'M AFRAID.
YOU MIGHT WANT TO WASH UP.
Y-YEAH.
"ALTHOUGH HE SEEMS AS RESOURCEFUL AS EVER.
SAY, MY RIDE'S LEAVING. I'LL DROP BY THE WAREHOUSE MONDAY AND SEE IF I CAN'T FINAGLE ANOTHER SHIPMENT OF THOSE NEW BERETTA SHOTGUNS.
THOSE BASTARDS FLY OFF THE SHELVES AT THE JOPLIN STORE.
"ONLY ONE
SURE, TERRY. YOU TAKE CARE NOW.
YOU, TOO.
"SO TRUE, MY BEAUTY.

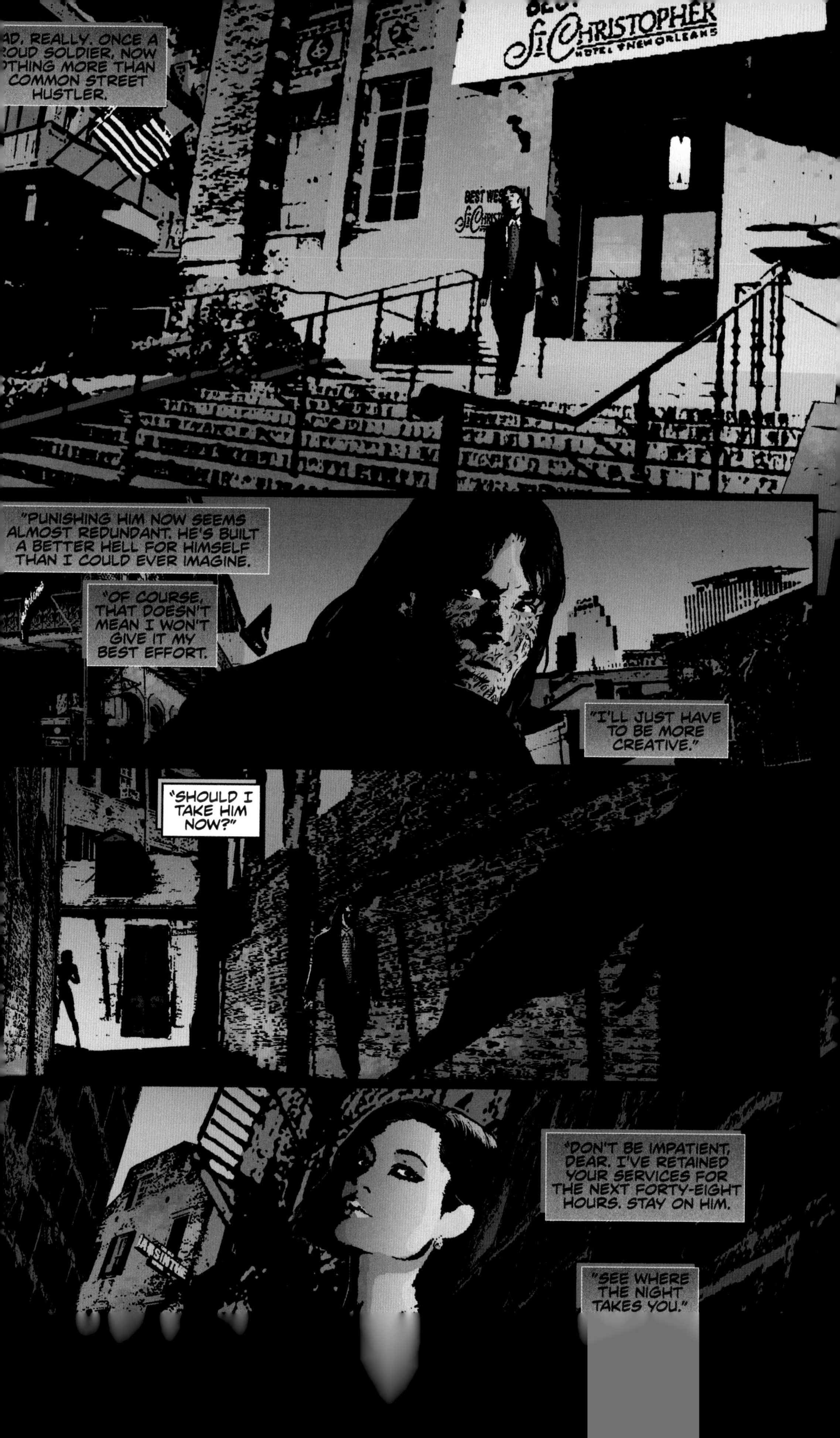

AD. REALLY. ONCE A ROUD SOLDIER, NOW THING MORE THAN COMMON STREET HUSTLER.
ST. CHRISTOPHER HOTEL NEW ORLEANS
"PUNISHING HIM NOW SEEMS ALMOST REDUNDANT. HE'S BUILT A BETTER HELL FOR HIMSELF THAN I COULD EVER IMAGINE.
"OF COURSE, THAT DOESN'T MEAN I WON'T GIVE IT MY BEST EFFORT.
"I'LL JUST HAVE TO BE MORE CREATIVE."
"SHOULD I TAKE HIM NOW?"
"DON'T BE IMPATIENT, DEAR. I'VE RETAINED YOUR SERVICES FOR THE NEXT FORTY-EIGHT HOURS. STAY ON HIM.
"SEE WHERE THE NIGHT TAKES YOU."

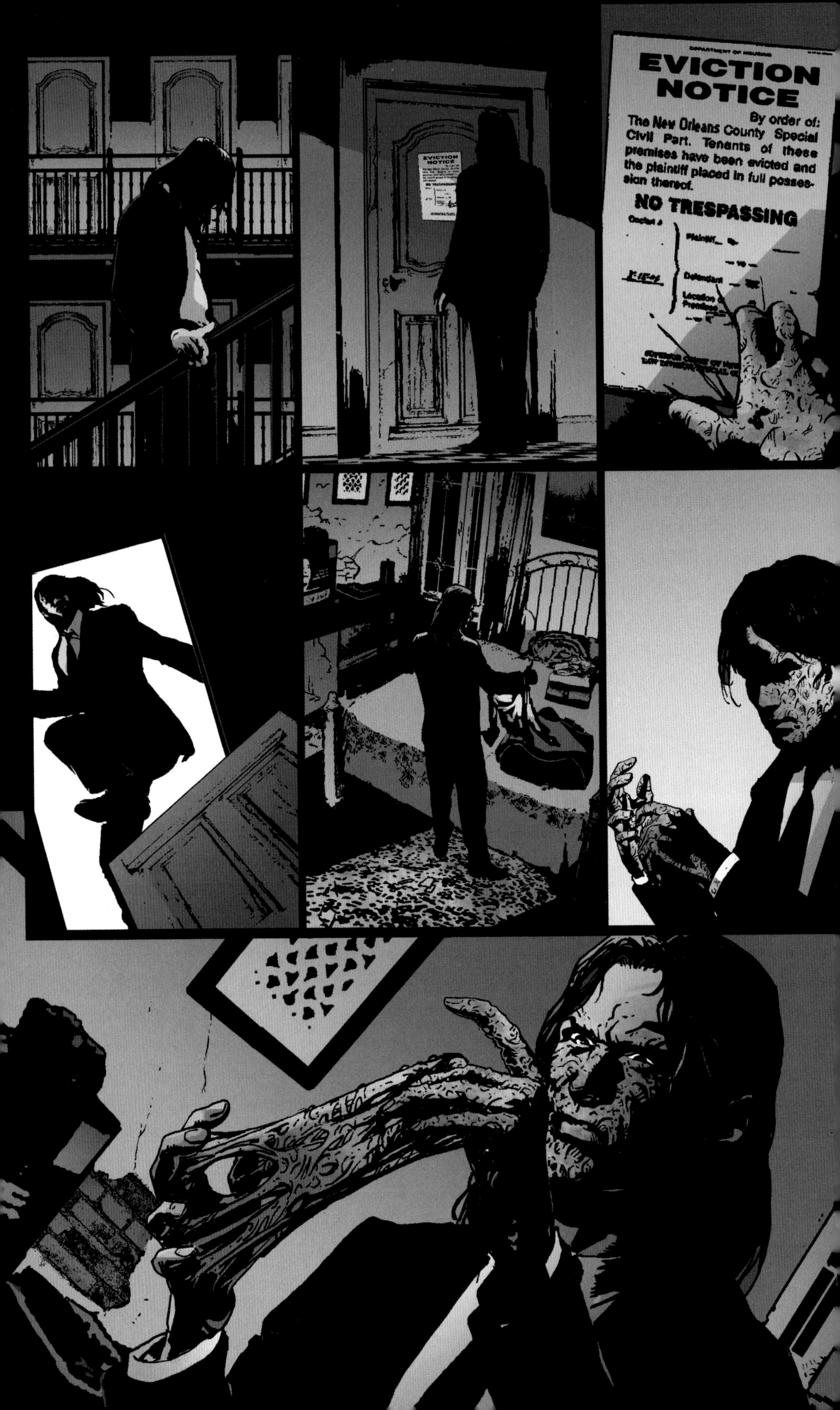
EVICTION NOTICE
By order of:
The New Orleans County Special Civil Part. Tenants of these premises have been evicted and the plaintiff placed in full possession thereof.
NO TRESPASSING
Plaintiff
Defendant

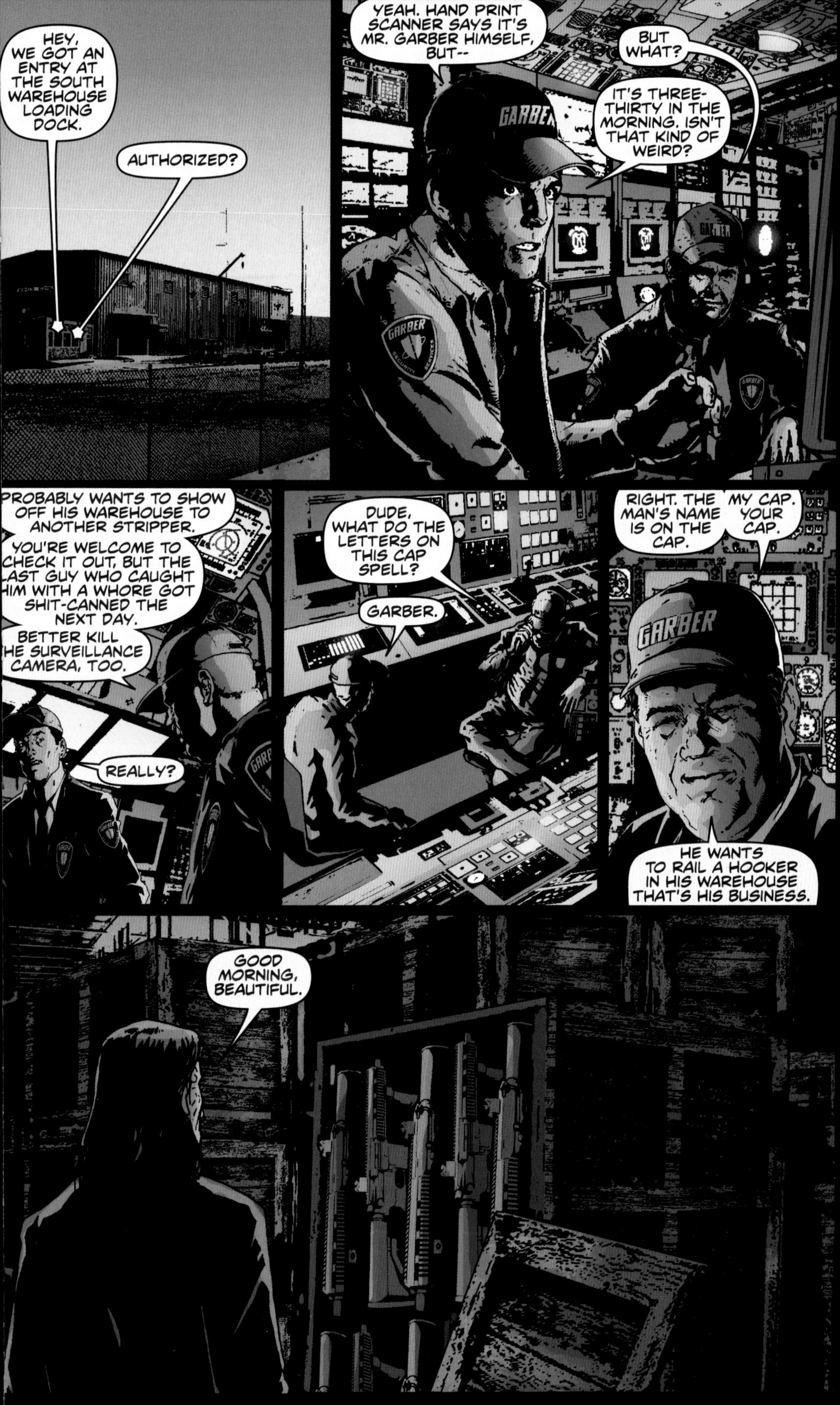
HEY, WE GOT AN ENTRY AT THE SOUTH WAREHOUSE LOADING DOCK.
AUTHORIZED?
YEAH. HAND PRINT SCANNER SAYS IT'S MR. GARBER HIMSELF, BUT--
BUT WHAT?
IT'S THREE-THIRTY IN THE MORNING. ISN'T THAT KIND OF WEIRD?
GARBER
PROBABLY WANTS TO SHOW OFF HIS WAREHOUSE TO ANOTHER STRIPPER.
YOU'RE WELCOME TO CHECK IT OUT, BUT THE LAST GUY WHO CAUGHT HIM WITH A WHORE GOT SHIT-CANNED THE NEXT DAY.
BETTER KILL THE SURVEILLANCE CAMERA, TOO.
REALLY?
DUDE, WHAT DO THE LETTERS ON THIS CAP SPELL?
GARBER.
RIGHT. THE MAN'S NAME IS ON THE CAP.
MY CAP. YOUR CAP.
GARBER
HE WANTS TO RAIL A HOOKER IN HIS WAREHOUSE THAT'S HIS BUSINESS.
GOOD MORNING, BEAUTIFUL.

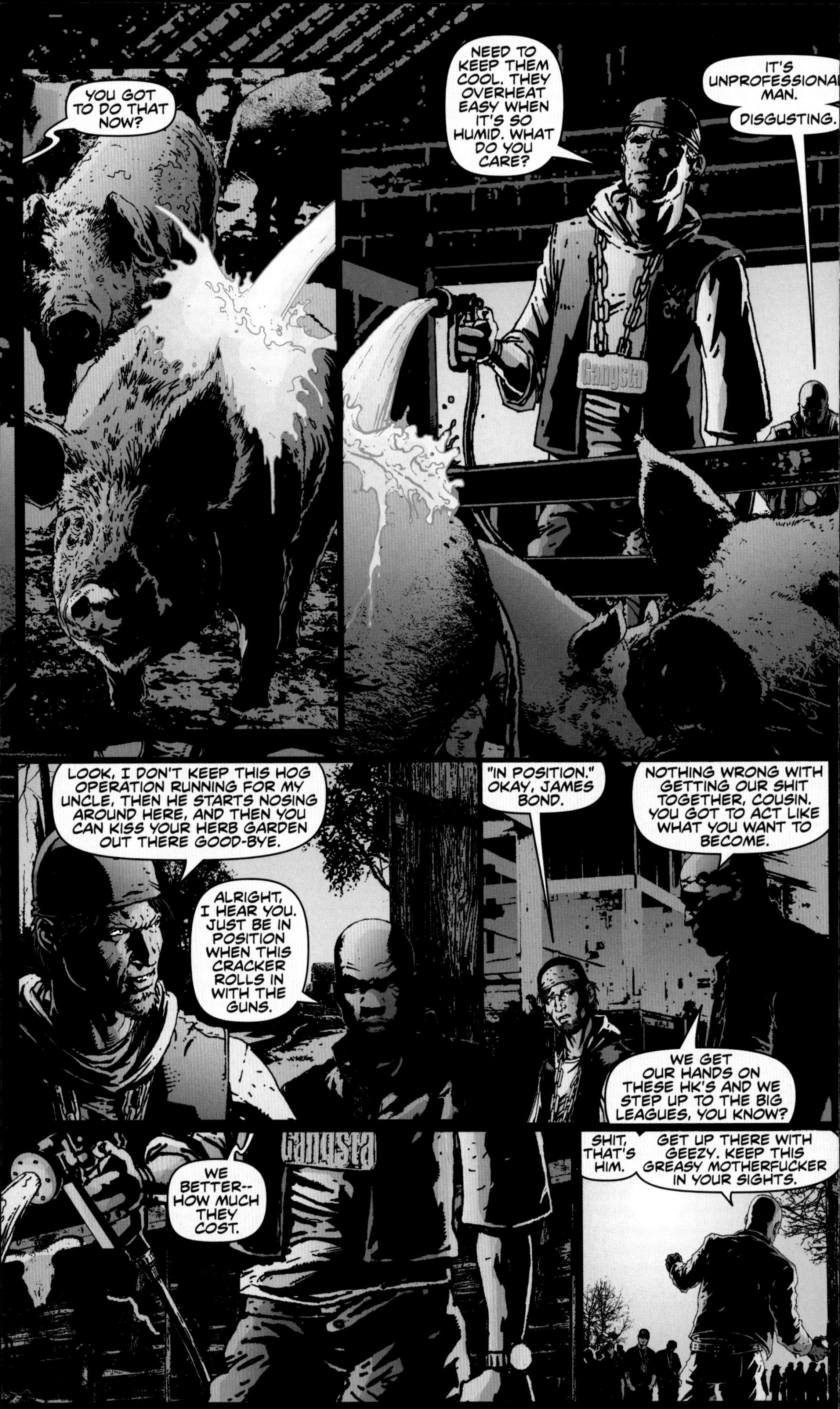
YOU GOT TO DO THAT NOW?
NEED TO KEEP THEM COOL. THEY OVERHEAT EASY WHEN IT'S SO HUMID. WHAT DO YOU CARE?
IT'S UNPROFESSIONAL MAN.
DISGUSTING.
Gangsta
LOOK, I DON'T KEEP THIS HOG OPERATION RUNNING FOR MY UNCLE, THEN HE STARTS NOSING AROUND HERE, AND THEN YOU CAN KISS YOUR HERB GARDEN OUT THERE GOOD-BYE.
ALRIGHT, I HEAR YOU. JUST BE IN POSITION WHEN THIS CRACKER ROLLS IN WITH THE GUNS.
"IN POSITION." OKAY, JAMES BOND.
NOTHING WRONG WITH GETTING OUR SHIT TOGETHER, COUSIN. YOU GOT TO ACT LIKE WHAT YOU WANT TO BECOME.
WE GET OUR HANDS ON THESE HK'S AND WE STEP UP TO THE BIG LEAGUES, YOU KNOW?
Gangsta
WE BETTER-- HOW MUCH THEY COST.
SHIT, THAT'S HIM.
GET UP THERE WITH GEEZY. KEEP THIS GREASY MOTHERFUCKER IN YOUR SIGHTS.

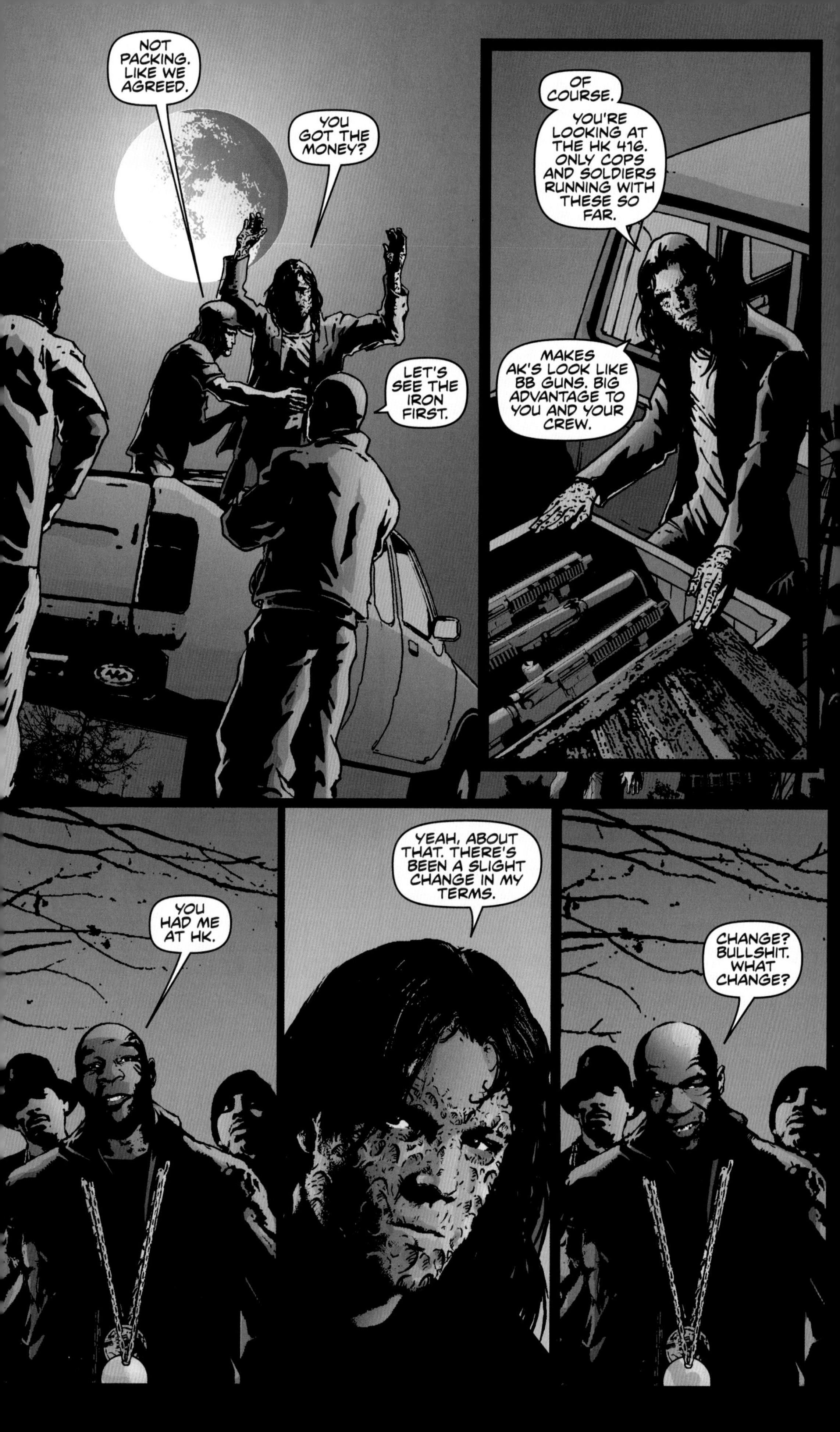
NOT PACKING. LIKE WE AGREED.
YOU GOT THE MONEY?
LET'S SEE THE IRON FIRST.
OF COURSE.
YOU'RE LOOKING AT THE HK 416. ONLY COPS AND SOLDIERS RUNNING WITH THESE SO FAR.
MAKES AK'S LOOK LIKE BB GUNS. BIG ADVANTAGE TO YOU AND YOUR CREW.
YOU HAD ME AT HK.
YEAH, ABOUT THAT. THERE'S BEEN A SLIGHT CHANGE IN MY TERMS.
CHANGE? BULLSHIT. WHAT CHANGE?

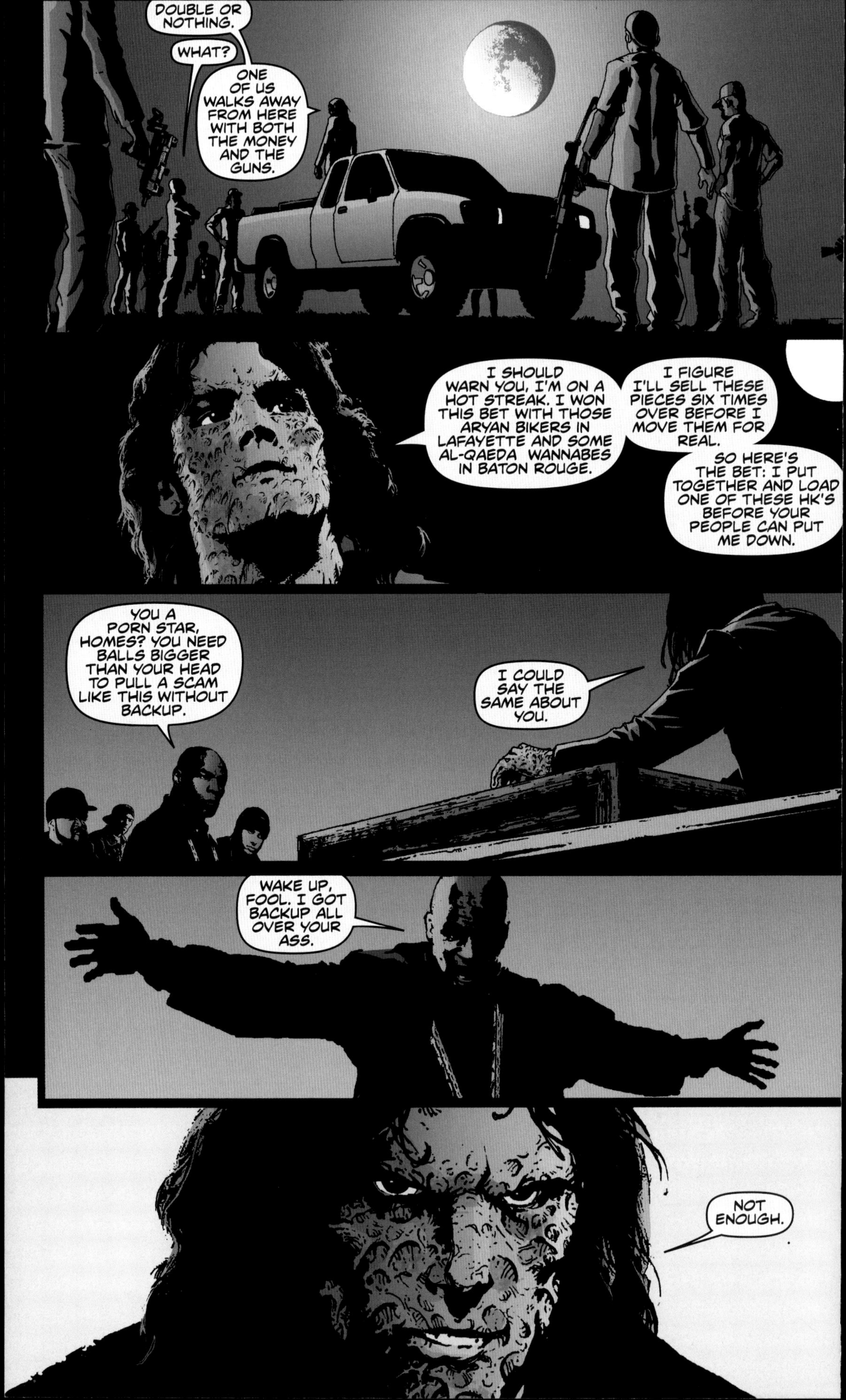
DOUBLE OR NOTHING.
WHAT?
ONE OF US WALKS AWAY FROM HERE WITH BOTH THE MONEY AND THE GUNS.
I SHOULD WARN YOU, I'M ON A HOT STREAK. I WON THIS BET WITH THOSE ARYAN BIKERS IN LAFAYETTE AND SOME AL-QAEDA WANNABES IN BATON ROUGE.
I FIGURE I'LL SELL THESE PIECES SIX TIMES OVER BEFORE I MOVE THEM FOR REAL.
SO HERE'S THE BET: I PUT TOGETHER AND LOAD ONE OF THESE HK'S BEFORE YOUR PEOPLE CAN PUT ME DOWN.
YOU A PORN STAR, HOMES? YOU NEED BALLS BIGGER THAN YOUR HEAD TO PULL A SCAM LIKE THIS WITHOUT BACKUP.
I COULD SAY THE SAME ABOUT YOU.
WAKE UP, FOOL. I GOT BACKUP ALL OVER YOUR ASS.
NOT ENOUGH.

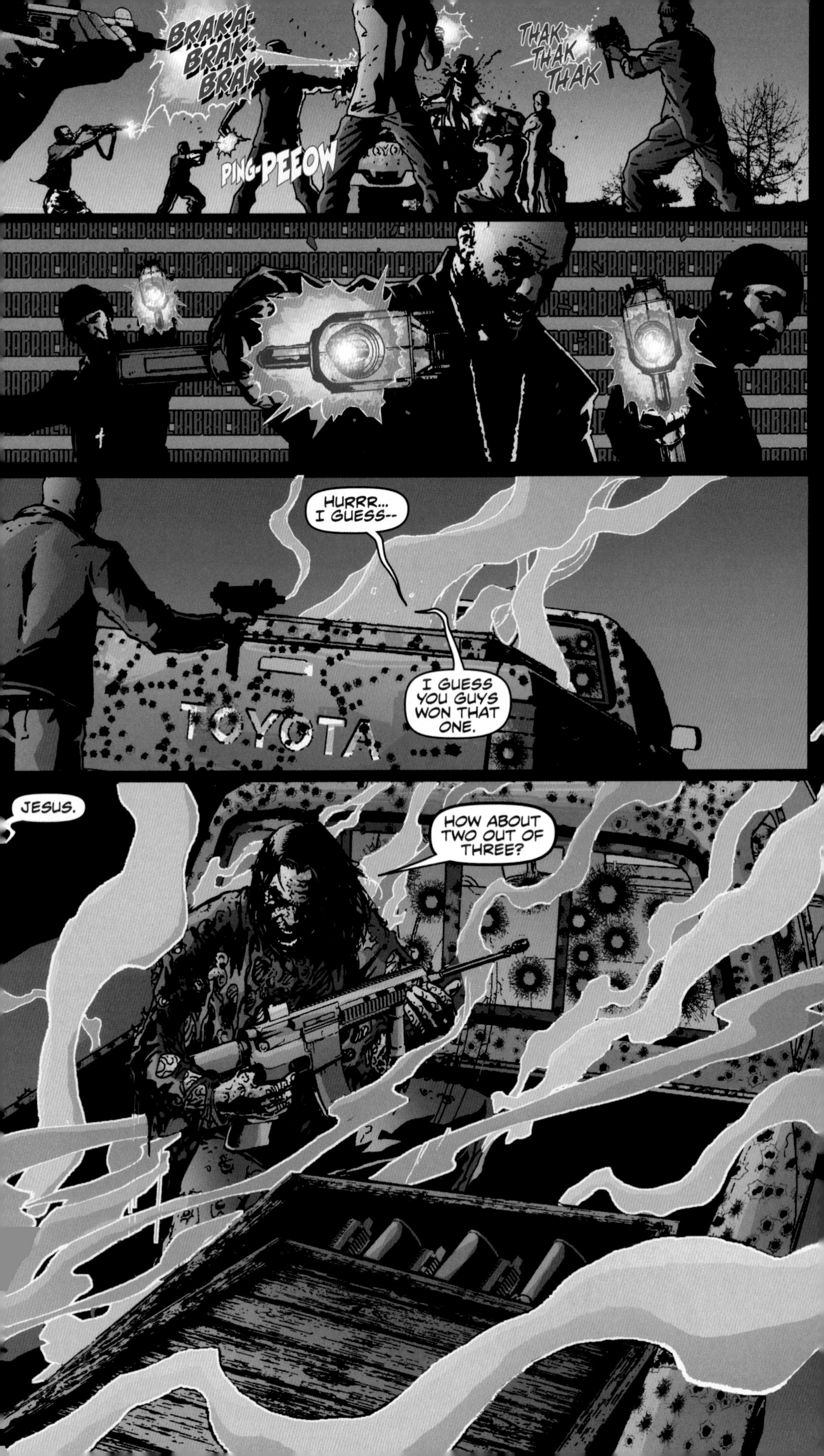
BRAKA-BRAK-BRAK
THAK THAK THAK
PING-PEEOW
HURRR... I GUESS--
I GUESS YOU GUYS WON THAT ONE.
TOYOTA
JESUS.
HOW ABOUT TWO OUT OF THREE?

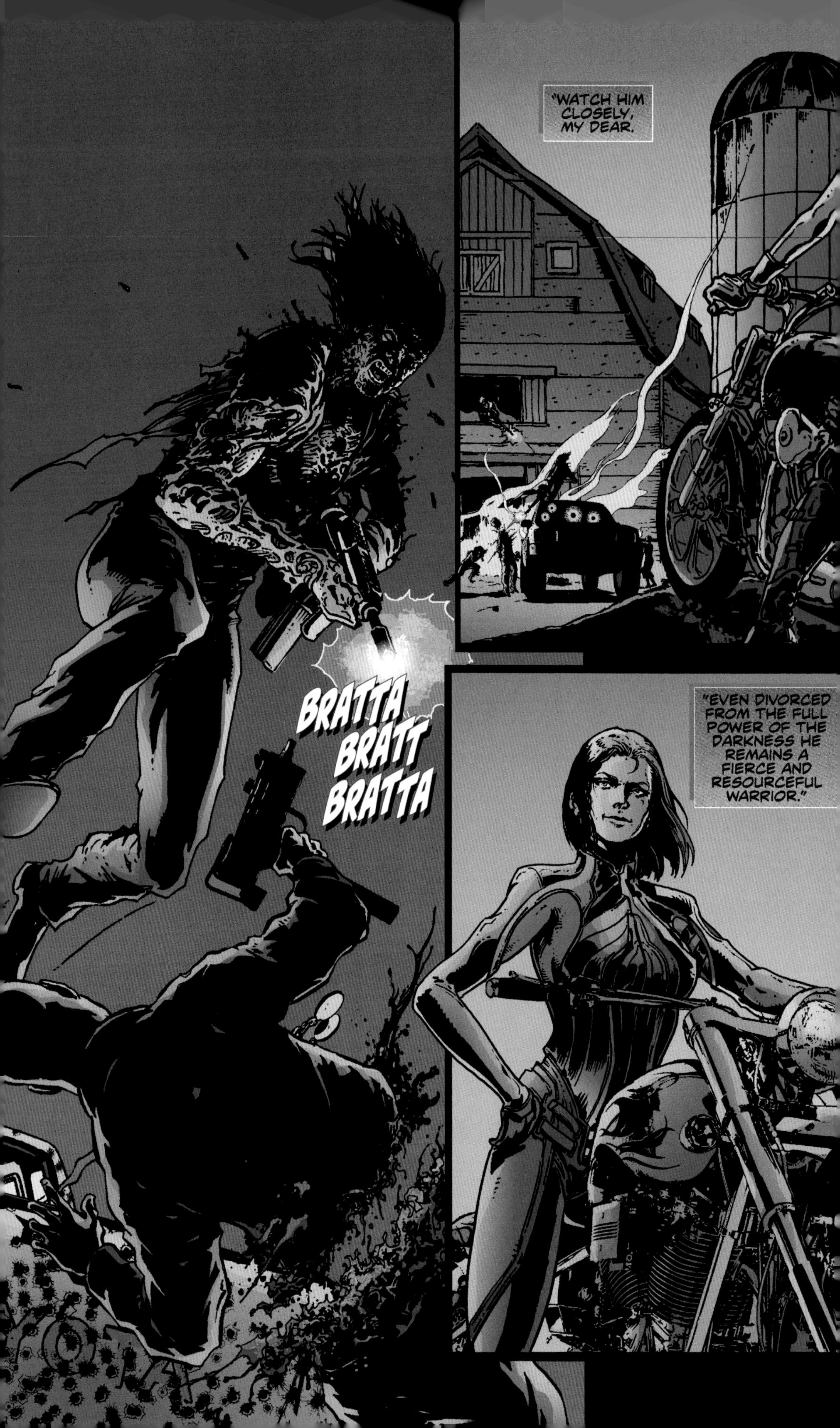

"WATCH HIM CLOSELY, MY DEAR.
BRATTA BRATT BRATTA
"EVEN DIVORCED FROM THE FULL POWER OF THE DARKNESS HE REMAINS A FIERCE AND RESOURCEFUL WARRIOR."

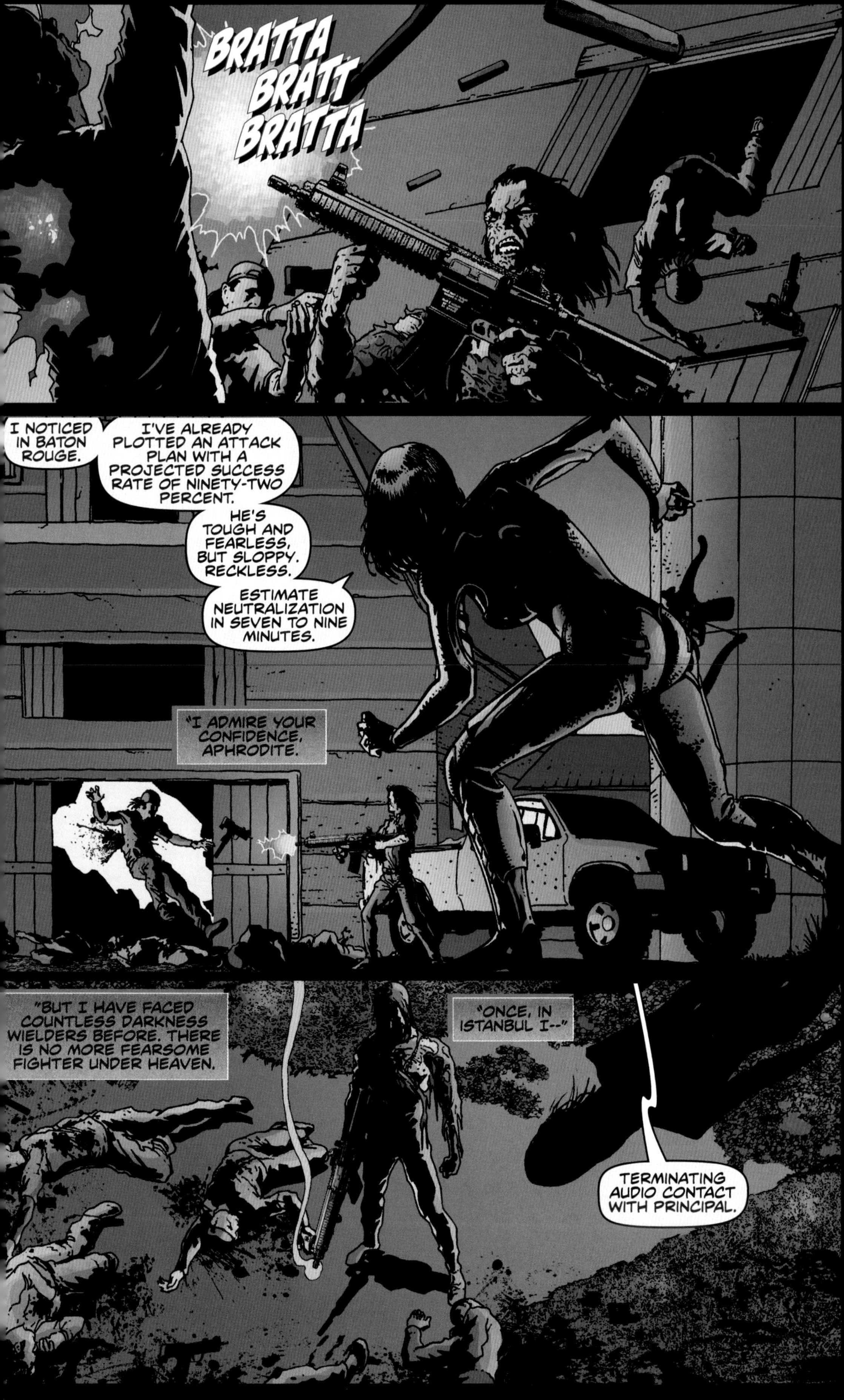
BRATTA BRATT BRATTA
I NOTICED IN BATON ROUGE.
I'VE ALREADY PLOTTED AN ATTACK PLAN WITH A PROJECTED SUCCESS RATE OF NINETY-TWO PERCENT.
HE'S TOUGH AND FEARLESS, BUT SLOPPY. RECKLESS.
ESTIMATE NEUTRALIZATION IN SEVEN TO NINE MINUTES.
"I ADMIRE YOUR CONFIDENCE, APHRODITE.
"BUT I HAVE FACED COUNTLESS DARKNESS WIELDERS BEFORE. THERE IS NO MORE FEARSOME FIGHTER UNDER HEAVEN.
"ONCE, IN ISTANBUL I--"
TERMINATING AUDIO CONTACT WITH PRINCIPAL.

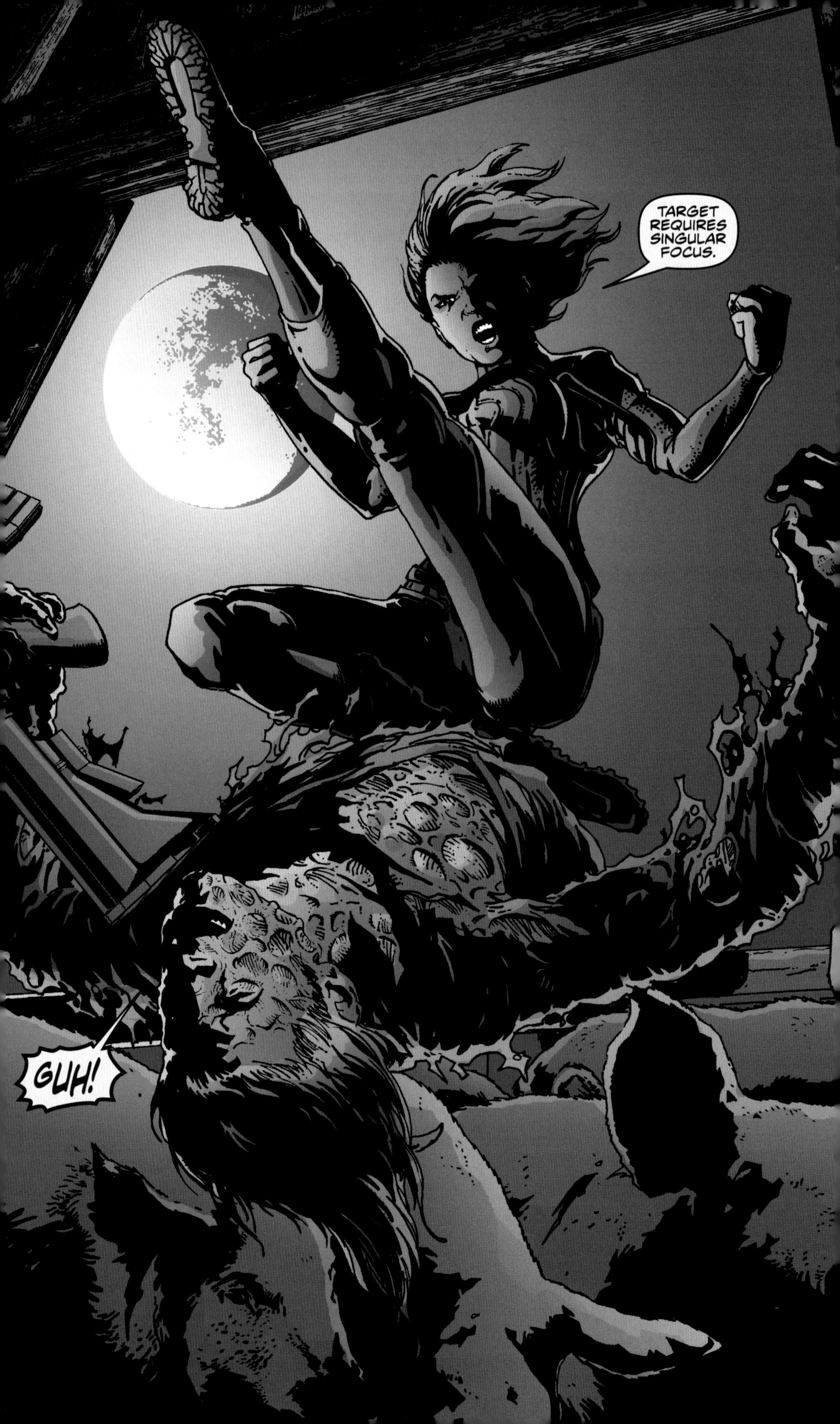
TARGET REQUIRES SINGULAR FOCUS.
GUH!

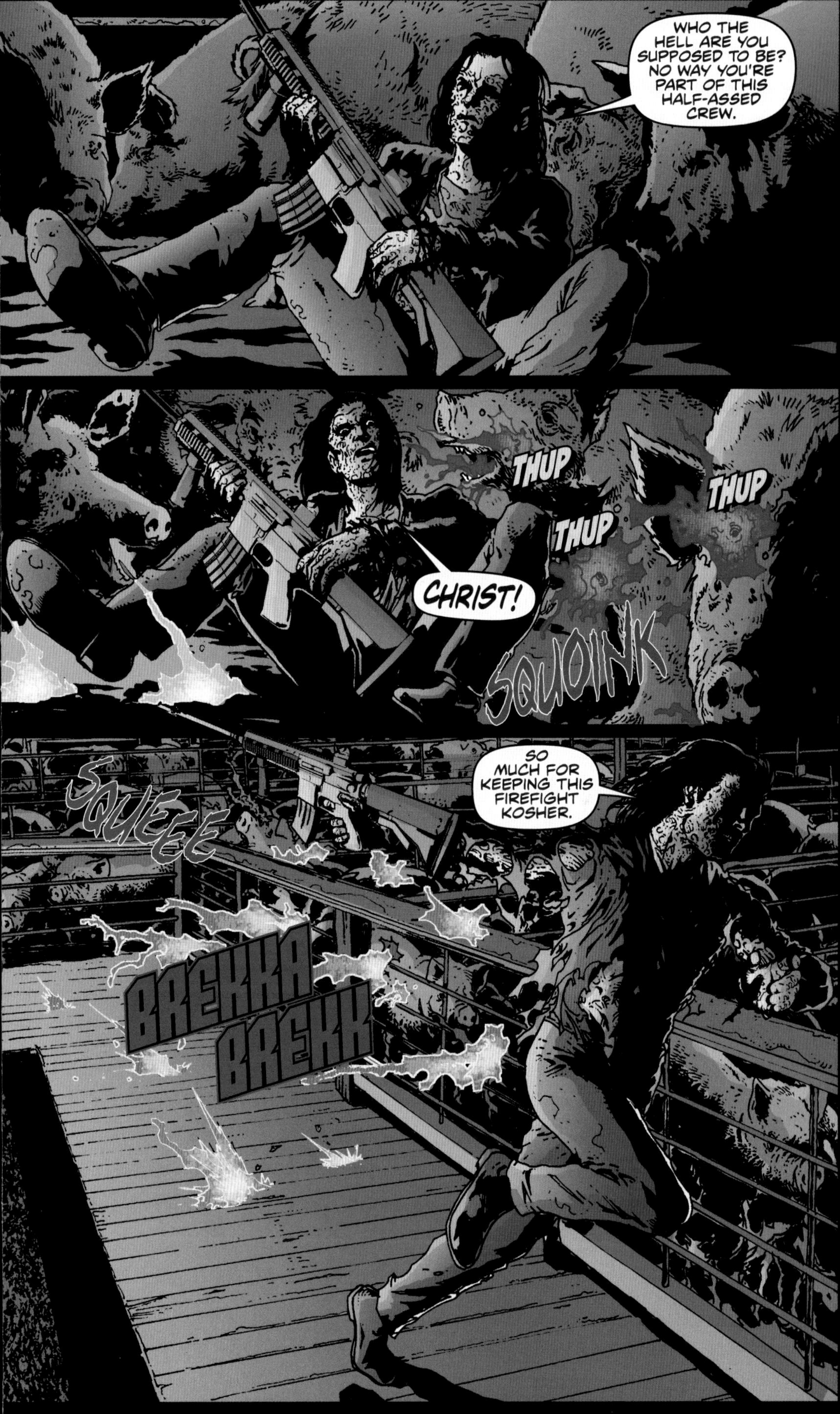
WHO THE HELL ARE YOU SUPPOSED TO BE? NO WAY YOU'RE PART OF THIS HALF-ASSED CREW.
THUP
THUP
THUP
CHRIST!
SQUOINK
SO MUCH FOR KEEPING THIS FIREFIGHT KOSHER.
SQUEEE
BREKKA BREKK

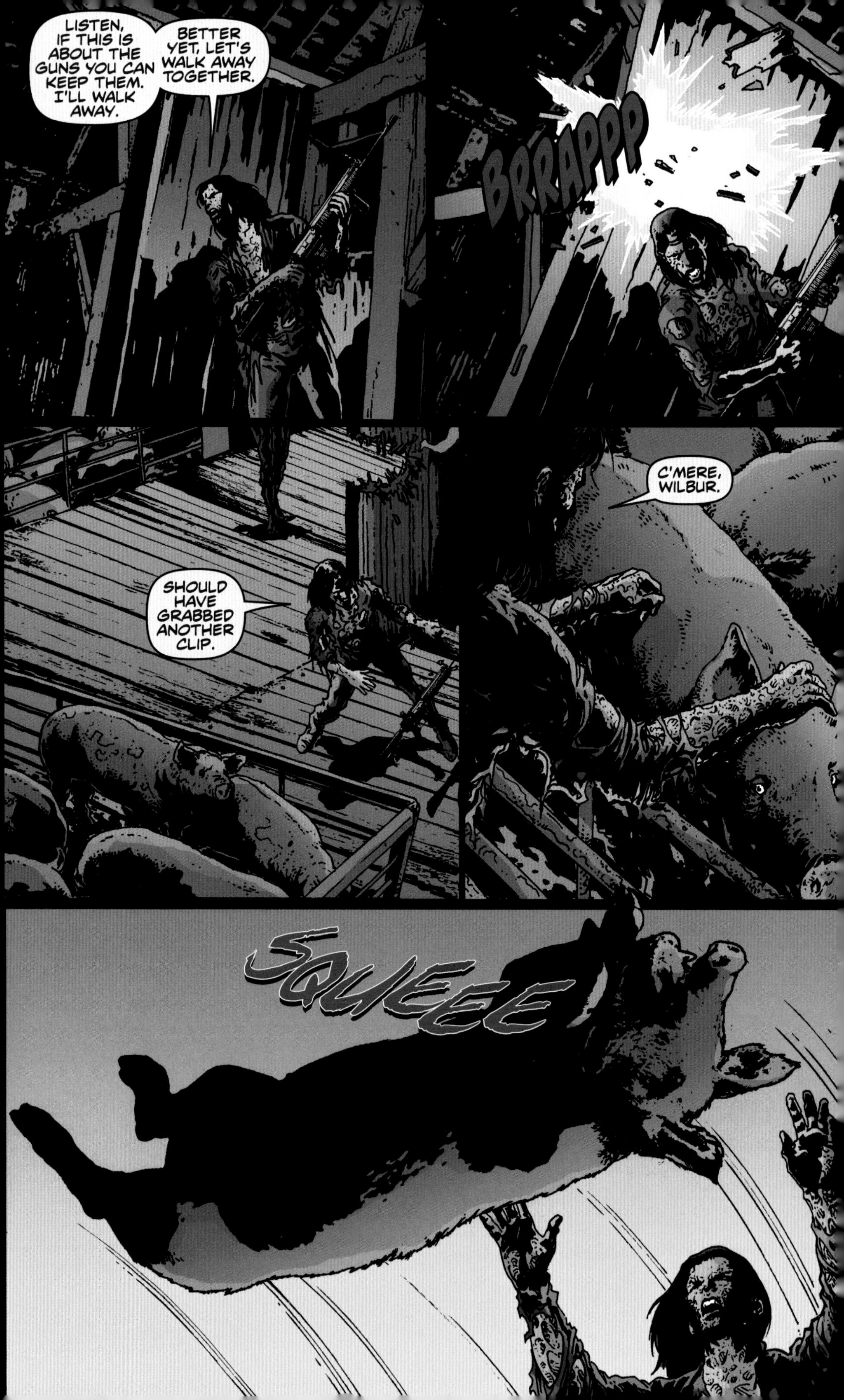
LISTEN, IF THIS IS ABOUT THE GUNS YOU CAN KEEP THEM. I'LL WALK AWAY.
BETTER YET, LET'S WALK AWAY TOGETHER.
BRRAPPP
SHOULD HAVE GRABBED ANOTHER CLIP.
C'MERE, WILBUR.
SQUEEE

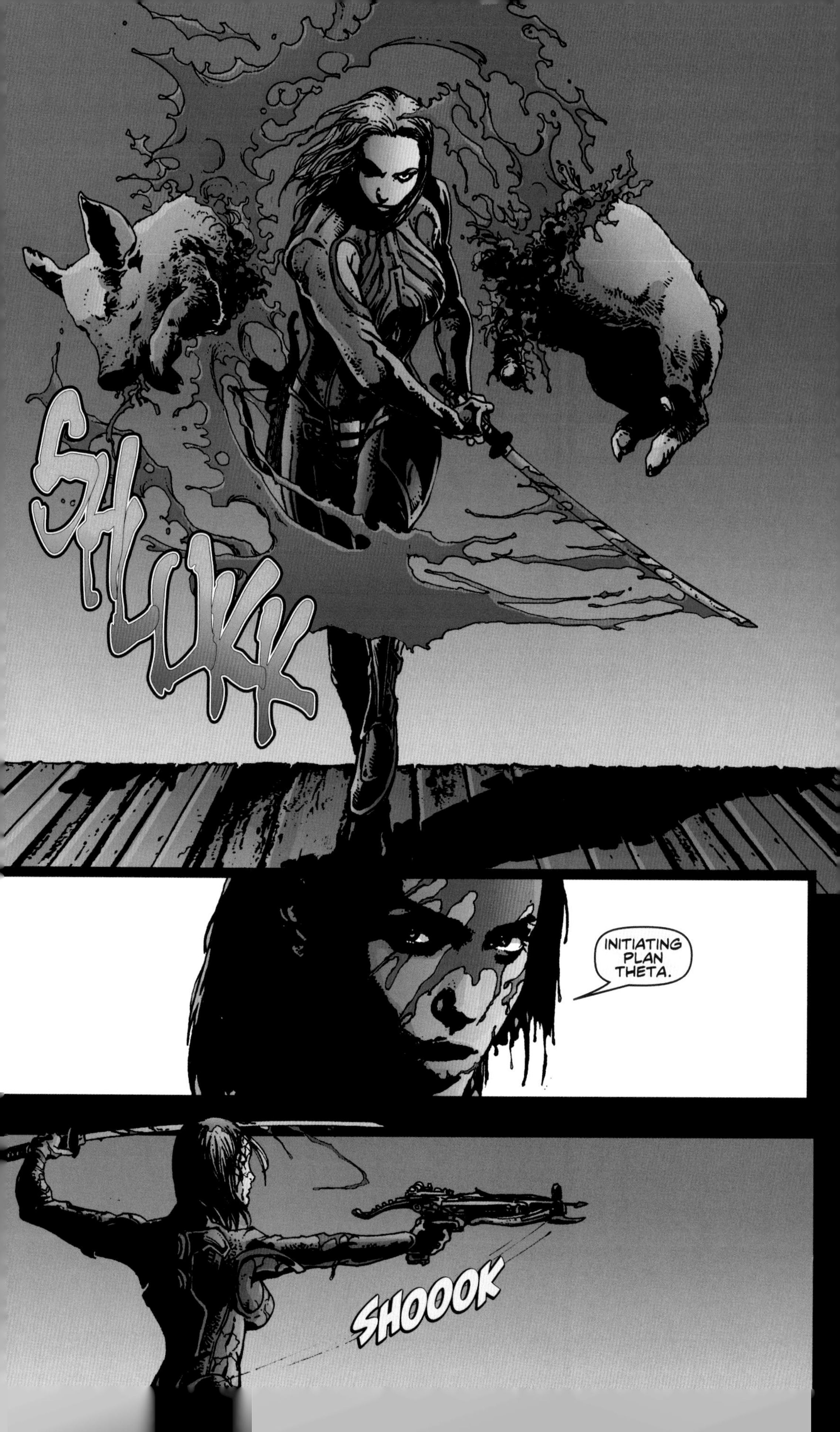
SHLUKK
INITIATING PLAN THETA.
SHOOOK

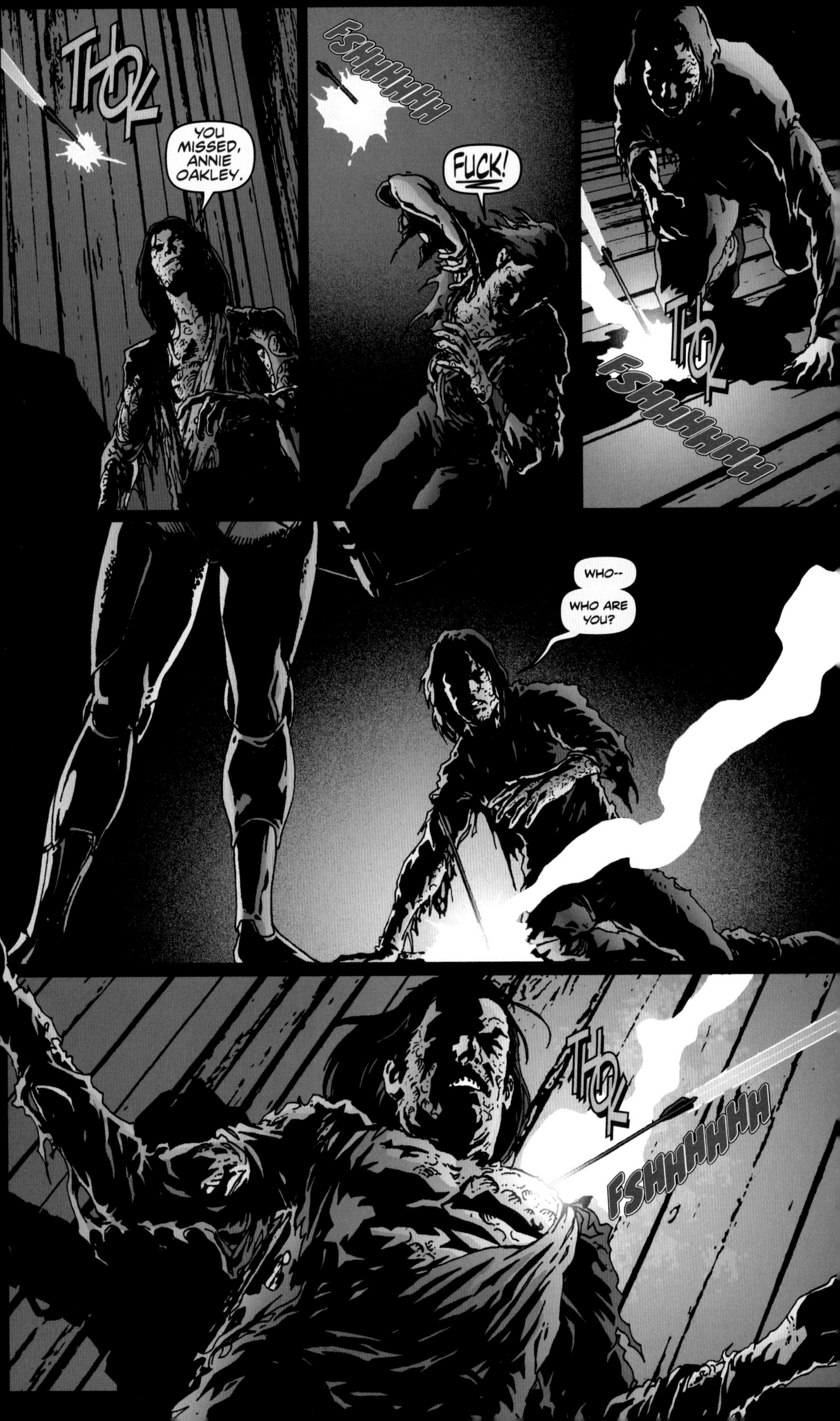
THOK
YOU MISSED, ANNIE OAKLEY.
FSHHHHHHH
FUCK!
THOK
FSHHHHHHH
WHO--
WHO ARE YOU?
THOK
FSHHHHHHH

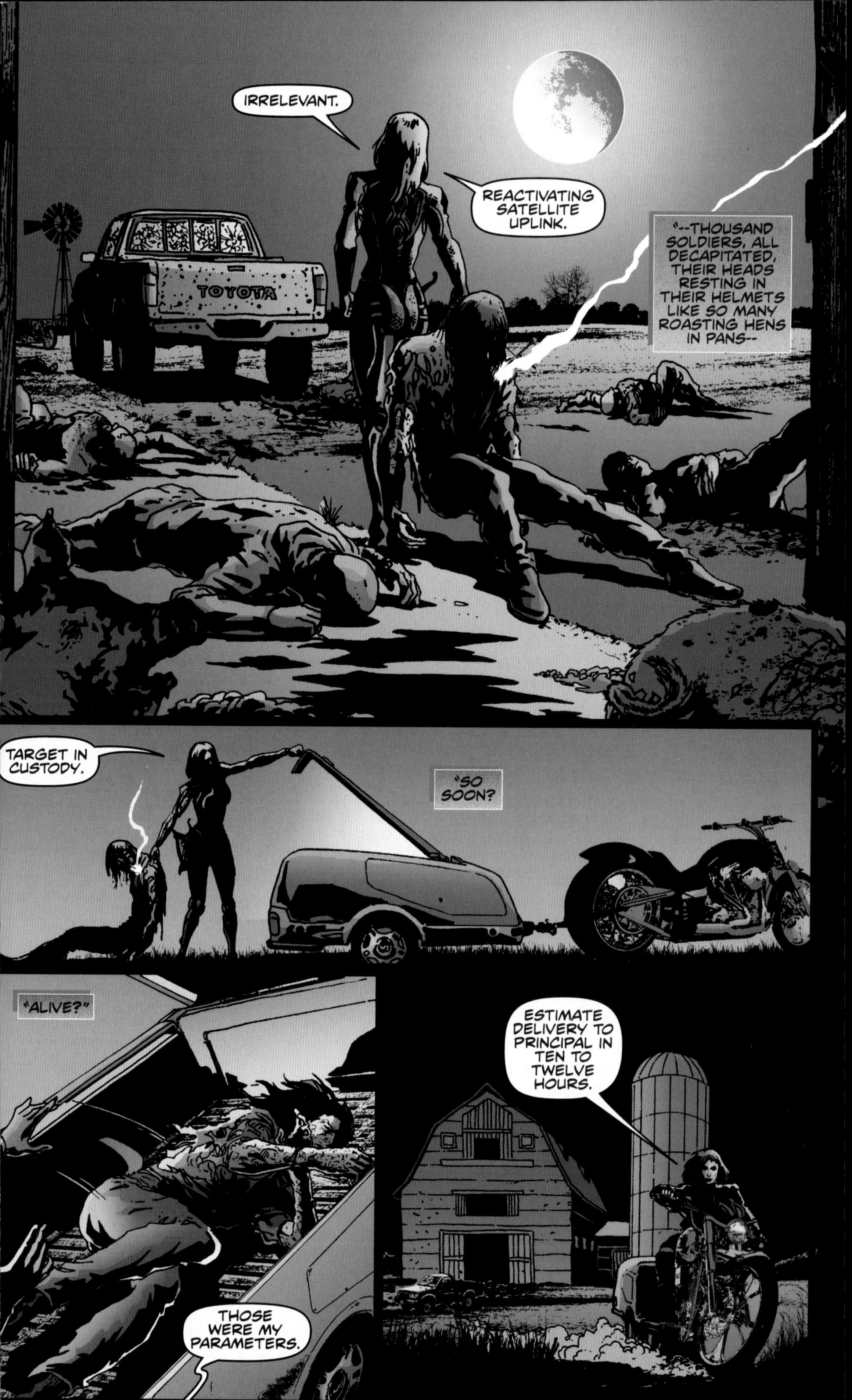
IRRELEVANT.
REACTIVATING SATELLITE UPLINK.
"--THOUSAND SOLDIERS, ALL DECAPITATED, THEIR HEADS RESTING IN THEIR HELMETS LIKE SO MANY ROASTING HENS IN PANS--
TOYOTA
TARGET IN CUSTODY.
"SO SOON?
"ALIVE?"
THOSE WERE MY PARAMETERS.
ESTIMATE DELIVERY TO PRINCIPAL IN TEN TO TWELVE HOURS.

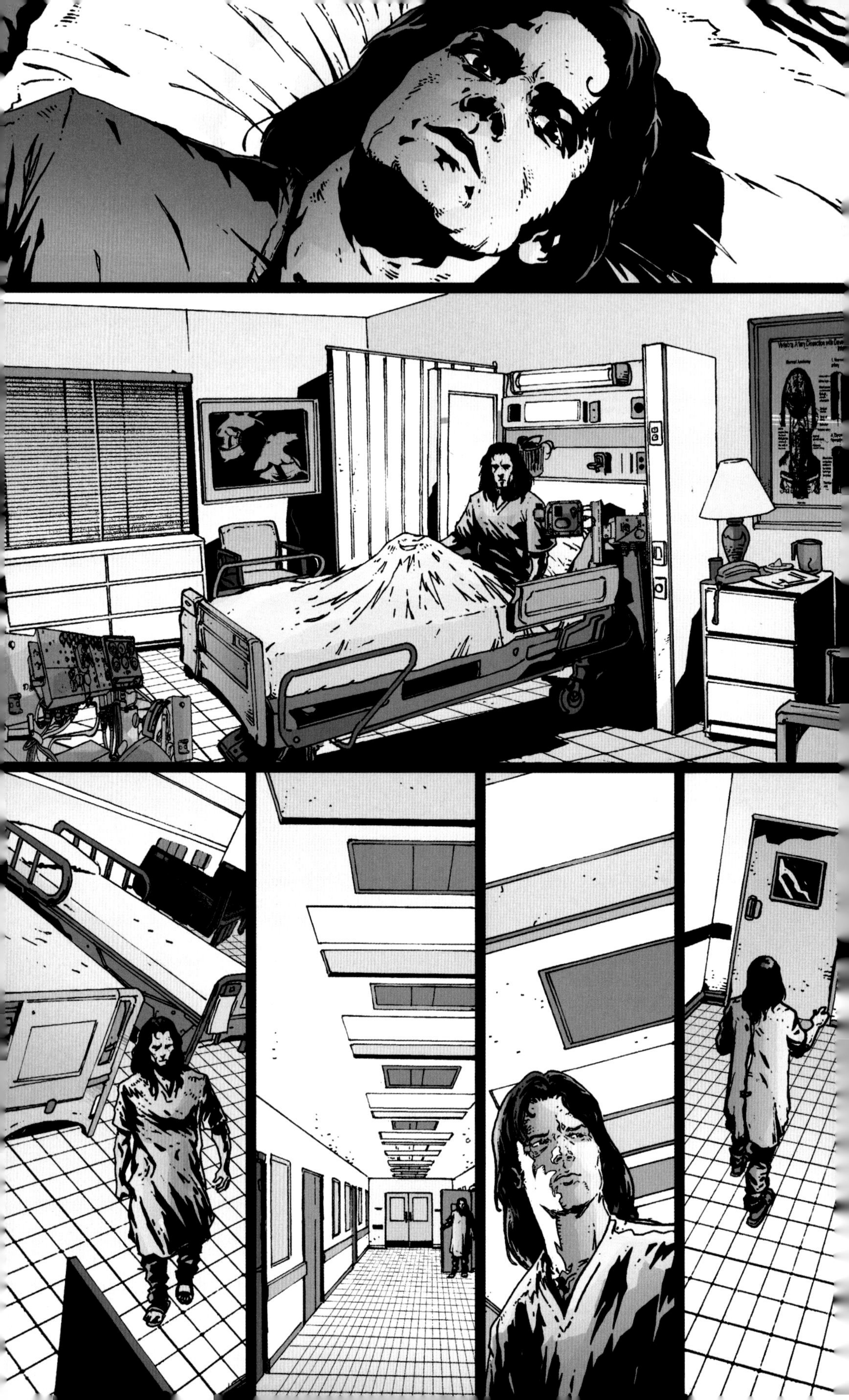

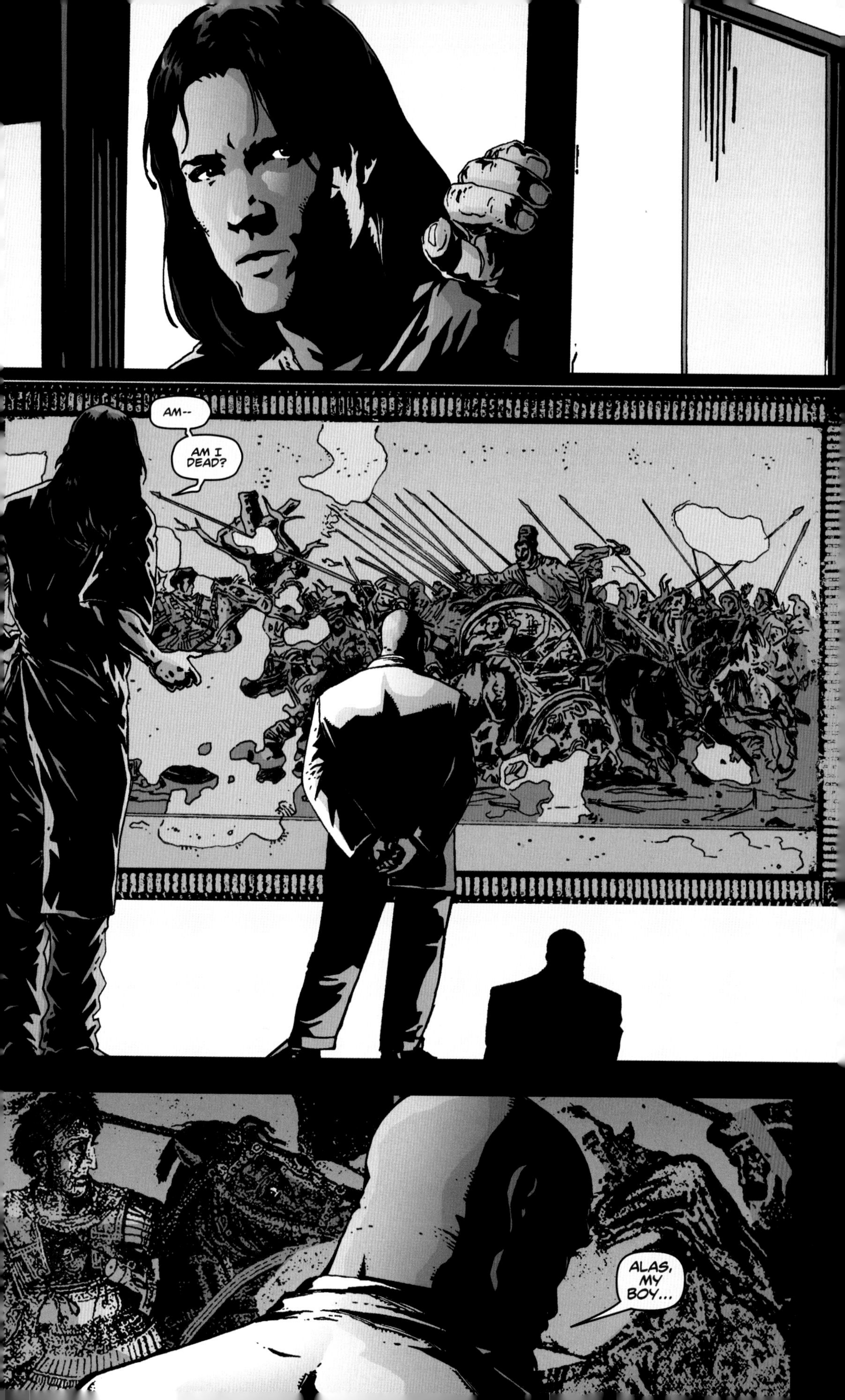
AM--
AM I DEAD?
ALAS, MY BOY...

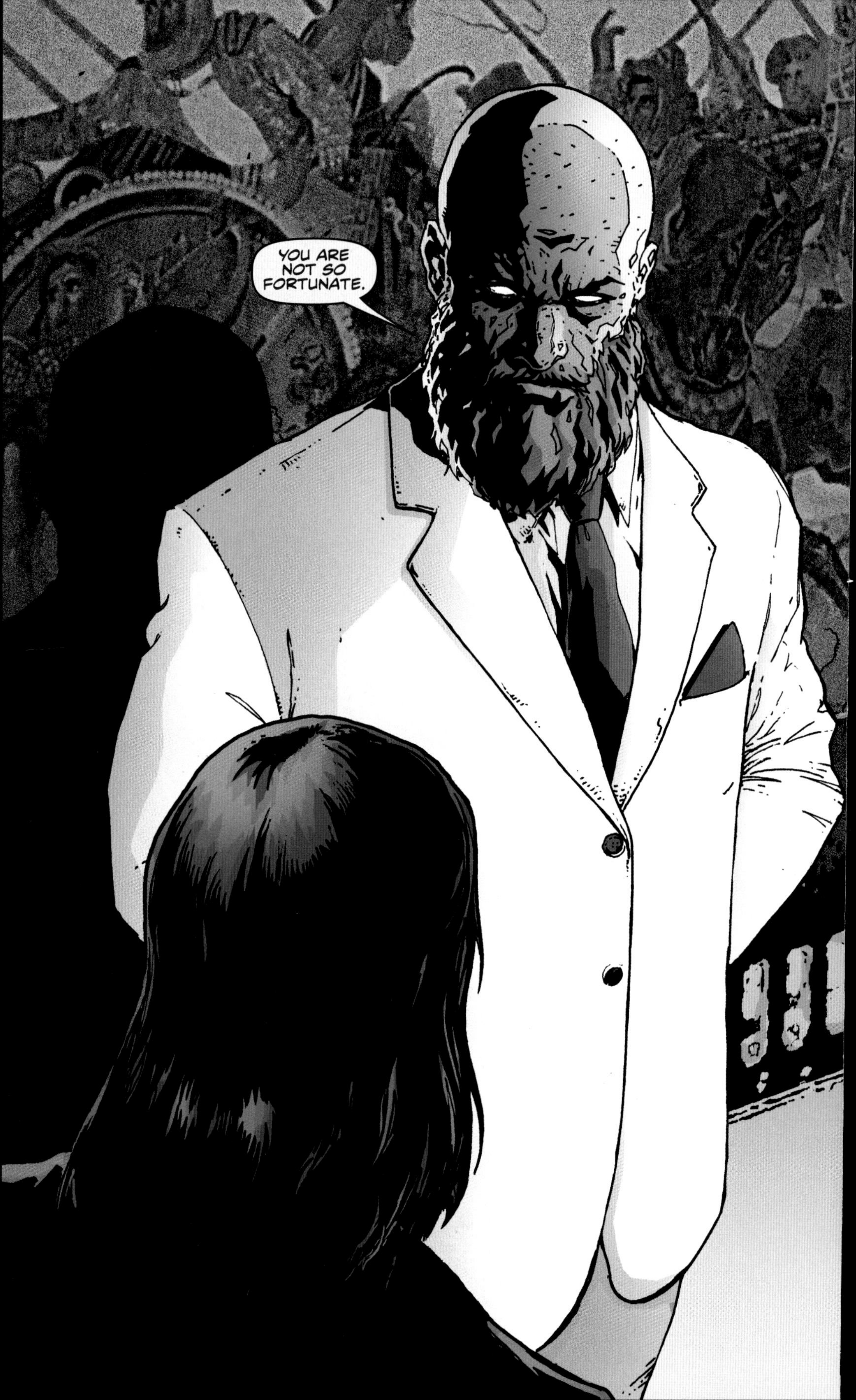
YOU ARE NOT SO FORTUNATE.

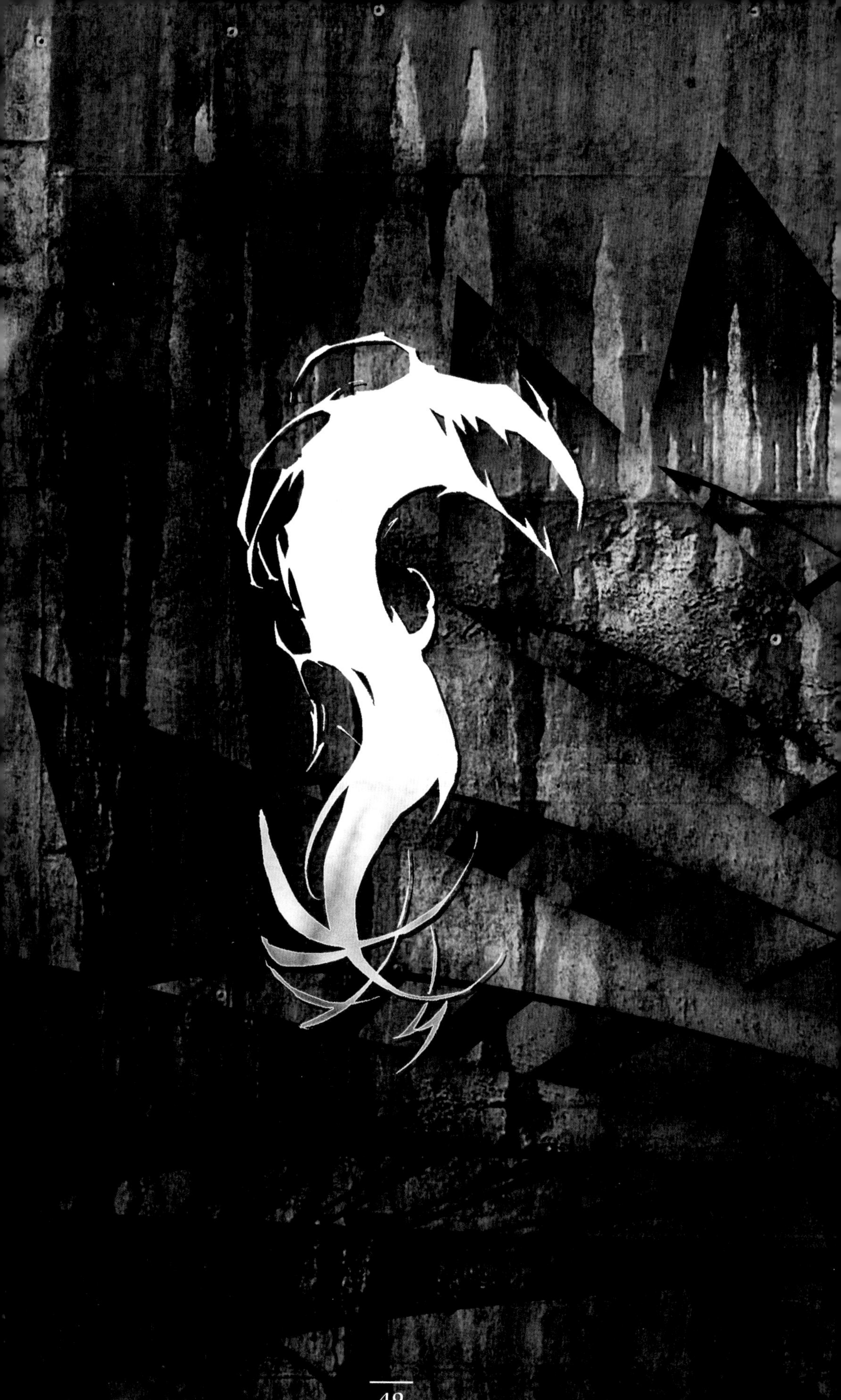

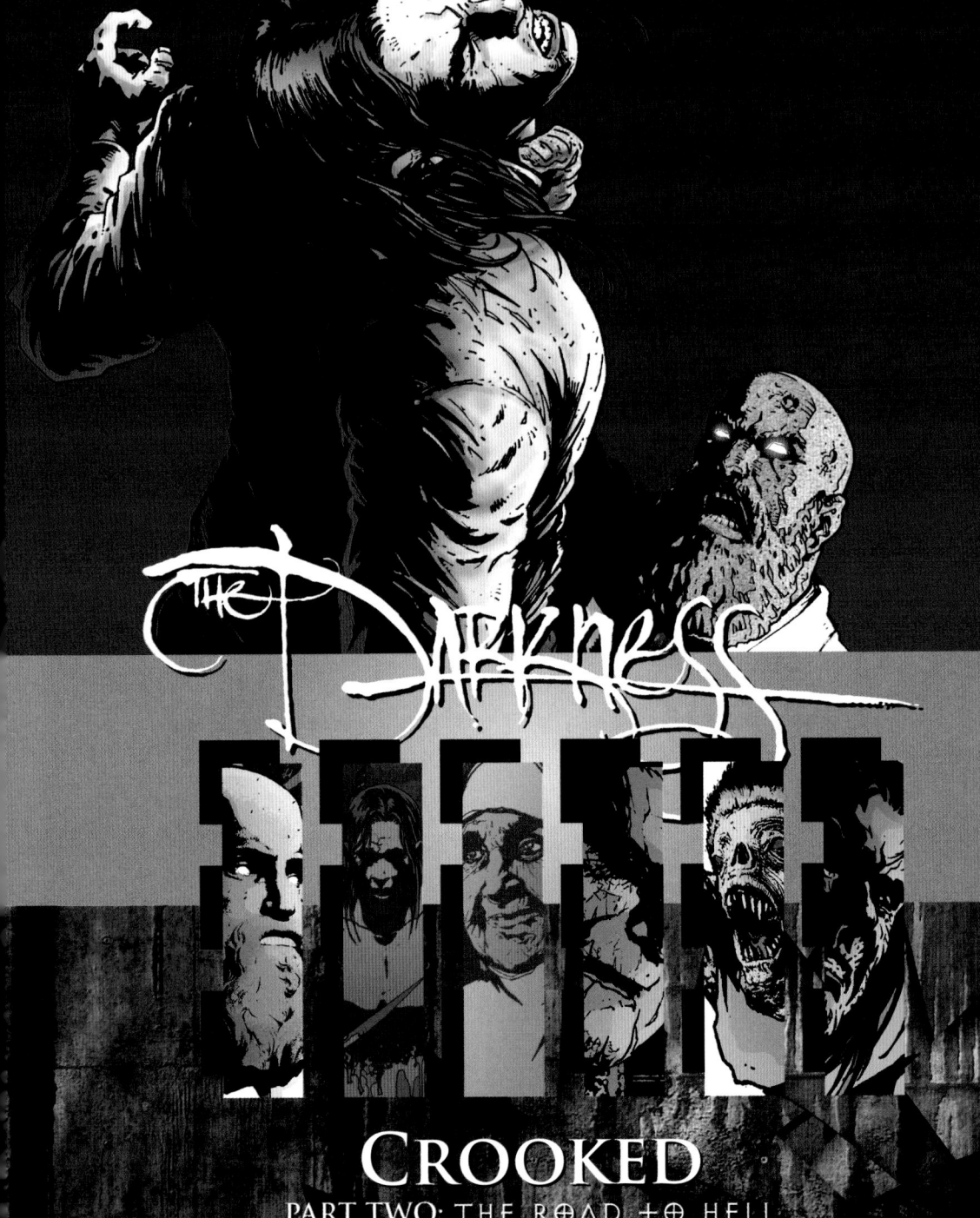

CROOKED

PART TWO: THE ROAD TO HELL

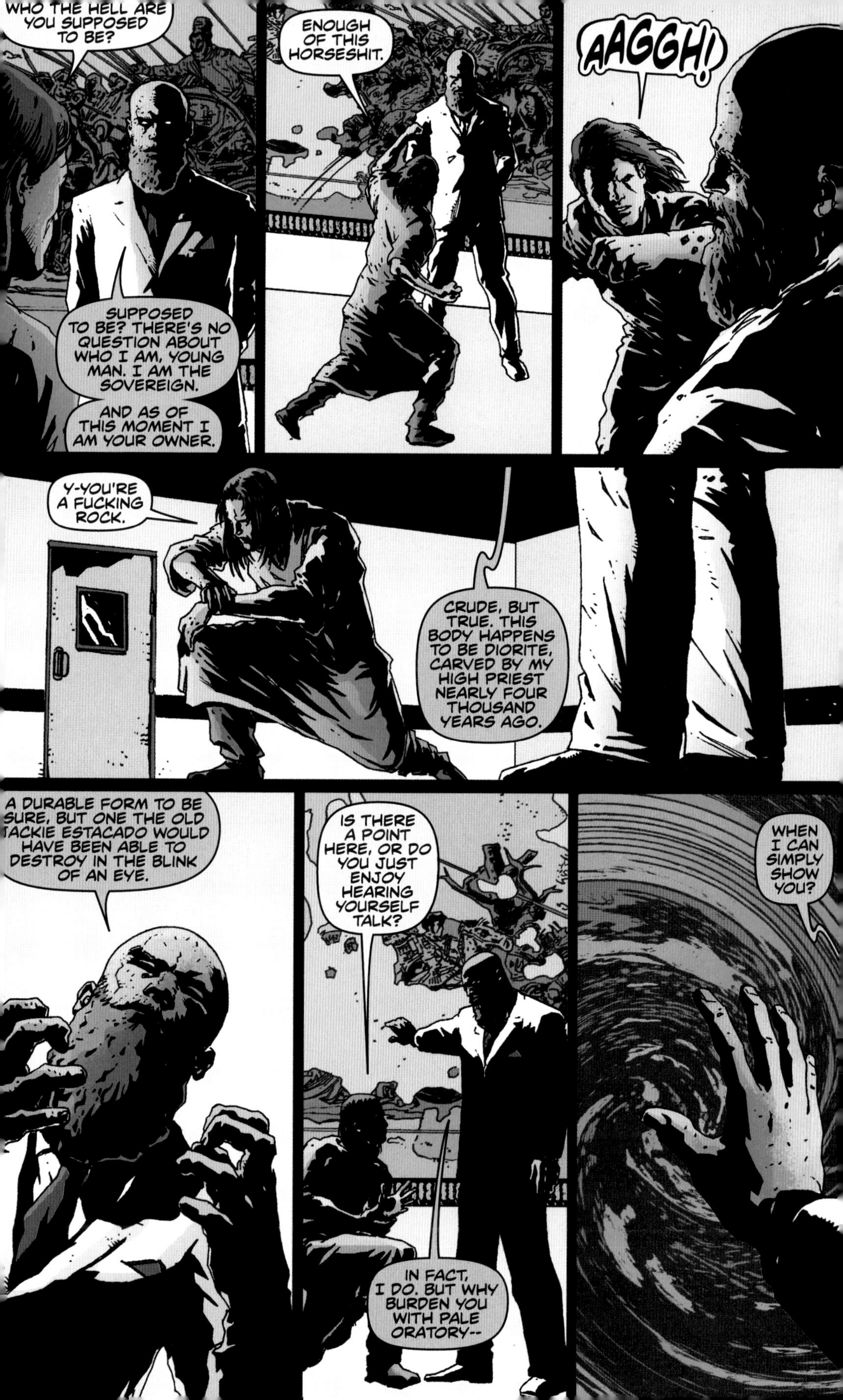
WHO THE HELL ARE YOU SUPPOSED TO BE?
SUPPOSED TO BE? THERE'S NO QUESTION ABOUT WHO I AM, YOUNG MAN. I AM THE SOVEREIGN.
AND AS OF THIS MOMENT I AM YOUR OWNER.
ENOUGH OF THIS HORSESHIT.
AAGGH!
Y-YOU'RE A FUCKING ROCK.
CRUDE, BUT TRUE. THIS BODY HAPPENS TO BE DIORITE, CARVED BY MY HIGH PRIEST NEARLY FOUR THOUSAND YEARS AGO.
A DURABLE FORM TO BE SURE, BUT ONE THE OLD JACKIE ESTACADO WOULD HAVE BEEN ABLE TO DESTROY IN THE BLINK OF AN EYE.
IS THERE A POINT HERE, OR DO YOU JUST ENJOY HEARING YOURSELF TALK?
IN FACT, I DO. BUT WHY BURDEN YOU WITH PALE ORATORY--
WHEN I CAN SIMPLY SHOW YOU?

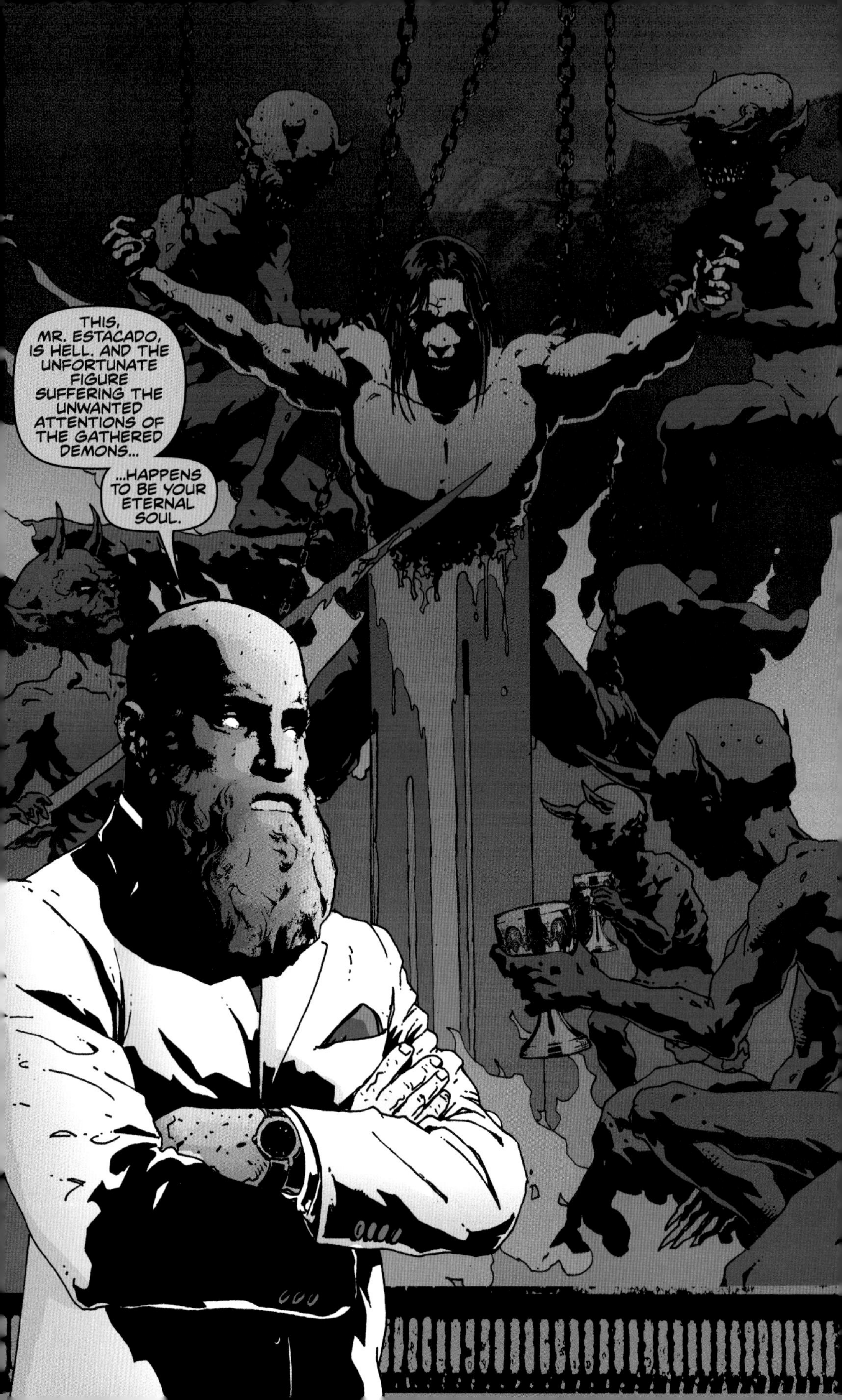
THIS, MR. ESTACADO, IS HELL. AND THE UNFORTUNATE FIGURE SUFFERING THE UNWANTED ATTENTIONS OF THE GATHERED DEMONS...
...HAPPENS TO BE YOUR ETERNAL SOUL.

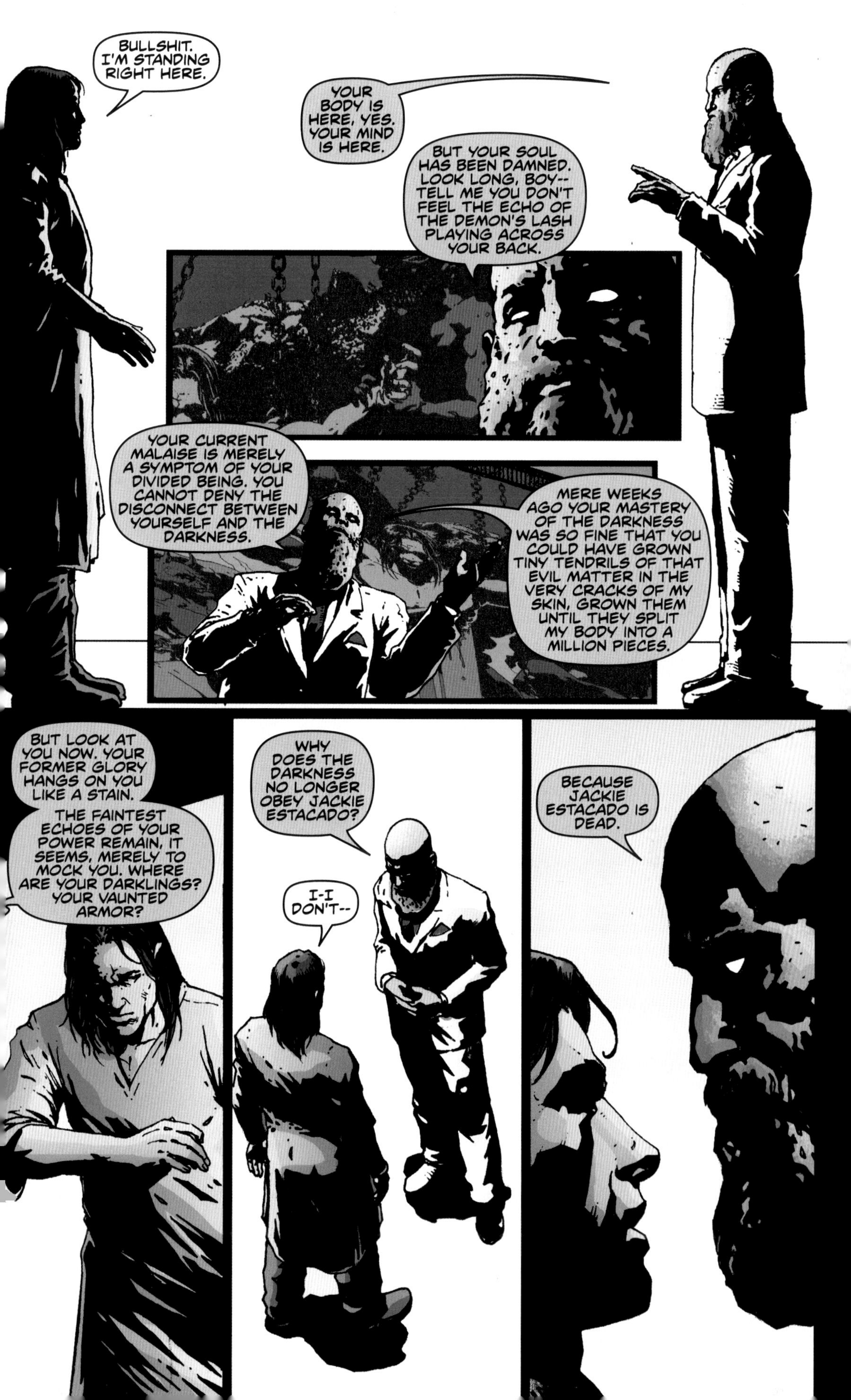
BULLSHIT. I'M STANDING RIGHT HERE.
YOUR BODY IS HERE, YES. YOUR MIND IS HERE.
BUT YOUR SOUL HAS BEEN DAMNED. LOOK LONG, BOY-- TELL ME YOU DON'T FEEL THE ECHO OF THE DEMON'S LASH PLAYING ACROSS YOUR BACK.
YOUR CURRENT MALAISE IS MERELY A SYMPTOM OF YOUR DIVIDED BEING. YOU CANNOT DENY THE DISCONNECT BETWEEN YOURSELF AND THE DARKNESS.
MERE WEEKS AGO YOUR MASTERY OF THE DARKNESS WAS SO FINE THAT YOU COULD HAVE GROWN TINY TENDRILS OF THAT EVIL MATTER IN THE VERY CRACKS OF MY SKIN, GROWN THEM UNTIL THEY SPLIT MY BODY INTO A MILLION PIECES.
BUT LOOK AT YOU NOW. YOUR FORMER GLORY HANGS ON YOU LIKE A STAIN.
THE FAINTEST ECHOES OF YOUR POWER REMAIN, IT SEEMS, MERELY TO MOCK YOU. WHERE ARE YOUR DARKLINGS? YOUR VAUNTED ARMOR?
WHY DOES THE DARKNESS NO LONGER OBEY JACKIE ESTACADO?
I-I DON'T--
BECAUSE JACKIE ESTACADO IS DEAD.

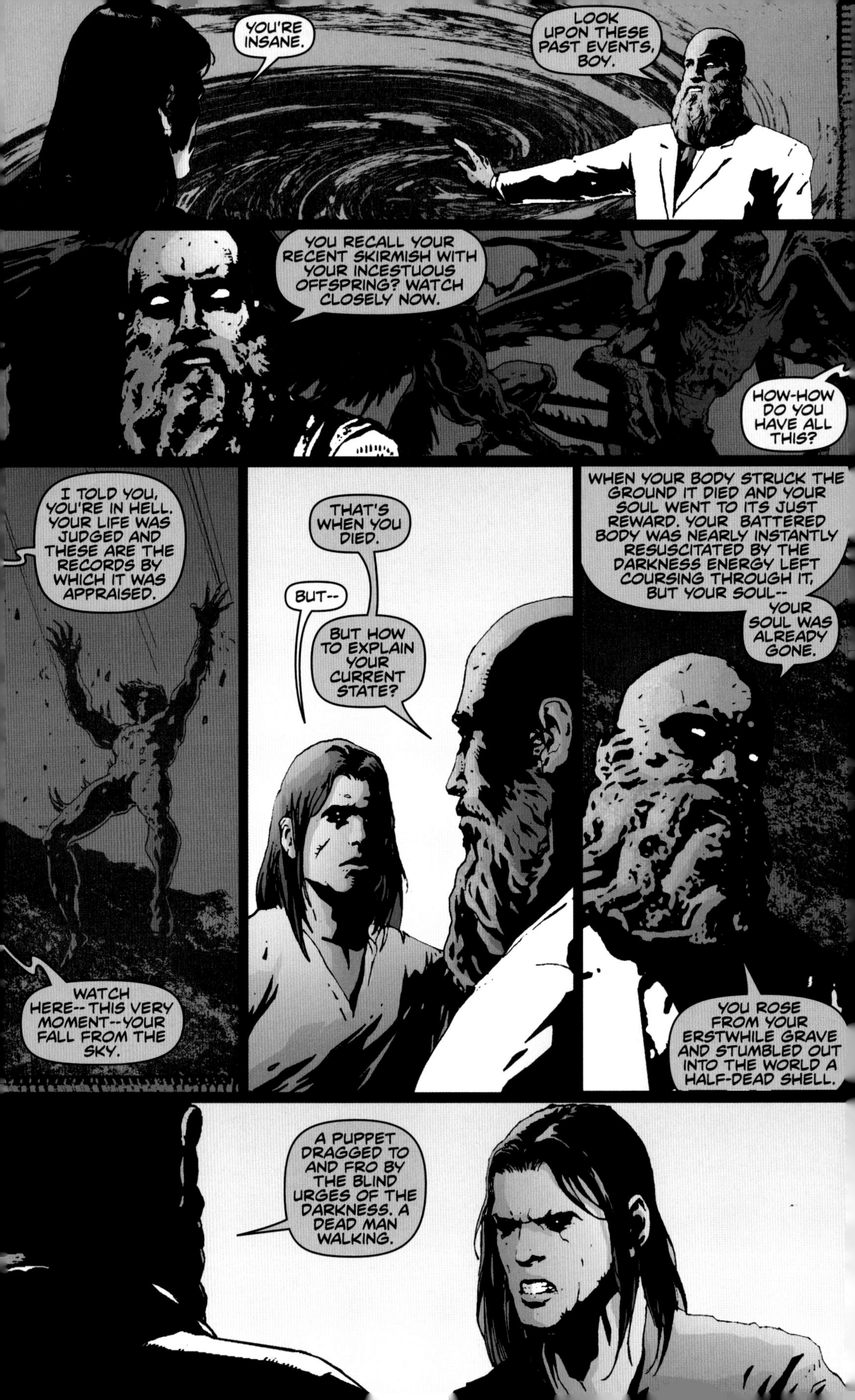
YOU'RE INSANE.
LOOK UPON THESE PAST EVENTS, BOY.
YOU RECALL YOUR RECENT SKIRMISH WITH YOUR INCESTUOUS OFFSPRING? WATCH CLOSELY NOW.
HOW-HOW DO YOU HAVE ALL THIS?
I TOLD YOU, YOU'RE IN HELL. YOUR LIFE WAS JUDGED AND THESE ARE THE RECORDS BY WHICH IT WAS APPRAISED.
WATCH HERE--THIS VERY MOMENT--YOUR FALL FROM THE SKY.
THAT'S WHEN YOU DIED.
BUT--
BUT HOW TO EXPLAIN YOUR CURRENT STATE?
WHEN YOUR BODY STRUCK THE GROUND IT DIED AND YOUR SOUL WENT TO ITS JUST REWARD. YOUR BATTERED BODY WAS NEARLY INSTANTLY RESUSCITATED BY THE DARKNESS ENERGY LEFT COURSING THROUGH IT, BUT YOUR SOUL--
YOUR SOUL WAS ALREADY GONE.
YOU ROSE FROM YOUR ERSTWHILE GRAVE AND STUMBLED OUT INTO THE WORLD A HALF-DEAD SHELL.
A PUPPET DRAGGED TO AND FRO BY THE BLIND URGES OF THE DARKNESS. A DEAD MAN WALKING.

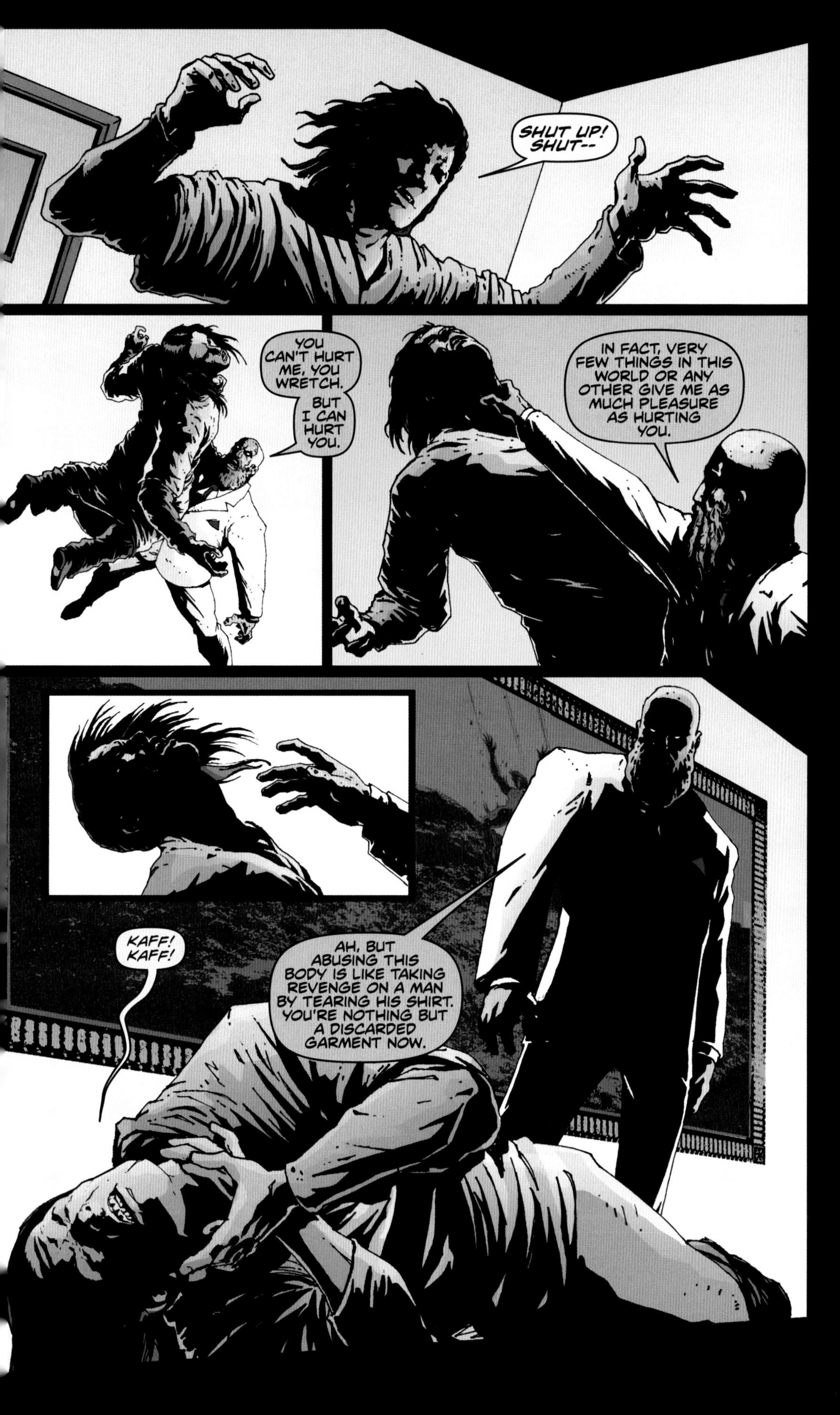
SHUT UP! SHUT--
YOU CAN'T HURT ME, YOU WRETCH.
BUT I CAN HURT YOU.
IN FACT, VERY FEW THINGS IN THIS WORLD OR ANY OTHER GIVE ME AS MUCH PLEASURE AS HURTING YOU.
KAFF! KAFF!
AH, BUT ABUSING THIS BODY IS LIKE TAKING REVENGE ON A MAN BY TEARING HIS SHIRT. YOU'RE NOTHING BUT A DISCARDED GARMENT NOW.

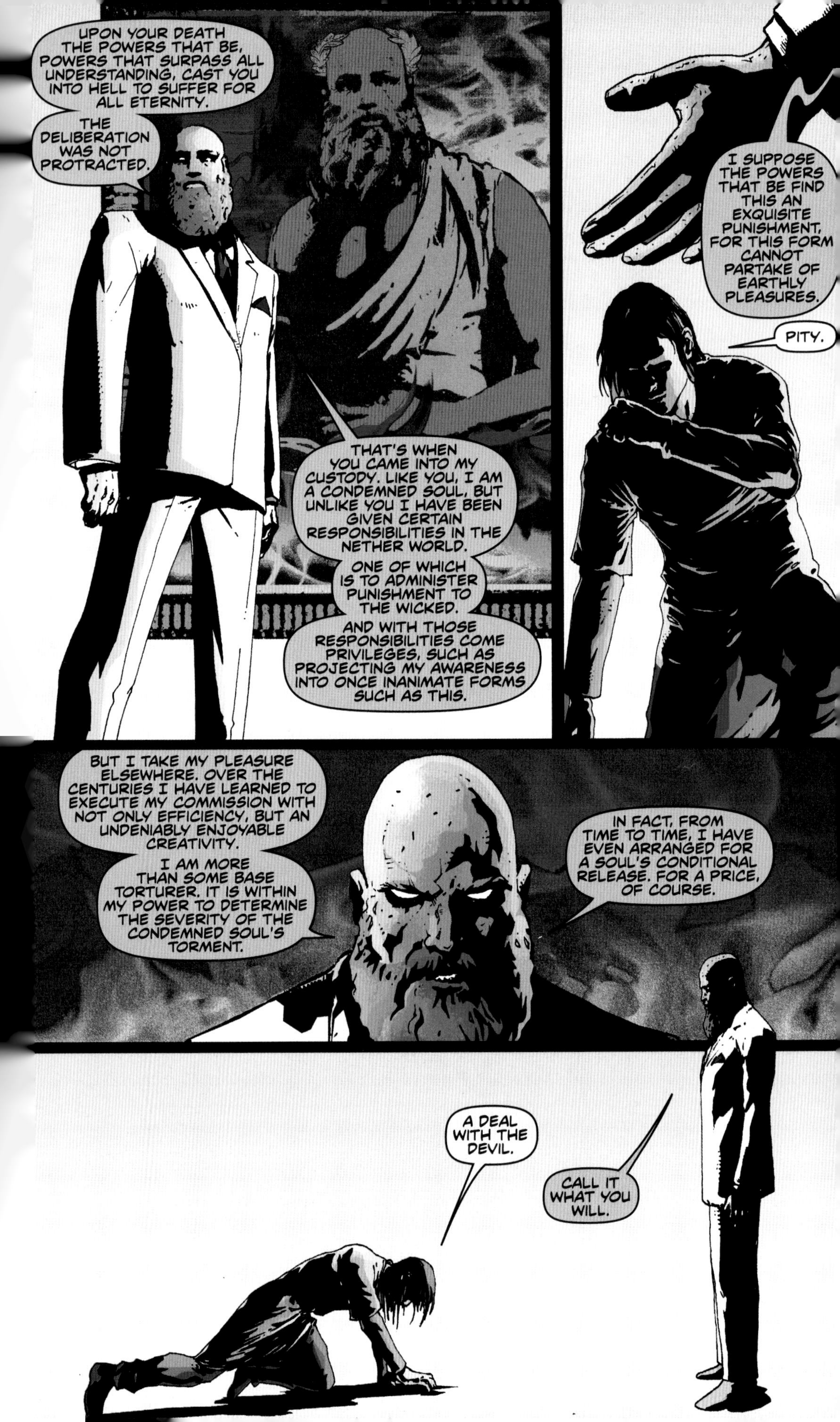

UPON YOUR DEATH THE POWERS THAT BE, POWERS THAT SURPASS ALL UNDERSTANDING, CAST YOU INTO HELL TO SUFFER FOR ALL ETERNITY.
THE DELIBERATION WAS NOT PROTRACTED.
THAT'S WHEN YOU CAME INTO MY CUSTODY. LIKE YOU, I AM A CONDEMNED SOUL, BUT UNLIKE YOU I HAVE BEEN GIVEN CERTAIN RESPONSIBILITIES IN THE NETHER WORLD.
ONE OF WHICH IS TO ADMINISTER PUNISHMENT TO THE WICKED.
AND WITH THOSE RESPONSIBILITIES COME PRIVILEGES, SUCH AS PROJECTING MY AWARENESS INTO ONCE INANIMATE FORMS SUCH AS THIS.
I SUPPOSE THE POWERS THAT BE FIND THIS AN EXQUISITE PUNISHMENT, FOR THIS FORM CANNOT PARTAKE OF EARTHLY PLEASURES.
PITY.
BUT I TAKE MY PLEASURE ELSEWHERE. OVER THE CENTURIES I HAVE LEARNED TO EXECUTE MY COMMISSION WITH NOT ONLY EFFICIENCY, BUT AN UNDENIABLY ENJOYABLE CREATIVITY.
I AM MORE THAN SOME BASE TORTURER. IT IS WITHIN MY POWER TO DETERMINE THE SEVERITY OF THE CONDEMNED SOUL'S TORMENT.
IN FACT, FROM TIME TO TIME, I HAVE EVEN ARRANGED FOR A SOUL'S CONDITIONAL RELEASE. FOR A PRICE, OF COURSE.
A DEAL WITH THE DEVIL.
CALL IT WHAT YOU WILL.

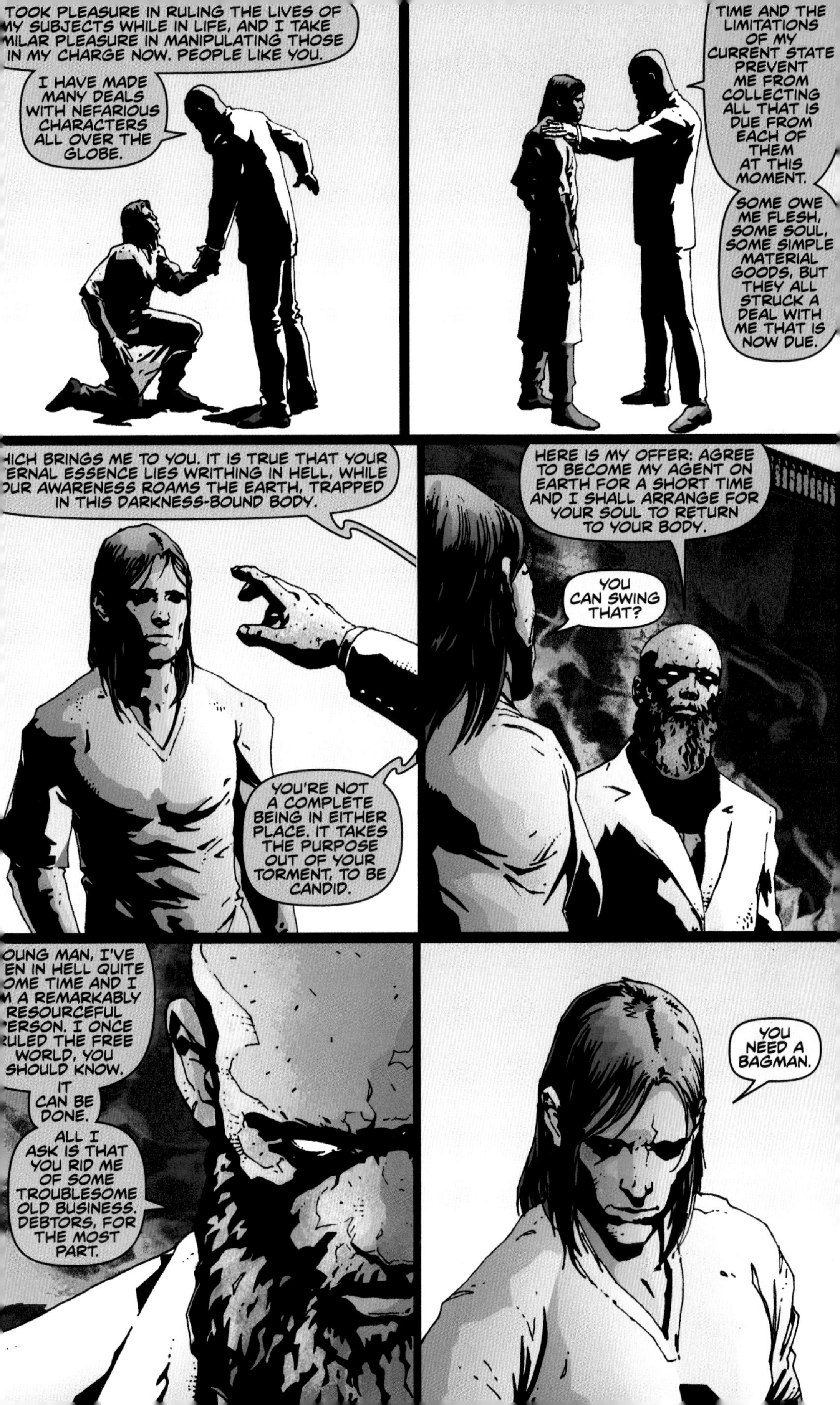
TOOK PLEASURE IN RULING THE LIVES OF MY SUBJECTS WHILE IN LIFE, AND I TAKE MILAR PLEASURE IN MANIPULATING THOSE IN MY CHARGE NOW. PEOPLE LIKE YOU.
I HAVE MADE MANY DEALS WITH NEFARIOUS CHARACTERS ALL OVER THE GLOBE.
TIME AND THE LIMITATIONS OF MY CURRENT STATE PREVENT ME FROM COLLECTING ALL THAT IS DUE FROM EACH OF THEM AT THIS MOMENT.
SOME OWE ME FLESH, SOME SOUL, SOME SIMPLE MATERIAL GOODS, BUT THEY ALL STRUCK A DEAL WITH ME THAT IS NOW DUE.
HICH BRINGS ME TO YOU. IT IS TRUE THAT YOUR ERNAL ESSENCE LIES WRITHING IN HELL, WHILE OUR AWARENESS ROAMS THE EARTH, TRAPPED IN THIS DARKNESS-BOUND BODY.
YOU'RE NOT A COMPLETE BEING IN EITHER PLACE. IT TAKES THE PURPOSE OUT OF YOUR TORMENT, TO BE CANDID.
HERE IS MY OFFER: AGREE TO BECOME MY AGENT ON EARTH FOR A SHORT TIME AND I SHALL ARRANGE FOR YOUR SOUL TO RETURN TO YOUR BODY.
YOU CAN SWING THAT?
OUNG MAN, I'VE EN IN HELL QUITE OME TIME AND I M A REMARKABLY RESOURCEFUL ERSON. I ONCE ULED THE FREE WORLD, YOU SHOULD KNOW.
IT CAN BE DONE.
ALL I ASK IS THAT YOU RID ME OF SOME TROUBLESOME OLD BUSINESS. DEBTORS, FOR THE MOST PART.
YOU NEED A BAGMAN.

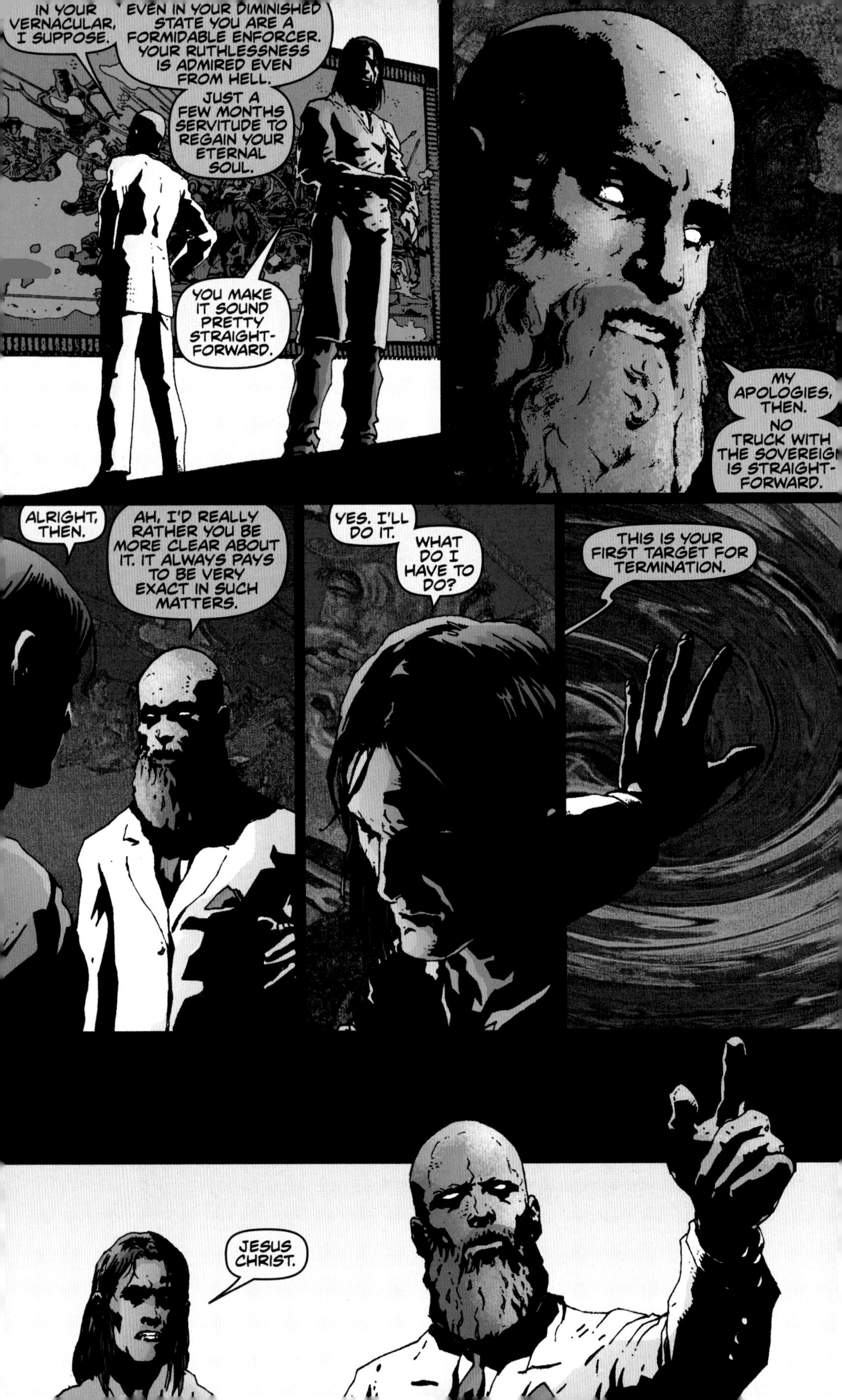
IN YOUR VERNACULAR, I SUPPOSE.
EVEN IN YOUR DIMINISHED STATE YOU ARE A FORMIDABLE ENFORCER. YOUR RUTHLESSNESS IS ADMIRED EVEN FROM HELL.
JUST A FEW MONTHS SERVITUDE TO REGAIN YOUR ETERNAL SOUL.
YOU MAKE IT SOUND PRETTY STRAIGHT-FORWARD.
MY APOLOGIES, THEN.
NO TRUCK WITH THE SOVEREIG IS STRAIGHT-FORWARD.
ALRIGHT, THEN.
AH, I'D REALLY RATHER YOU BE MORE CLEAR ABOUT IT. IT ALWAYS PAYS TO BE VERY EXACT IN SUCH MATTERS.
YES. I'LL DO IT.
WHAT DO I HAVE TO DO?
THIS IS YOUR FIRST TARGET FOR TERMINATION.
JESUS CHRIST.

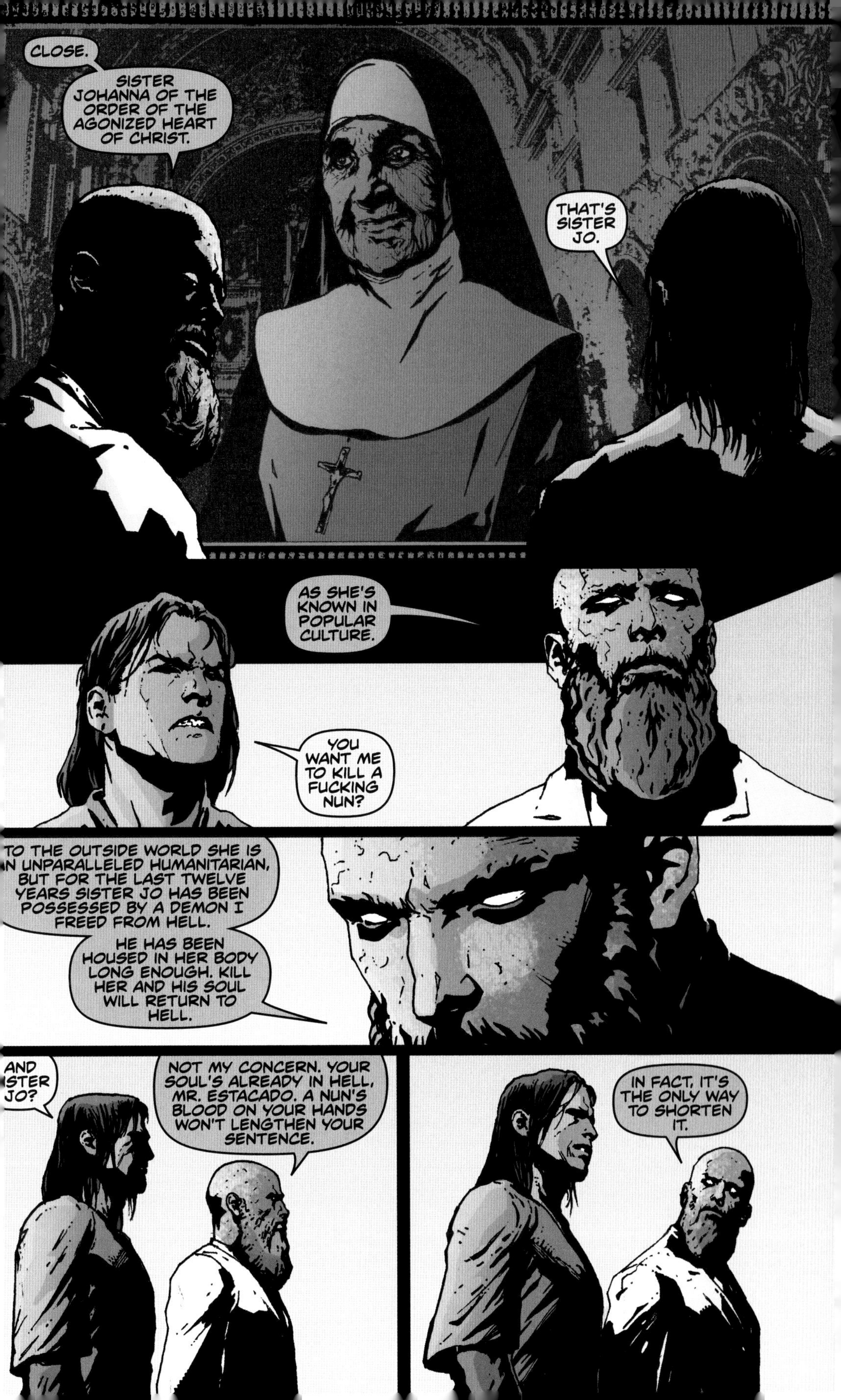
CLOSE.
SISTER JOHANNA OF THE ORDER OF THE AGONIZED HEART OF CHRIST.
THAT'S SISTER JO.
AS SHE'S KNOWN IN POPULAR CULTURE.
YOU WANT ME TO KILL A FUCKING NUN?
TO THE OUTSIDE WORLD SHE IS N UNPARALLELED HUMANITARIAN, BUT FOR THE LAST TWELVE YEARS SISTER JO HAS BEEN POSSESSED BY A DEMON I FREED FROM HELL.
HE HAS BEEN HOUSED IN HER BODY LONG ENOUGH. KILL HER AND HIS SOUL WILL RETURN TO HELL.
AND STER JO?
NOT MY CONCERN. YOUR SOUL'S ALREADY IN HELL, MR. ESTACADO. A NUN'S BLOOD ON YOUR HANDS WON'T LENGTHEN YOUR SENTENCE.
IN FACT, IT'S THE ONLY WAY TO SHORTEN IT.

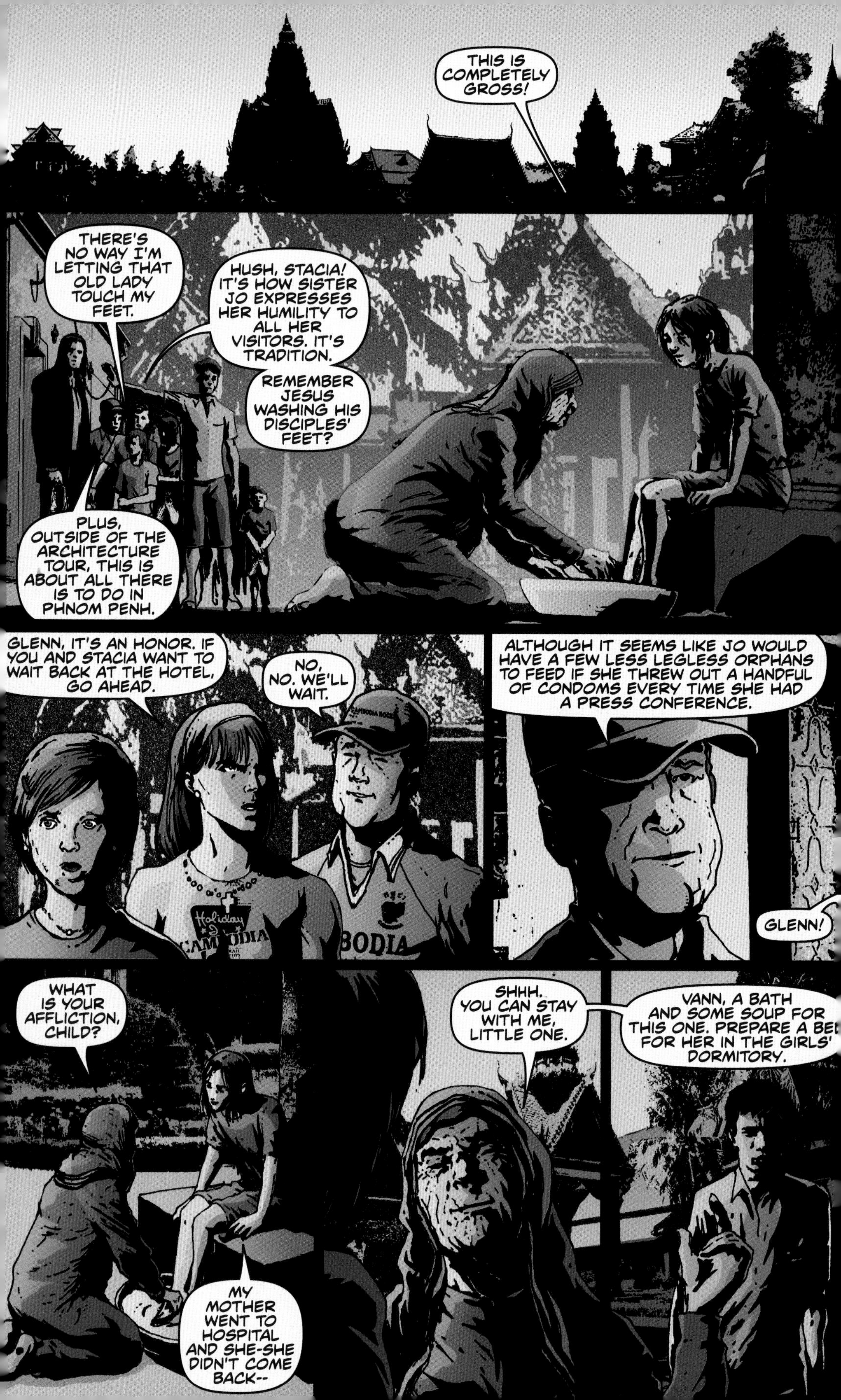
THIS IS COMPLETELY GROSS!
THERE'S NO WAY I'M LETTING THAT OLD LADY TOUCH MY FEET.
HUSH, STACIA! IT'S HOW SISTER JO EXPRESSES HER HUMILITY TO ALL HER VISITORS. IT'S TRADITION.
REMEMBER JESUS WASHING HIS DISCIPLES' FEET?
PLUS, OUTSIDE OF THE ARCHITECTURE TOUR, THIS IS ABOUT ALL THERE IS TO DO IN PHNOM PENH.
GLENN, IT'S AN HONOR. IF YOU AND STACIA WANT TO WAIT BACK AT THE HOTEL, GO AHEAD.
NO, NO. WE'LL WAIT.
ALTHOUGH IT SEEMS LIKE JO WOULD HAVE A FEW LESS LEGLESS ORPHANS TO FEED IF SHE THREW OUT A HANDFUL OF CONDOMS EVERY TIME SHE HAD A PRESS CONFERENCE.
GLENN!
WHAT IS YOUR AFFLICTION, CHILD?
MY MOTHER WENT TO HOSPITAL AND SHE-SHE DIDN'T COME BACK--
SHHH. YOU CAN STAY WITH ME, LITTLE ONE.
VANN, A BATH AND SOME SOUP FOR THIS ONE. PREPARE A BE FOR HER IN THE GIRLS' DORMITORY.

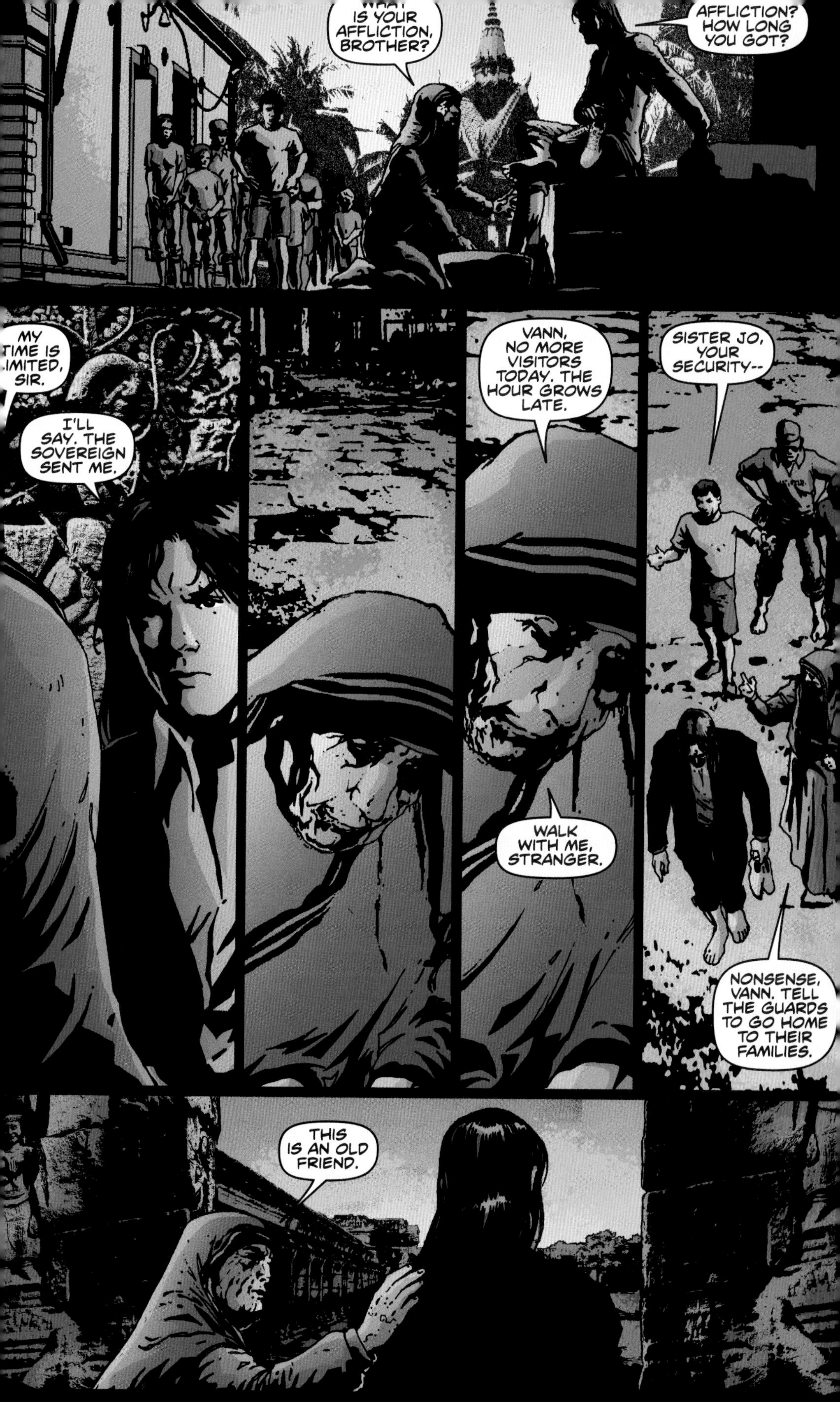
WHAT IS YOUR AFFLICTION, BROTHER?
AFFLICTION? HOW LONG YOU GOT?
MY TIME IS LIMITED, SIR.
I'LL SAY. THE SOVEREIGN SENT ME.
VANN, NO MORE VISITORS TODAY. THE HOUR GROWS LATE.
WALK WITH ME, STRANGER.
SISTER JO, YOUR SECURITY--
NONSENSE, VANN. TELL THE GUARDS TO GO HOME TO THEIR FAMILIES.
THIS IS AN OLD FRIEND.

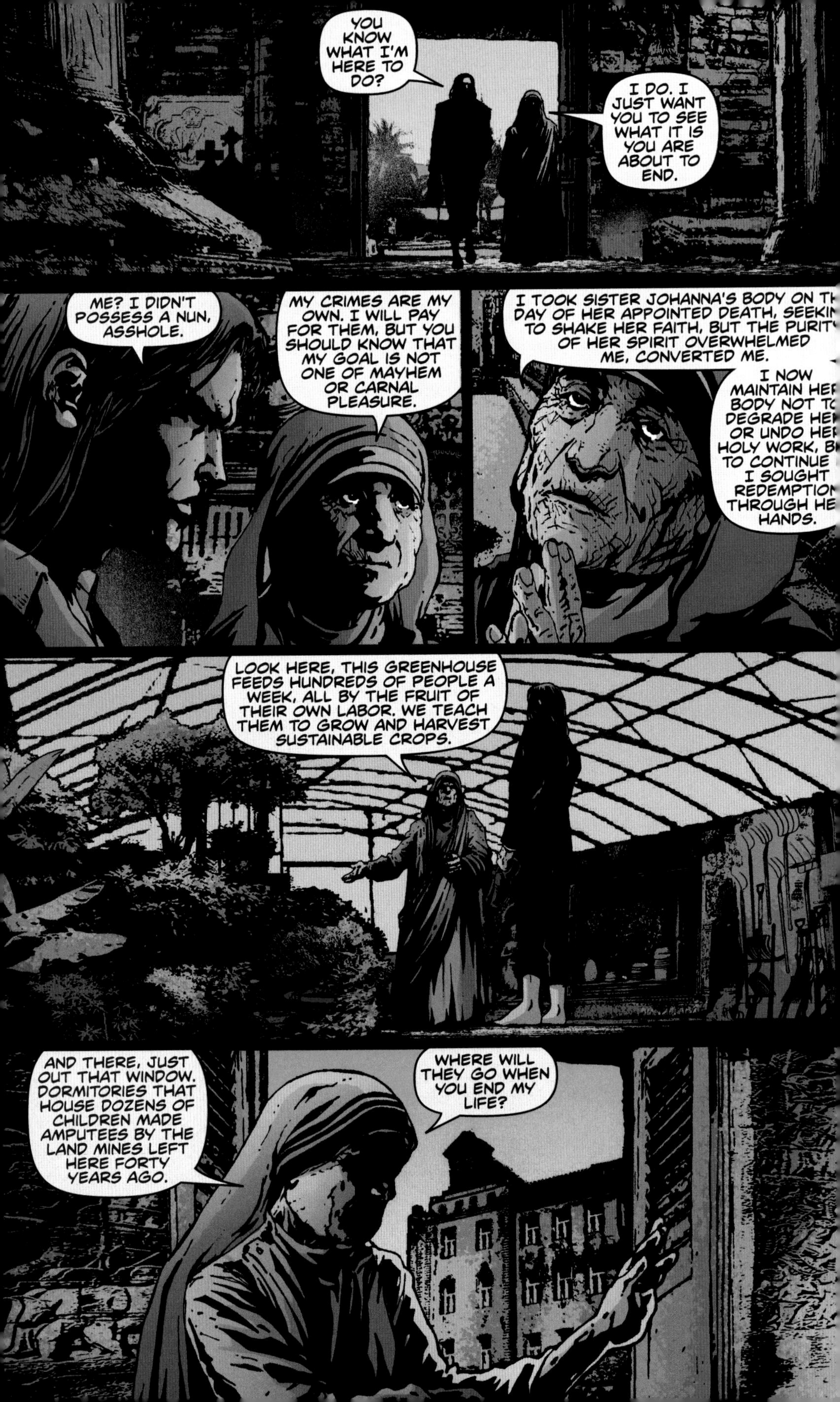

YOU KNOW WHAT I'M HERE TO DO?
I DO. I JUST WANT YOU TO SEE WHAT IT IS YOU ARE ABOUT TO END.
ME? I DIDN'T POSSESS A NUN, ASSHOLE.
MY CRIMES ARE MY OWN. I WILL PAY FOR THEM, BUT YOU SHOULD KNOW THAT MY GOAL IS NOT ONE OF MAYHEM OR CARNAL PLEASURE.
I TOOK SISTER JOHANNA'S BODY ON TH DAY OF HER APPOINTED DEATH, SEEKIN TO SHAKE HER FAITH, BUT THE PURIT OF HER SPIRIT OVERWHELMED ME, CONVERTED ME.
I NOW MAINTAIN HER BODY NOT TO DEGRADE HE OR UNDO HE HOLY WORK, B TO CONTINUE I SOUGHT REDEMPTIO THROUGH HE HANDS.
LOOK HERE, THIS GREENHOUSE FEEDS HUNDREDS OF PEOPLE A WEEK, ALL BY THE FRUIT OF THEIR OWN LABOR. WE TEACH THEM TO GROW AND HARVEST SUSTAINABLE CROPS.
AND THERE, JUST OUT THAT WINDOW. DORMITORIES THAT HOUSE DOZENS OF CHILDREN MADE AMPUTEES BY THE LAND MINES LEFT HERE FORTY YEARS AGO.
WHERE WILL THEY GO WHEN YOU END MY LIFE?

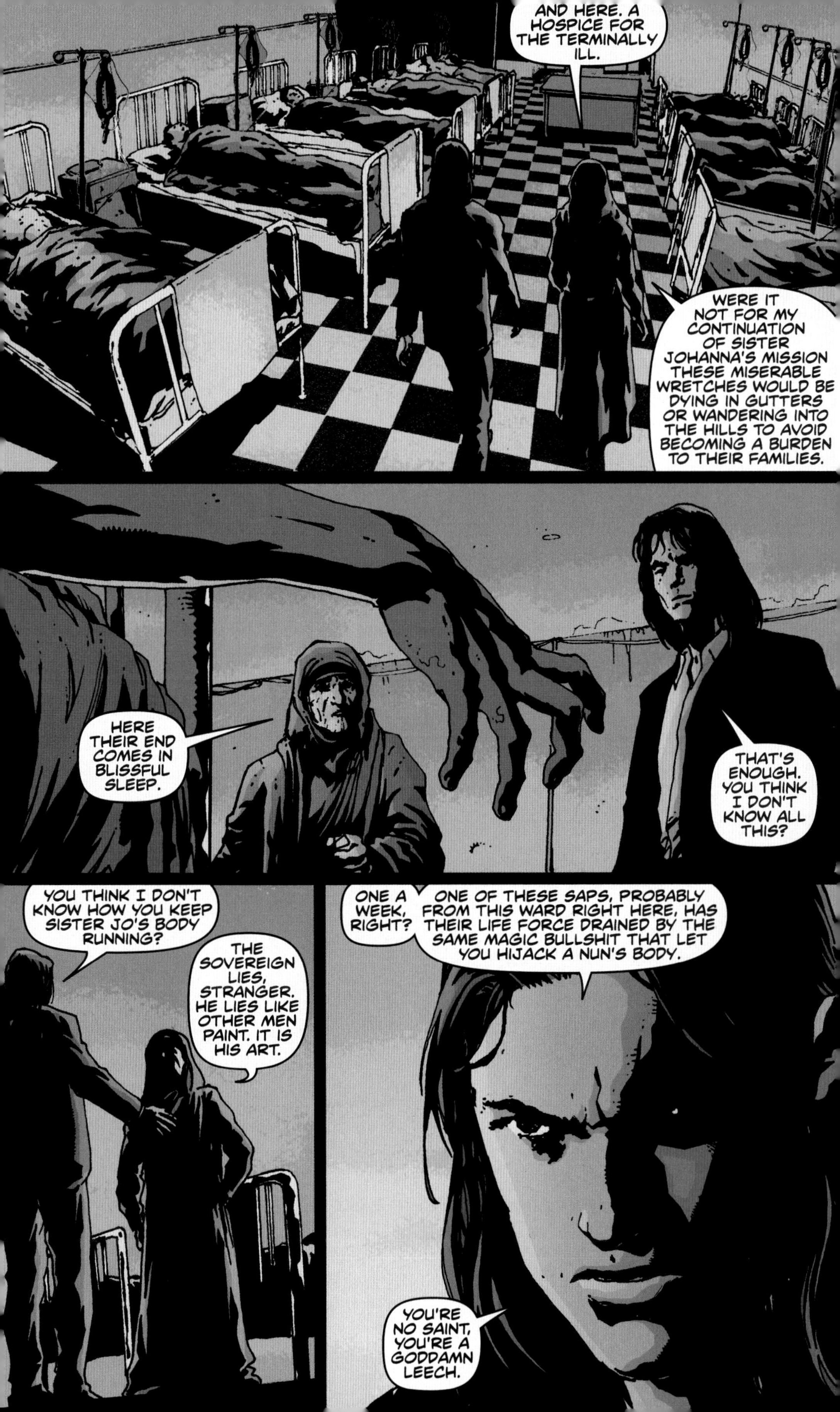
AND HERE. A HOSPICE FOR THE TERMINALLY ILL.
WERE IT NOT FOR MY CONTINUATION OF SISTER JOHANNA'S MISSION THESE MISERABLE WRETCHES WOULD BE DYING IN GUTTERS OR WANDERING INTO THE HILLS TO AVOID BECOMING A BURDEN TO THEIR FAMILIES.
HERE THEIR END COMES IN BLISSFUL SLEEP.
THAT'S ENOUGH. YOU THINK I DON'T KNOW ALL THIS?
YOU THINK I DON'T KNOW HOW YOU KEEP SISTER JO'S BODY RUNNING?
THE SOVEREIGN LIES, STRANGER. HE LIES LIKE OTHER MEN PAINT. IT IS HIS ART.
ONE A WEEK, RIGHT?
ONE OF THESE SAPS, PROBABLY FROM THIS WARD RIGHT HERE, HAS THEIR LIFE FORCE DRAINED BY THE SAME MAGIC BULLSHIT THAT LET YOU HIJACK A NUN'S BODY.
YOU'RE NO SAINT, YOU'RE A GODDAMN LEECH.

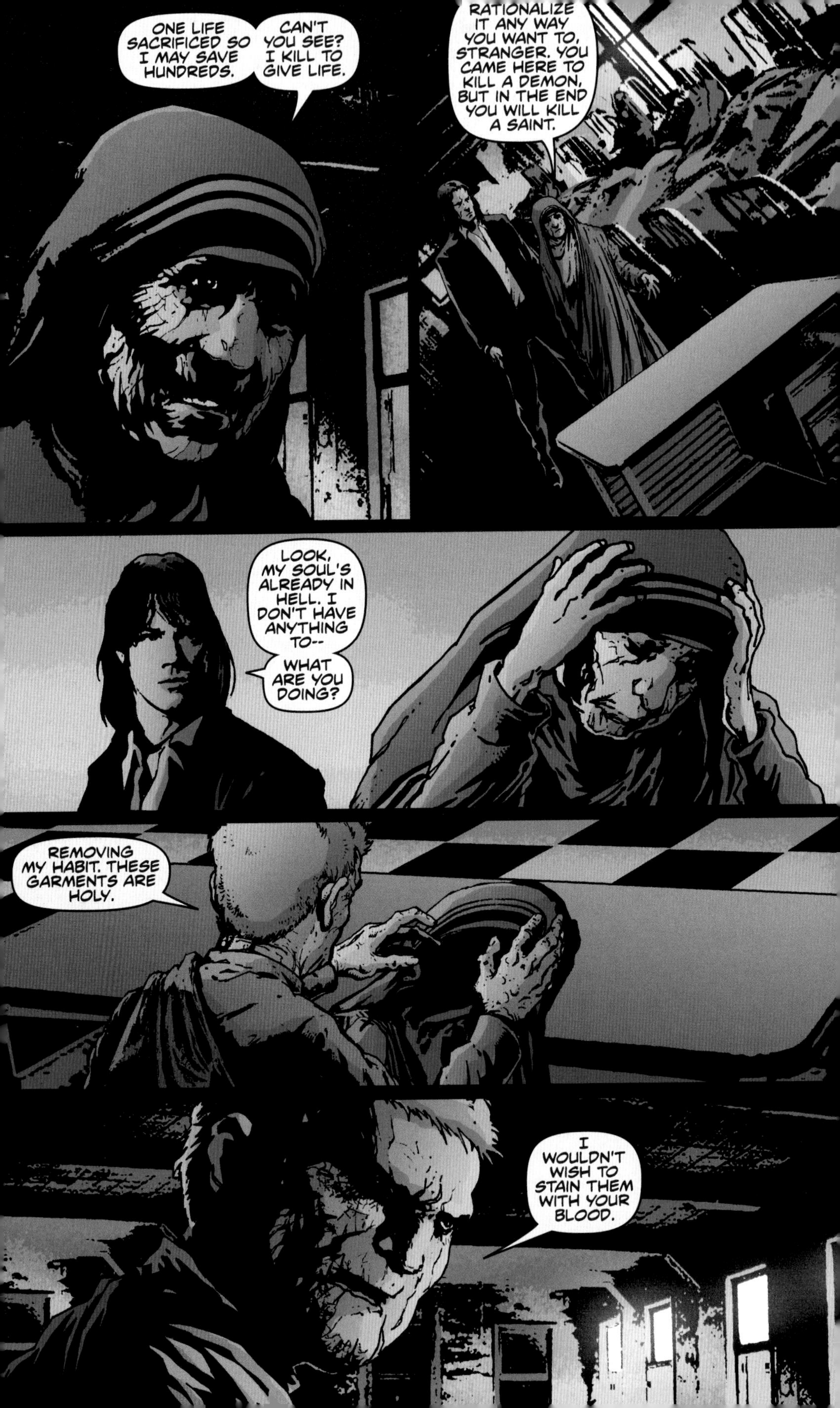

ONE LIFE SACRIFICED SO I MAY SAVE HUNDREDS.
CAN'T YOU SEE? I KILL TO GIVE LIFE.
RATIONALIZE IT ANY WAY YOU WANT TO, STRANGER. YOU CAME HERE TO KILL A DEMON, BUT IN THE END YOU WILL KILL A SAINT.
LOOK, MY SOUL'S ALREADY IN HELL. I DON'T HAVE ANYTHING TO--
WHAT ARE YOU DOING?
REMOVING MY HABIT. THESE GARMENTS ARE HOLY.
I WOULDN'T WISH TO STAIN THEM WITH YOUR BLOOD.

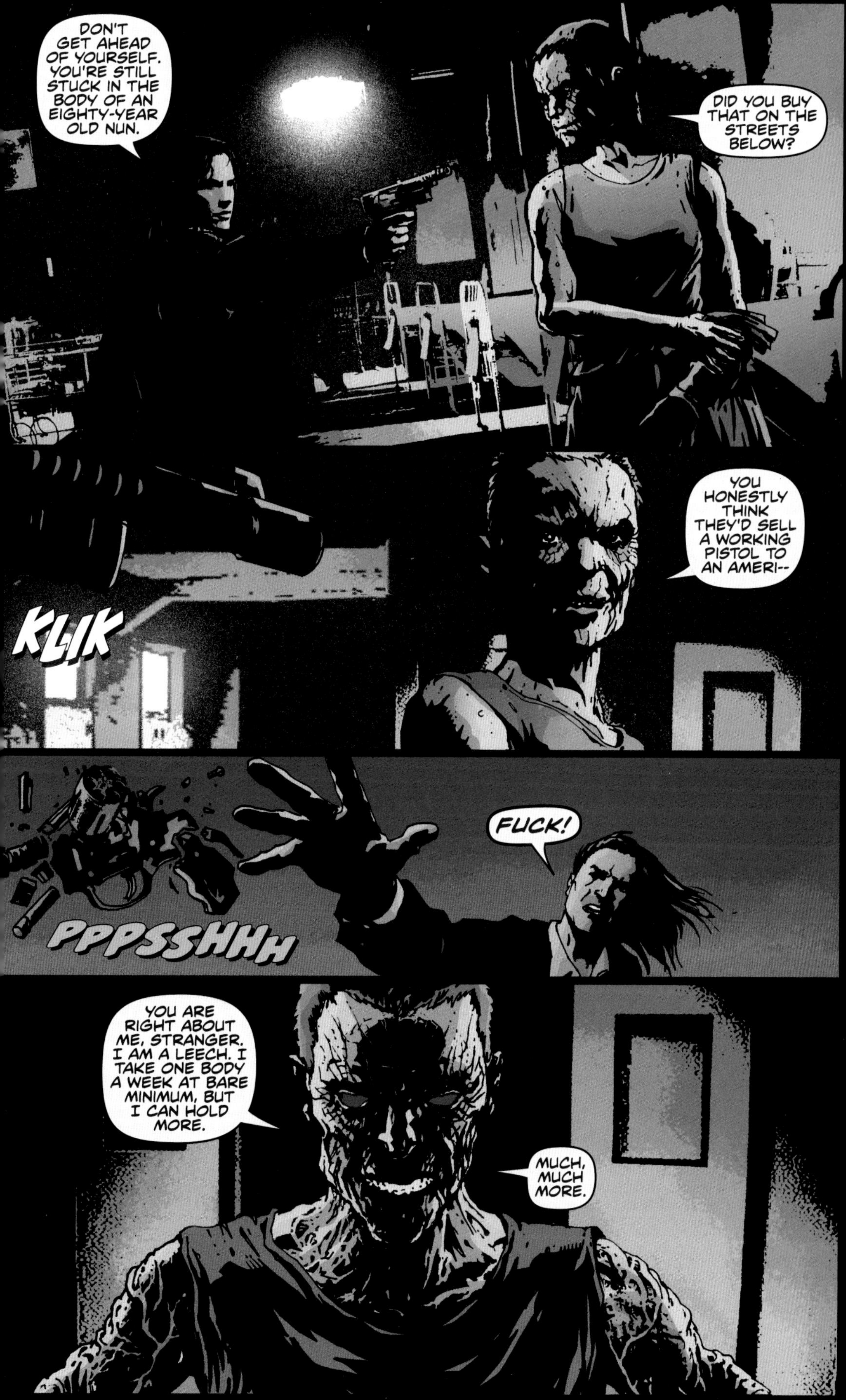
DON'T GET AHEAD OF YOURSELF. YOU'RE STILL STUCK IN THE BODY OF AN EIGHTY-YEAR OLD NUN.
DID YOU BUY THAT ON THE STREETS BELOW?
YOU HONESTLY THINK THEY'D SELL A WORKING PISTOL TO AN AMERI--
KLIK
FUCK!
PPPSSHHH
YOU ARE RIGHT ABOUT ME, STRANGER. I AM A LEECH. I TAKE ONE BODY A WEEK AT BARE MINIMUM, BUT I CAN HOLD MORE.
MUCH, MUCH MORE.

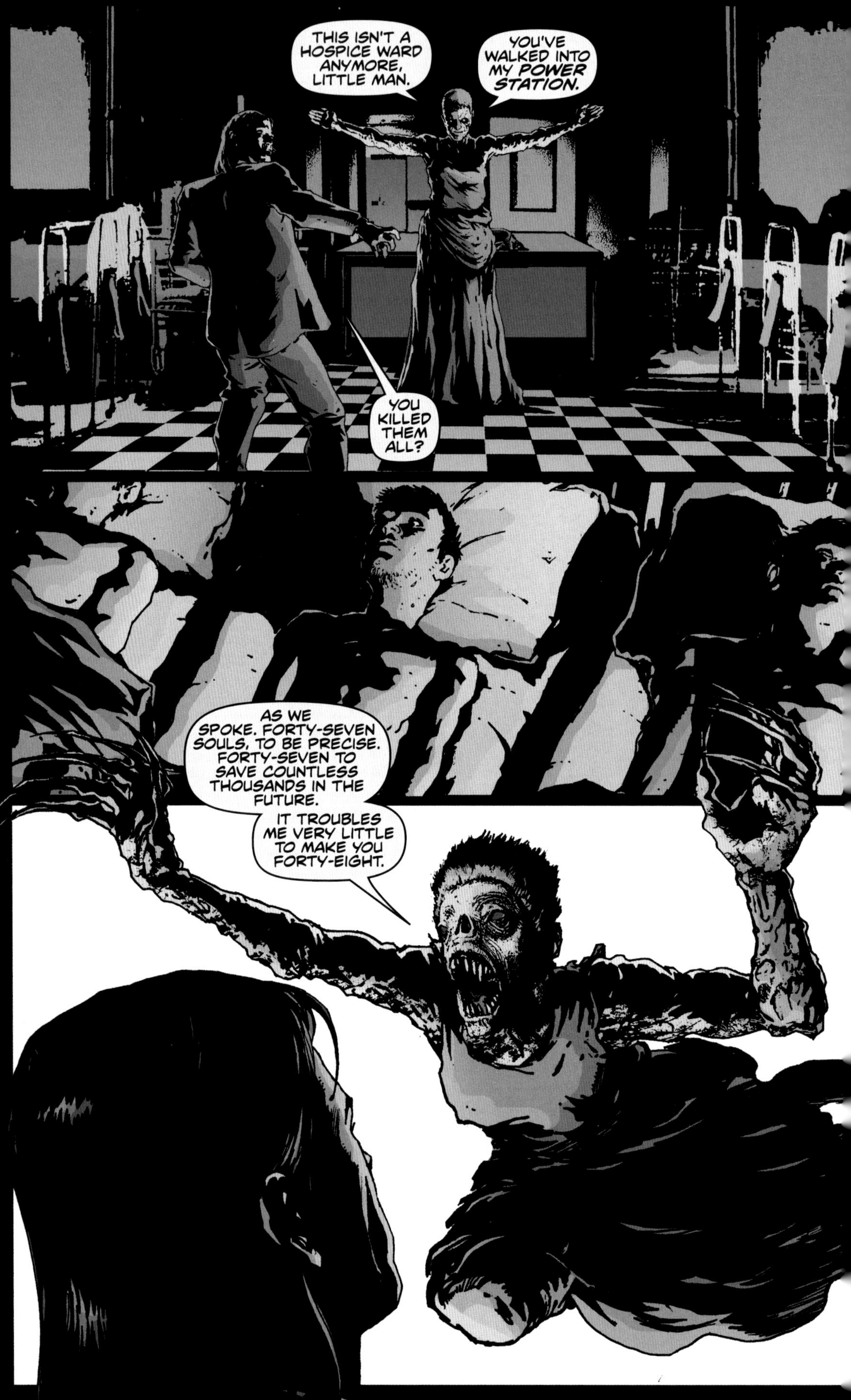
THIS ISN'T A HOSPICE WARD ANYMORE, LITTLE MAN.
YOU'VE WALKED INTO MY POWER STATION.
YOU KILLED THEM ALL?
AS WE SPOKE. FORTY-SEVEN SOULS, TO BE PRECISE. FORTY-SEVEN TO SAVE COUNTLESS THOUSANDS IN THE FUTURE.
IT TROUBLES ME VERY LITTLE TO MAKE YOU FORTY-EIGHT.

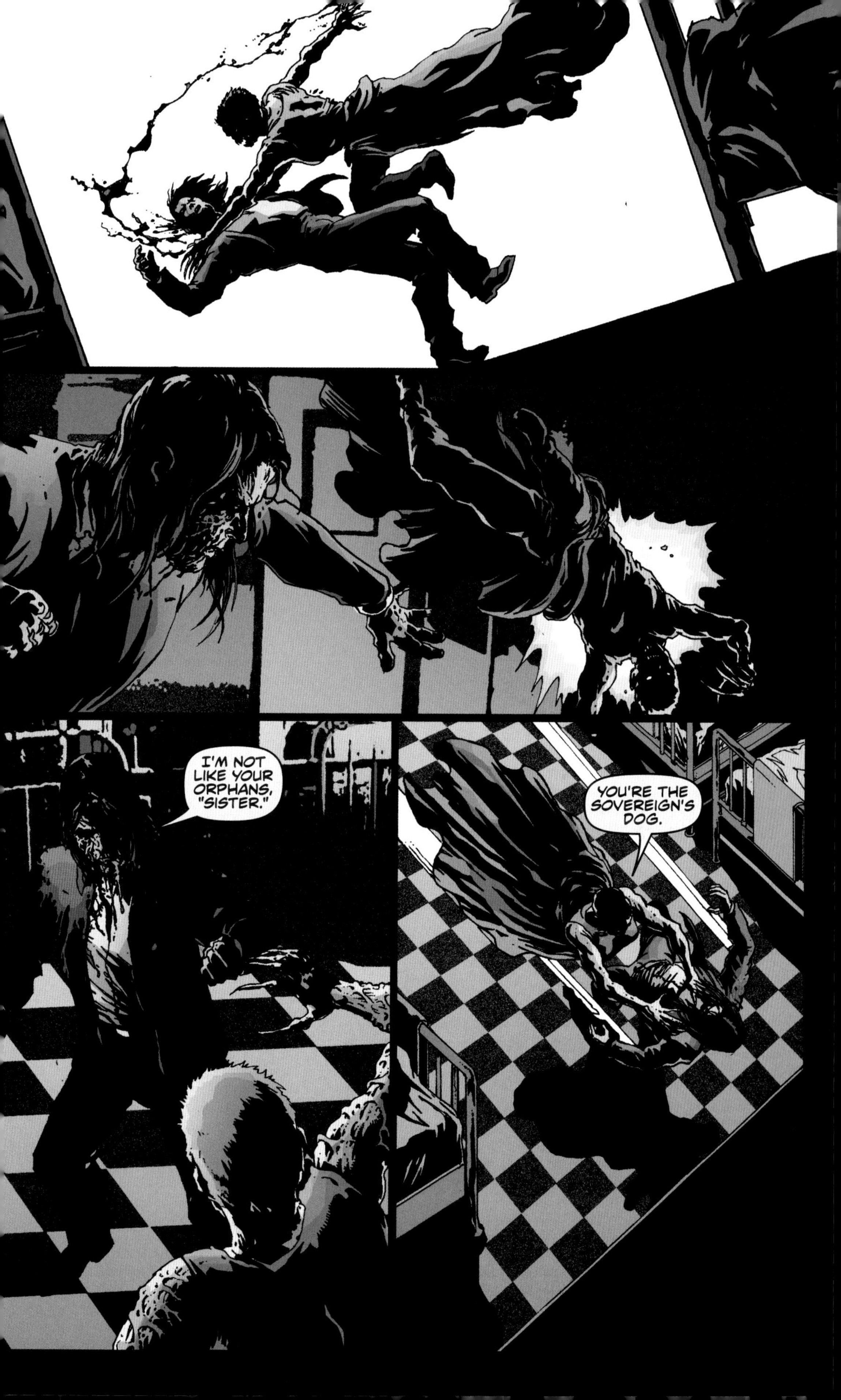
I'M NOT LIKE YOUR ORPHANS, "SISTER."
YOU'RE THE SOVEREIGN'S DOG.

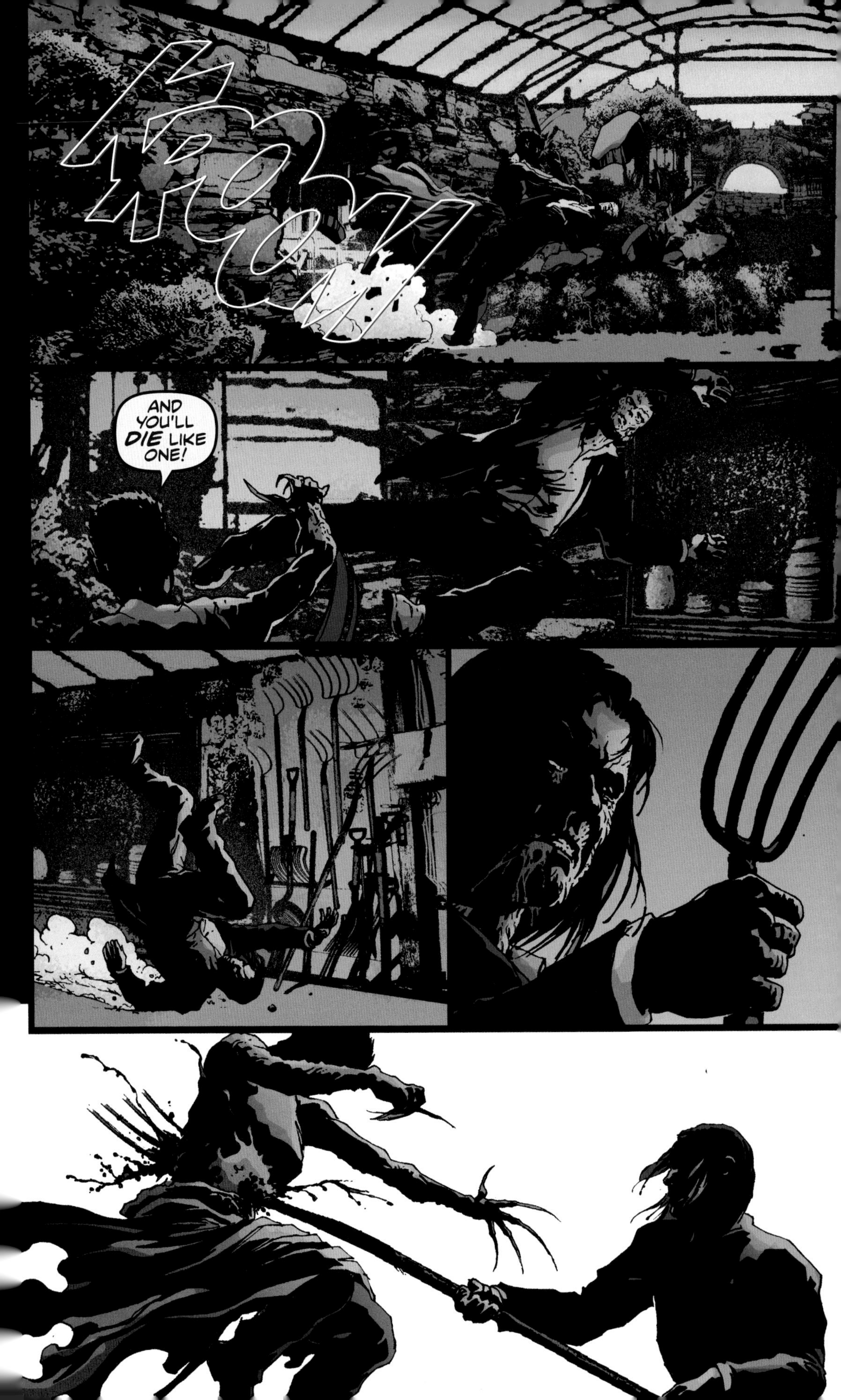
KROOM
AND YOU'LL DIE LIKE ONE!

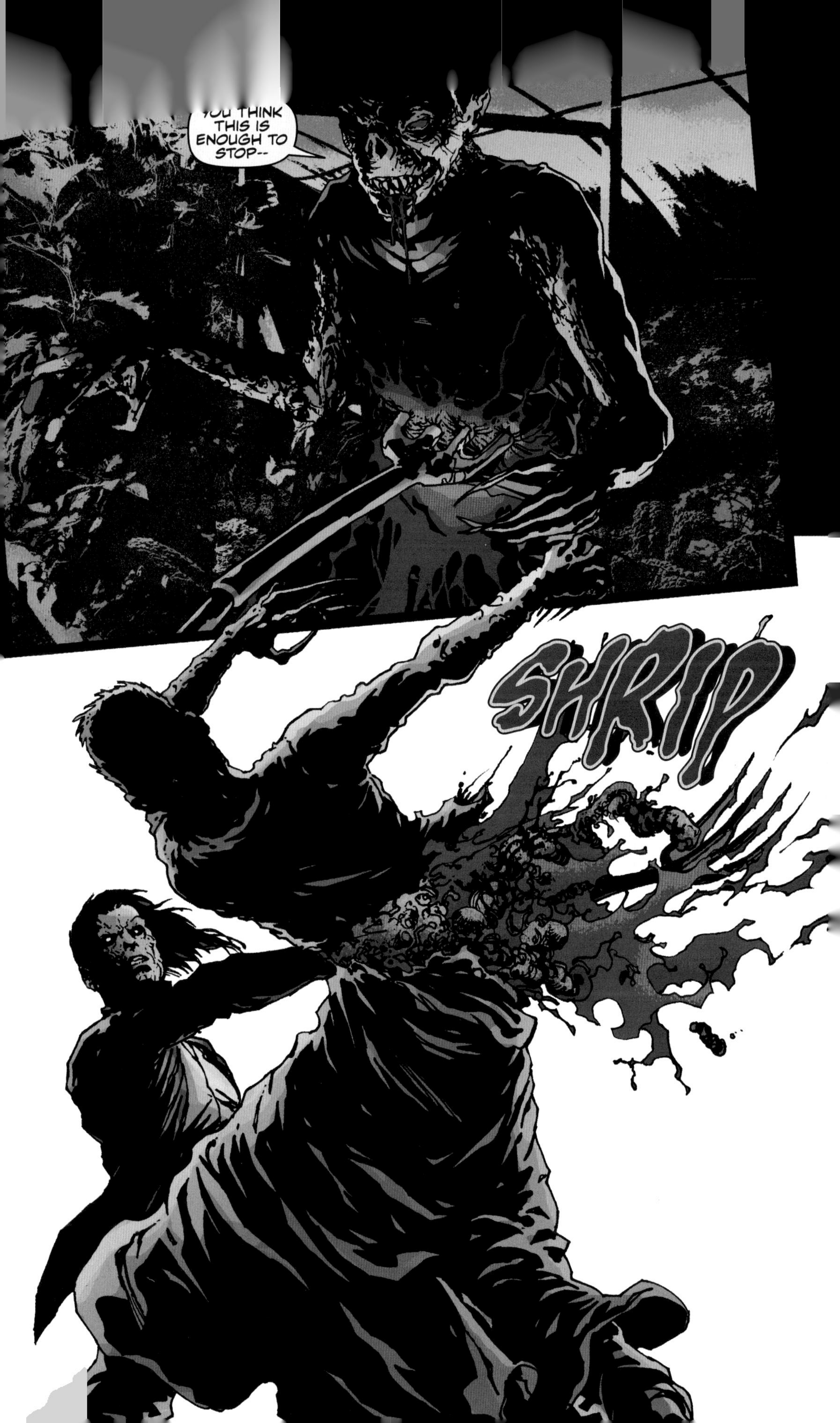
YOU THINK THIS IS ENOUGH TO STOP--
SHRIP

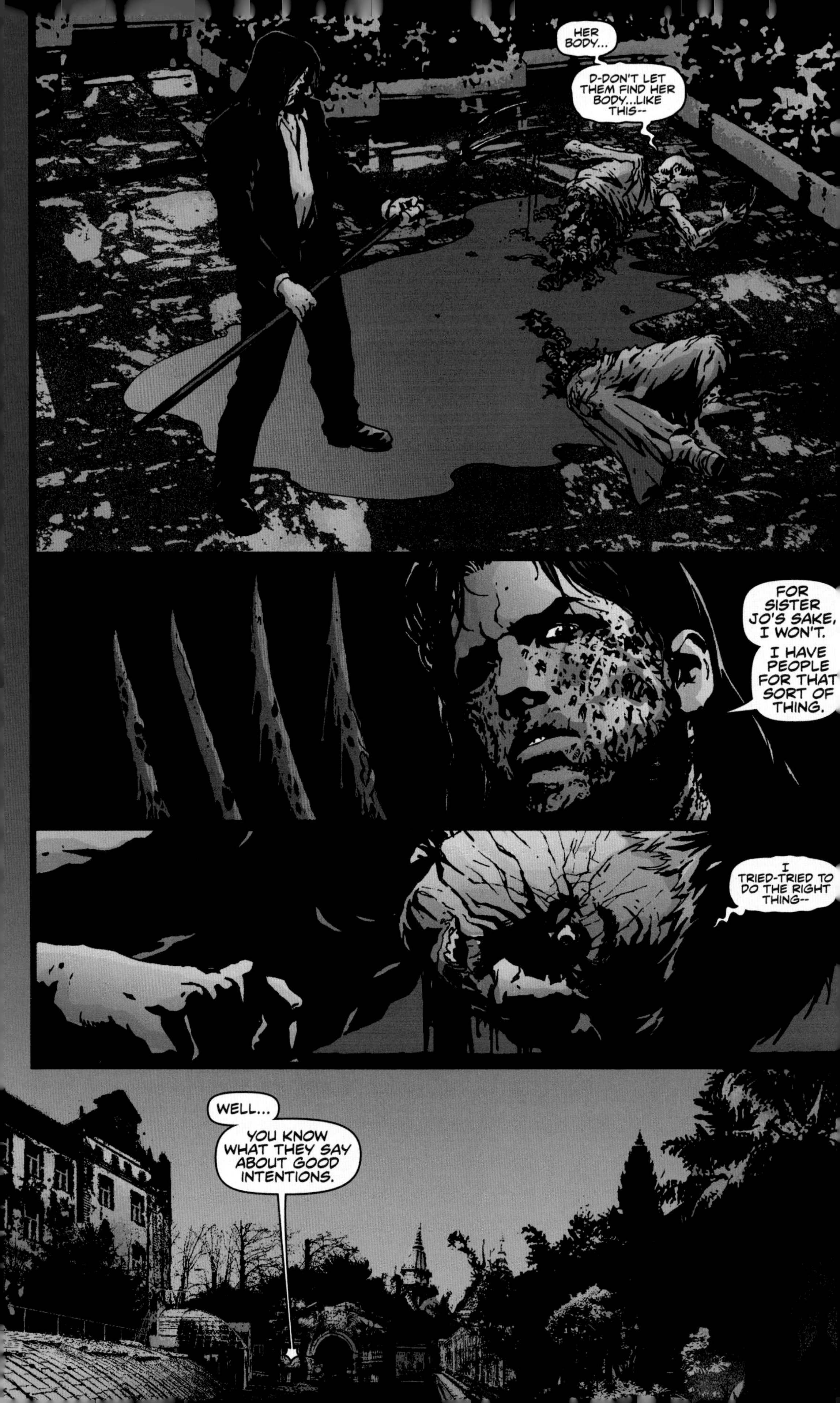
HER BODY...
D-DON'T LET THEM FIND HER BODY...LIKE THIS--
FOR SISTER JO'S SAKE, I WON'T.
I HAVE PEOPLE FOR THAT SORT OF THING.
I TRIED-TRIED TO DO THE RIGHT THING--
WELL...
YOU KNOW WHAT THEY SAY ABOUT GOOD INTENTIONS.

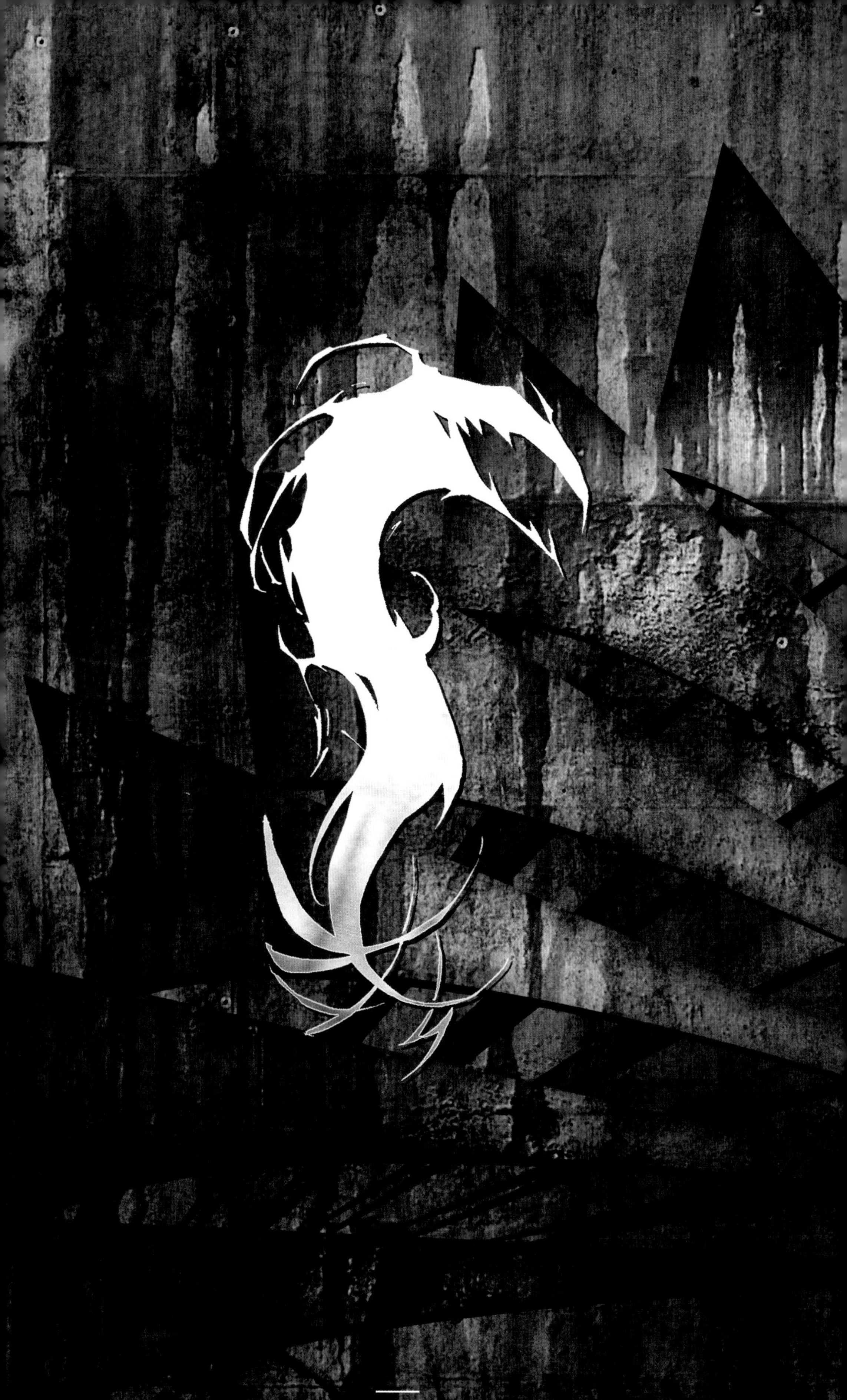

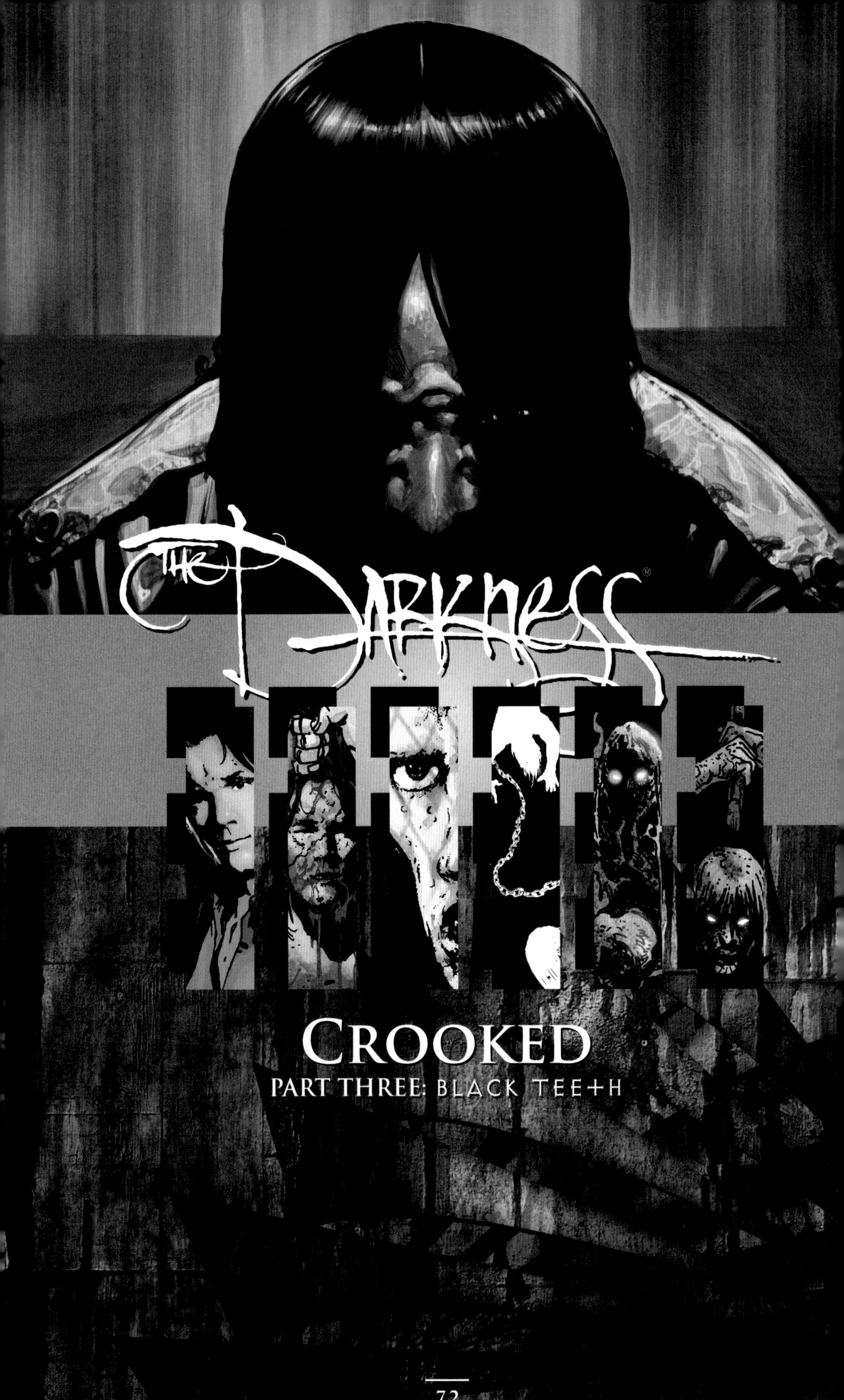
The Darkness®
CROOKED
PART THREE: BLACK TEE+H

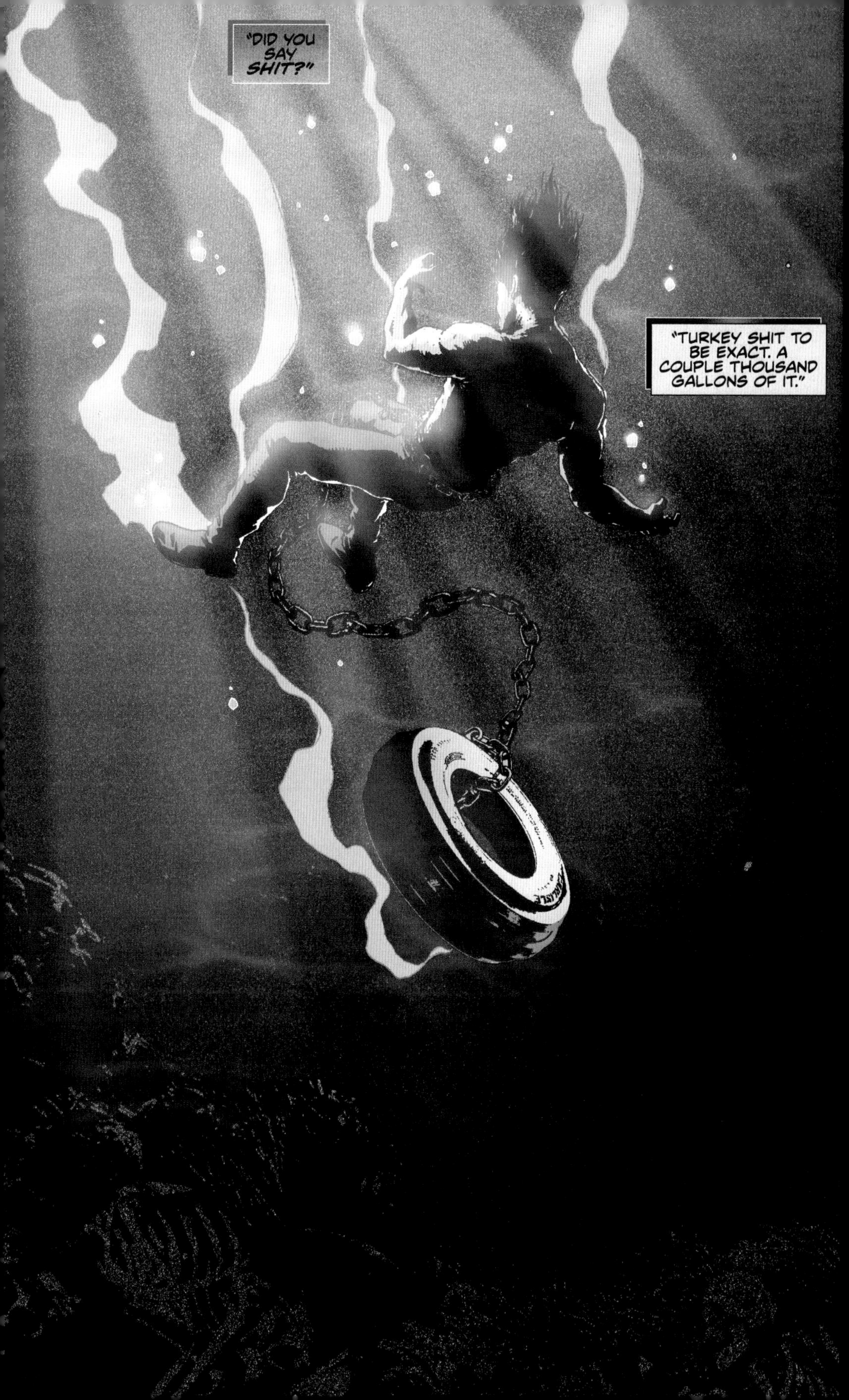
"DID YOU SAY SHIT?"
"TURKEY SHIT TO BE EXACT. A COUPLE THOUSAND GALLONS OF IT."

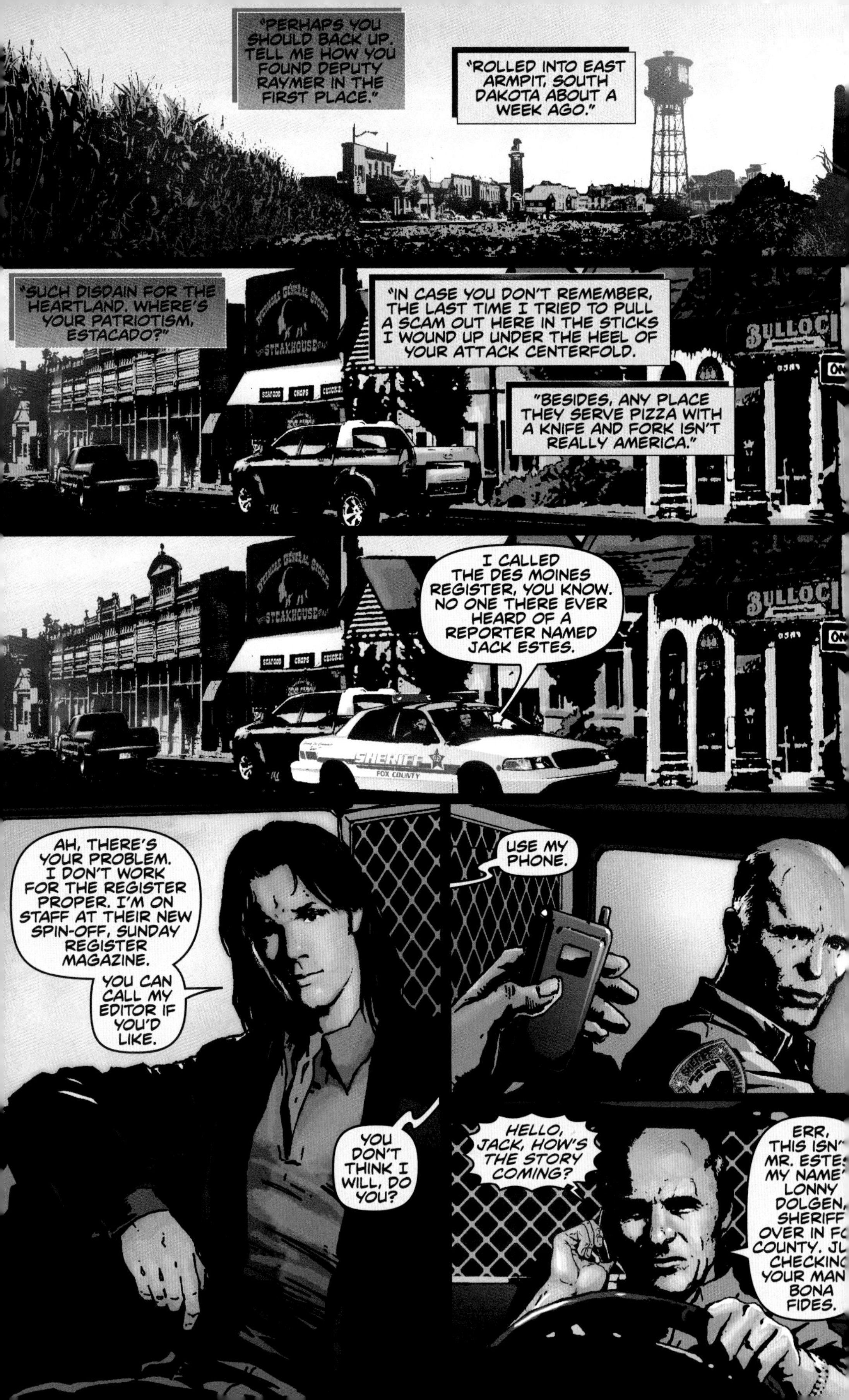
"PERHAPS YOU SHOULD BACK UP. TELL ME HOW YOU FOUND DEPUTY RAYMER IN THE FIRST PLACE."
"ROLLED INTO EAST ARMPIT, SOUTH DAKOTA ABOUT A WEEK AGO."
"SUCH DISDAIN FOR THE HEARTLAND. WHERE'S YOUR PATRIOTISM, ESTACADO?"
"IN CASE YOU DON'T REMEMBER, THE LAST TIME I TRIED TO PULL A SCAM OUT HERE IN THE STICKS I WOUND UP UNDER THE HEEL OF YOUR ATTACK CENTERFOLD.
"BESIDES, ANY PLACE THEY SERVE PIZZA WITH A KNIFE AND FORK ISN'T REALLY AMERICA."
STEAKHOUSE
SEAFOOD
CHOPS
I CALLED THE DES MOINES REGISTER, YOU KNOW. NO ONE THERE EVER HEARD OF A REPORTER NAMED JACK ESTES.
SHERIFF
FOX COUNTY
AH, THERE'S YOUR PROBLEM. I DON'T WORK FOR THE REGISTER PROPER. I'M ON STAFF AT THEIR NEW SPIN-OFF, SUNDAY REGISTER MAGAZINE.
YOU CAN CALL MY EDITOR IF YOU'D LIKE.
USE MY PHONE.
YOU DON'T THINK I WILL, DO YOU?
HELLO, JACK, HOW'S THE STORY COMING?
ERR, THIS ISN' MR. ESTE MY NAME' LONNY DOLGEN, SHERIFF OVER IN F COUNTY. J CHECKIN YOUR MAN BONA FIDES.

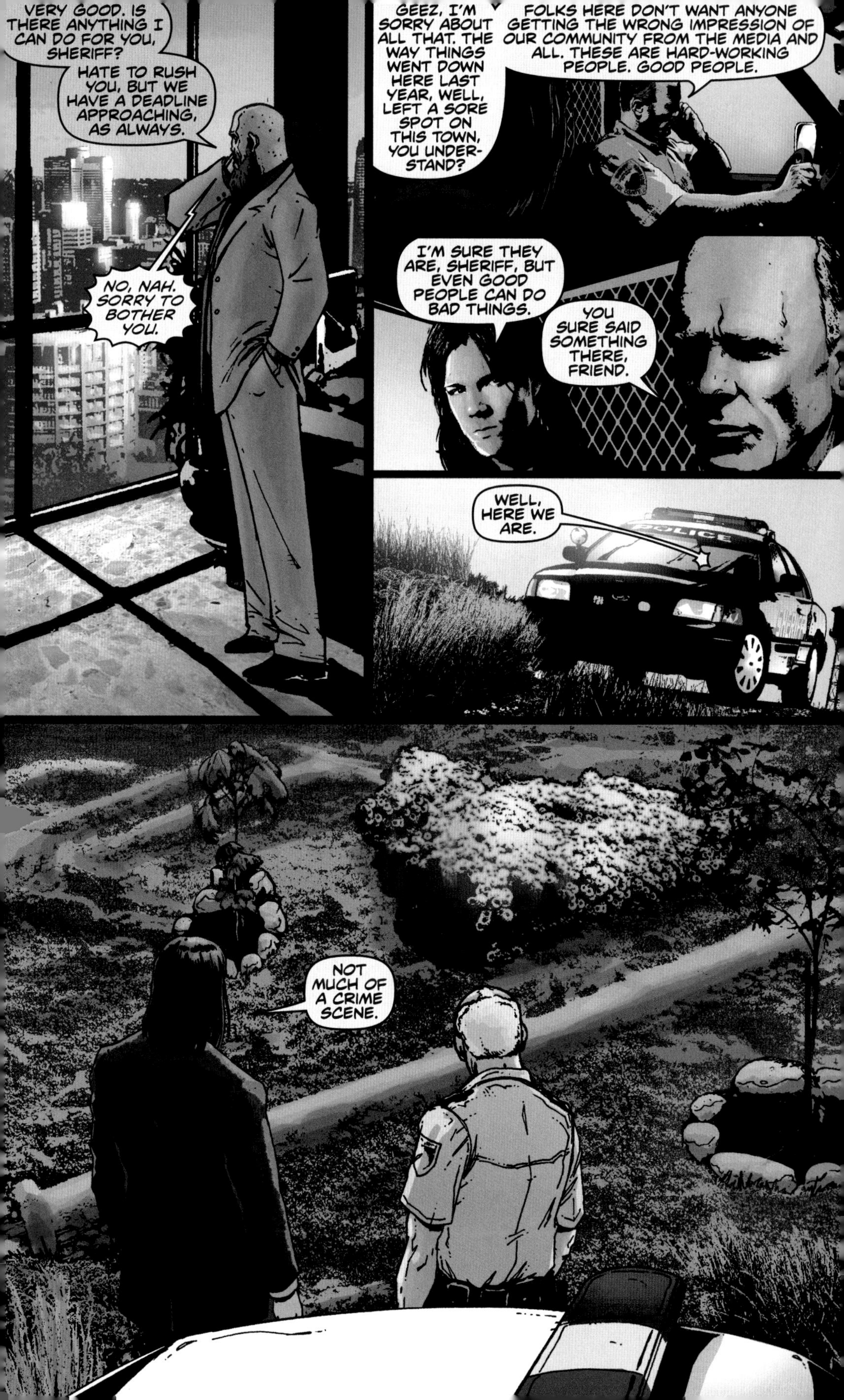
VERY GOOD. IS THERE ANYTHING I CAN DO FOR YOU, SHERIFF?
HATE TO RUSH YOU, BUT WE HAVE A DEADLINE APPROACHING, AS ALWAYS.
NO, NAH. SORRY TO BOTHER YOU.
GEEZ, I'M SORRY ABOUT ALL THAT. THE WAY THINGS WENT DOWN HERE LAST YEAR, WELL, LEFT A SORE SPOT ON THIS TOWN, YOU UNDER-STAND?
FOLKS HERE DON'T WANT ANYONE GETTING THE WRONG IMPRESSION OF OUR COMMUNITY FROM THE MEDIA AND ALL. THESE ARE HARD-WORKING PEOPLE. GOOD PEOPLE.
I'M SURE THEY ARE, SHERIFF, BUT EVEN GOOD PEOPLE CAN DO BAD THINGS.
YOU SURE SAID SOMETHING THERE, FRIEND.
WELL, HERE WE ARE.
POLICE
NOT MUCH OF A CRIME SCENE.

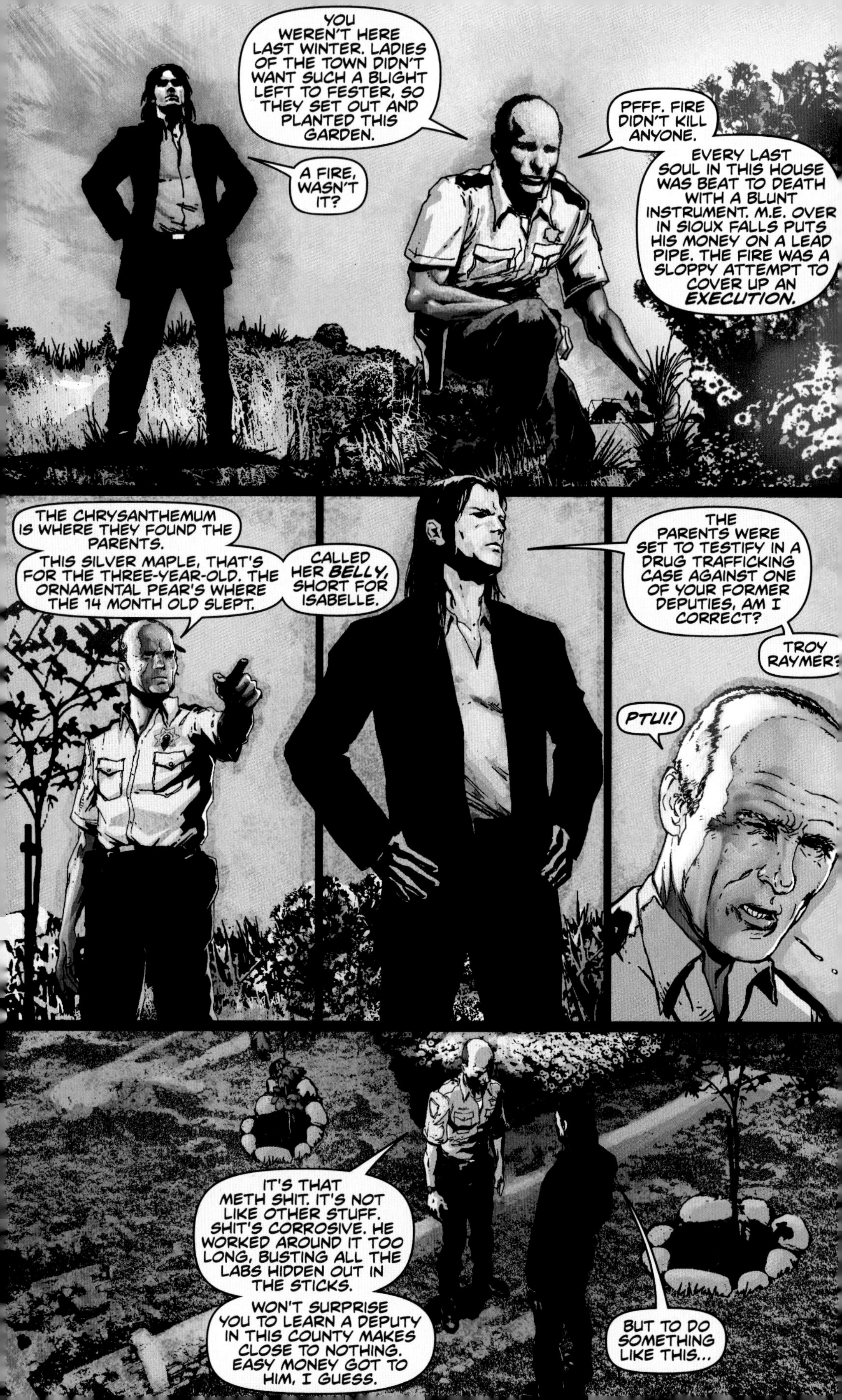

YOU WEREN'T HERE LAST WINTER. LADIES OF THE TOWN DIDN'T WANT SUCH A BLIGHT LEFT TO FESTER, SO THEY SET OUT AND PLANTED THIS GARDEN.
A FIRE, WASN'T IT?
PFFF. FIRE DIDN'T KILL ANYONE.
EVERY LAST SOUL IN THIS HOUSE WAS BEAT TO DEATH WITH A BLUNT INSTRUMENT. M.E. OVER IN SIOUX FALLS PUTS HIS MONEY ON A LEAD PIPE. THE FIRE WAS A SLOPPY ATTEMPT TO COVER UP AN EXECUTION.
THE CHRYSANTHEMUM IS WHERE THEY FOUND THE PARENTS.
THIS SILVER MAPLE, THAT'S FOR THE THREE-YEAR-OLD. THE ORNAMENTAL PEAR'S WHERE THE 14 MONTH OLD SLEPT.
CALLED HER BELLY, SHORT FOR ISABELLE.
THE PARENTS WERE SET TO TESTIFY IN A DRUG TRAFFICKING CASE AGAINST ONE OF YOUR FORMER DEPUTIES, AM I CORRECT?
TROY RAYMER?
PTUI!
IT'S THAT METH SHIT. IT'S NOT LIKE OTHER STUFF. SHIT'S CORROSIVE. HE WORKED AROUND IT TOO LONG, BUSTING ALL THE LABS HIDDEN OUT IN THE STICKS.
WON'T SURPRISE YOU TO LEARN A DEPUTY IN THIS COUNTY MAKES CLOSE TO NOTHING. EASY MONEY GOT TO HIM, I GUESS.
BUT TO DO SOMETHING LIKE THIS...

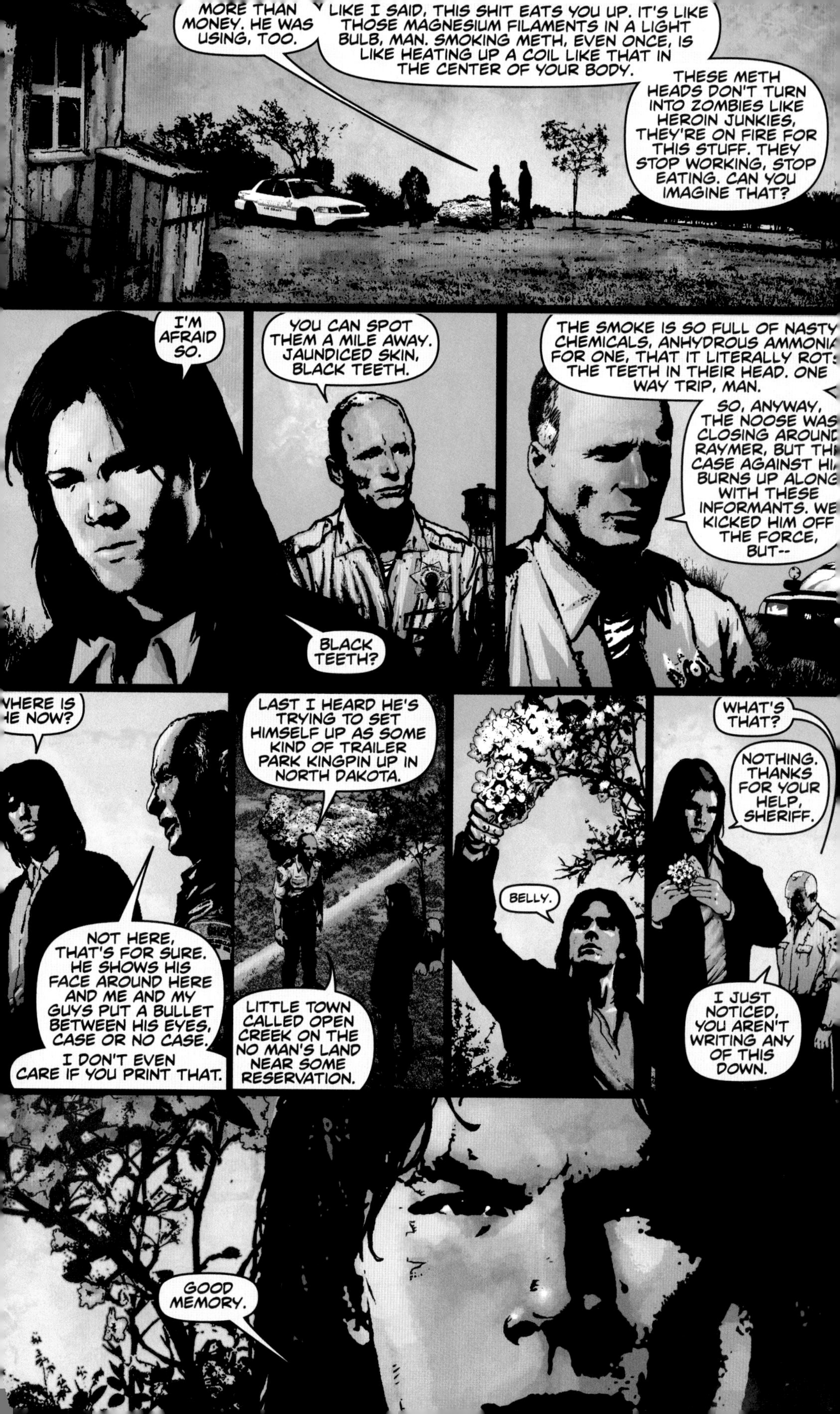
MORE THAN MONEY. HE WAS USING, TOO.
LIKE I SAID, THIS SHIT EATS YOU UP. IT'S LIKE THOSE MAGNESIUM FILAMENTS IN A LIGHT BULB, MAN. SMOKING METH, EVEN ONCE, IS LIKE HEATING UP A COIL LIKE THAT IN THE CENTER OF YOUR BODY.
THESE METH HEADS DON'T TURN INTO ZOMBIES LIKE HEROIN JUNKIES, THEY'RE ON FIRE FOR THIS STUFF. THEY STOP WORKING, STOP EATING. CAN YOU IMAGINE THAT?
I'M AFRAID SO.
YOU CAN SPOT THEM A MILE AWAY. JAUNDICED SKIN, BLACK TEETH.
BLACK TEETH?
THE SMOKE IS SO FULL OF NASTY CHEMICALS, ANHYDROUS AMMONIA FOR ONE, THAT IT LITERALLY ROTS THE TEETH IN THEIR HEAD. ONE WAY TRIP, MAN.
SO, ANYWAY, THE NOOSE WAS CLOSING AROUND RAYMER, BUT THE CASE AGAINST HIM BURNS UP ALONG WITH THESE INFORMANTS. WE KICKED HIM OFF THE FORCE, BUT--
WHERE IS HE NOW?
NOT HERE, THAT'S FOR SURE. HE SHOWS HIS FACE AROUND HERE AND ME AND MY GUYS PUT A BULLET BETWEEN HIS EYES, CASE OR NO CASE.
I DON'T EVEN CARE IF YOU PRINT THAT.
LAST I HEARD HE'S TRYING TO SET HIMSELF UP AS SOME KIND OF TRAILER PARK KINGPIN UP IN NORTH DAKOTA.
LITTLE TOWN CALLED OPEN CREEK ON THE NO MAN'S LAND NEAR SOME RESERVATION.
BELLY.
WHAT'S THAT?
NOTHING. THANKS FOR YOUR HELP, SHERIFF.
I JUST NOTICED, YOU AREN'T WRITING ANY OF THIS DOWN.
GOOD MEMORY.

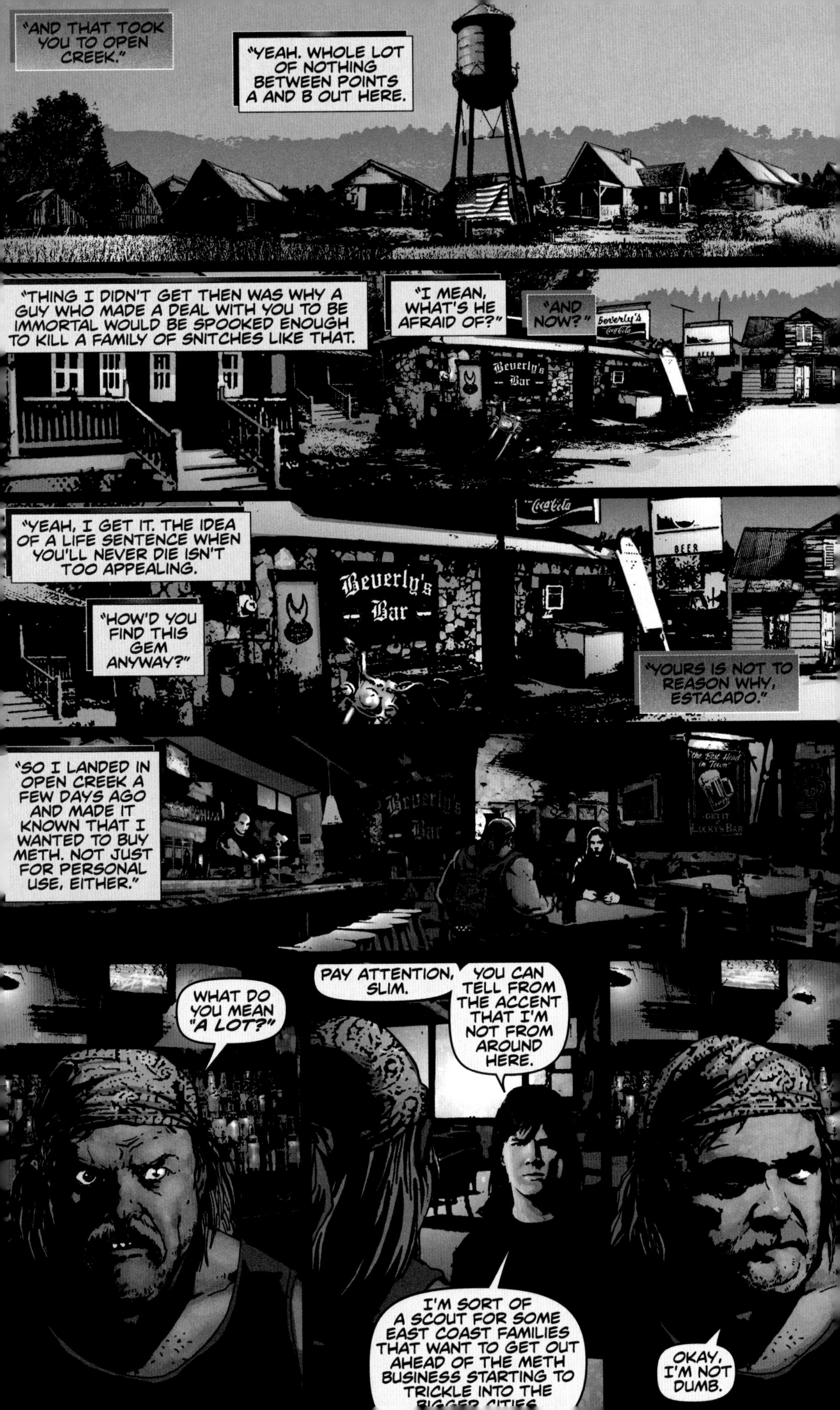
"AND THAT TOOK YOU TO OPEN CREEK."
"YEAH. WHOLE LOT OF NOTHING BETWEEN POINTS A AND B OUT HERE.
"THING I DIDN'T GET THEN WAS WHY A GUY WHO MADE A DEAL WITH YOU TO BE IMMORTAL WOULD BE SPOOKED ENOUGH TO KILL A FAMILY OF SNITCHES LIKE THAT.
"I MEAN, WHAT'S HE AFRAID OF?"
"AND NOW?"
Beverly's
Beverly's Bar
"YEAH, I GET IT. THE IDEA OF A LIFE SENTENCE WHEN YOU'LL NEVER DIE ISN'T TOO APPEALING.
Coca-Cola
BEER
"HOW'D YOU FIND THIS GEM ANYWAY?"
Beverly's Bar
"YOURS IS NOT TO REASON WHY, ESTACADO."
"SO I LANDED IN OPEN CREEK A FEW DAYS AGO AND MADE IT KNOWN THAT I WANTED TO BUY METH. NOT JUST FOR PERSONAL USE, EITHER."
the Best Head in Town
GET IT
LUCKY'S BAR
WHAT DO YOU MEAN "A LOT?"
PAY ATTENTION, SLIM.
YOU CAN TELL FROM THE ACCENT THAT I'M NOT FROM AROUND HERE.
I'M SORT OF A SCOUT FOR SOME EAST COAST FAMILIES THAT WANT TO GET OUT AHEAD OF THE METH BUSINESS STARTING TO TRICKLE INTO THE
OKAY, I'M NOT DUMB.

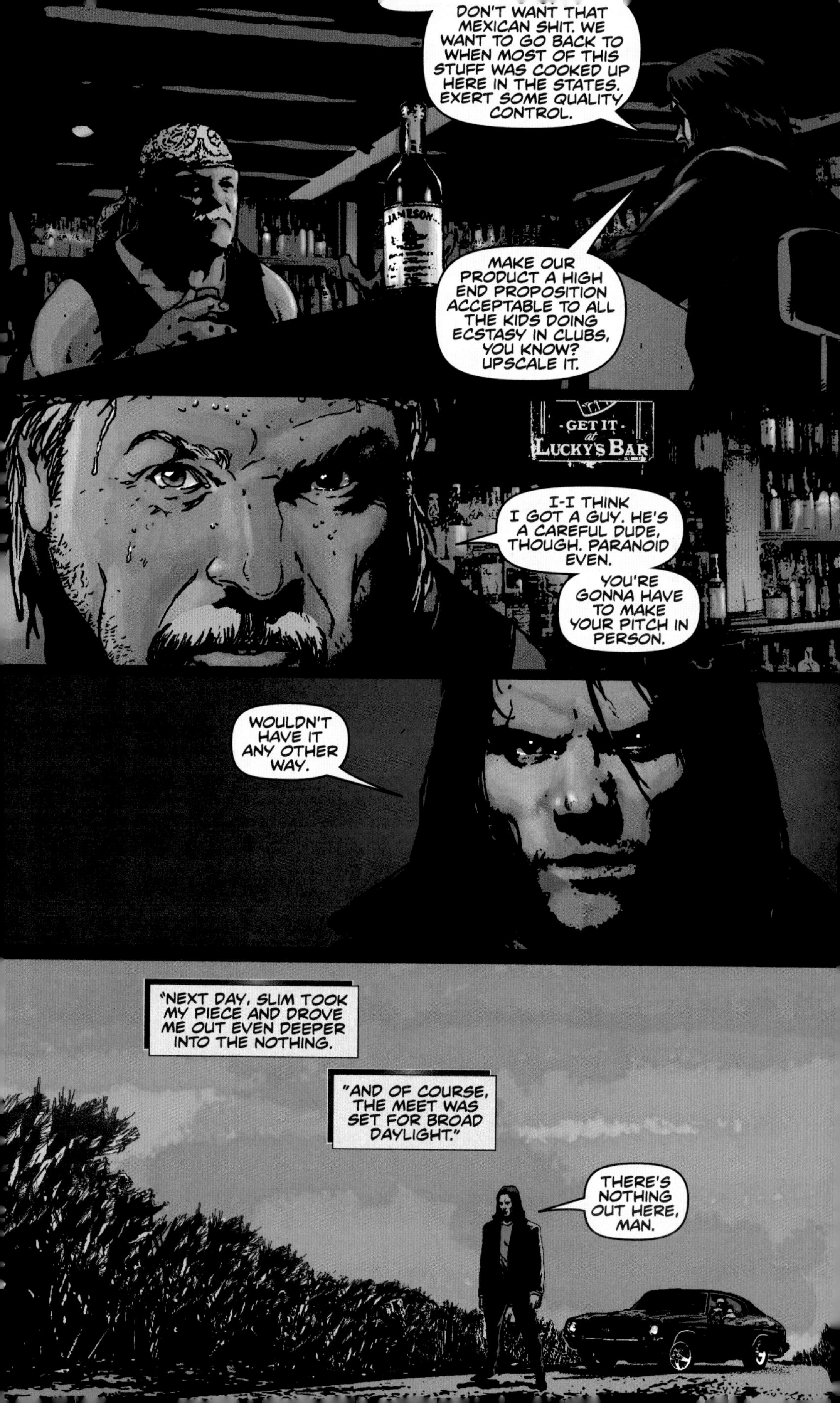
DON'T WANT THAT MEXICAN SHIT. WE WANT TO GO BACK TO WHEN MOST OF THIS STUFF WAS COOKED UP HERE IN THE STATES. EXERT SOME QUALITY CONTROL.
JAMESON
MAKE OUR PRODUCT A HIGH END PROPOSITION ACCEPTABLE TO ALL THE KIDS DOING ECSTASY IN CLUBS, YOU KNOW? UPSCALE IT.
GET IT at LUCKY'S BAR
I-I THINK I GOT A GUY. HE'S A CAREFUL DUDE, THOUGH. PARANOID EVEN.
YOU'RE GONNA HAVE TO MAKE YOUR PITCH IN PERSON.
WOULDN'T HAVE IT ANY OTHER WAY.
"NEXT DAY, SLIM TOOK MY PIECE AND DROVE ME OUT EVEN DEEPER INTO THE NOTHING.
"AND OF COURSE, THE MEET WAS SET FOR BROAD DAYLIGHT."
THERE'S NOTHING OUT HERE, MAN.

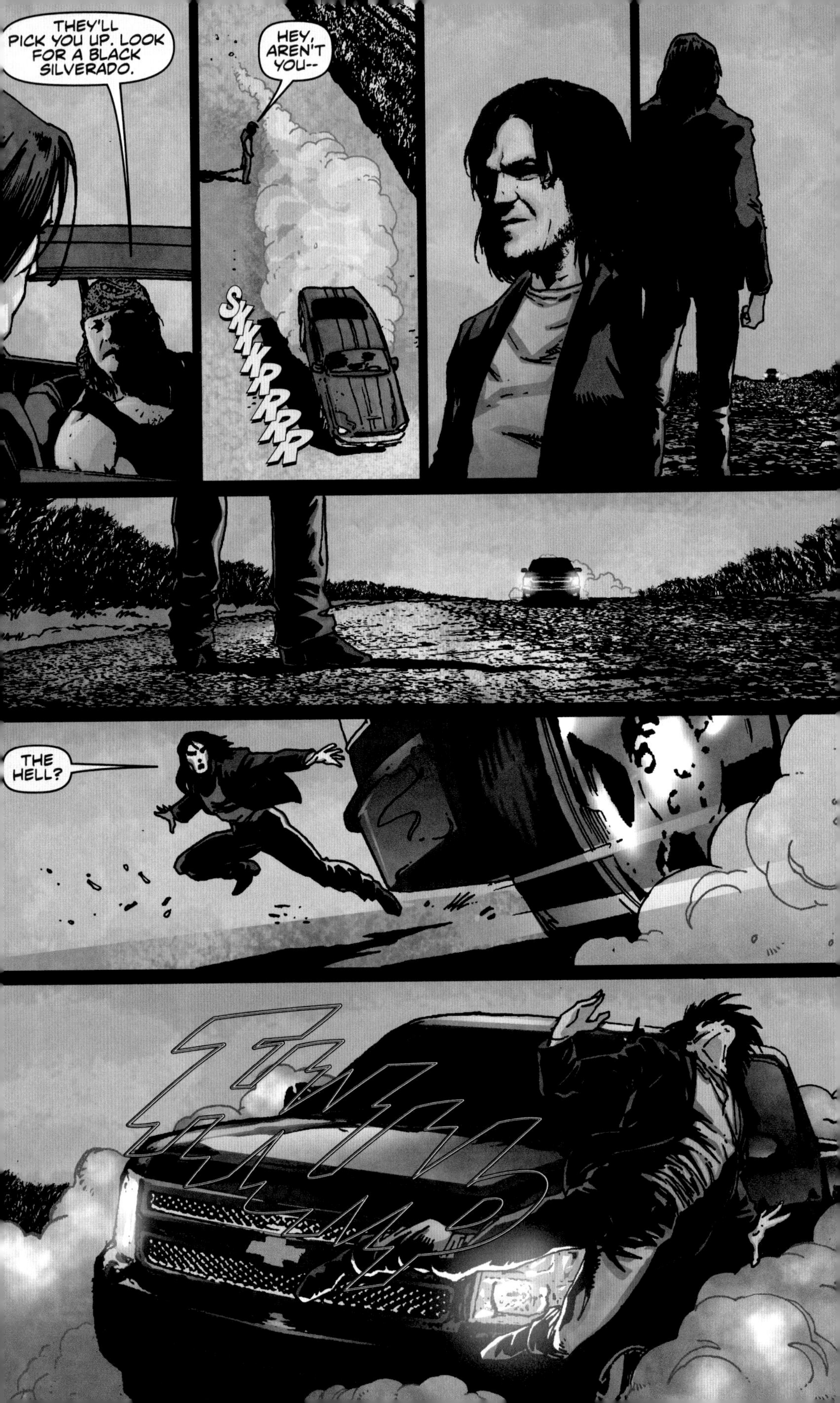
THEY'LL PICK YOU UP. LOOK FOR A BLACK SILVERADO.
HEY, AREN'T YOU--
SKKKRRRRR
THE HELL?
THUMP

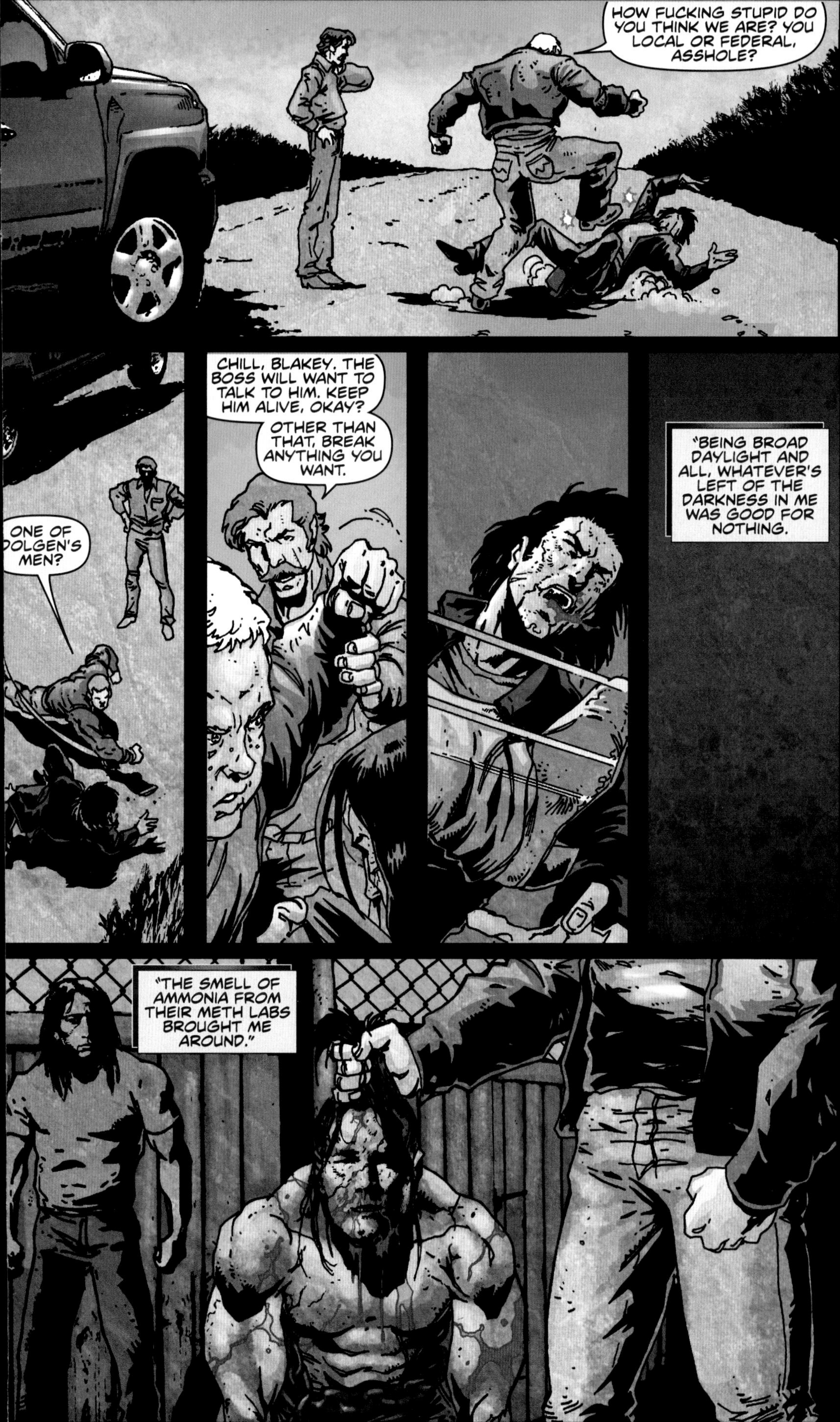
HOW FUCKING STUPID DO YOU THINK WE ARE? YOU LOCAL OR FEDERAL, ASSHOLE?
ONE OF DOLGEN'S MEN?
CHILL, BLAKEY. THE BOSS WILL WANT TO TALK TO HIM. KEEP HIM ALIVE, OKAY?
OTHER THAN THAT, BREAK ANYTHING YOU WANT.
"BEING BROAD DAYLIGHT AND ALL, WHATEVER'S LEFT OF THE DARKNESS IN ME WAS GOOD FOR NOTHING.
"THE SMELL OF AMMONIA FROM THEIR METH LABS BROUGHT ME AROUND."

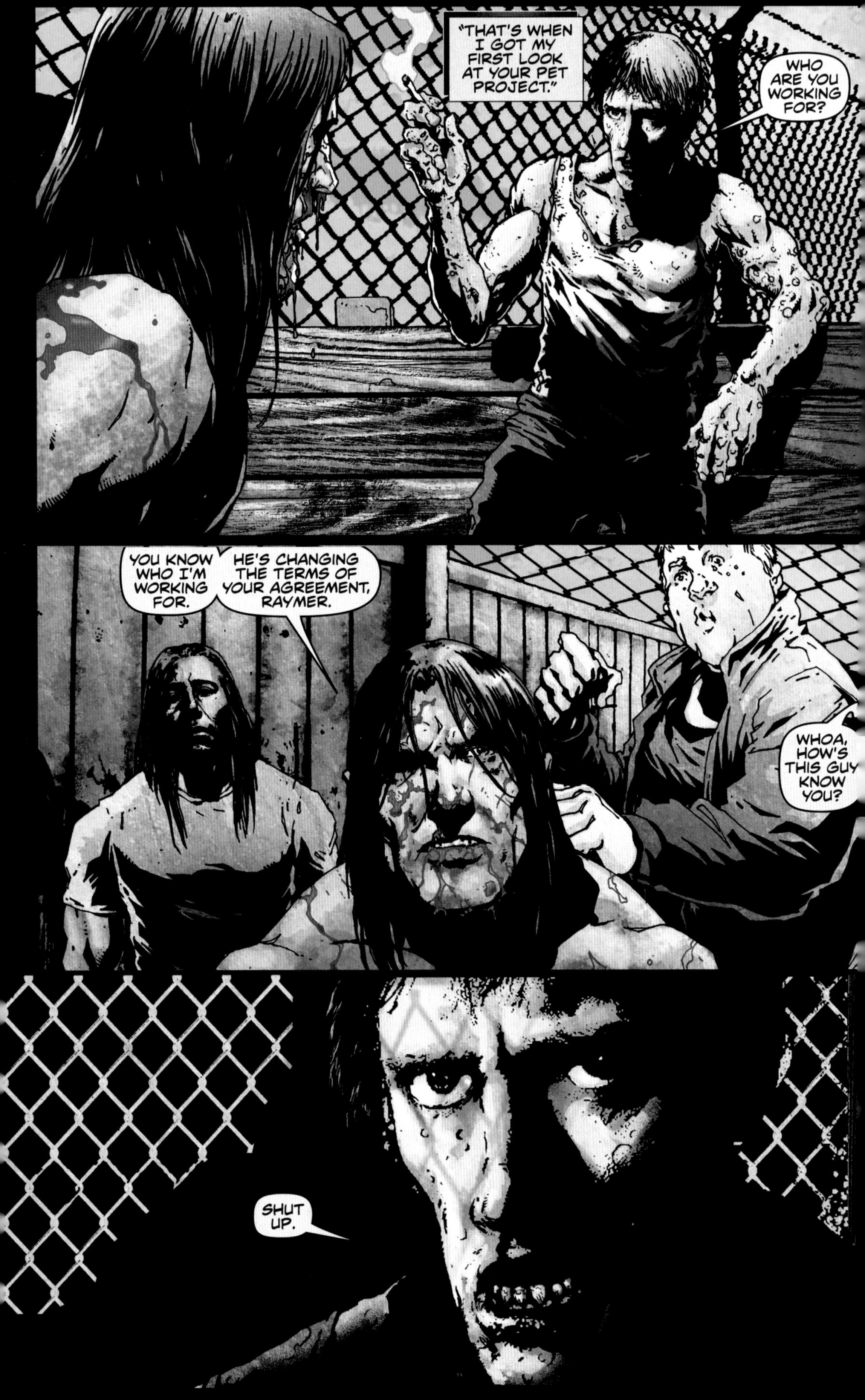
"THAT'S WHEN I GOT MY FIRST LOOK AT YOUR PET PROJECT."
WHO ARE YOU WORKING FOR?
YOU KNOW WHO I'M WORKING FOR.
HE'S CHANGING THE TERMS OF YOUR AGREEMENT, RAYMER.
WHOA, HOW'S THIS GUY KNOW YOU?
SHUT UP.

THE SOVEREIGN SAYS HE SOLD YOU YOUR GIFT WHEN YOU WERE A COP AND DESPERATE TO COME HOME TO YOUR FAMILY EVERY NIGHT.

SAYS ONCE YOU LEARNED YOU COULDN'T DIE YOU STARTED TO LOSE YOUR MORAL COMPASS, AS THEY SAY.

COULDN'T DIE? WHAT'S THIS GUY TALKING ABOUT?

NOTHING. NOTHING. HE'S CRAZY. SOME JUNKIE LOOKING FOR REVENGE.

HE GOES SWIMMING, GOT IT?

LAST CHANCE, RAYMER.

LAST CHANCE FOR YOU, DIPSHIT. LOOK AROUND. THIS HUGE BUILDING USED TO HOLD TURKEYS. THOUSANDS OF THEM.

RAYMER BUSTED OUT THE FARMER WHO OWNED THE PLACE AND TOOK OVER, MADE IT HIS LITTLE FORTRESS ON THE PLAINS.

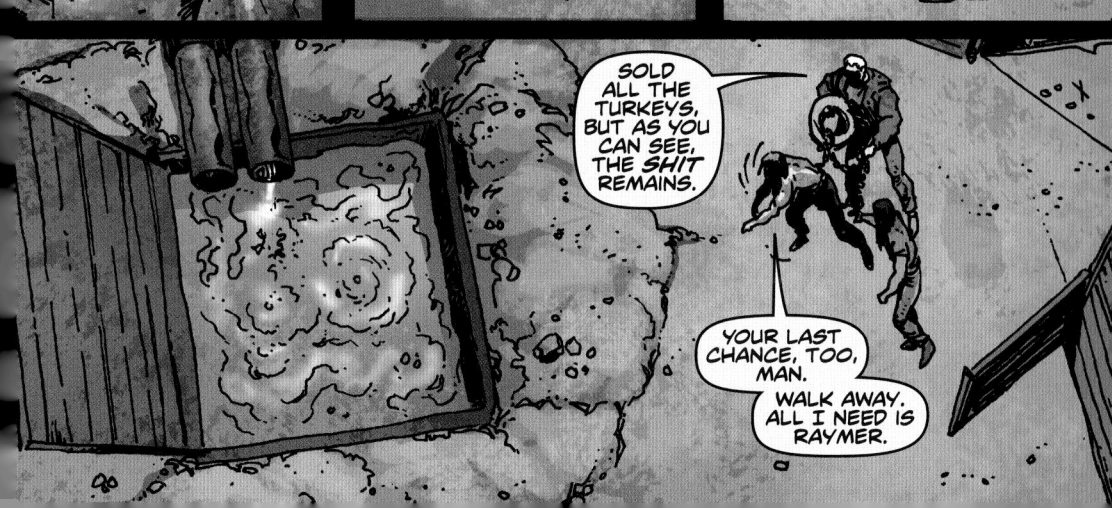

SOLD ALL THE TURKEYS, BUT AS YOU CAN SEE, THE *SHIT* REMAINS.

YOUR LAST CHANCE, TOO, MAN.

WALK AWAY. ALL I NEED IS RAYMER.

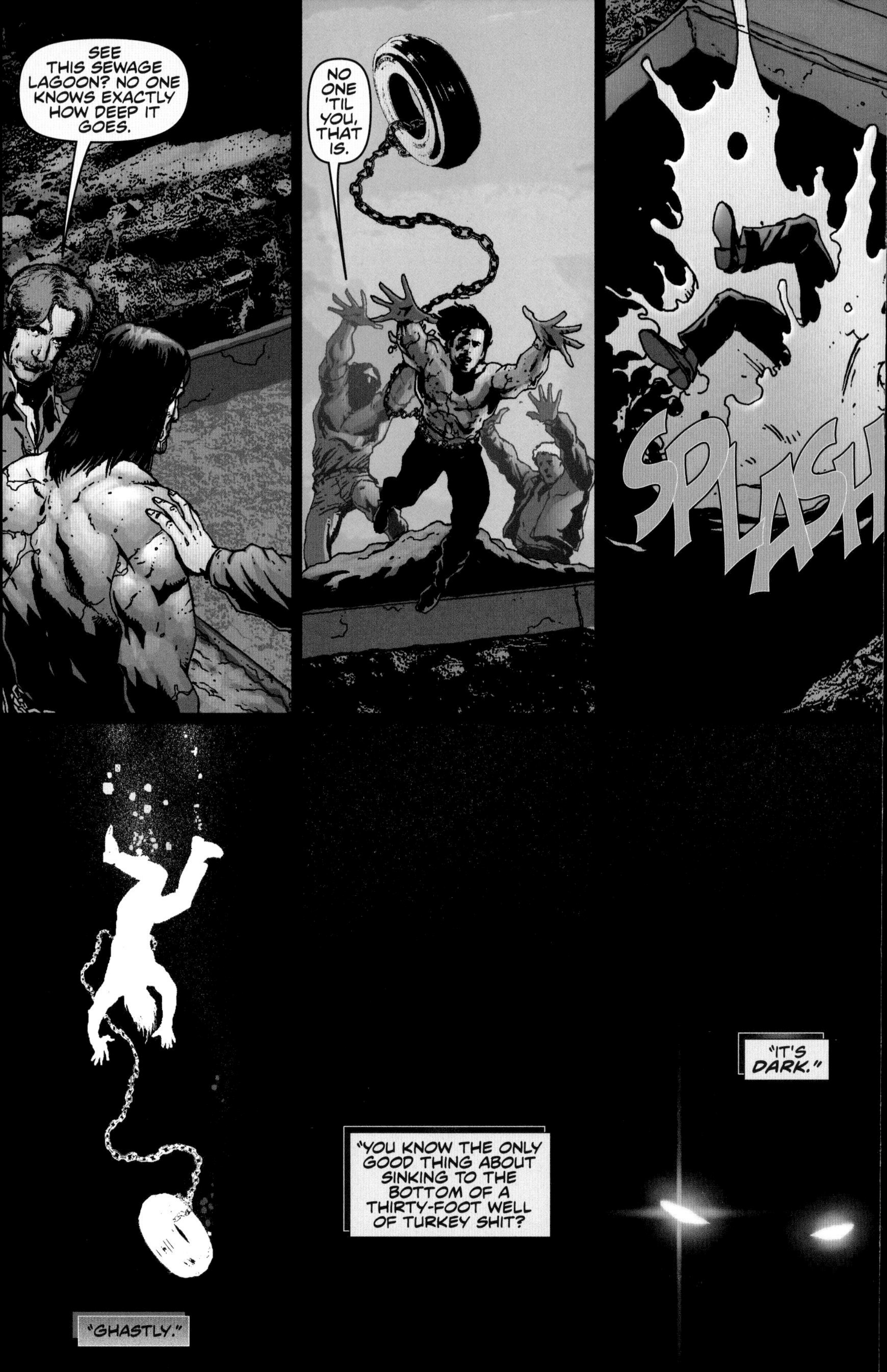
SEE THIS SEWAGE LAGOON? NO ONE KNOWS EXACTLY HOW DEEP IT GOES.
NO ONE 'TIL YOU, THAT IS.
SPLASH
"GHASTLY."
"YOU KNOW THE ONLY GOOD THING ABOUT SINKING TO THE BOTTOM OF A THIRTY-FOOT WELL OF TURKEY SHIT?
"IT'S DARK."

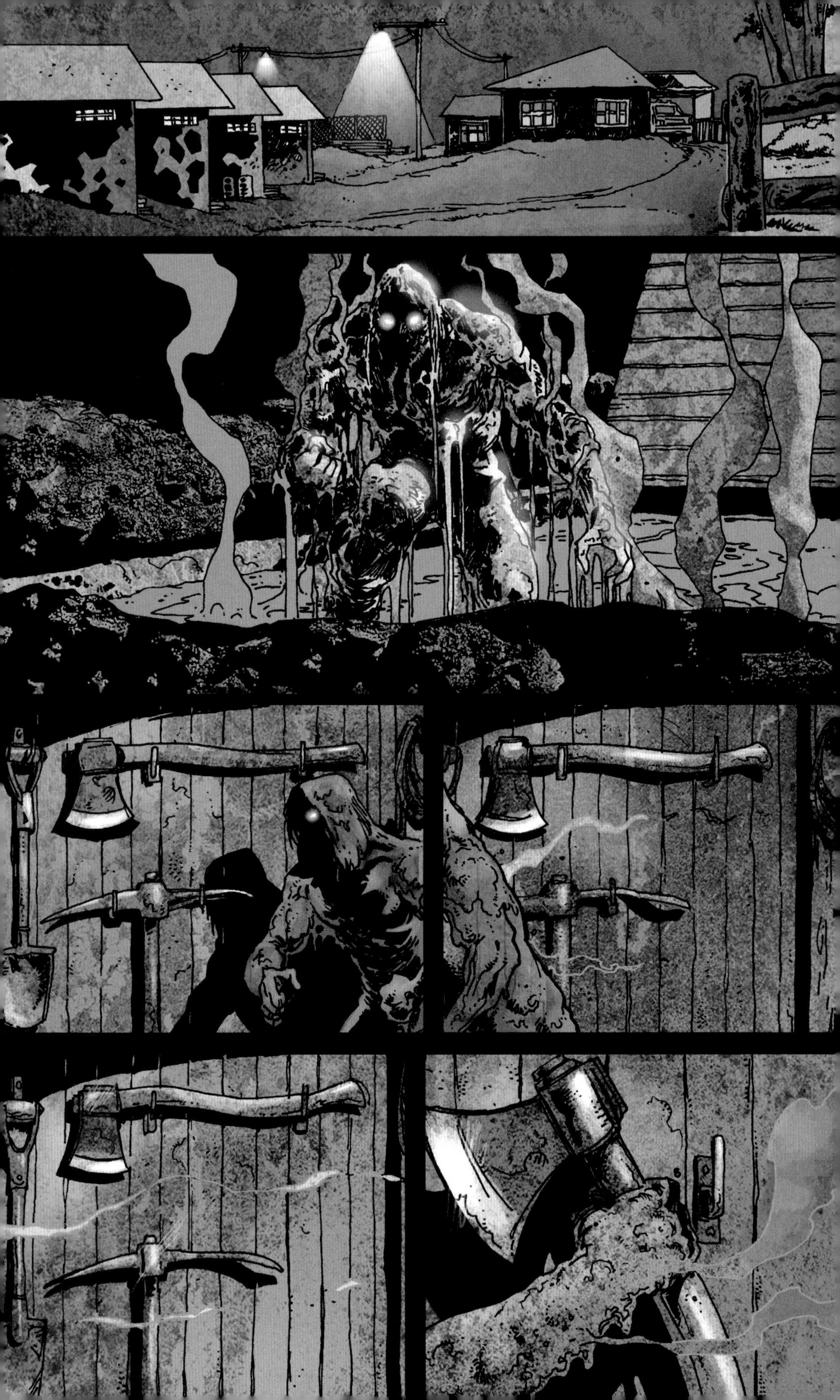

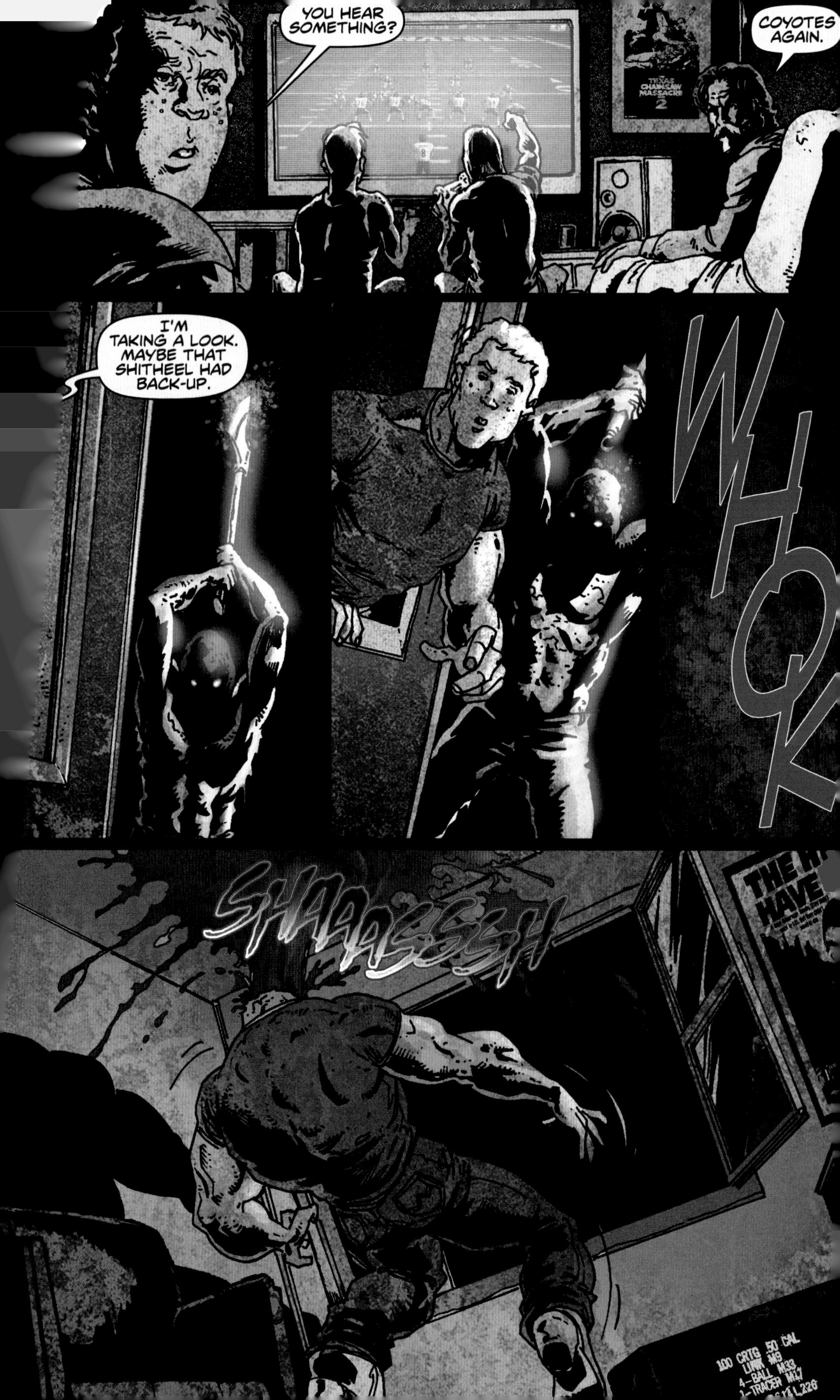
YOU HEAR SOMETHING?
THE TEXAS CHAINSAW MASSACRE 2
COYOTES AGAIN.
I'M TAKING A LOOK. MAYBE THAT SHITHEEL HAD BACK-UP.
WHOK
SHAAASSSH
THE
HAVE
100 CRTG .50 CAL
LINK M9
4-BALL M33
1-TRACER M17

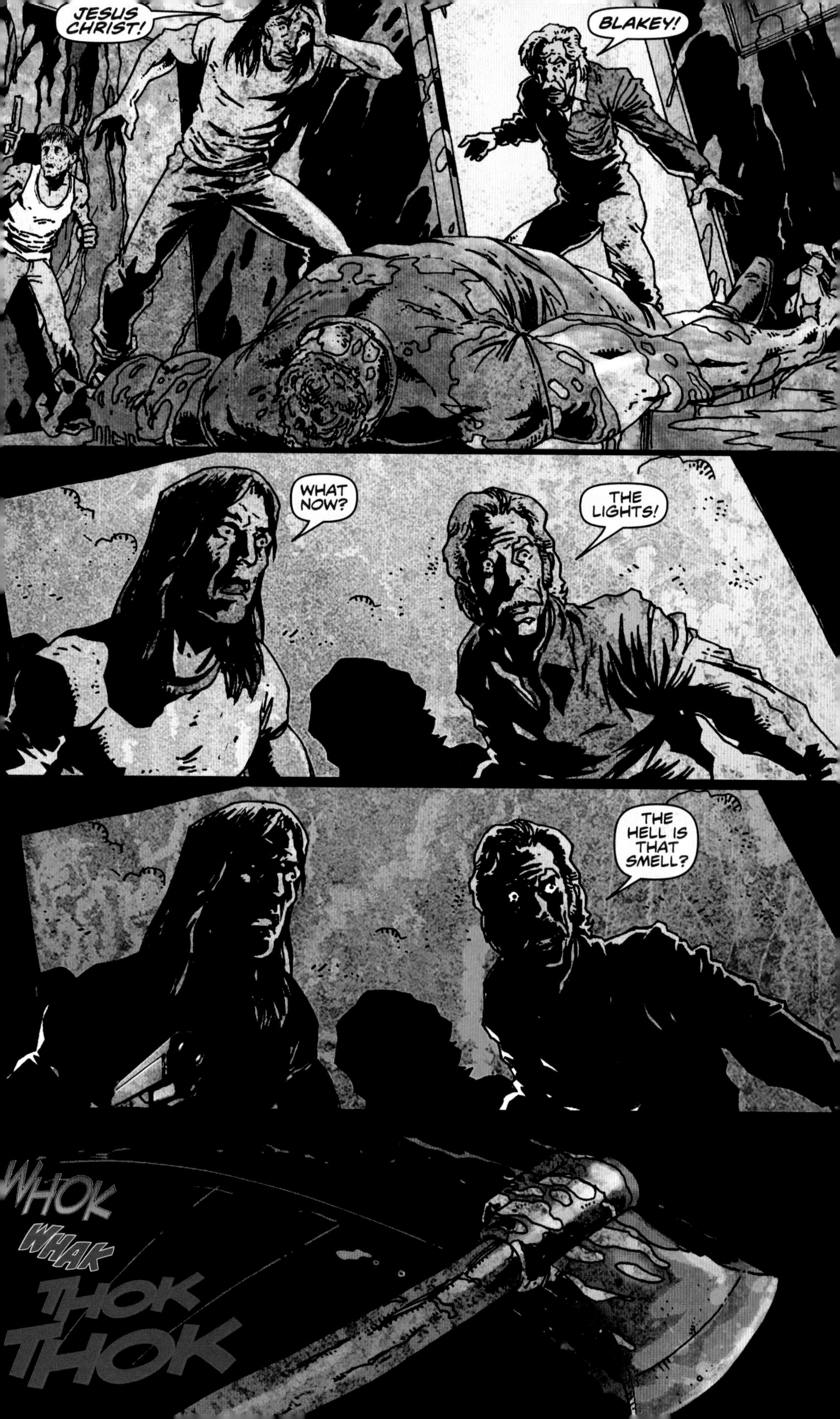

JESUS CHRIST!
BLAKEY!
WHAT NOW?
THE LIGHTS!
THE HELL IS THAT SMELL?
WHOK
WHAK
THOK
THOK

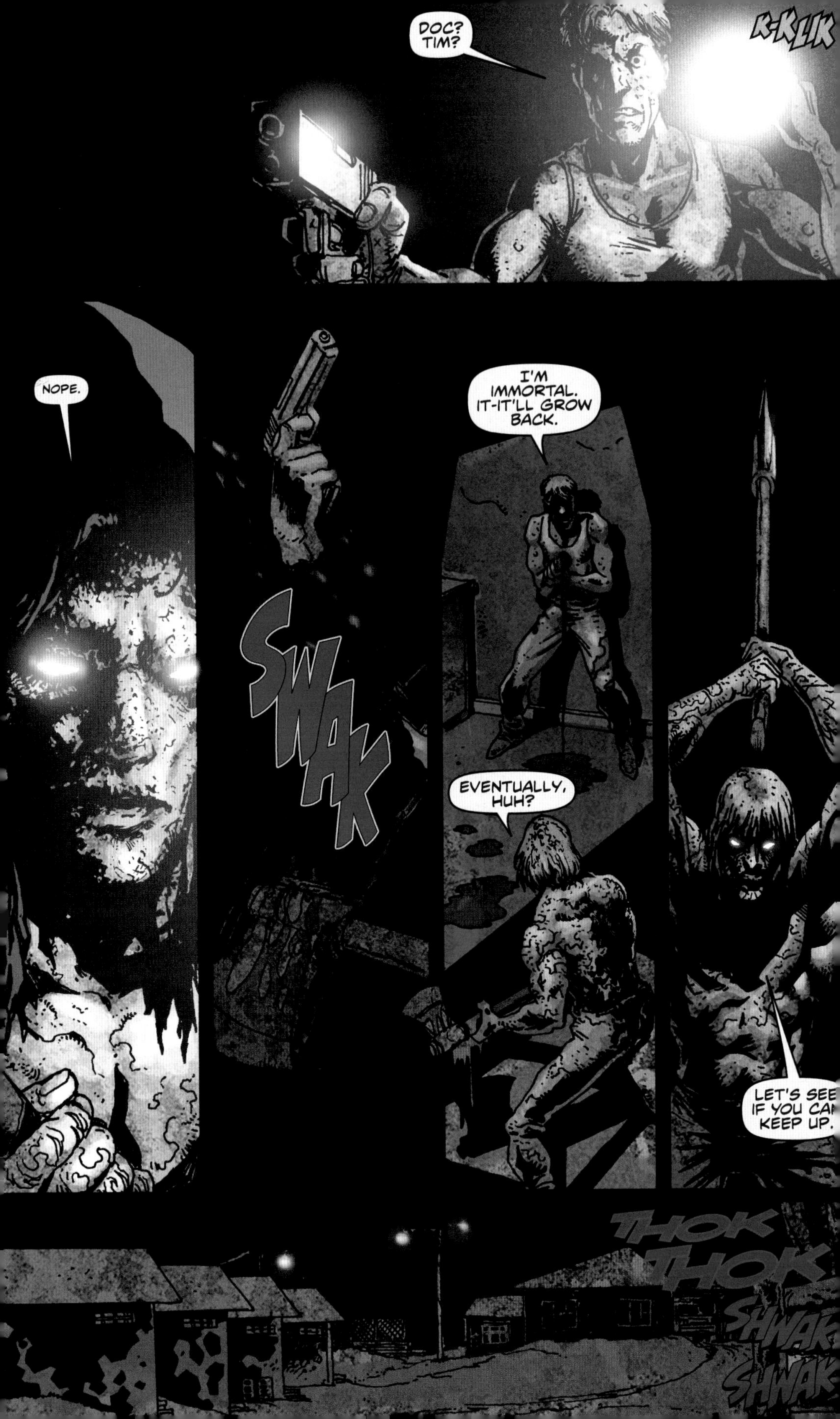
DOC? TIM?
K-KLIK
NOPE.
SWAK
I'M IMMORTAL. IT-IT'LL GROW BACK.
EVENTUALLY, HUH?
LET'S SEE IF YOU CA KEEP UP.
THOK
THOK
SHWAK
SHWAK

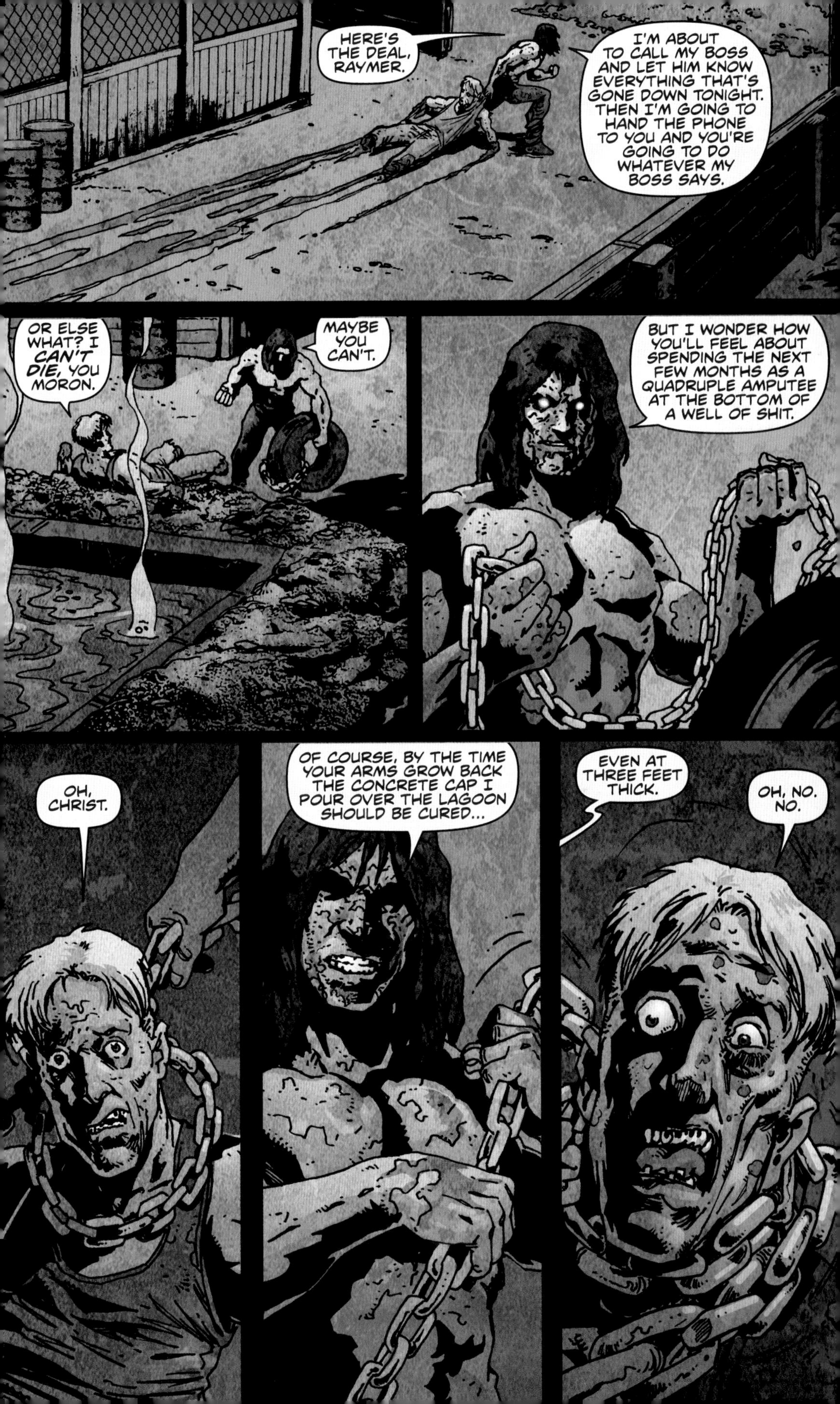
HERE'S THE DEAL, RAYMER.
I'M ABOUT TO CALL MY BOSS AND LET HIM KNOW EVERYTHING THAT'S GONE DOWN TONIGHT. THEN I'M GOING TO HAND THE PHONE TO YOU AND YOU'RE GOING TO DO WHATEVER MY BOSS SAYS.
OR ELSE WHAT? I *CAN'T DIE,* YOU MORON.
MAYBE YOU CAN'T.
BUT I WONDER HOW YOU'LL FEEL ABOUT SPENDING THE NEXT FEW MONTHS AS A QUADRUPLE AMPUTEE AT THE BOTTOM OF A WELL OF SHIT.
OH, CHRIST.
OF COURSE, BY THE TIME YOUR ARMS GROW BACK THE CONCRETE CAP I POUR OVER THE LAGOON SHOULD BE CURED...
EVEN AT THREE FEET THICK.
OH, NO. NO.

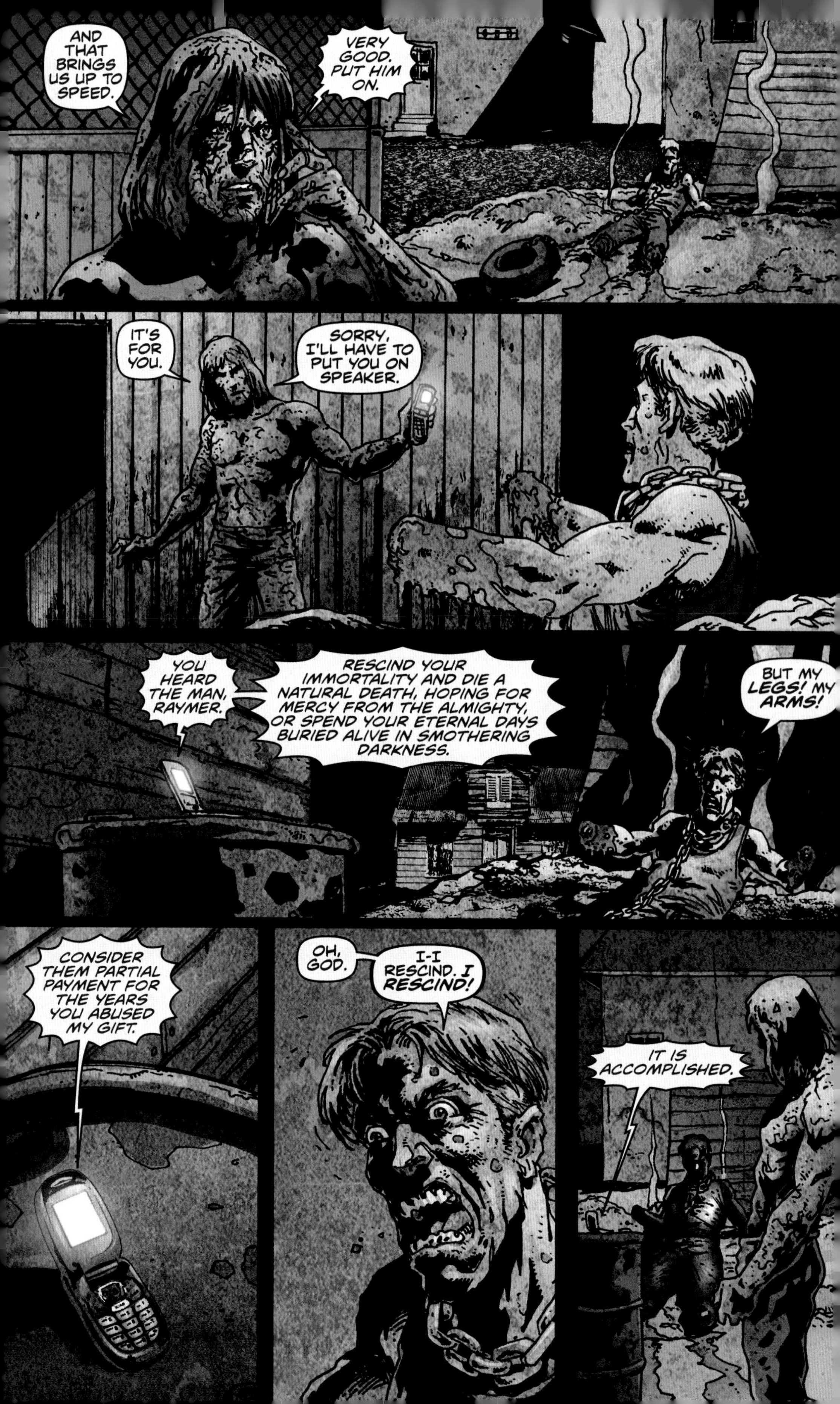
AND THAT BRINGS US UP TO SPEED.
VERY GOOD. PUT HIM ON.
IT'S FOR YOU.
SORRY, I'LL HAVE TO PUT YOU ON SPEAKER.
YOU HEARD THE MAN, RAYMER.
RESCIND YOUR IMMORTALITY AND DIE A NATURAL DEATH, HOPING FOR MERCY FROM THE ALMIGHTY, OR SPEND YOUR ETERNAL DAYS BURIED ALIVE IN SMOTHERING DARKNESS.
BUT MY LEGS! MY ARMS!
CONSIDER THEM PARTIAL PAYMENT FOR THE YEARS YOU ABUSED MY GIFT.
OH, GOD.
I-I RESCIND. I RESCIND!
IT IS ACCOMPLISHED.

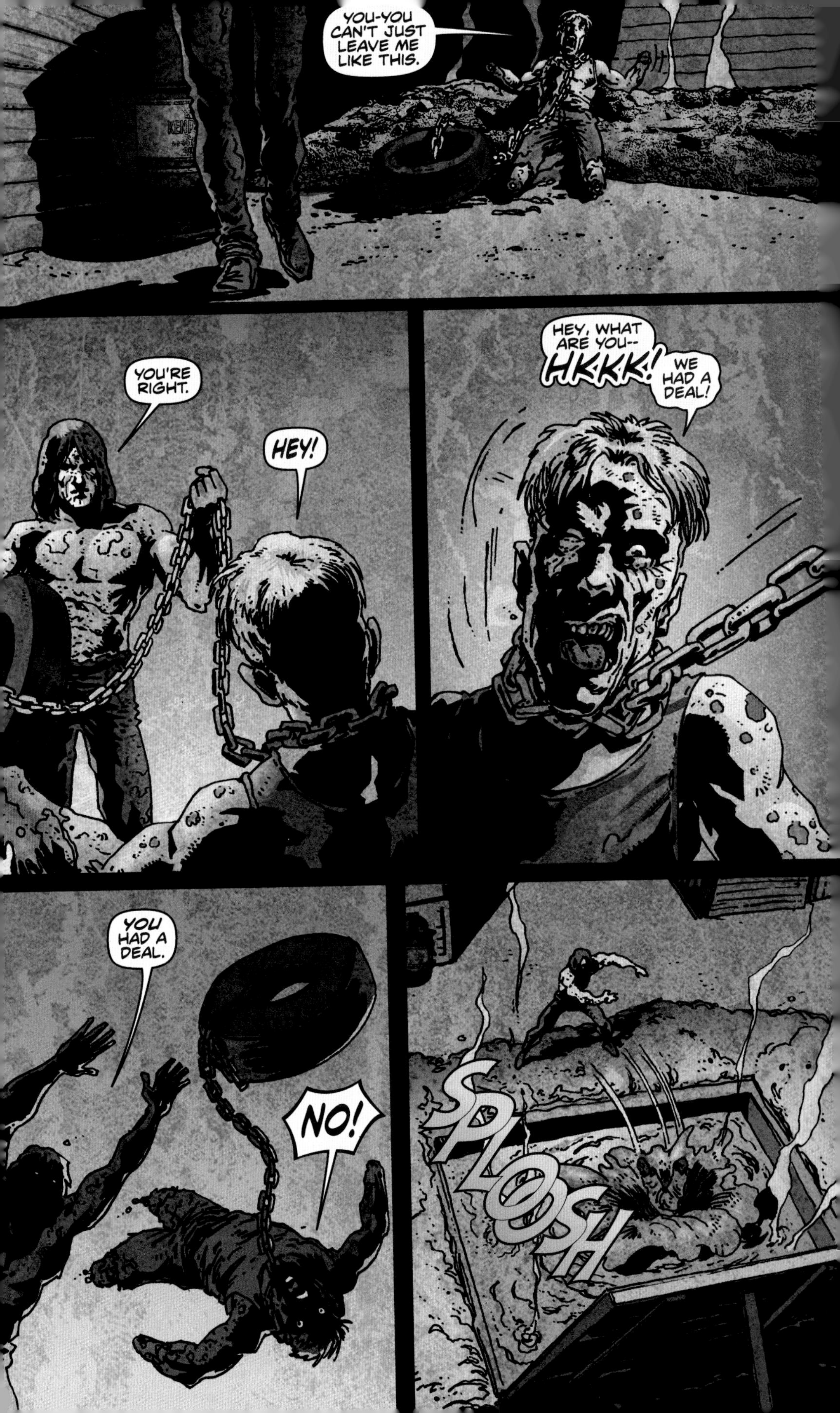
YOU-YOU CAN'T JUST LEAVE ME LIKE THIS.
YOU'RE RIGHT.
HEY!
HEY, WHAT ARE YOU--
HKKK!
WE HAD A DEAL!
YOU HAD A DEAL.
NO!
SPLOOSH

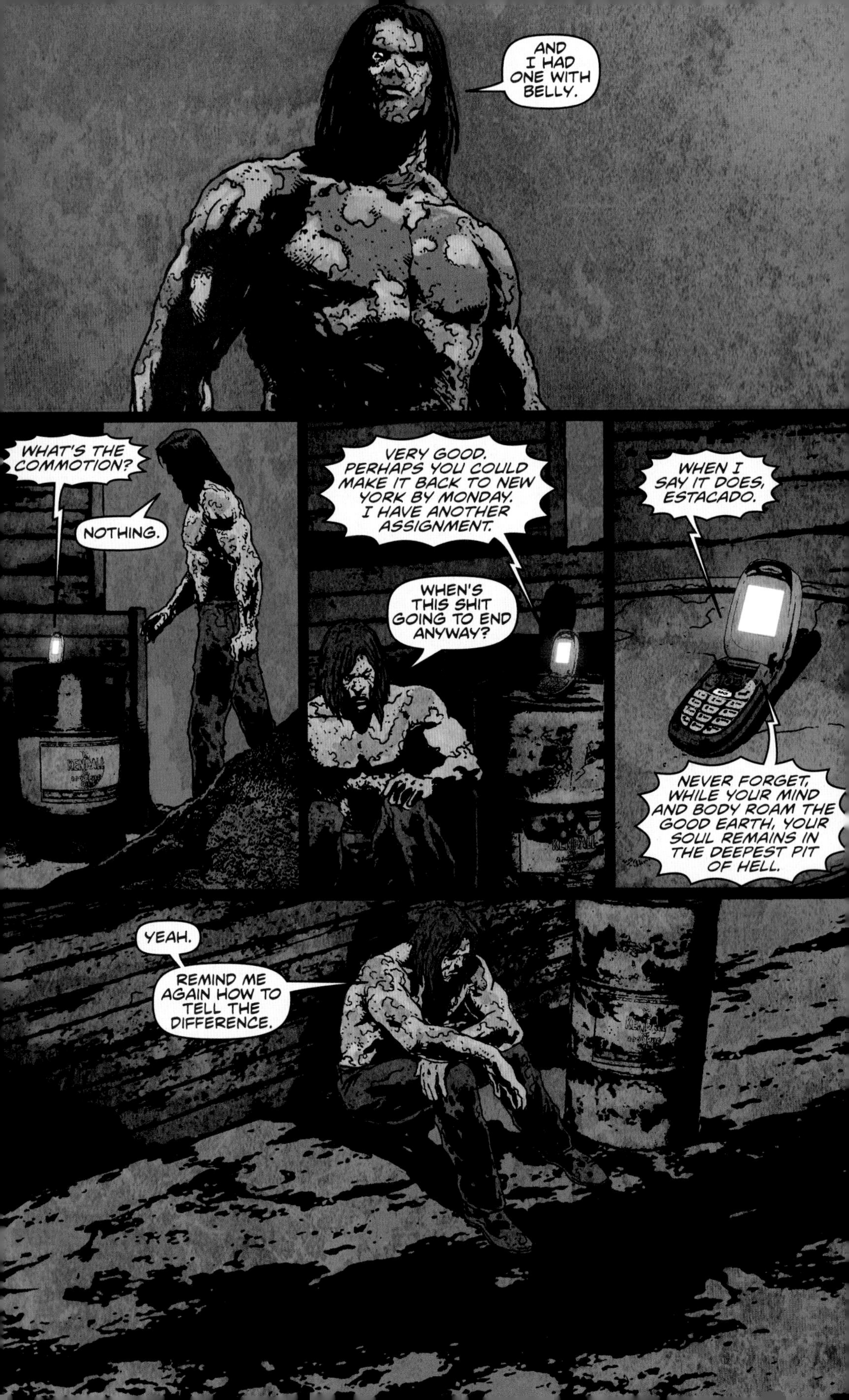
AND I HAD ONE WITH BELLY.
WHAT'S THE COMMOTION?
NOTHING.
VERY GOOD. PERHAPS YOU COULD MAKE IT BACK TO NEW YORK BY MONDAY. I HAVE ANOTHER ASSIGNMENT.
WHEN'S THIS SHIT GOING TO END ANYWAY?
WHEN I SAY IT DOES, ESTACADO.
NEVER FORGET, WHILE YOUR MIND AND BODY ROAM THE GOOD EARTH, YOUR SOUL REMAINS IN THE DEEPEST PIT OF HELL.
YEAH.
REMIND ME AGAIN HOW TO TELL THE DIFFERENCE.

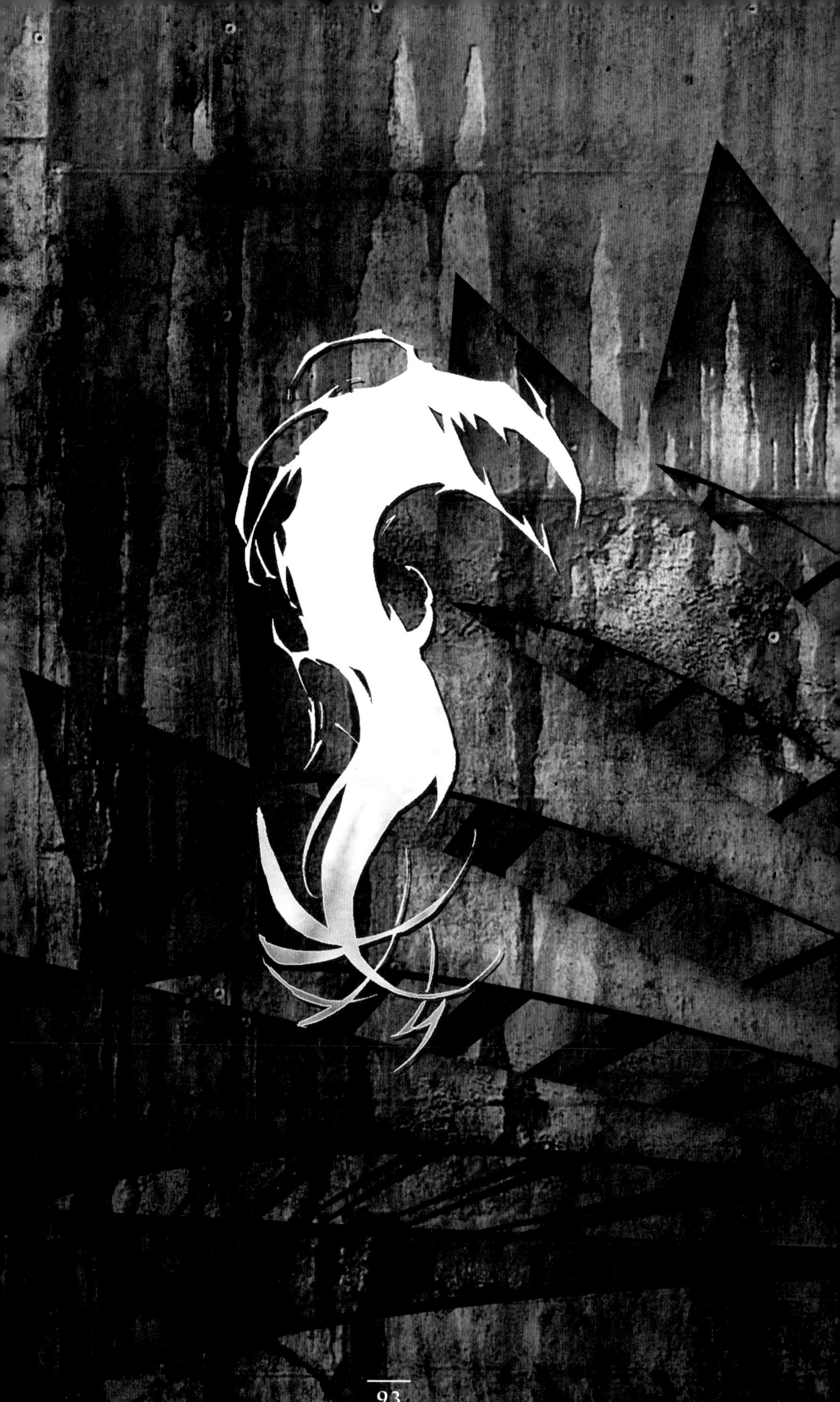

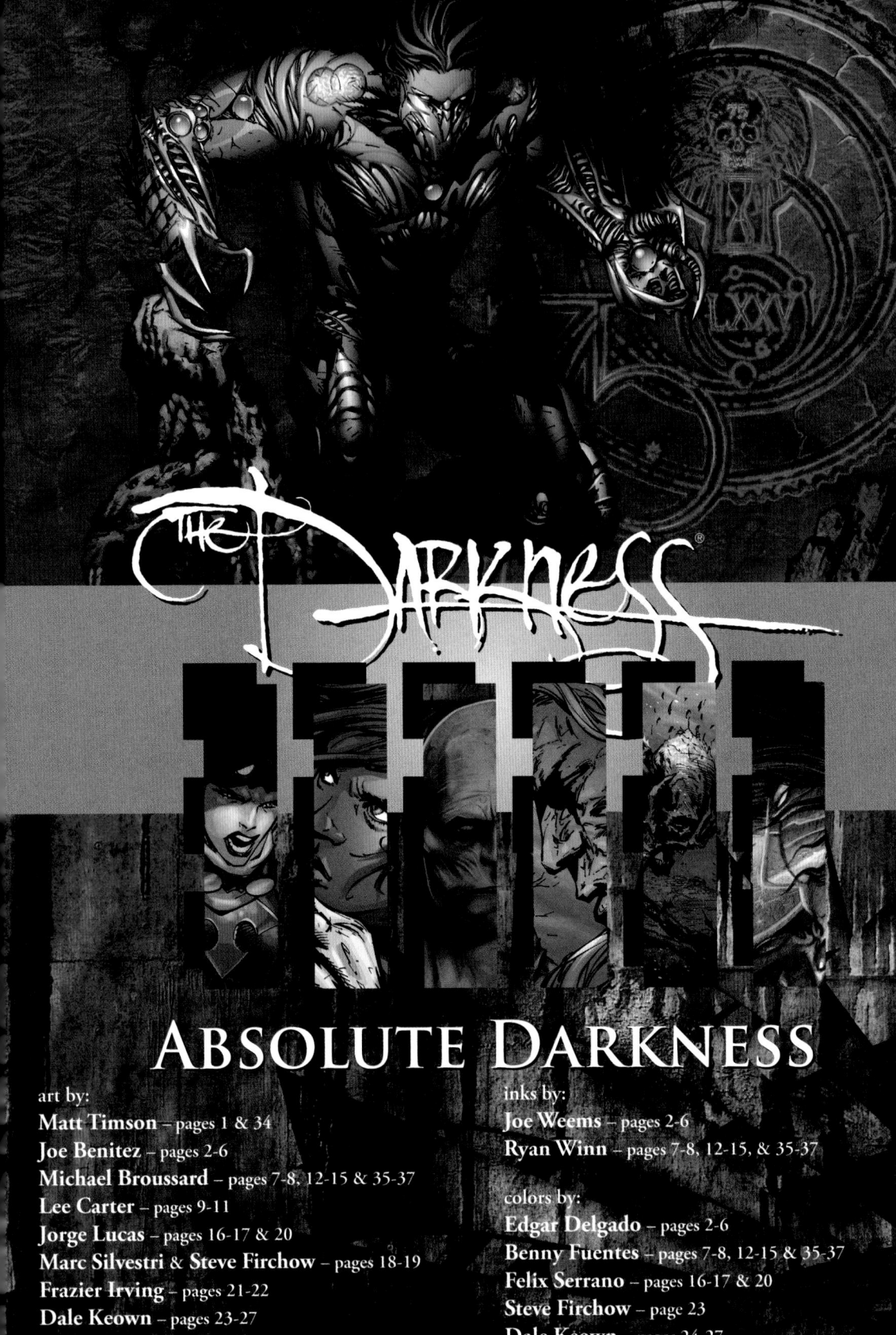

ABSOLUTE DARKNESS

art by:

Matt Timson – pages 1 & 34
Joe Benitez – pages 2-6
Michael Broussard – pages 7-8, 12-15 & 35-37
Lee Carter – pages 9-11
Jorge Lucas – pages 16-17 & 20
Marc Silvestri & Steve Firchow – pages 18-19
Frazier Irving – pages 21-22
Dale Keown – pages 23-27
Ryan Sook – pages 28-32
Stjepan Sejic – page 33

inks by:

Joe Weems – pages 2-6
Ryan Winn – pages 7-8, 12-15, & 35-37

colors by:

Edgar Delgado – pages 2-6
Benny Fuentes – pages 7-8, 12-15 & 35-37
Felix Serrano – pages 16-17 & 20
Steve Firchow – page 23
Dale Keown – pages 24-27
Dave McCaig – pages 28-32

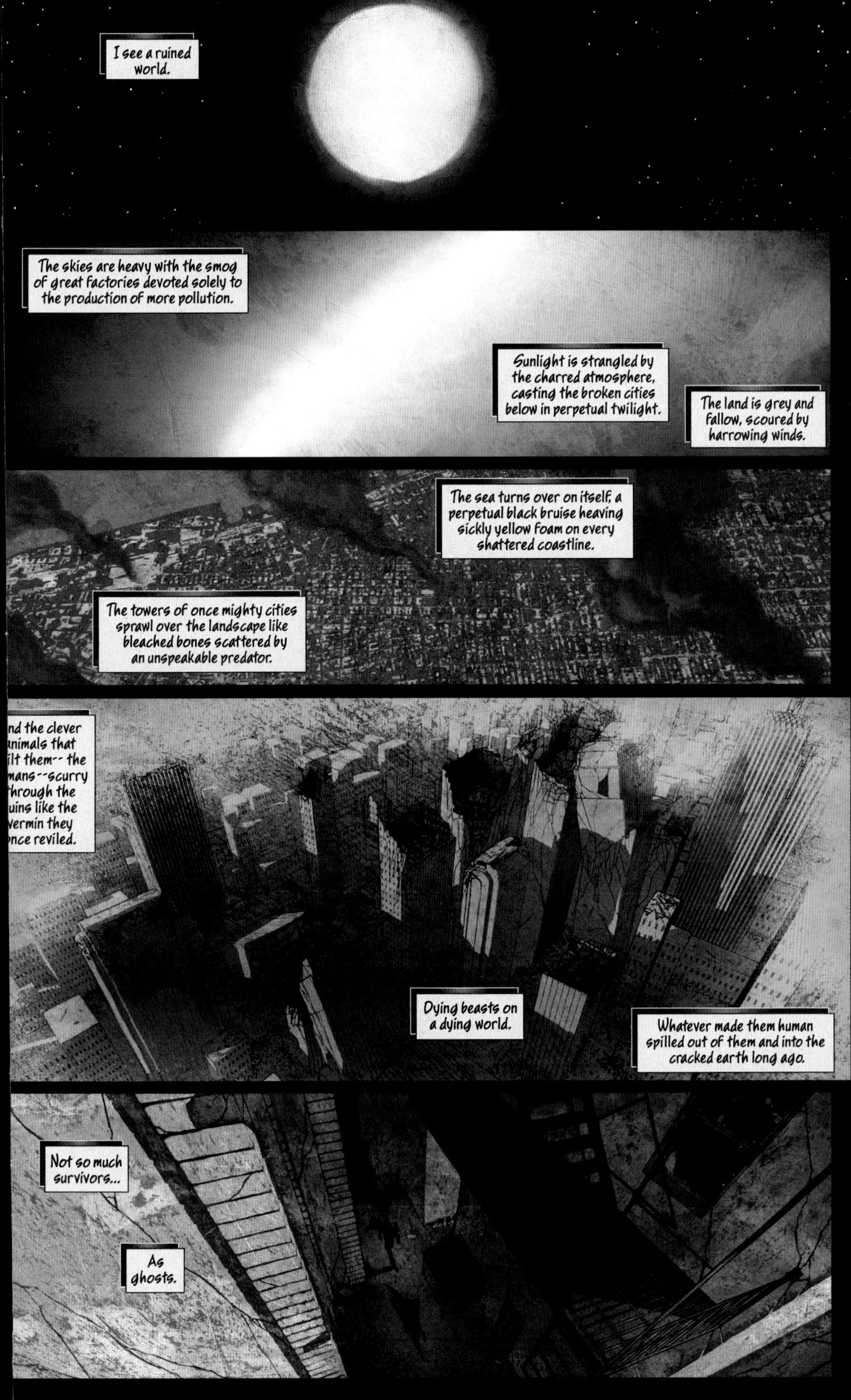
I see a ruined world.
The skies are heavy with the smog of great factories devoted solely to the production of more pollution.
Sunlight is strangled by the charred atmosphere, casting the broken cities below in perpetual twilight.
The land is grey and fallow, scoured by harrowing winds.
The sea turns over on itself, a perpetual black bruise heaving sickly yellow foam on every shattered coastline.
The towers of once mighty cities sprawl over the landscape like bleached bones scattered by an unspeakable predator.
nd the clever nimals that ilt them-- the mans--scurry through the uins like the vermin they nce reviled.
Dying beasts on a dying world.
Whatever made them human spilled out of them and into the cracked earth long ago.
Not so much survivors...
As ghosts.

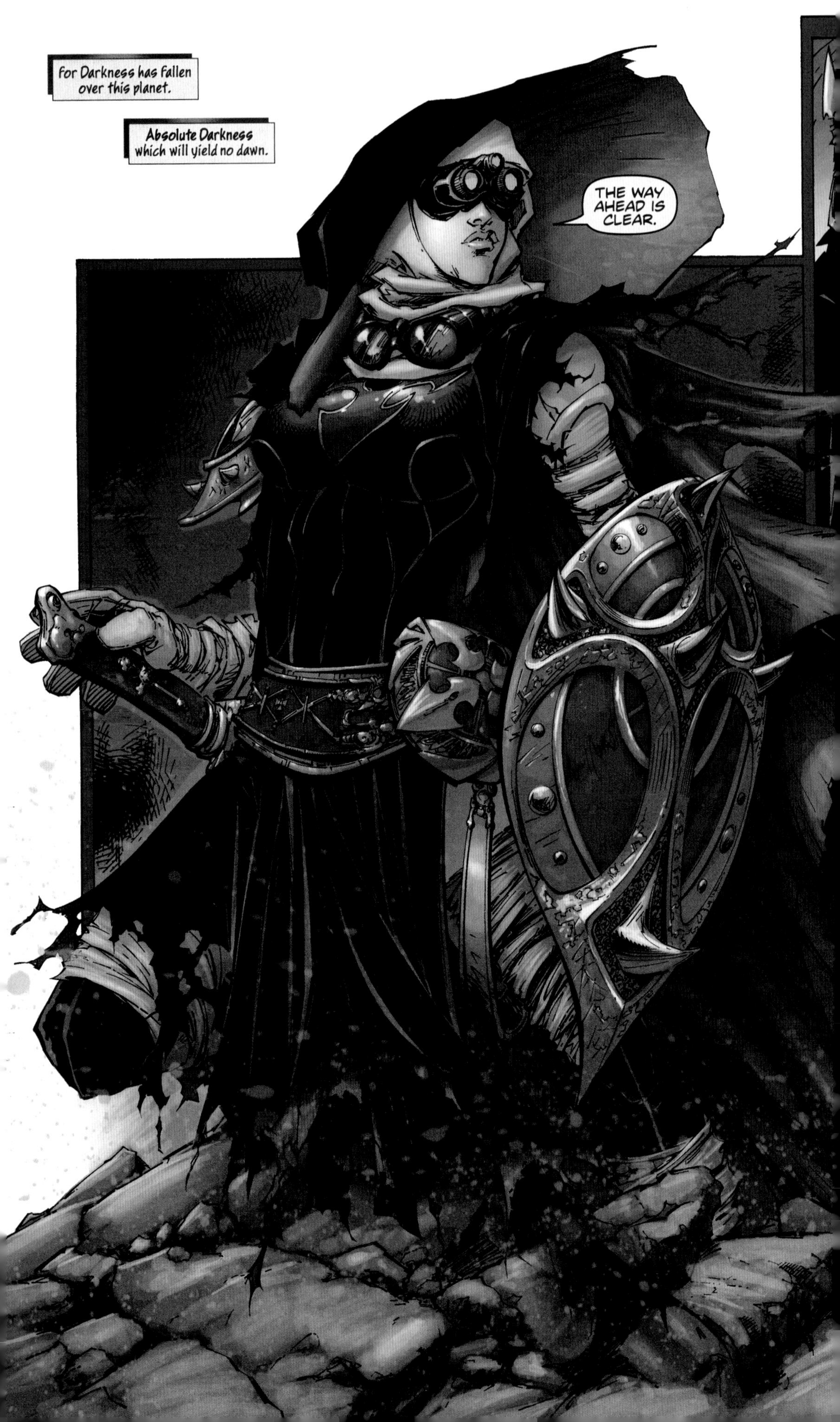
For Darkness has fallen over this planet.
Absolute Darkness which will yield no dawn.
THE WAY AHEAD IS CLEAR.

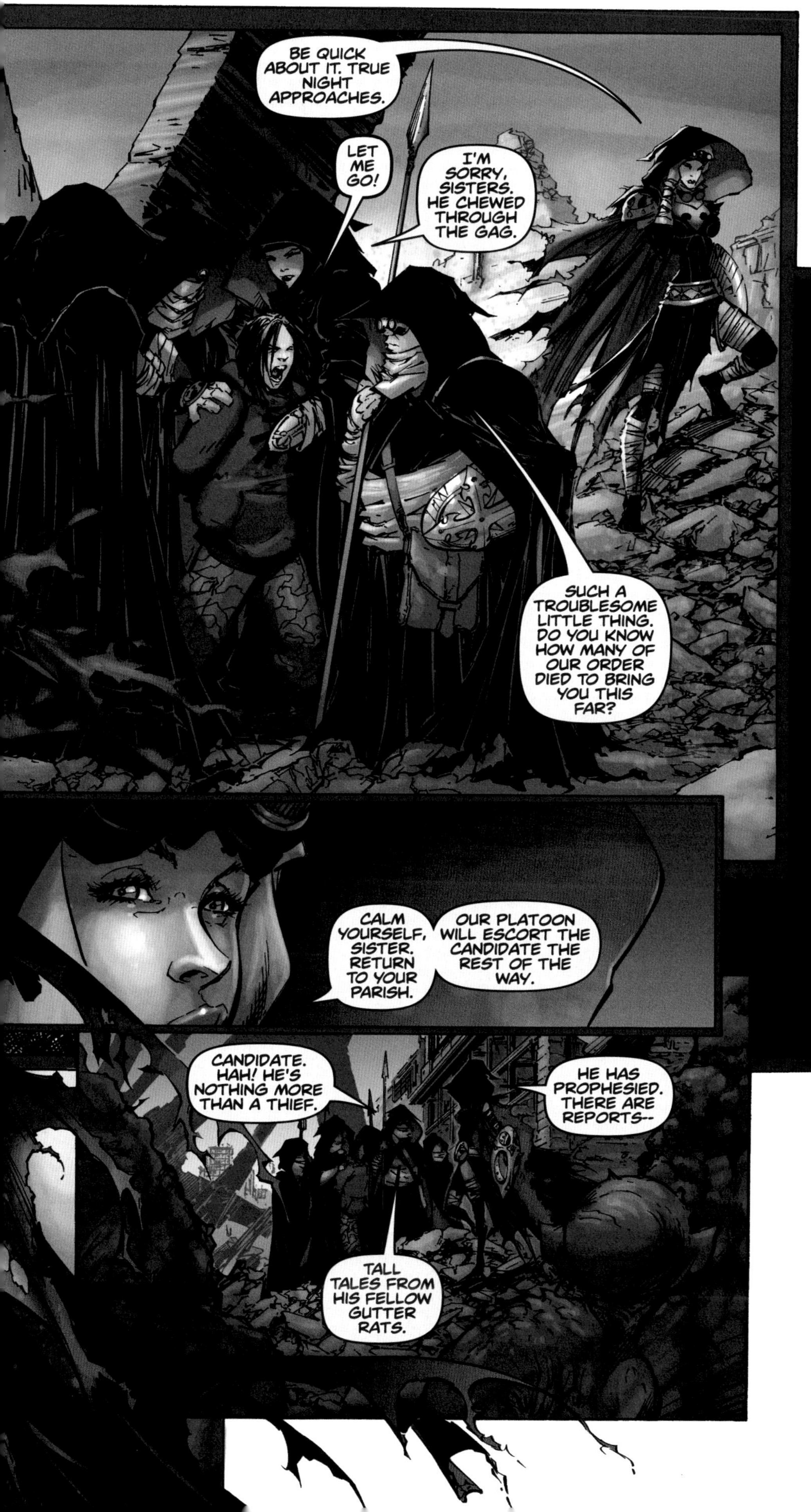
BE QUICK ABOUT IT. TRUE NIGHT APPROACHES.
LET ME GO!
I'M SORRY, SISTERS. HE CHEWED THROUGH THE GAG.
SUCH A TROUBLESOME LITTLE THING. DO YOU KNOW HOW MANY OF OUR ORDER DIED TO BRING YOU THIS FAR?
CALM YOURSELF, SISTER. RETURN TO YOUR PARISH.
OUR PLATOON WILL ESCORT THE CANDIDATE THE REST OF THE WAY.
CANDIDATE. HAH! HE'S NOTHING MORE THAN A THIEF.
HE HAS PROPHESIED. THERE ARE REPORTS--
TALL TALES FROM HIS FELLOW GUTTER RATS.

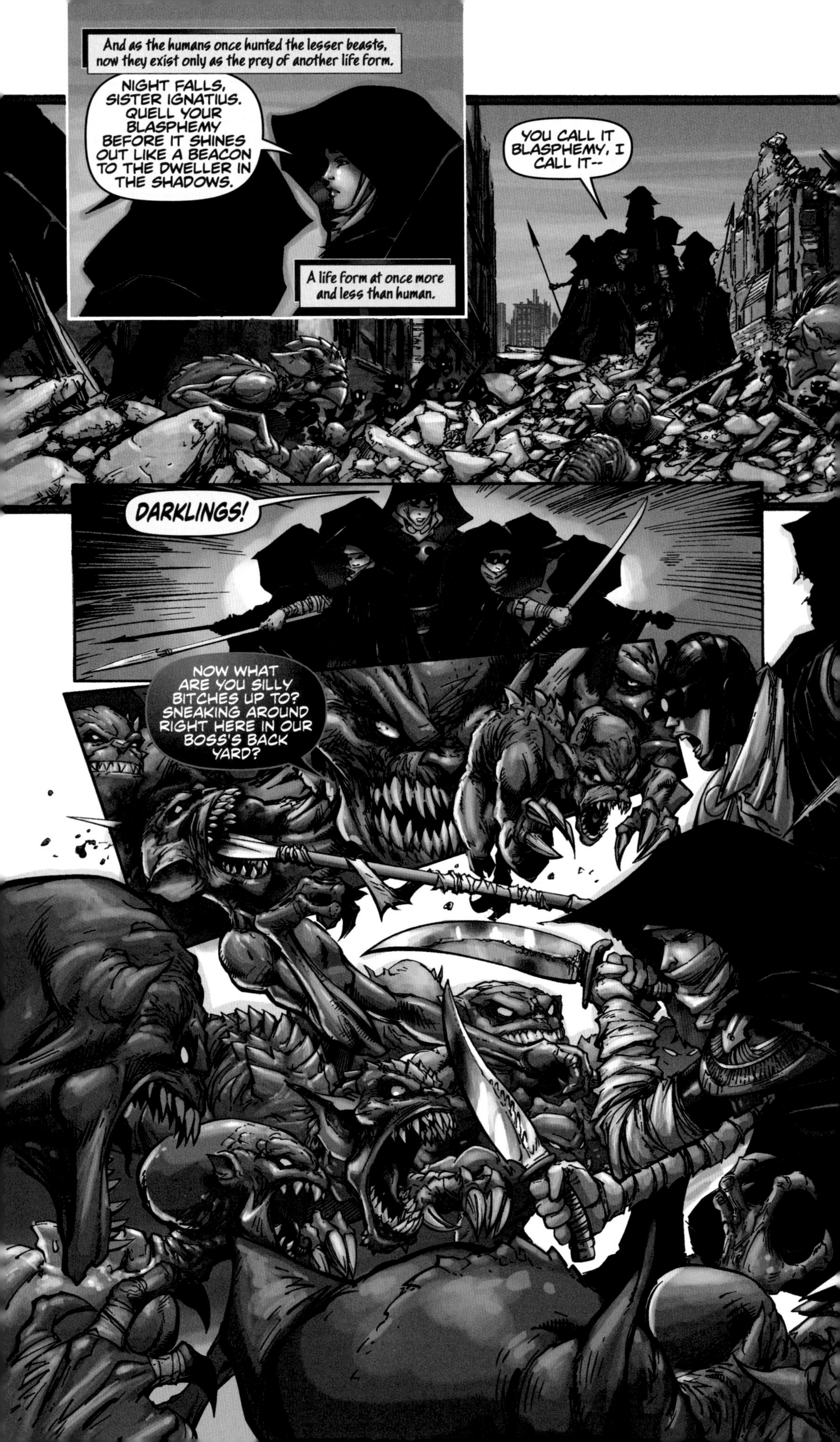
And as the humans once hunted the lesser beasts, now they exist only as the prey of another life form.
NIGHT FALLS, SISTER IGNATIUS. QUELL YOUR BLASPHEMY BEFORE IT SHINES OUT LIKE A BEACON TO THE DWELLER IN THE SHADOWS.
A life form at once more and less than human.
YOU CALL IT BLASPHEMY, I CALL IT--
DARKLINGS!
NOW WHAT ARE YOU SILLY BITCHES UP TO? SNEAKING AROUND RIGHT HERE IN OUR BOSS'S BACK YARD?

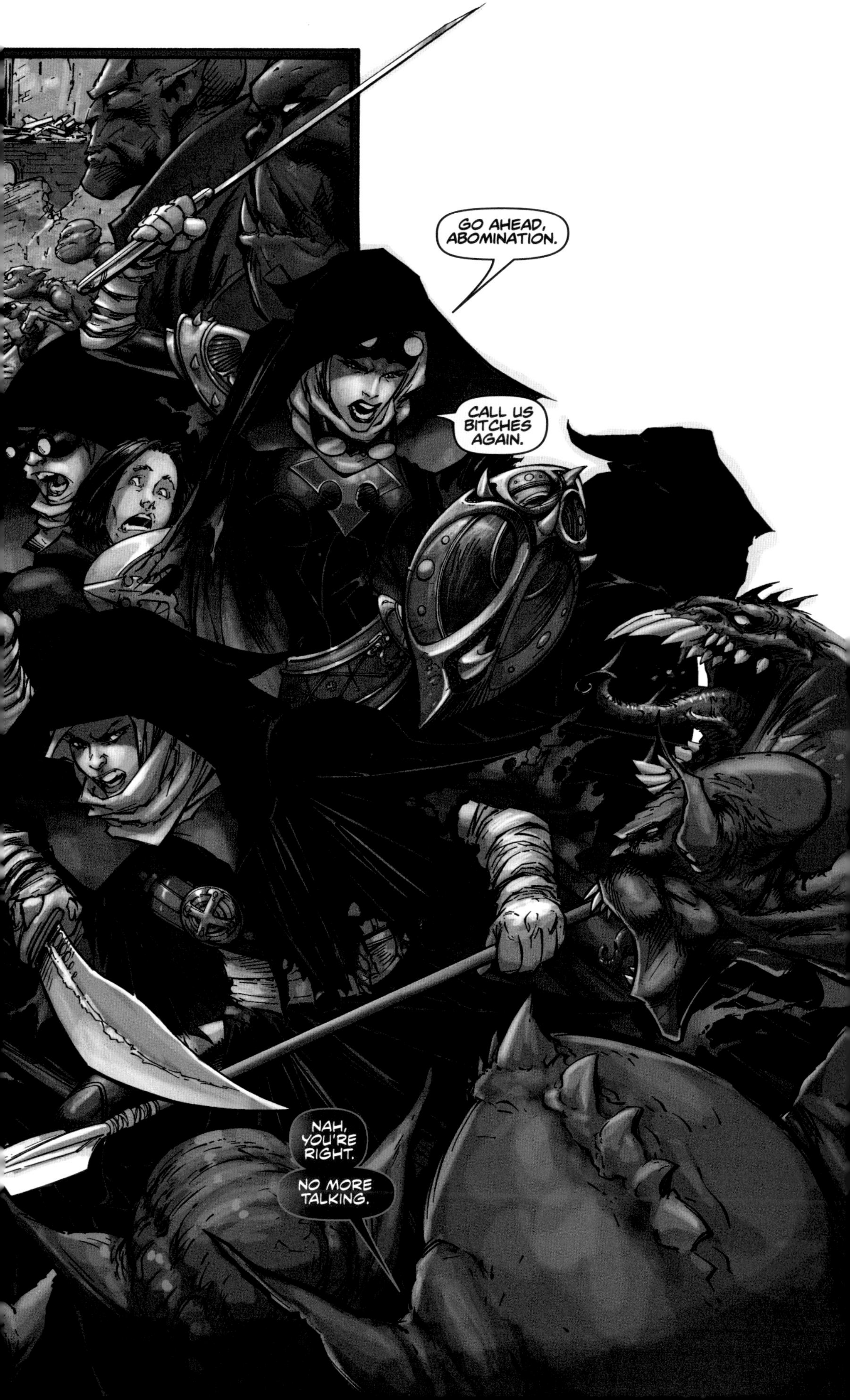
GO AHEAD, ABOMINATION.
CALL US BITCHES AGAIN.
NAH, YOU'RE RIGHT.
NO MORE TALKING.

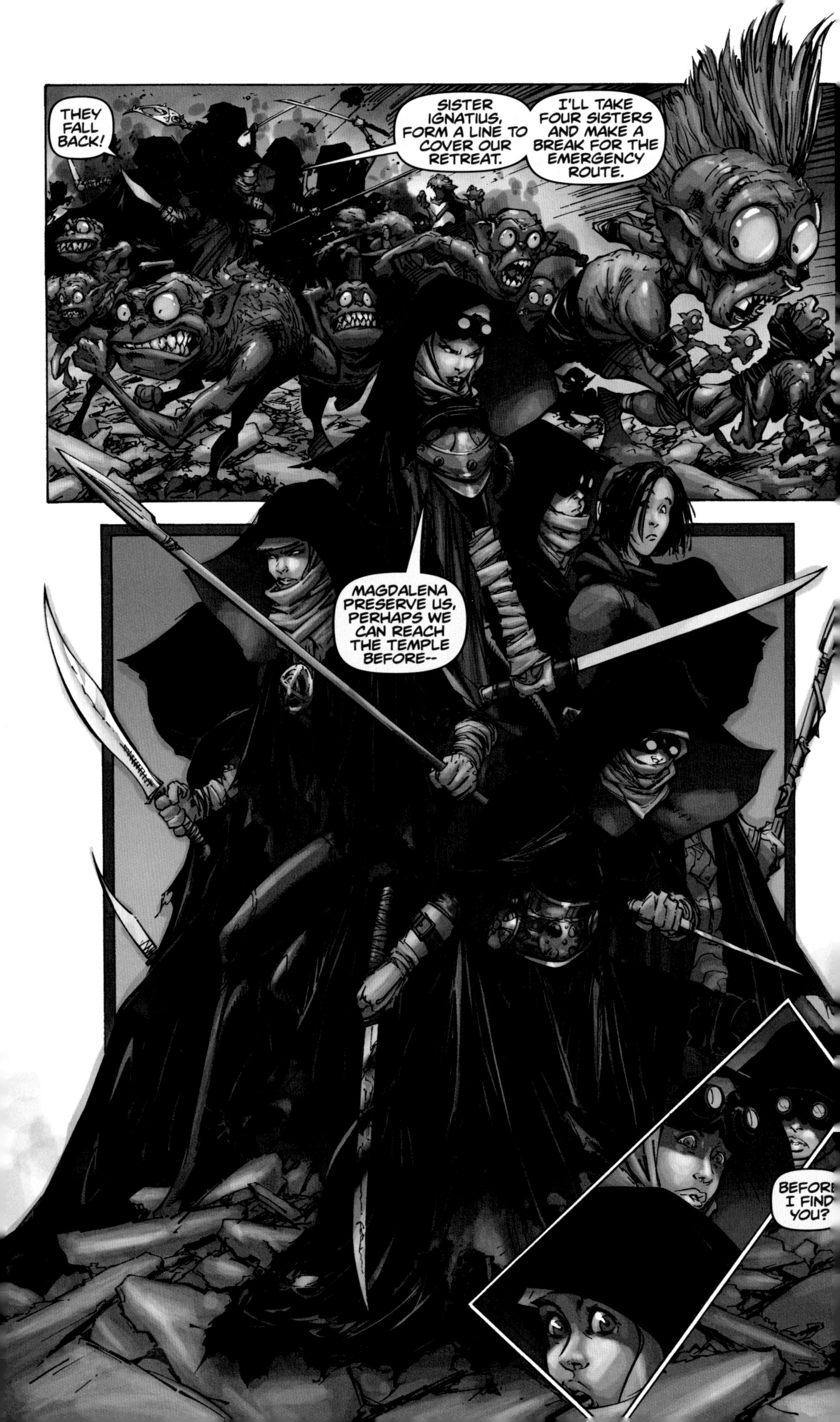
THEY FALL BACK!
SISTER IGNATIUS, FORM A LINE TO COVER OUR RETREAT.
I'LL TAKE FOUR SISTERS AND MAKE A BREAK FOR THE EMERGENCY ROUTE.
MAGDALENA PRESERVE US, PERHAPS WE CAN REACH THE TEMPLE BEFORE--
BEFOR I FIND YOU?

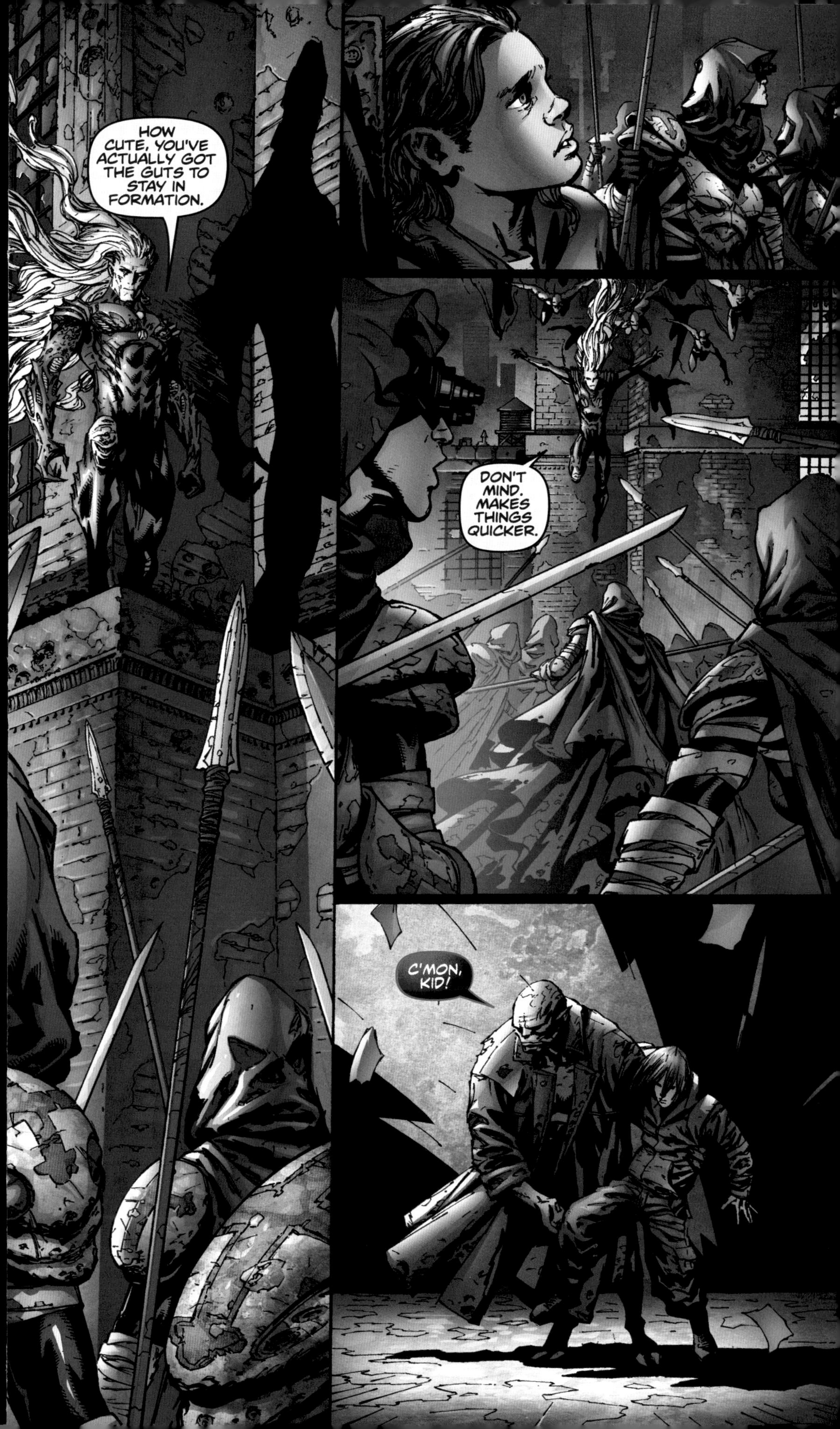
HOW CUTE, YOU'VE ACTUALLY GOT THE GUTS TO STAY IN FORMATION.
DON'T MIND. MAKES THINGS QUICKER.
C'MON, KID!

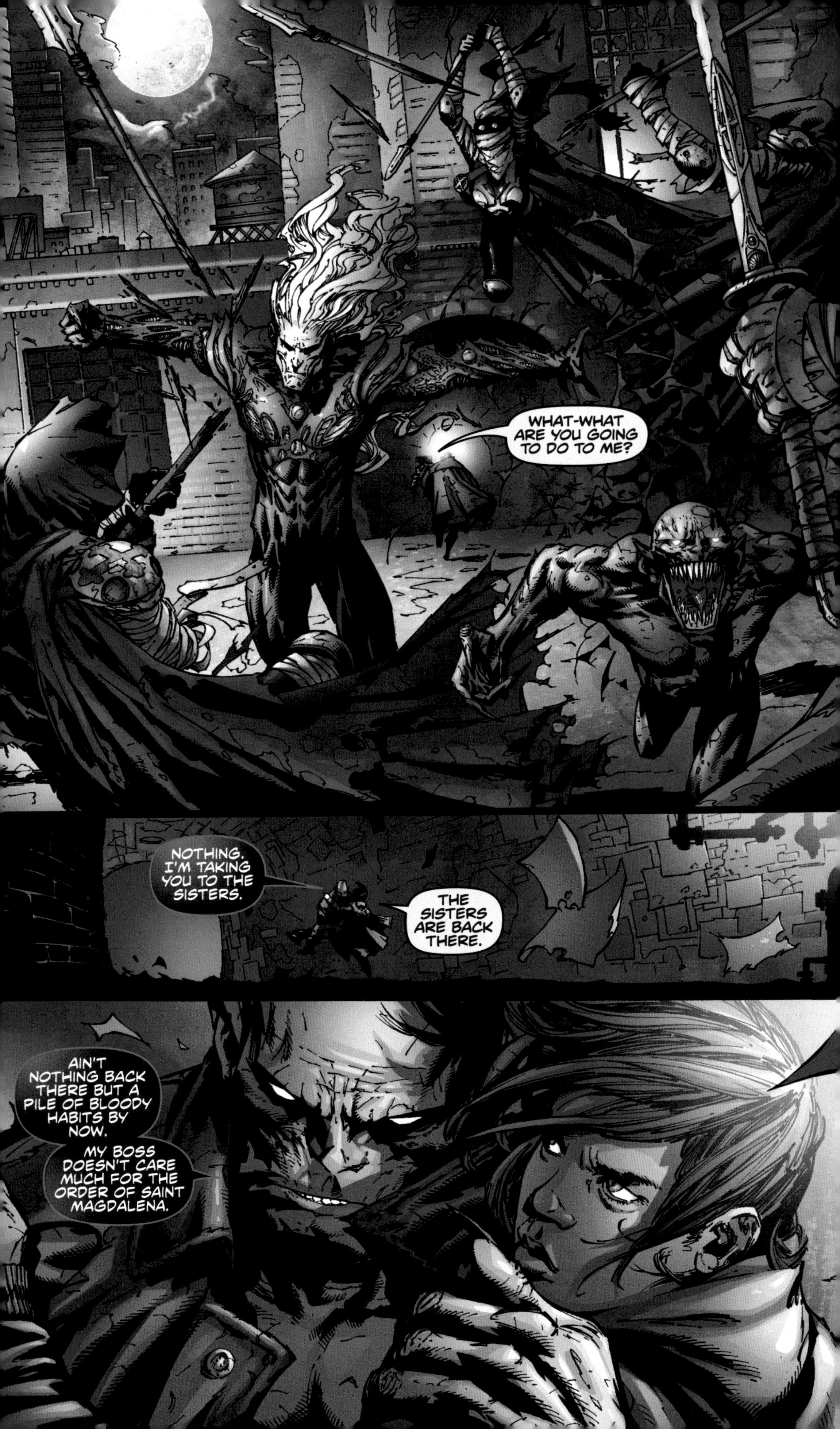
WHAT-WHAT ARE YOU GOING TO DO TO ME?
NOTHING. I'M TAKING YOU TO THE SISTERS.
THE SISTERS ARE BACK THERE.
AIN'T NOTHING BACK THERE BUT A PILE OF BLOODY HABITS BY NOW.
MY BOSS DOESN'T CARE MUCH FOR THE ORDER OF SAINT MAGDALENA.

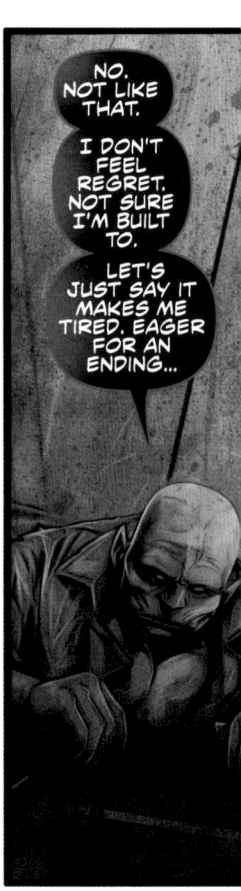

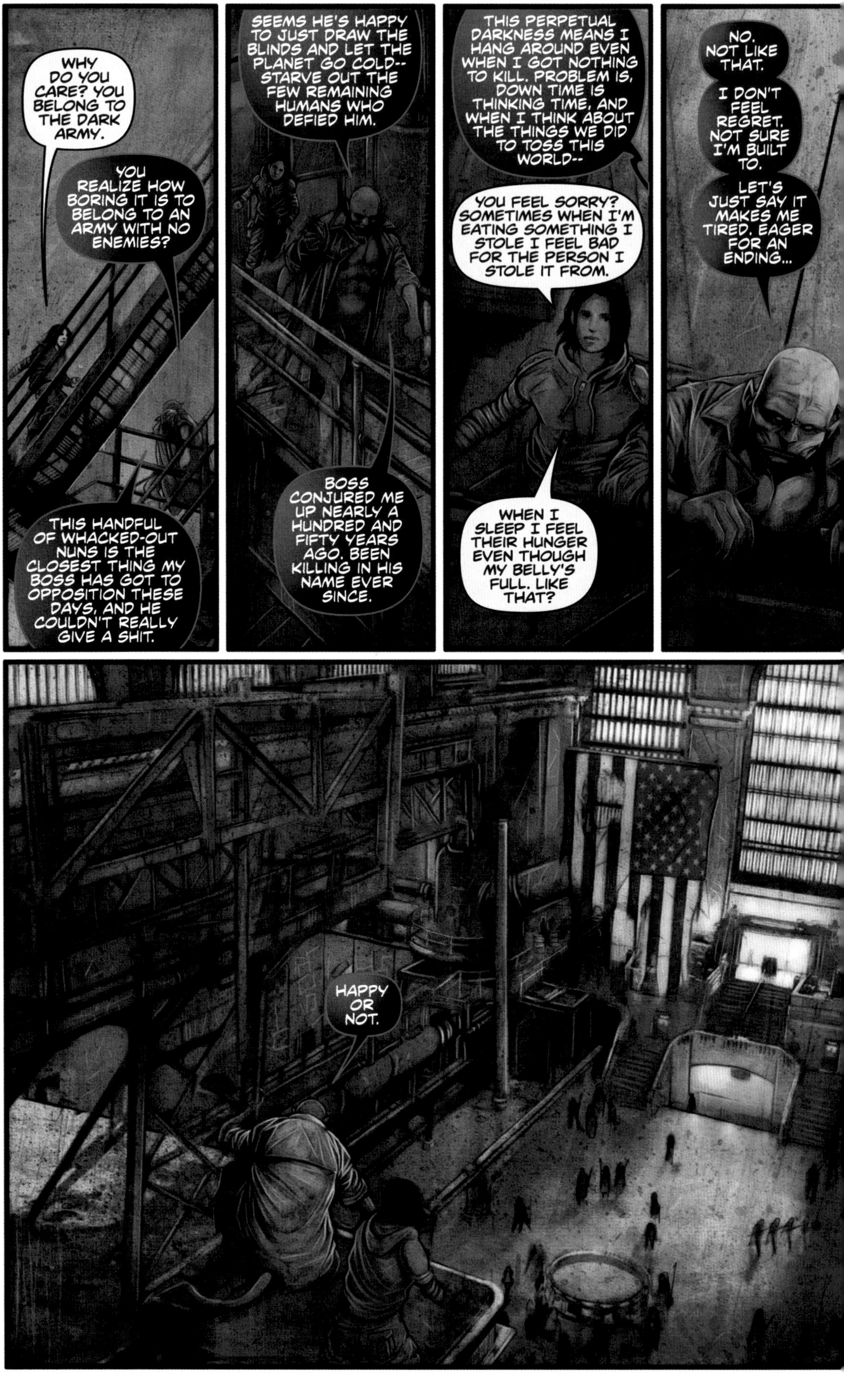

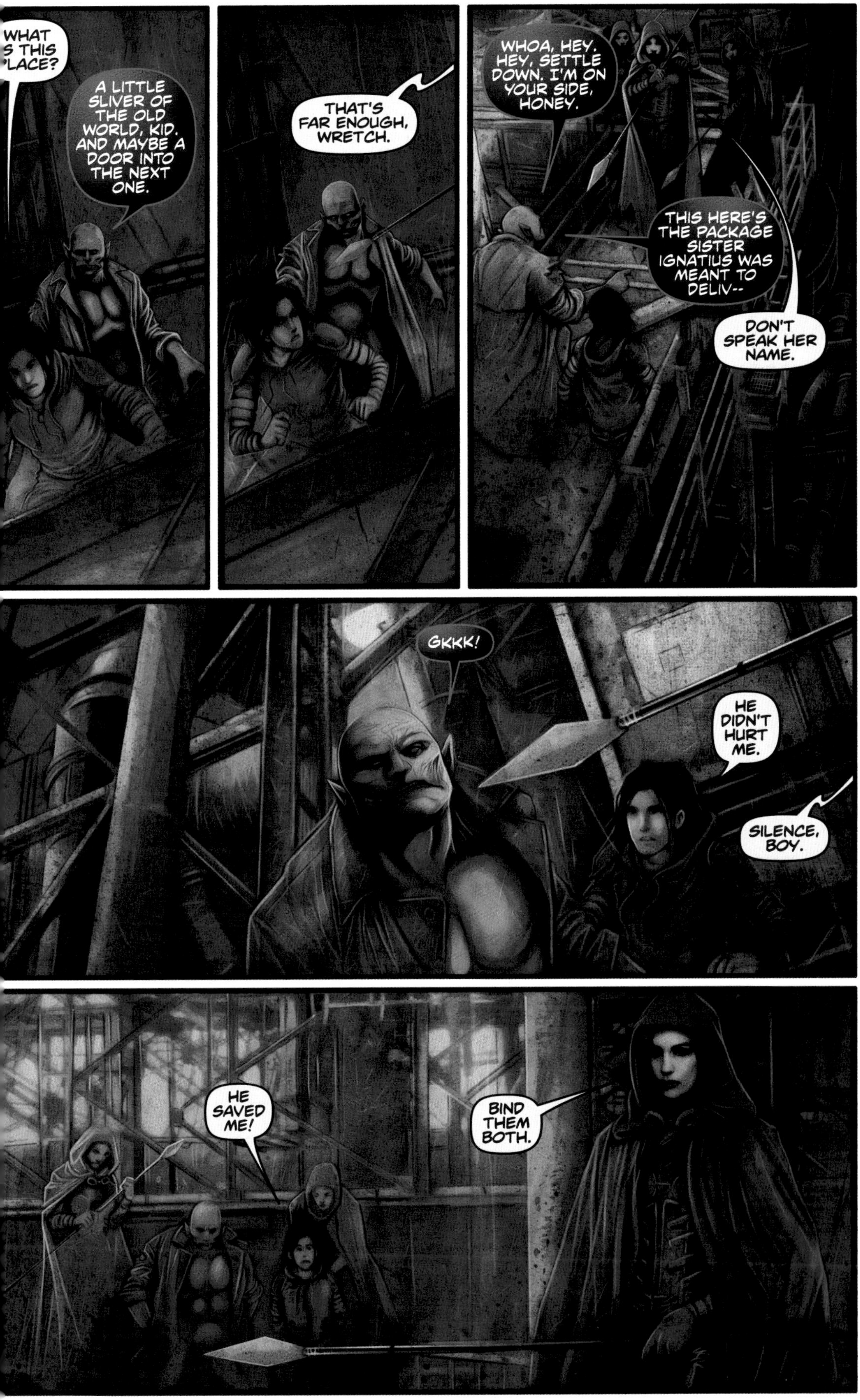
WHAT S THIS 'LACE?
A LITTLE SLIVER OF THE OLD WORLD, KID. AND MAYBE A DOOR INTO THE NEXT ONE.
THAT'S FAR ENOUGH, WRETCH.
WHOA, HEY. HEY, SETTLE DOWN. I'M ON YOUR SIDE, HONEY.
THIS HERE'S THE PACKAGE SISTER IGNATIUS WAS MEANT TO DELIV--
DON'T SPEAK HER NAME.
GKKK!
HE DIDN'T HURT ME.
SILENCE, BOY.
HE SAVED ME!
BIND THEM BOTH.

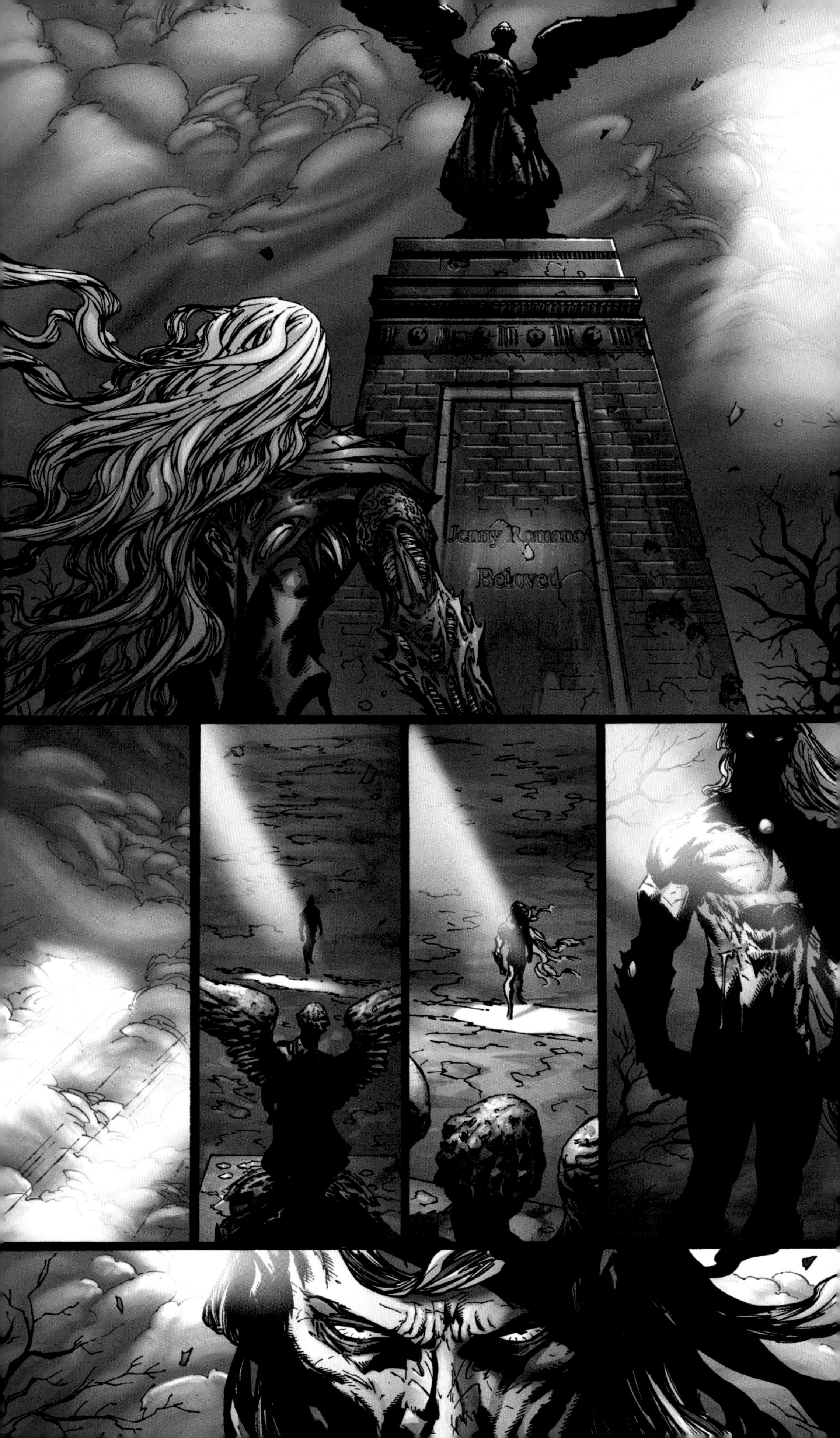
Jenny Romano
Beloved

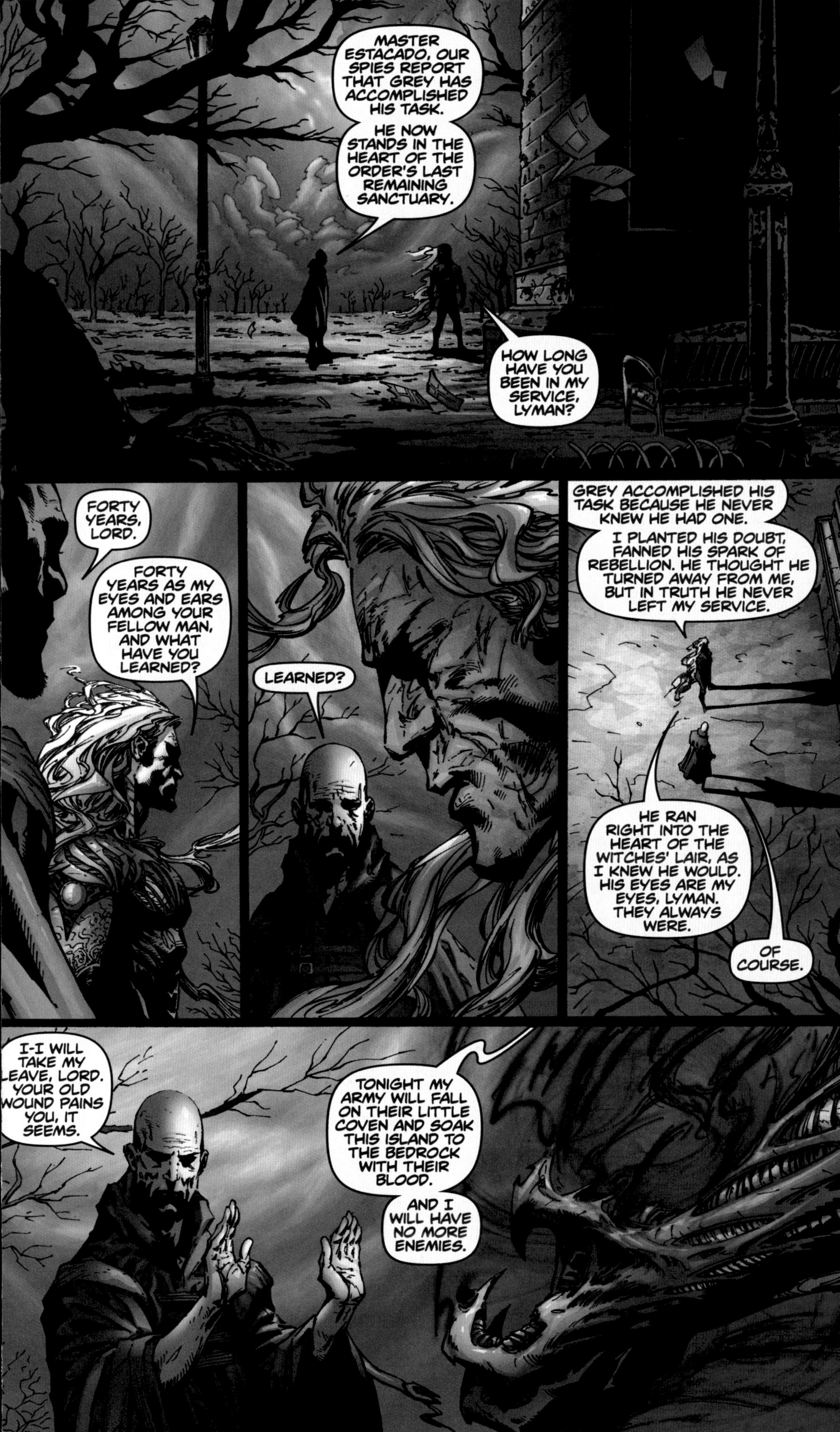
MASTER ESTACADO, OUR SPIES REPORT THAT GREY HAS ACCOMPLISHED HIS TASK.
HE NOW STANDS IN THE HEART OF THE ORDER'S LAST REMAINING SANCTUARY.
HOW LONG HAVE YOU BEEN IN MY SERVICE, LYMAN?
FORTY YEARS, LORD.
FORTY YEARS AS MY EYES AND EARS AMONG YOUR FELLOW MAN, AND WHAT HAVE YOU LEARNED?
LEARNED?
GREY ACCOMPLISHED HIS TASK BECAUSE HE NEVER KNEW HE HAD ONE.
I PLANTED HIS DOUBT, FANNED HIS SPARK OF REBELLION. HE THOUGHT HE TURNED AWAY FROM ME, BUT IN TRUTH HE NEVER LEFT MY SERVICE.
HE RAN RIGHT INTO THE HEART OF THE WITCHES' LAIR, AS I KNEW HE WOULD. HIS EYES ARE MY EYES, LYMAN. THEY ALWAYS WERE.
OF COURSE.
I-I WILL TAKE MY LEAVE, LORD. YOUR OLD WOUND PAINS YOU, IT SEEMS.
TONIGHT MY ARMY WILL FALL ON THEIR LITTLE COVEN AND SOAK THIS ISLAND TO THE BEDROCK WITH THEIR BLOOD.
AND I WILL HAVE NO MORE ENEMIES.

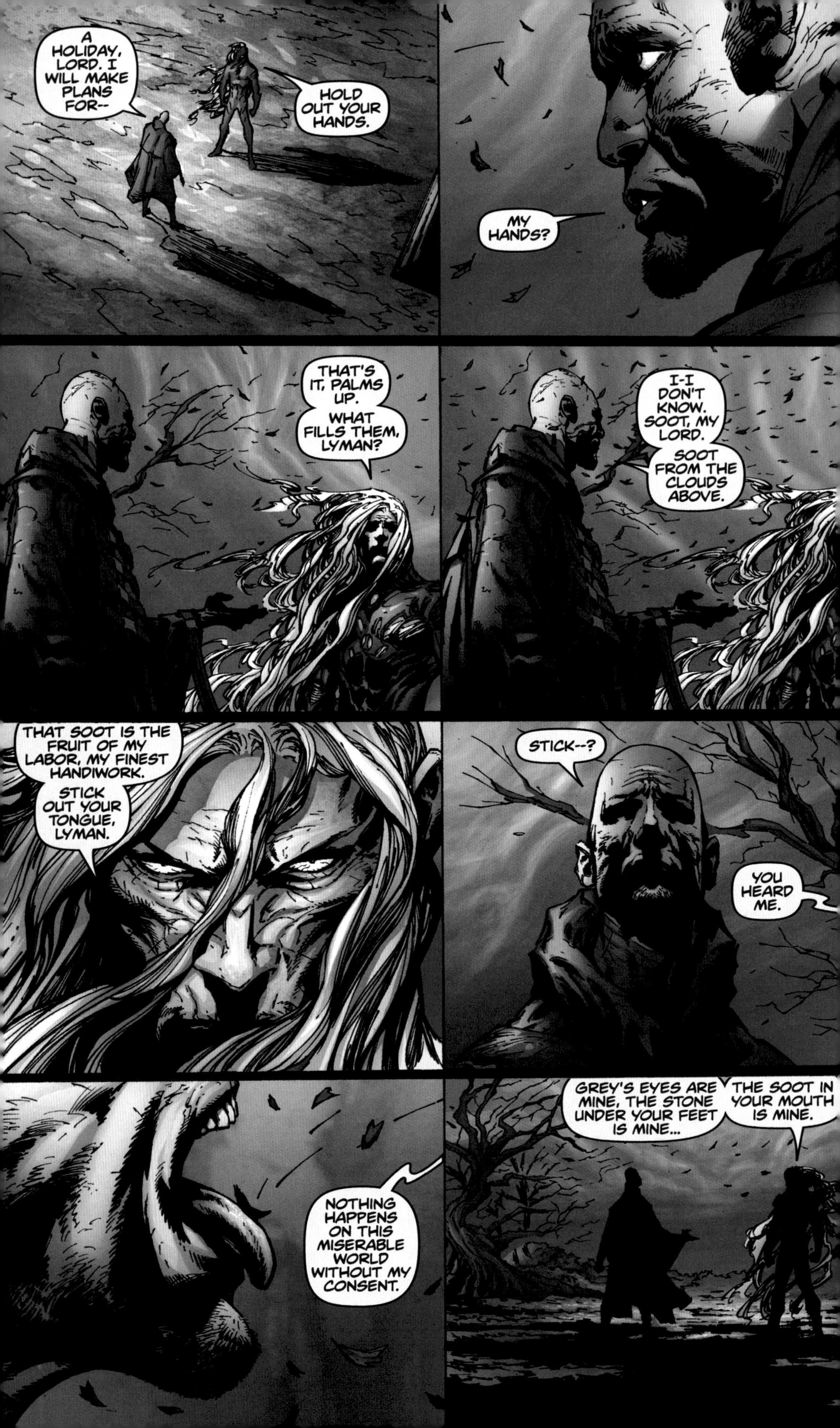
A HOLIDAY, LORD. I WILL MAKE PLANS FOR--
HOLD OUT YOUR HANDS.
MY HANDS?
THAT'S IT, PALMS UP.
WHAT FILLS THEM, LYMAN?
I-I DON'T KNOW. SOOT, MY LORD.
SOOT FROM THE CLOUDS ABOVE.
THAT SOOT IS THE FRUIT OF MY LABOR, MY FINEST HANDIWORK.
STICK OUT YOUR TONGUE, LYMAN.
STICK--?
YOU HEARD ME.
NOTHING HAPPENS ON THIS MISERABLE WORLD WITHOUT MY CONSENT.
GREY'S EYES ARE MINE, THE STONE UNDER YOUR FEET IS MINE...
THE SOOT IN YOUR MOUTH IS MINE.

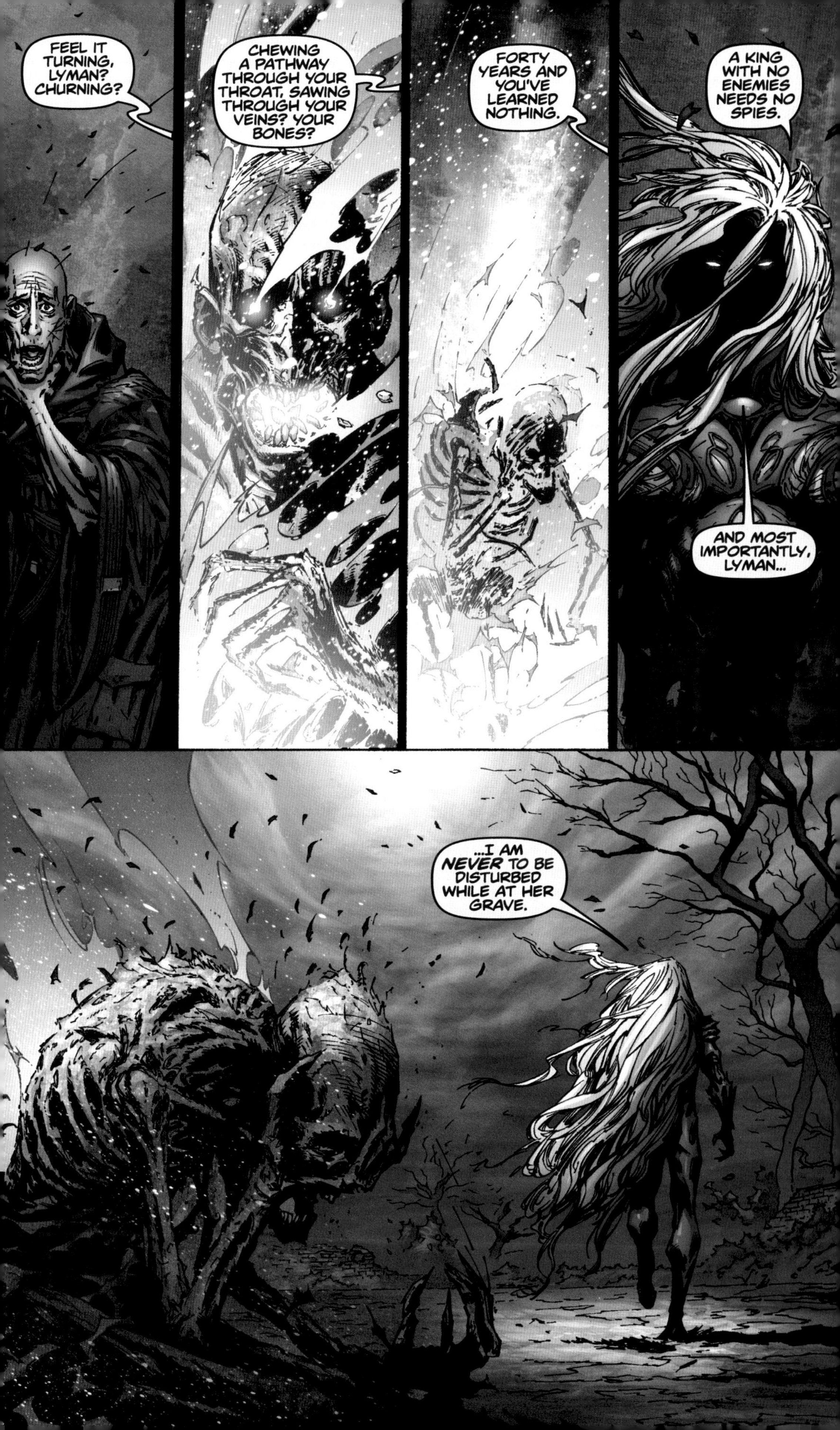
FEEL IT TURNING, LYMAN? CHURNING?
CHEWING A PATHWAY THROUGH YOUR THROAT, SAWING THROUGH YOUR VEINS? YOUR BONES?
FORTY YEARS AND YOU'VE LEARNED NOTHING.
A KING WITH NO ENEMIES NEEDS NO SPIES.
AND MOST IMPORTANTLY, LYMAN...
...I AM *NEVER* TO BE DISTURBED WHILE AT HER GRAVE.

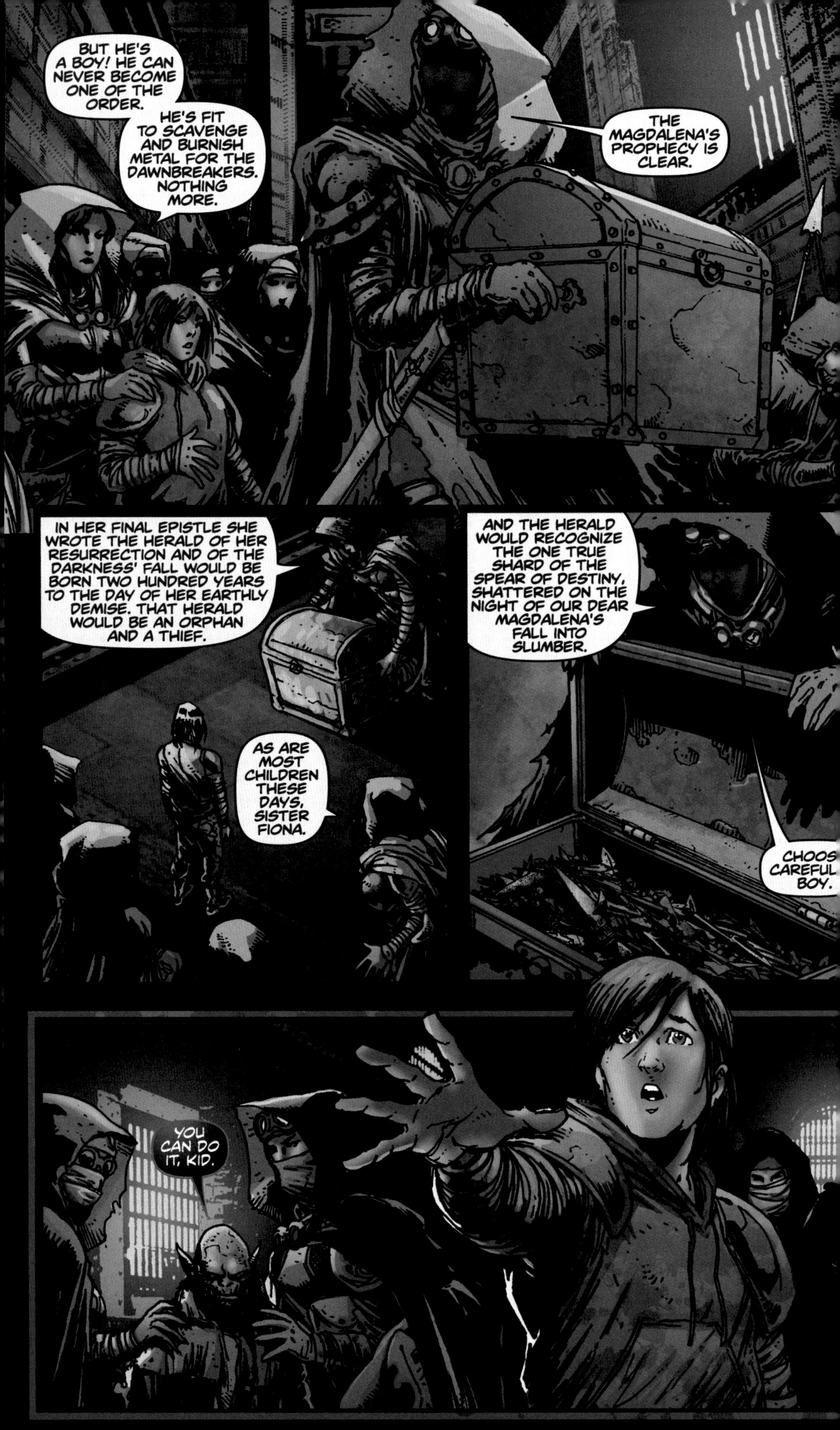
BUT HE'S A BOY! HE CAN NEVER BECOME ONE OF THE ORDER.
HE'S FIT TO SCAVENGE AND BURNISH METAL FOR THE DAWNBREAKERS. NOTHING MORE.
THE MAGDALENA'S PROPHECY IS CLEAR.
IN HER FINAL EPISTLE SHE WROTE THE HERALD OF HER RESURRECTION AND OF THE DARKNESS' FALL WOULD BE BORN TWO HUNDRED YEARS TO THE DAY OF HER EARTHLY DEMISE. THAT HERALD WOULD BE AN ORPHAN AND A THIEF.
AS ARE MOST CHILDREN THESE DAYS, SISTER FIONA.
AND THE HERALD WOULD RECOGNIZE THE ONE TRUE SHARD OF THE SPEAR OF DESTINY, SHATTERED ON THE NIGHT OF OUR DEAR MAGDALENA'S FALL INTO SLUMBER.
CHOOS CAREFUL BOY.
YOU CAN DO IT, KID.

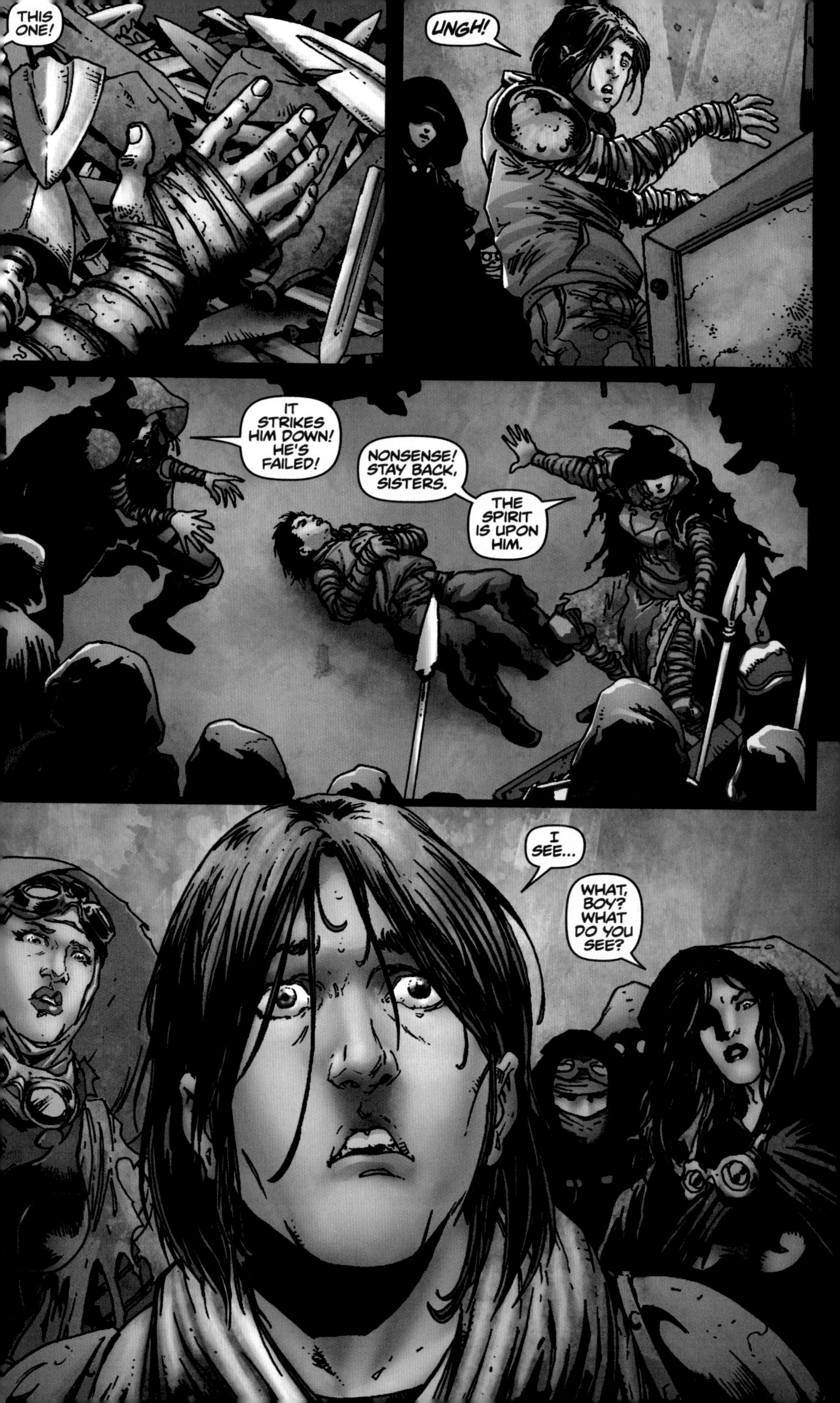
THIS ONE!
UNGH!
IT STRIKES HIM DOWN! HE'S FAILED!
NONSENSE! STAY BACK, SISTERS.
THE SPIRIT IS UPON HIM.
I SEE...
WHAT, BOY? WHAT DO YOU SEE?

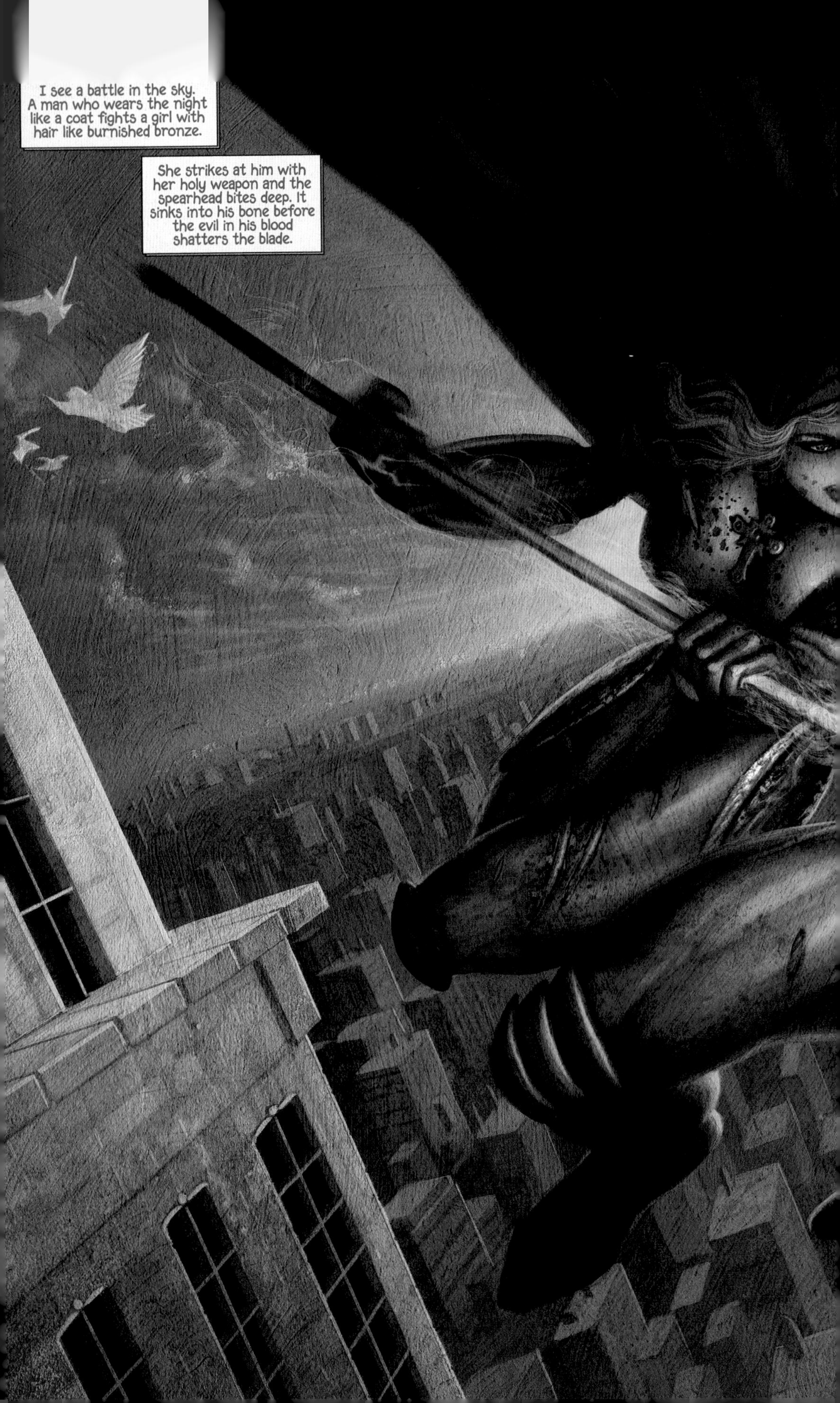
I see a battle in the sky. A man who wears the night like a coat fights a girl with hair like burnished bronze.
She strikes at him with her holy weapon and the spearhead bites deep. It sinks into his bone before the evil in his blood shatters the blade.

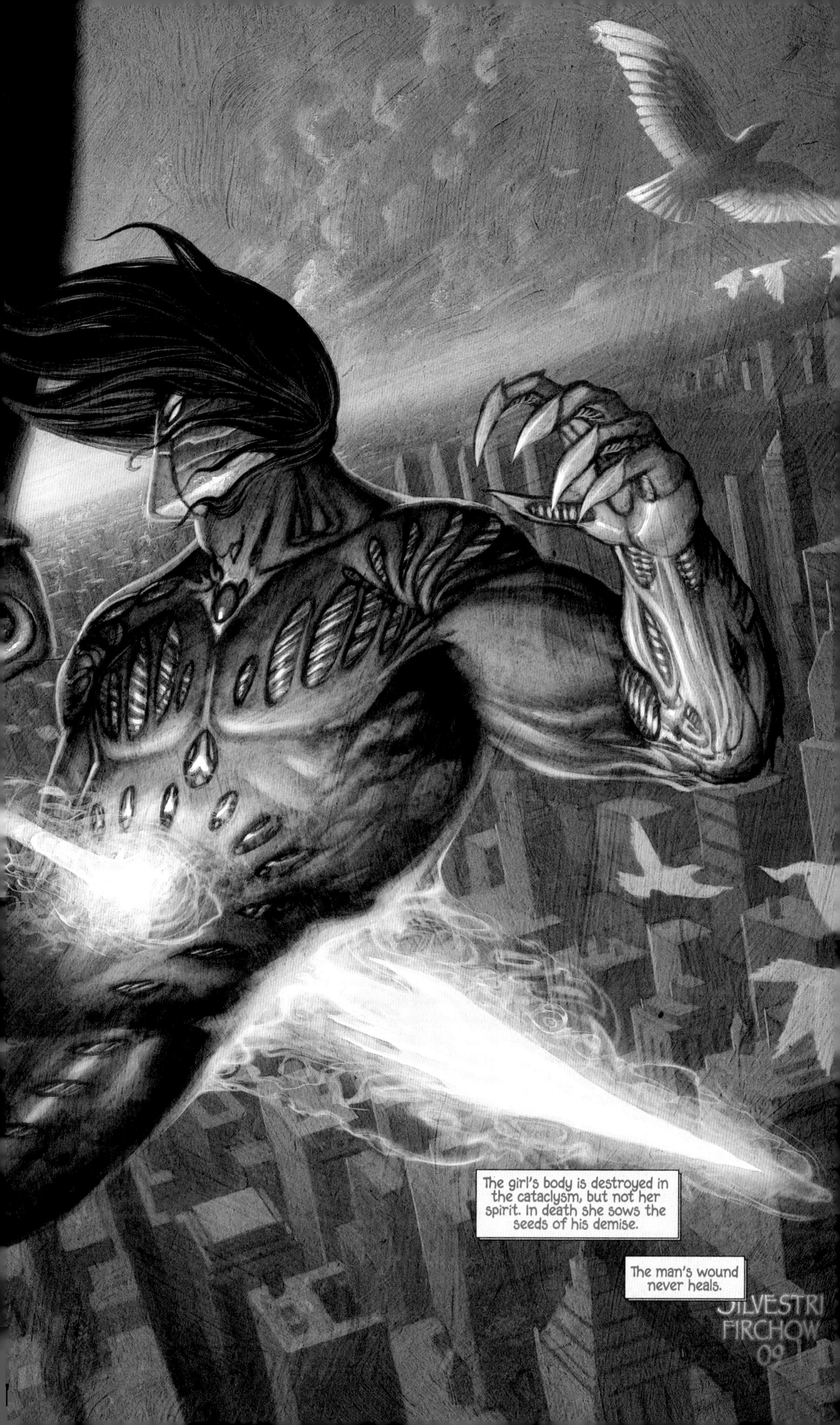
The girl's body is destroyed in the cataclysm, but not her spirit. In death she sows the seeds of his demise.
The man's wound never heals.
SILVESTRI
FIRCHOW
09

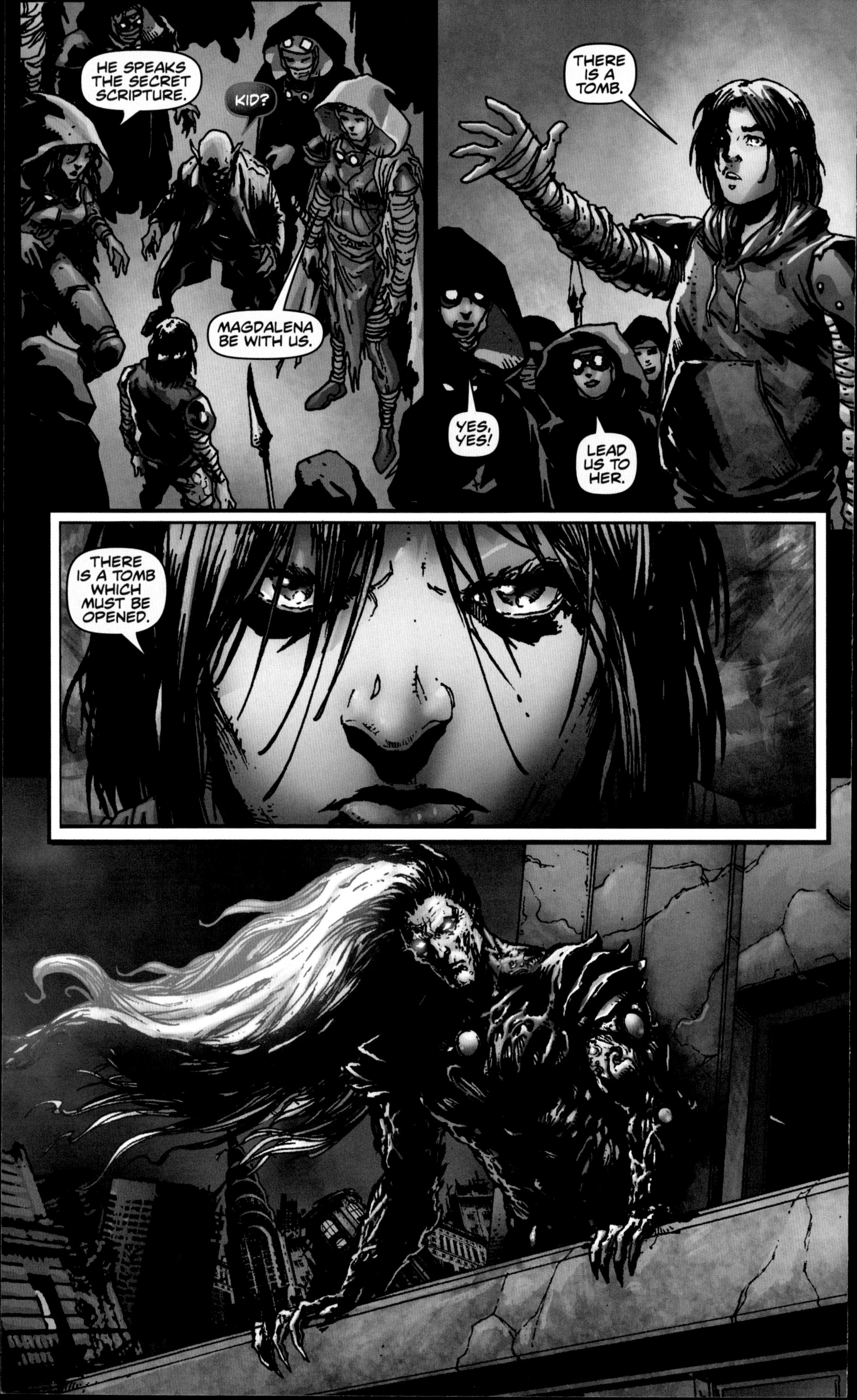
HE SPEAKS THE SECRET SCRIPTURE.
KID?
MAGDALENA BE WITH US.
THERE IS A TOMB.
YES, YES!
LEAD US TO HER.
THERE IS A TOMB WHICH MUST BE OPENED.

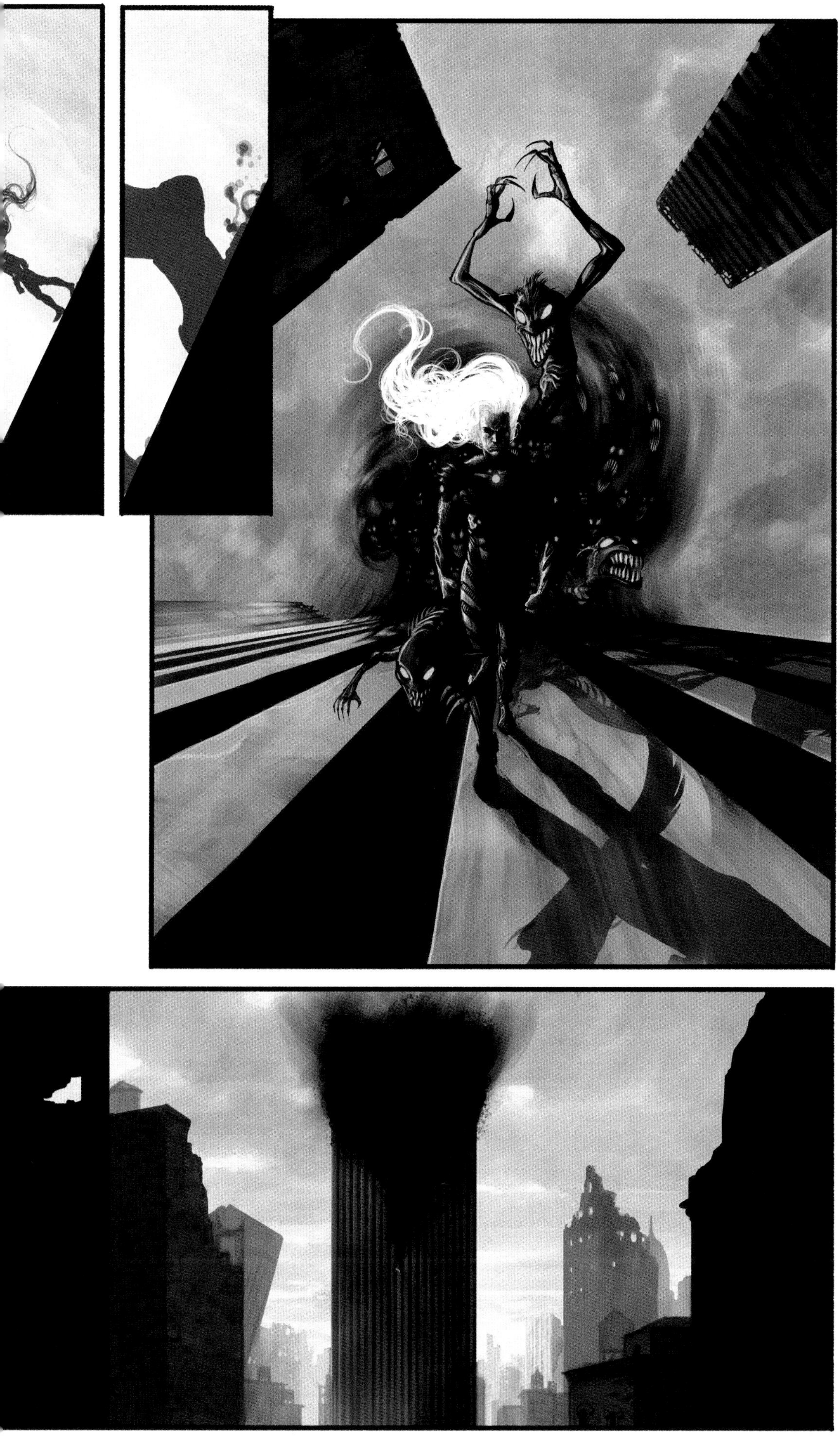

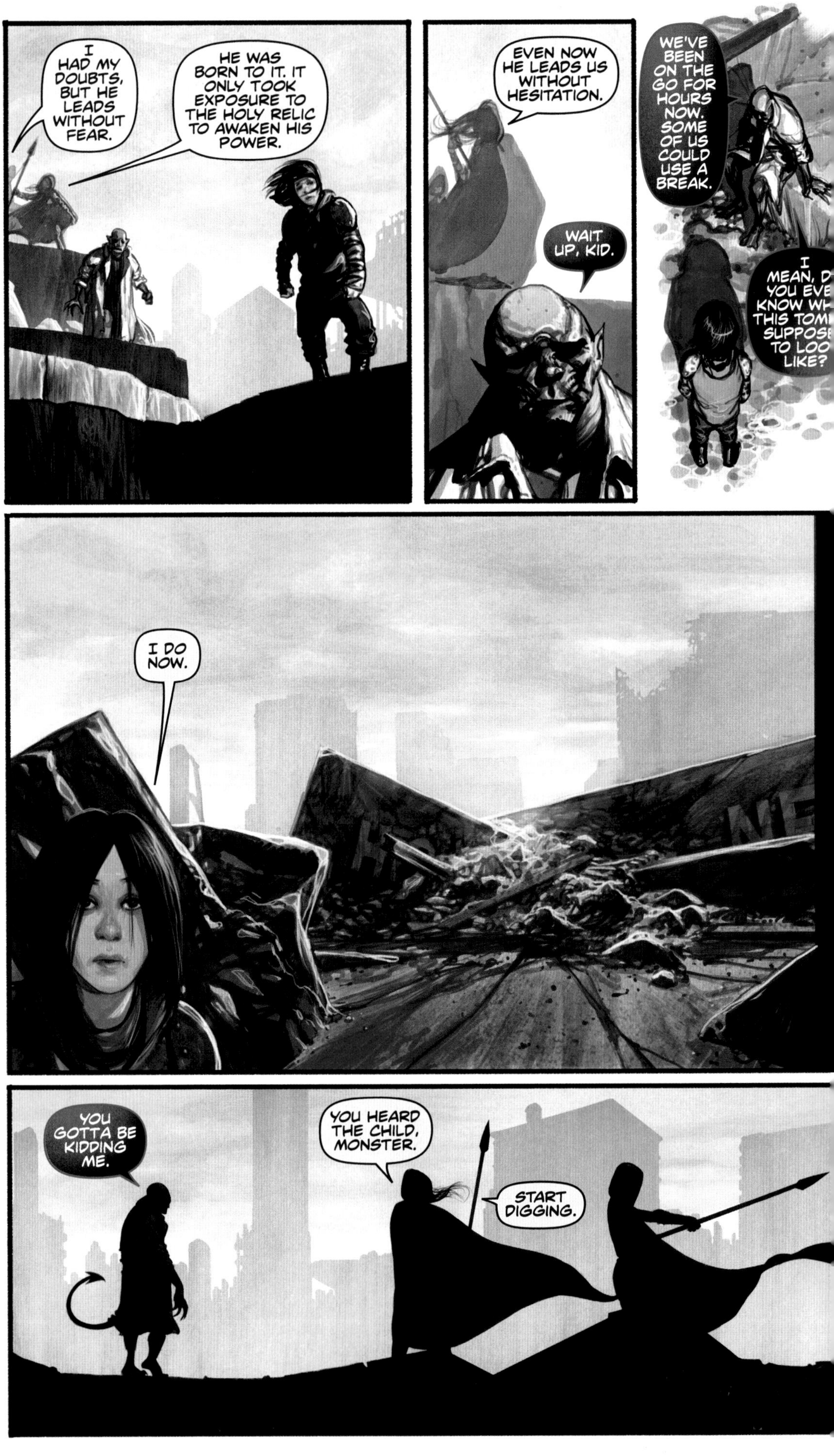
I HAD MY DOUBTS, BUT HE LEADS WITHOUT FEAR.
HE WAS BORN TO IT. IT ONLY TOOK EXPOSURE TO THE HOLY RELIC TO AWAKEN HIS POWER.
EVEN NOW HE LEADS US WITHOUT HESITATION.
WAIT UP, KID.
WE'VE BEEN ON THE GO FOR HOURS NOW. SOME OF US COULD USE A BREAK.
I MEAN, D
YOU EVE
KNOW WH
THIS TOM
SUPPOSE
TO LOO
LIKE?
I DO NOW.
YOU GOTTA BE KIDDING ME.
YOU HEARD THE CHILD, MONSTER.
START DIGGING.

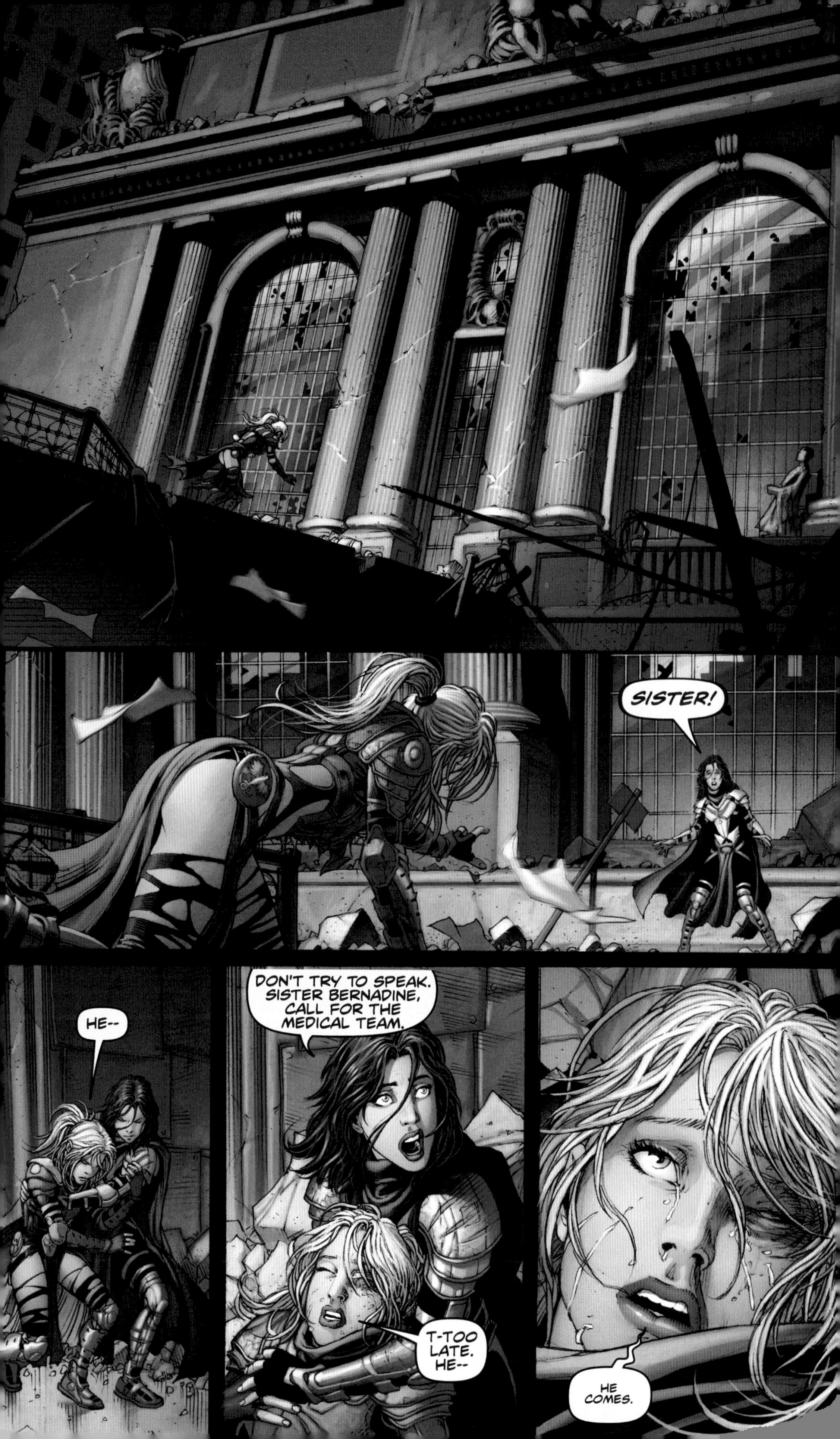
SISTER!
HE--
DON'T TRY TO SPEAK. SISTER BERNADINE, CALL FOR THE MEDICAL TEAM.
T-TOO LATE. HE--
HE COMES.

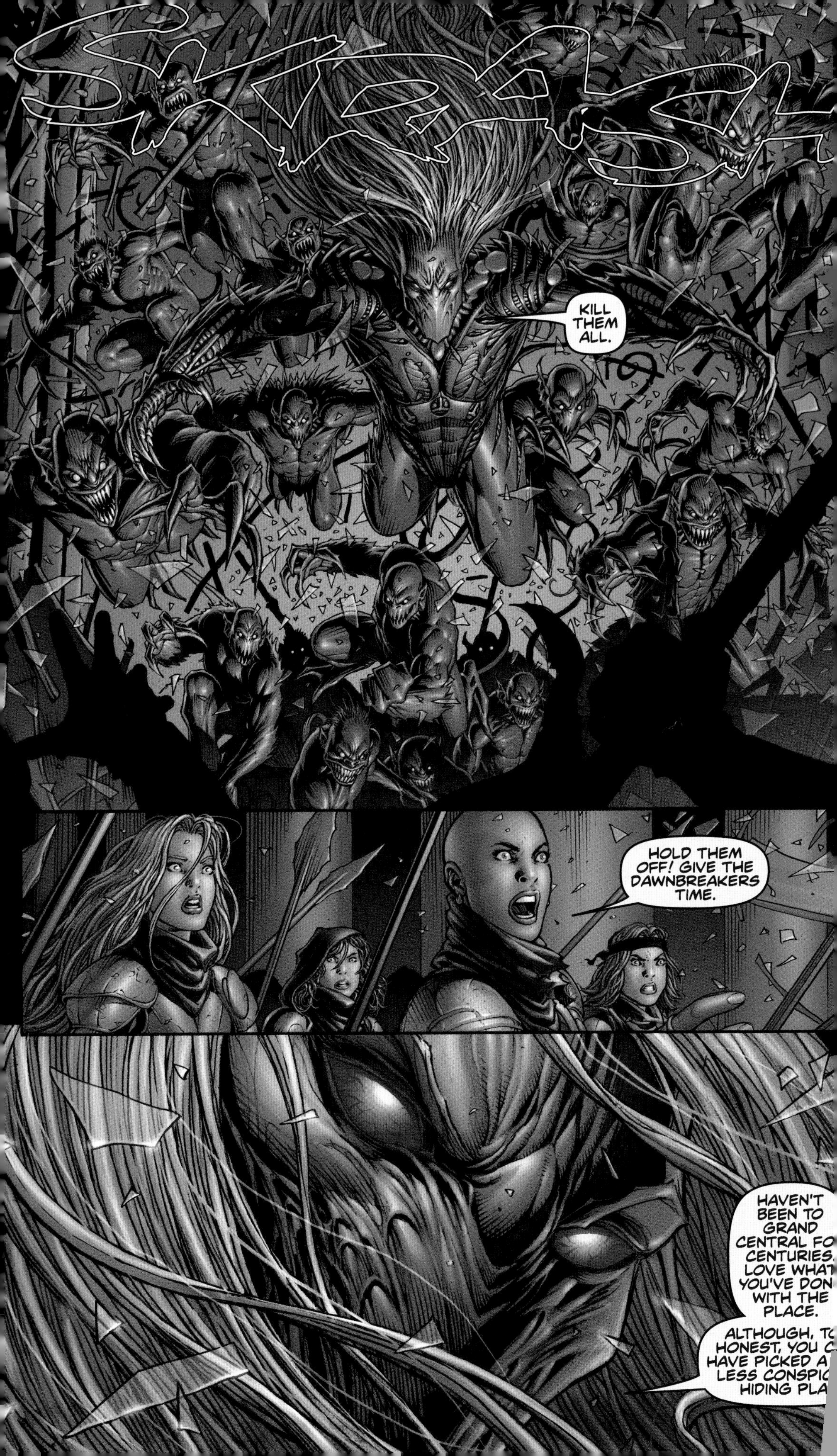
KILL THEM ALL.
HOLD THEM OFF! GIVE THE DAWNBREAKERS TIME.
HAVEN'T BEEN TO GRAND CENTRAL FO CENTURIES. LOVE WHAT YOU'VE DON WITH THE PLACE.
ALTHOUGH, T HONEST, YOU C HAVE PICKED A LESS CONSPIC HIDING PLA

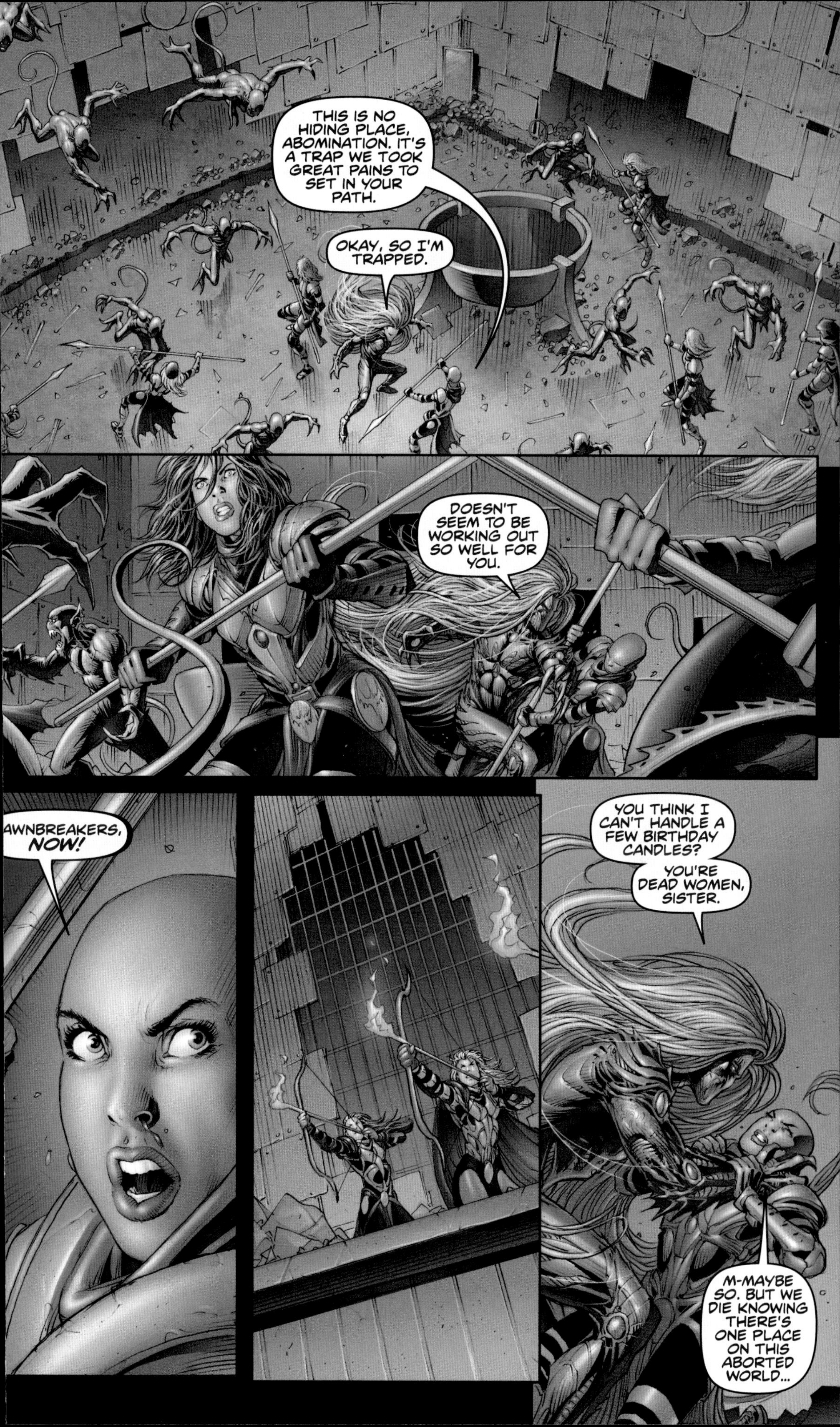
THIS IS NO HIDING PLACE, ABOMINATION. IT'S A TRAP WE TOOK GREAT PAINS TO SET IN YOUR PATH.
OKAY, SO I'M TRAPPED.
DOESN'T SEEM TO BE WORKING OUT SO WELL FOR YOU.
AWNBREAKERS, NOW!
YOU THINK I CAN'T HANDLE A FEW BIRTHDAY CANDLES?
YOU'RE DEAD WOMEN, SISTER.
M-MAYBE SO. BUT WE DIE KNOWING THERE'S ONE PLACE ON THIS ABORTED WORLD...

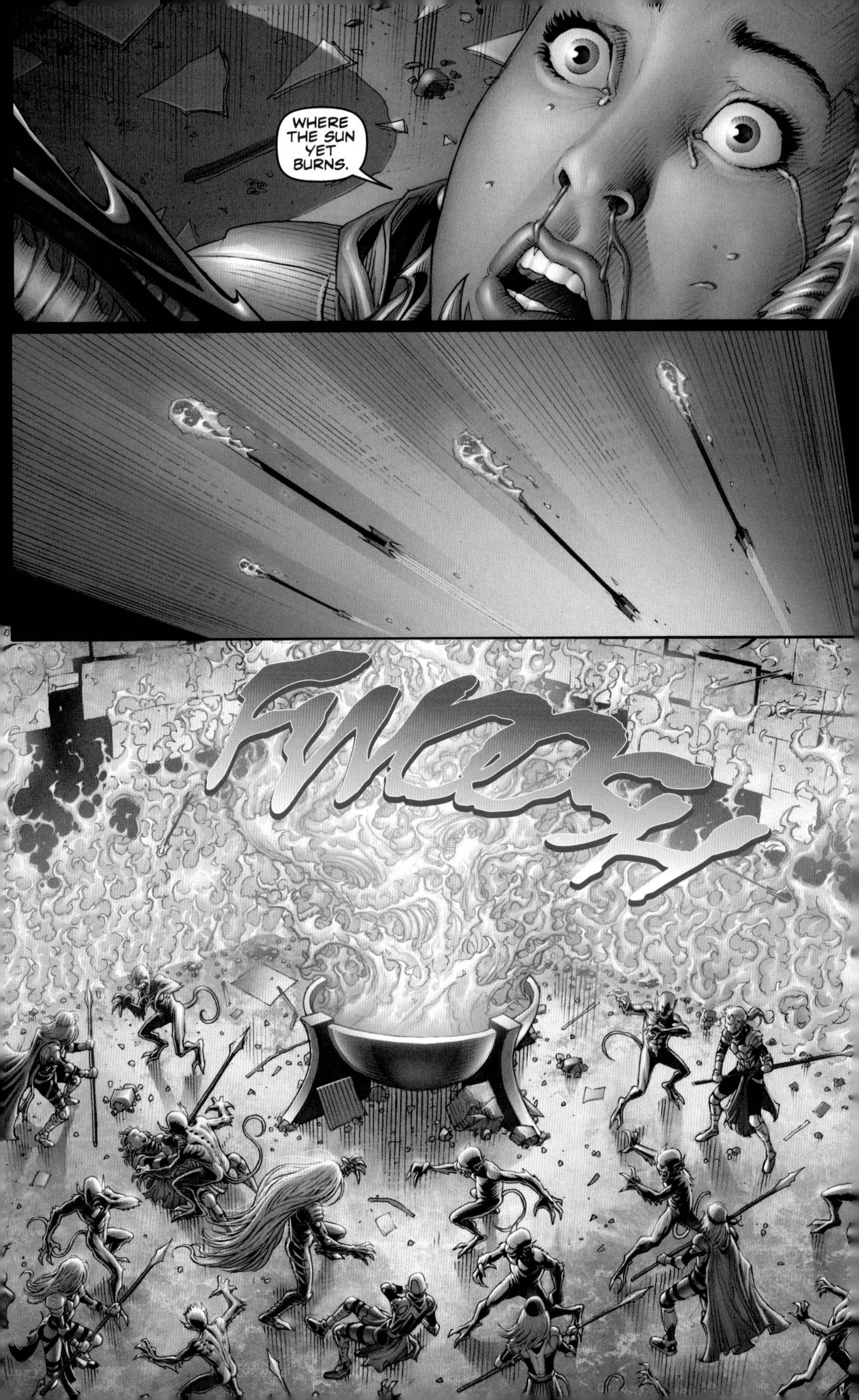
WHERE THE SUN YET BURNS.

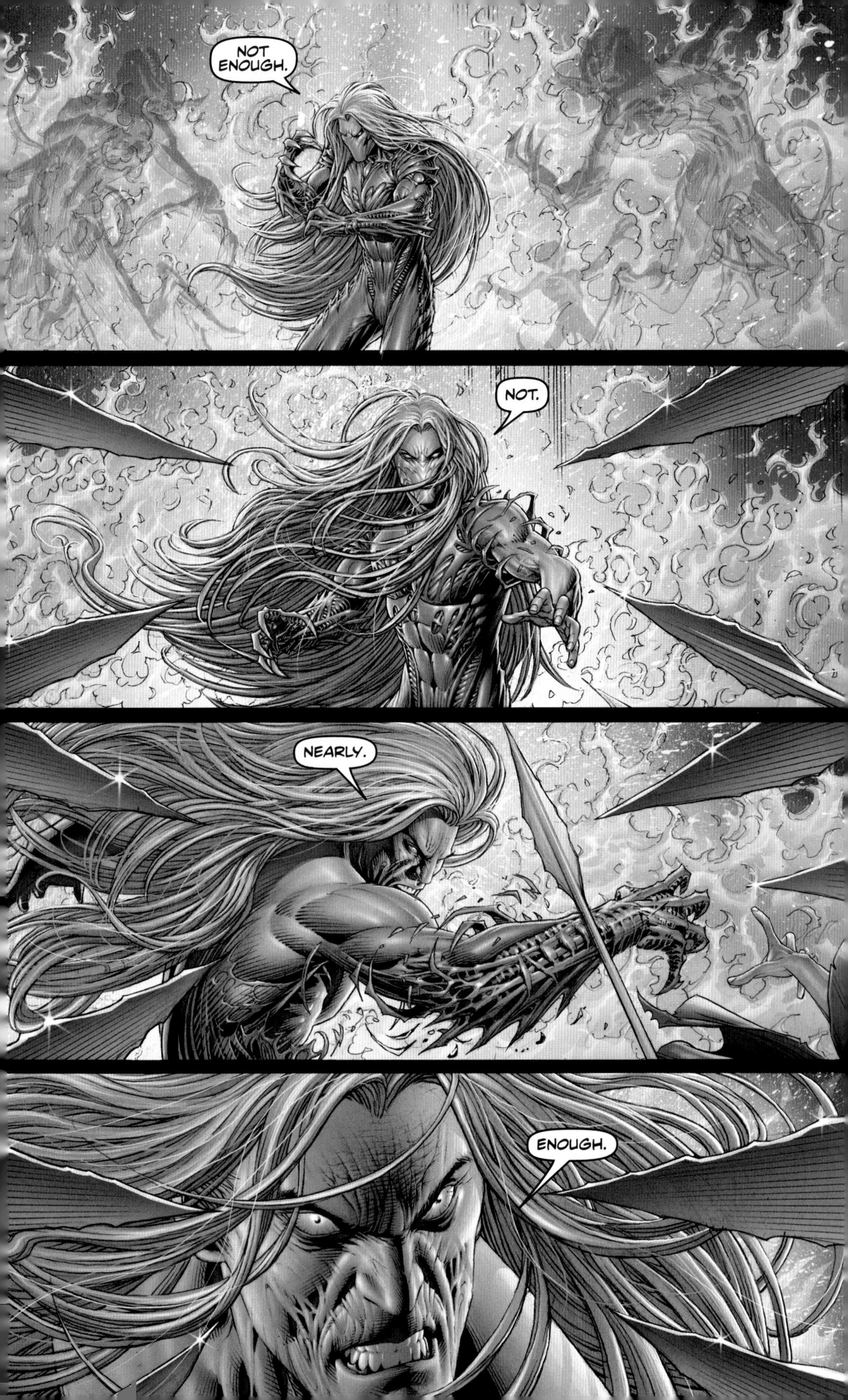
NOT ENOUGH.
NOT.
NEARLY.
ENOUGH.

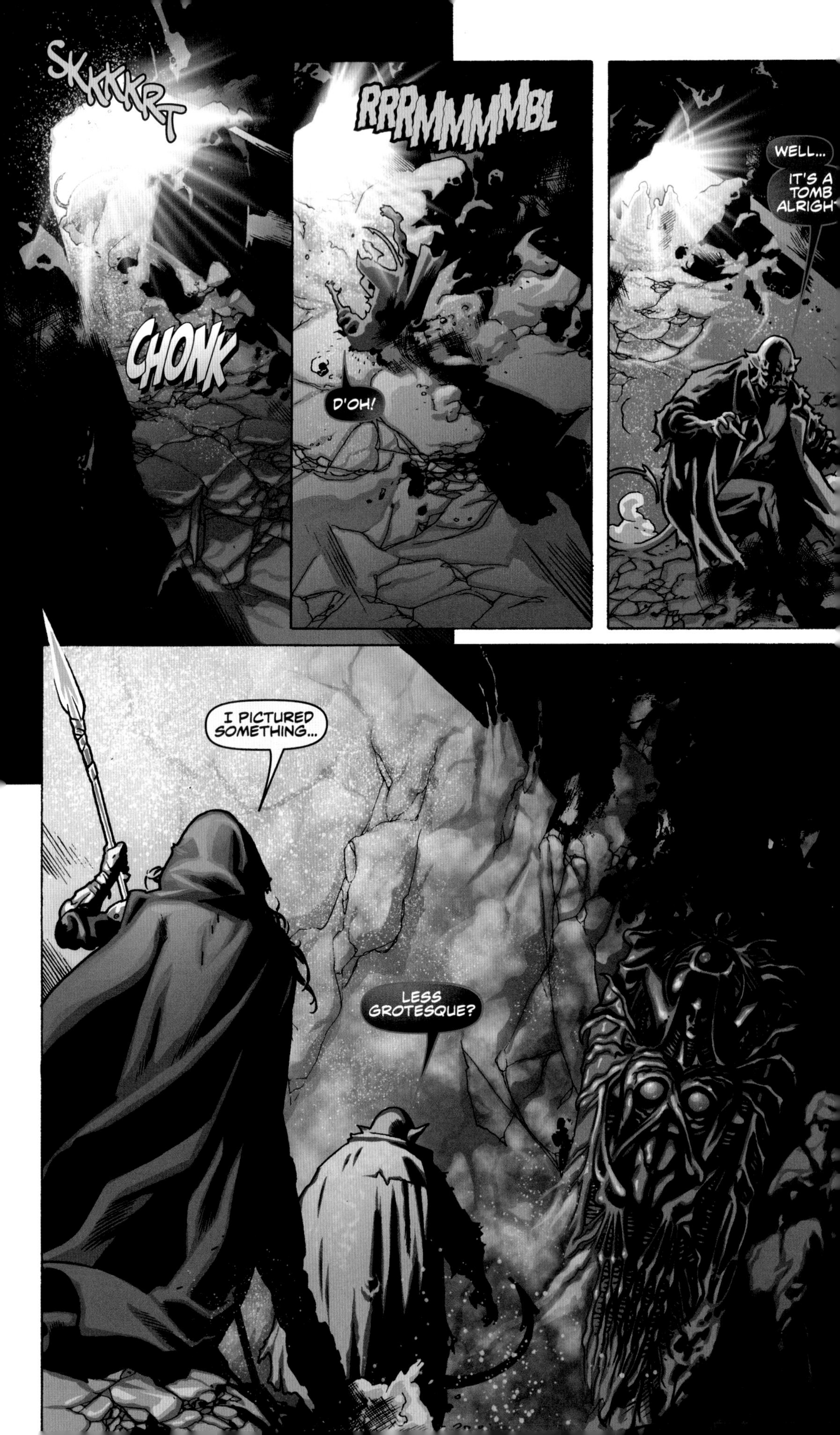
SKKKKRT
CHONK
RRRMMMMBL
D'OH!
WELL...
IT'S A TOMB ALRIGH
I PICTURED SOMETHING...
LESS GROTESQUE?

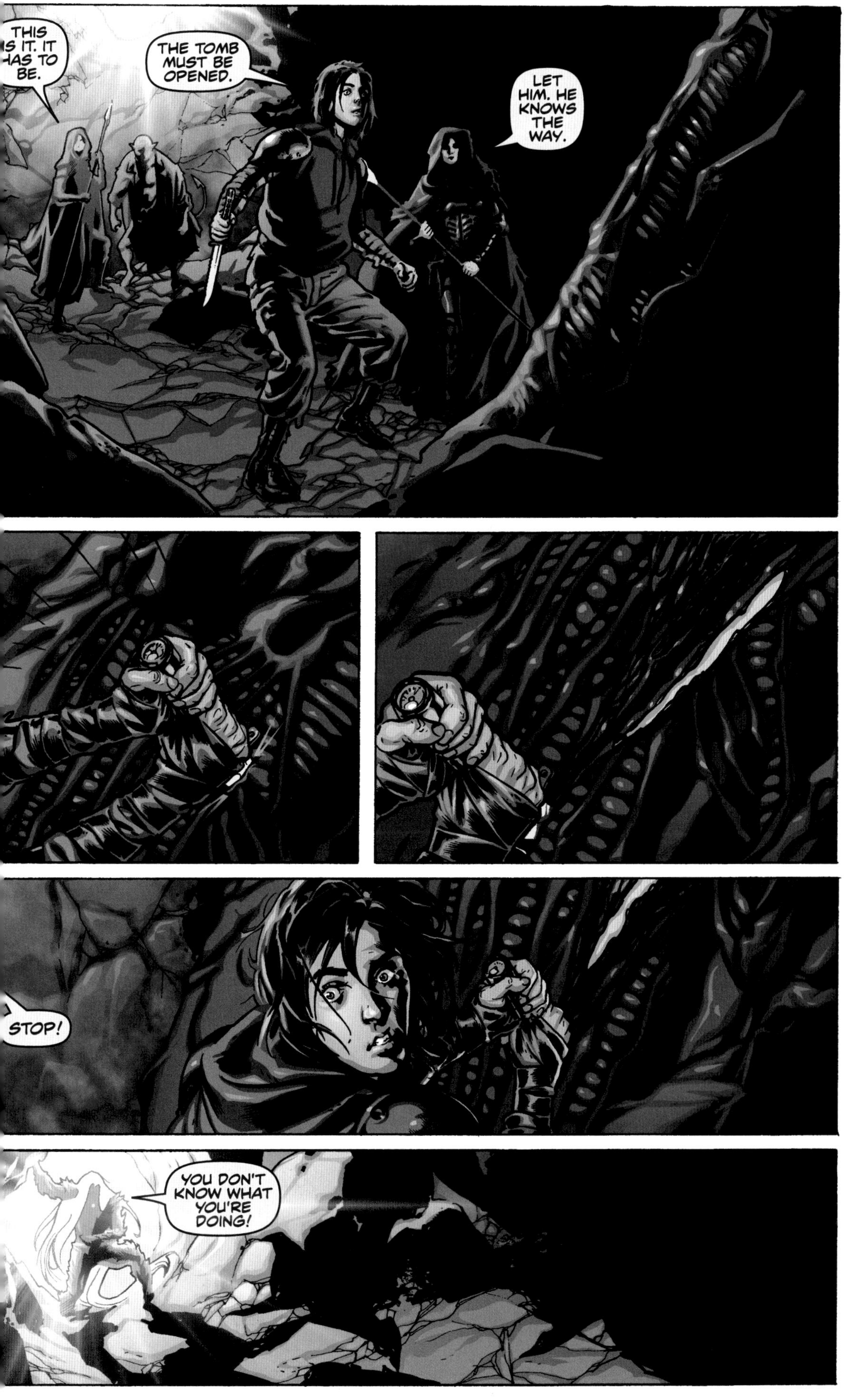
THIS IS IT. IT HAS TO BE.
THE TOMB MUST BE OPENED.
LET HIM. HE KNOWS THE WAY.
STOP!
YOU DON'T KNOW WHAT YOU'RE DOING!

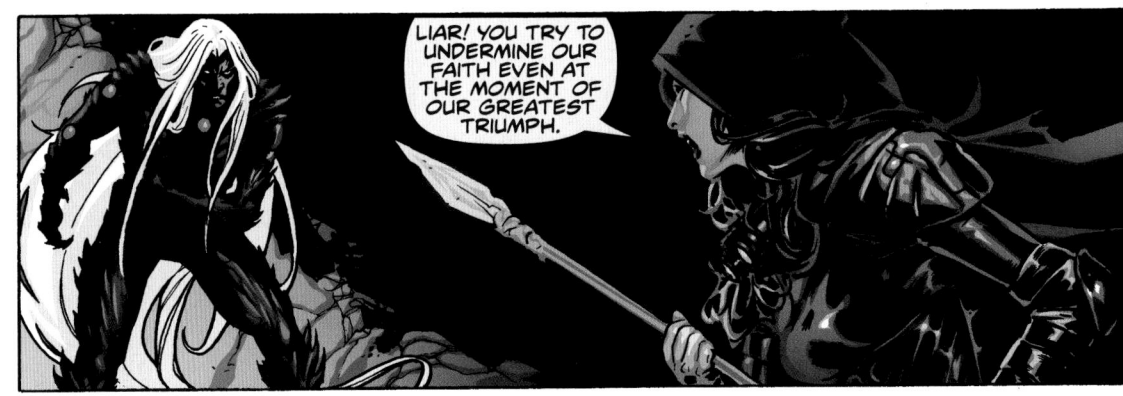

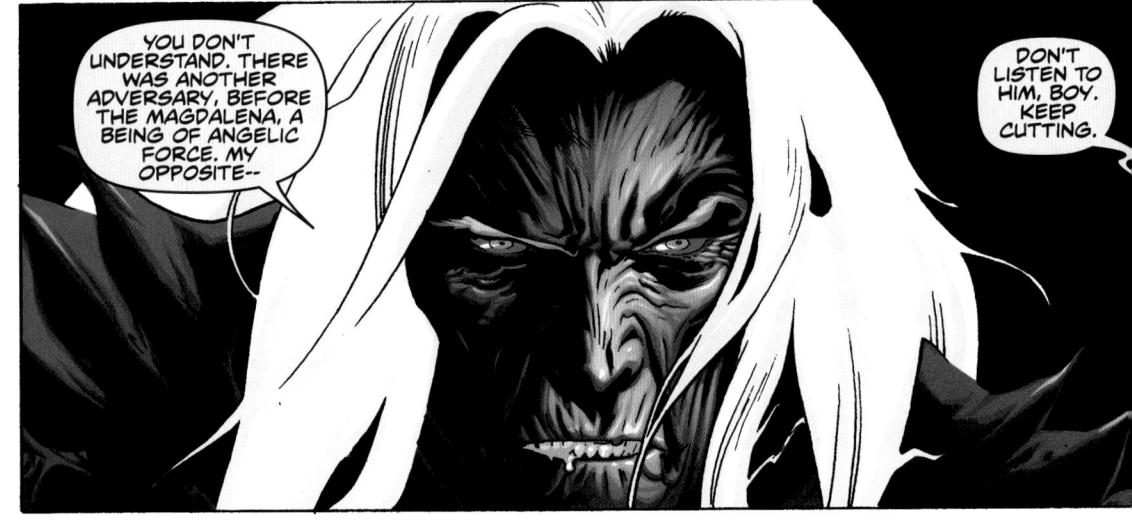

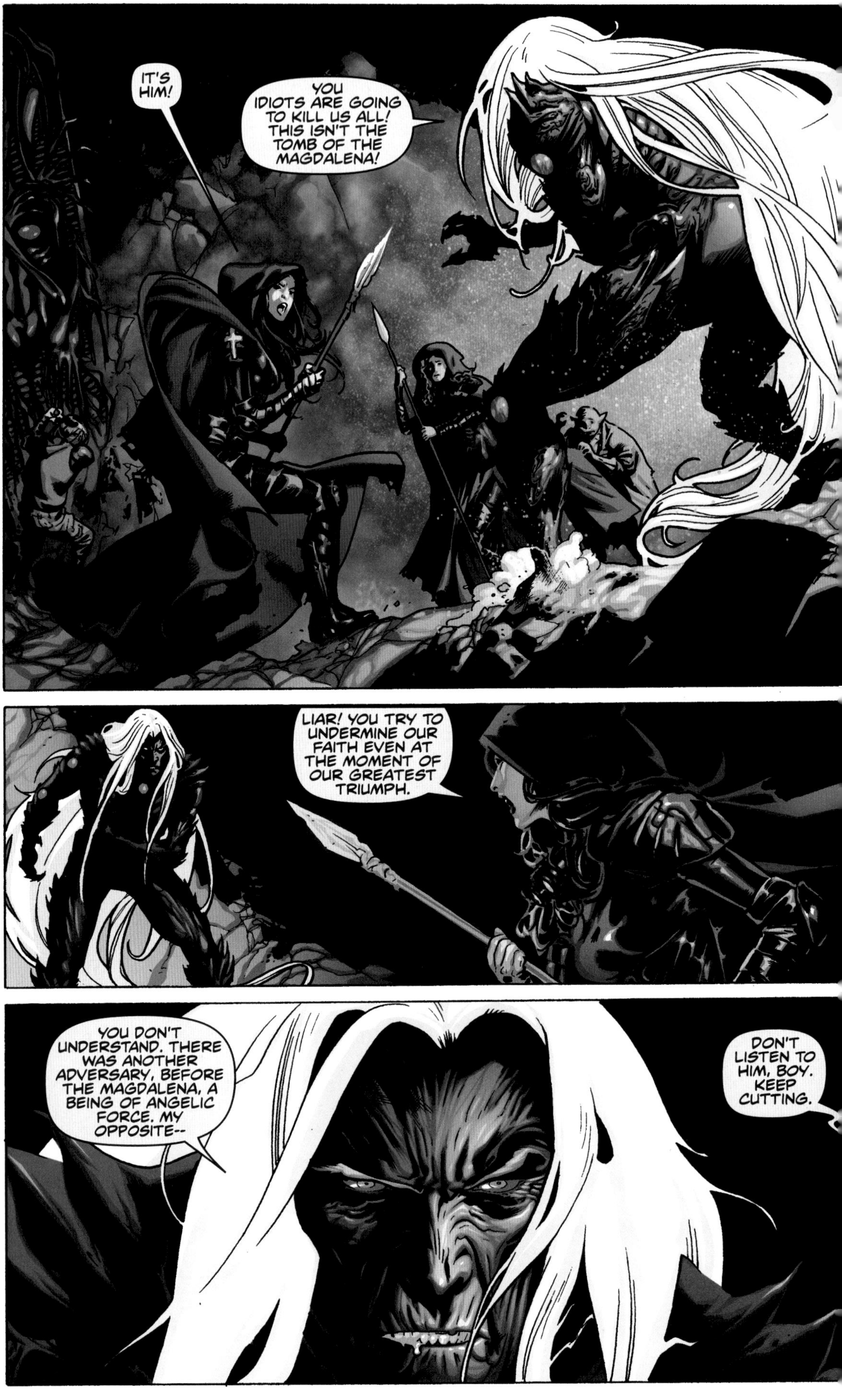
IT'S HIM!
YOU IDIOTS ARE GOING TO KILL US ALL! THIS ISN'T THE TOMB OF THE MAGDALENA!
LIAR! YOU TRY TO UNDERMINE OUR FAITH EVEN AT THE MOMENT OF OUR GREATEST TRIUMPH.
YOU DON'T UNDERSTAND. THERE WAS ANOTHER ADVERSARY, BEFORE THE MAGDALENA, A BEING OF ANGELIC FORCE. MY OPPOSITE--
DON'T LISTEN TO HIM, BOY. KEEP CUTTING.

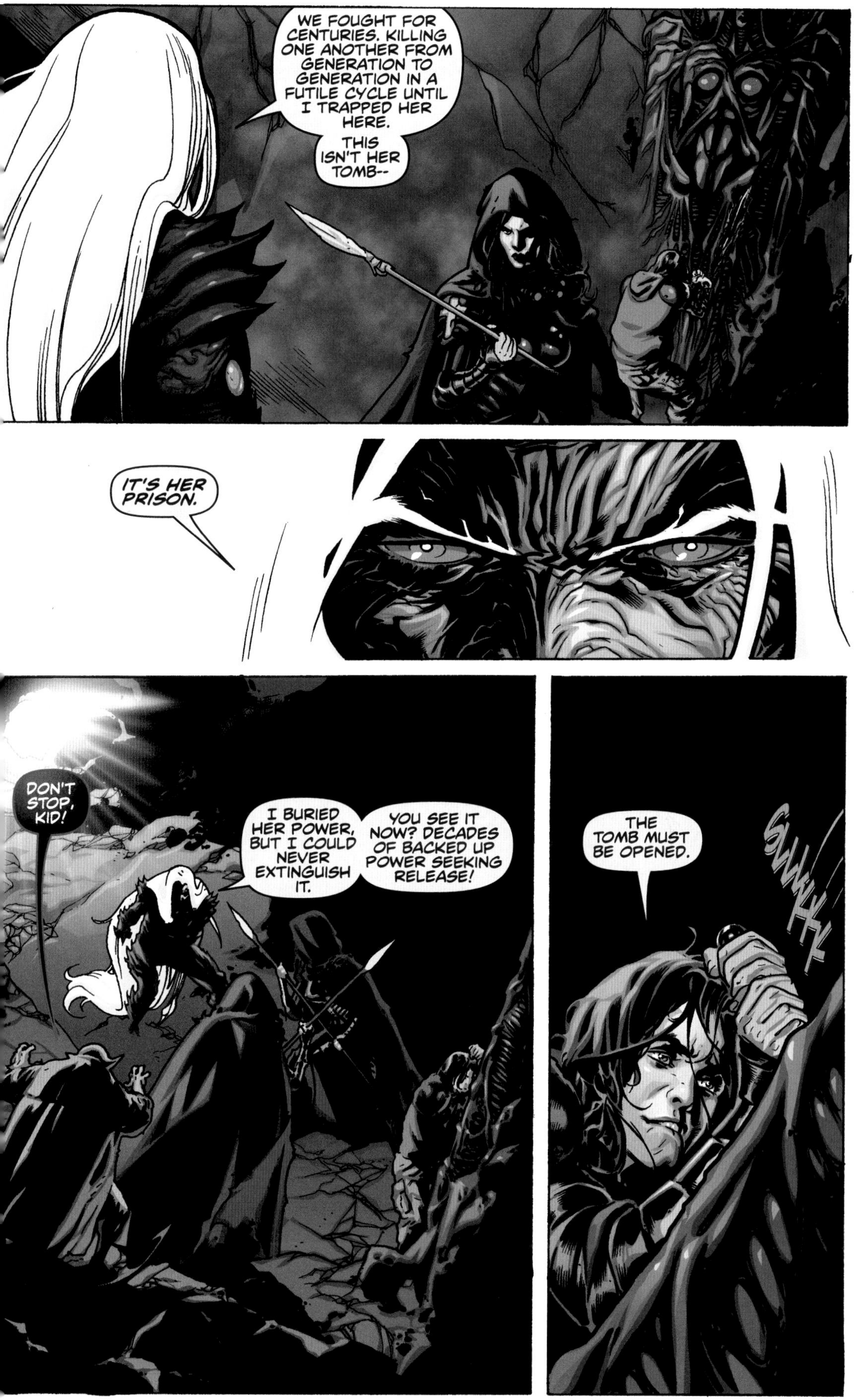
WE FOUGHT FOR CENTURIES. KILLING ONE ANOTHER FROM GENERATION TO GENERATION IN A FUTILE CYCLE UNTIL I TRAPPED HER HERE.
THIS ISN'T HER TOMB--
IT'S HER PRISON.
DON'T STOP, KID!
I BURIED HER POWER, BUT I COULD NEVER EXTINGUISH IT.
YOU SEE IT NOW? DECADES OF BACKED UP POWER SEEKING RELEASE!
THE TOMB MUST BE OPENED.
SHUNKK

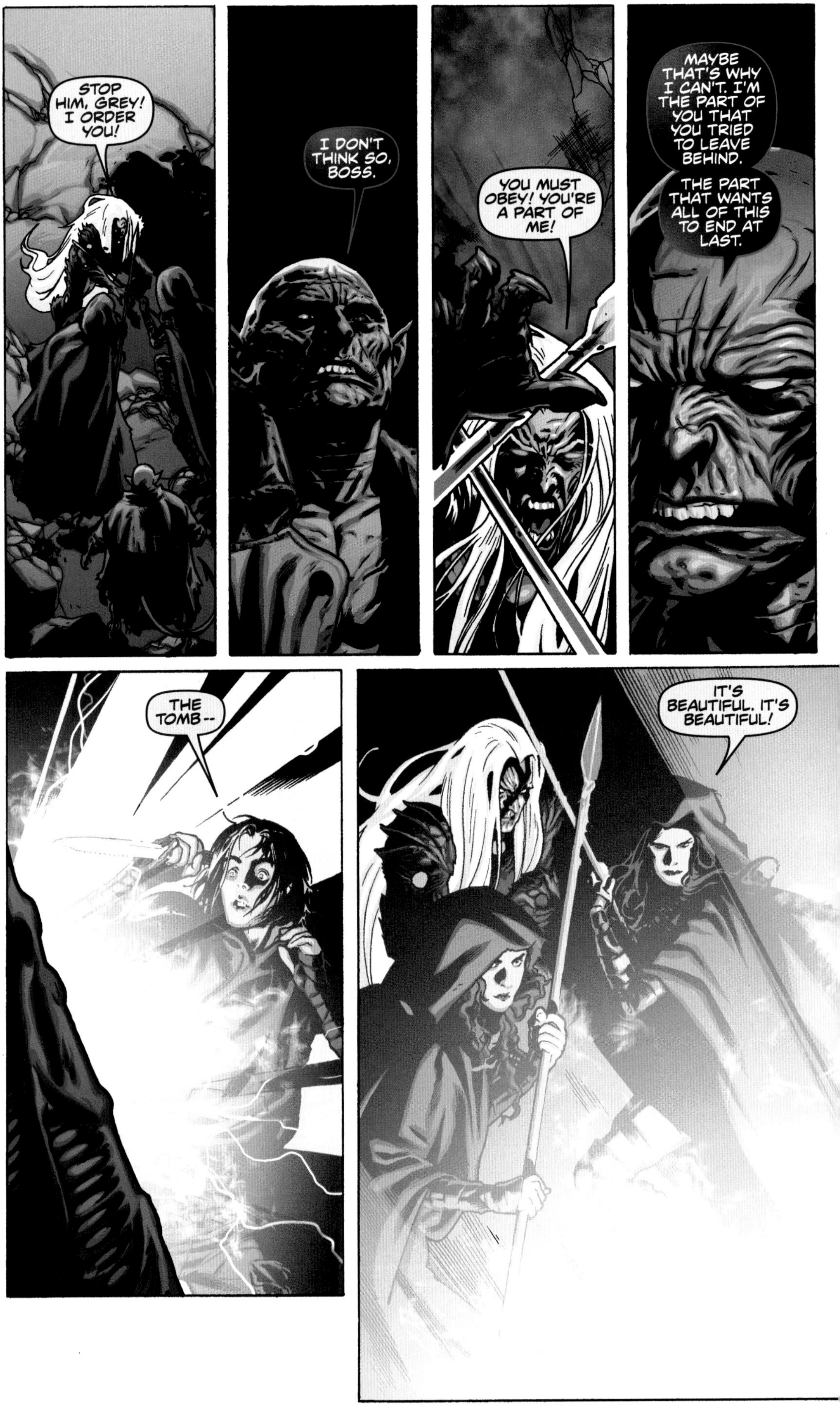
STOP HIM, GREY! I ORDER YOU!
I DON'T THINK SO, BOSS.
YOU MUST OBEY! YOU'RE A PART OF ME!
MAYBE THAT'S WHY I CAN'T. I'M THE PART OF YOU THAT YOU TRIED TO LEAVE BEHIND.
THE PART THAT WANTS ALL OF THIS TO END AT LAST.
THE TOMB --
IT'S BEAUTIFUL. IT'S BEAUTIFUL!

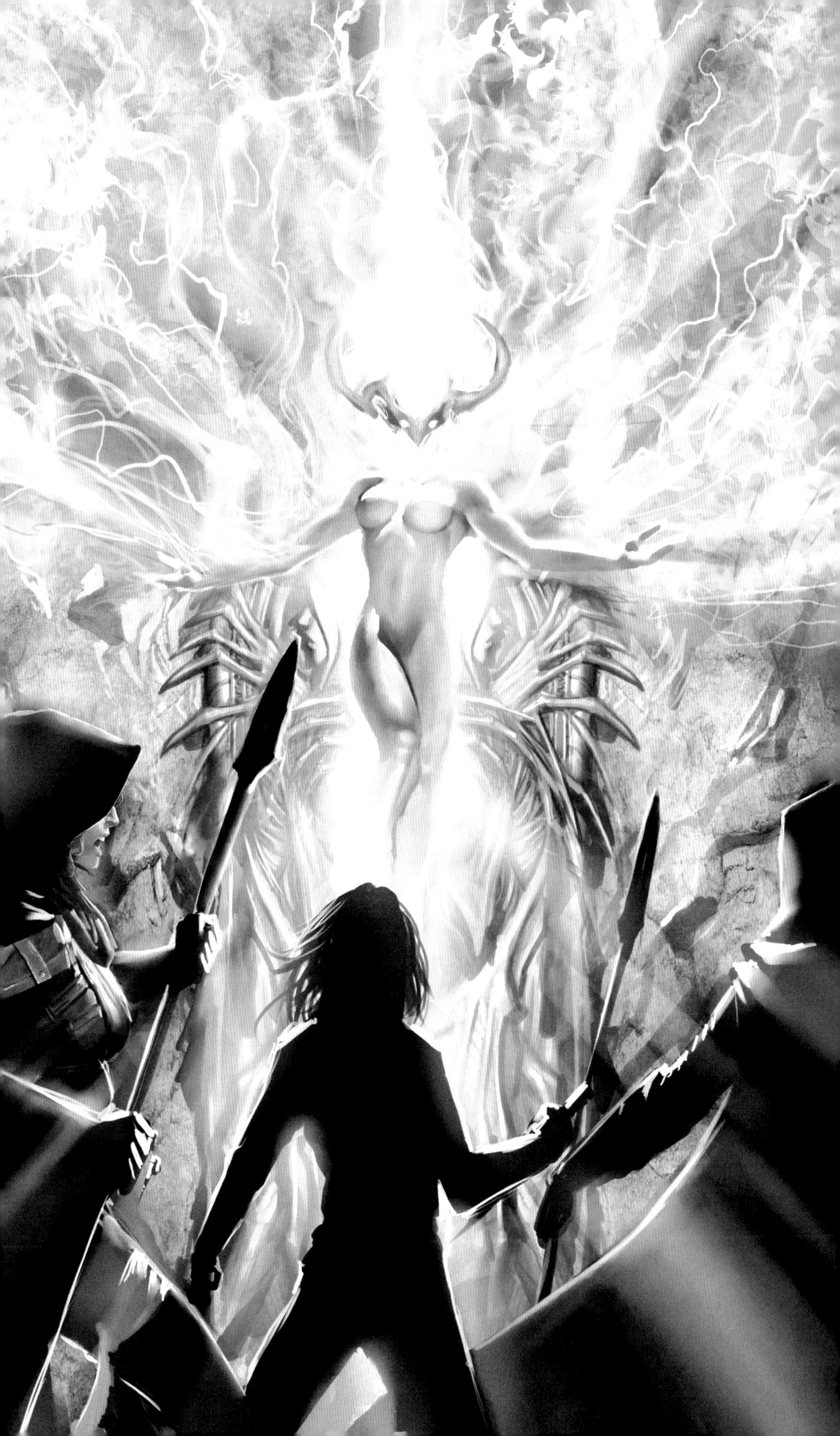

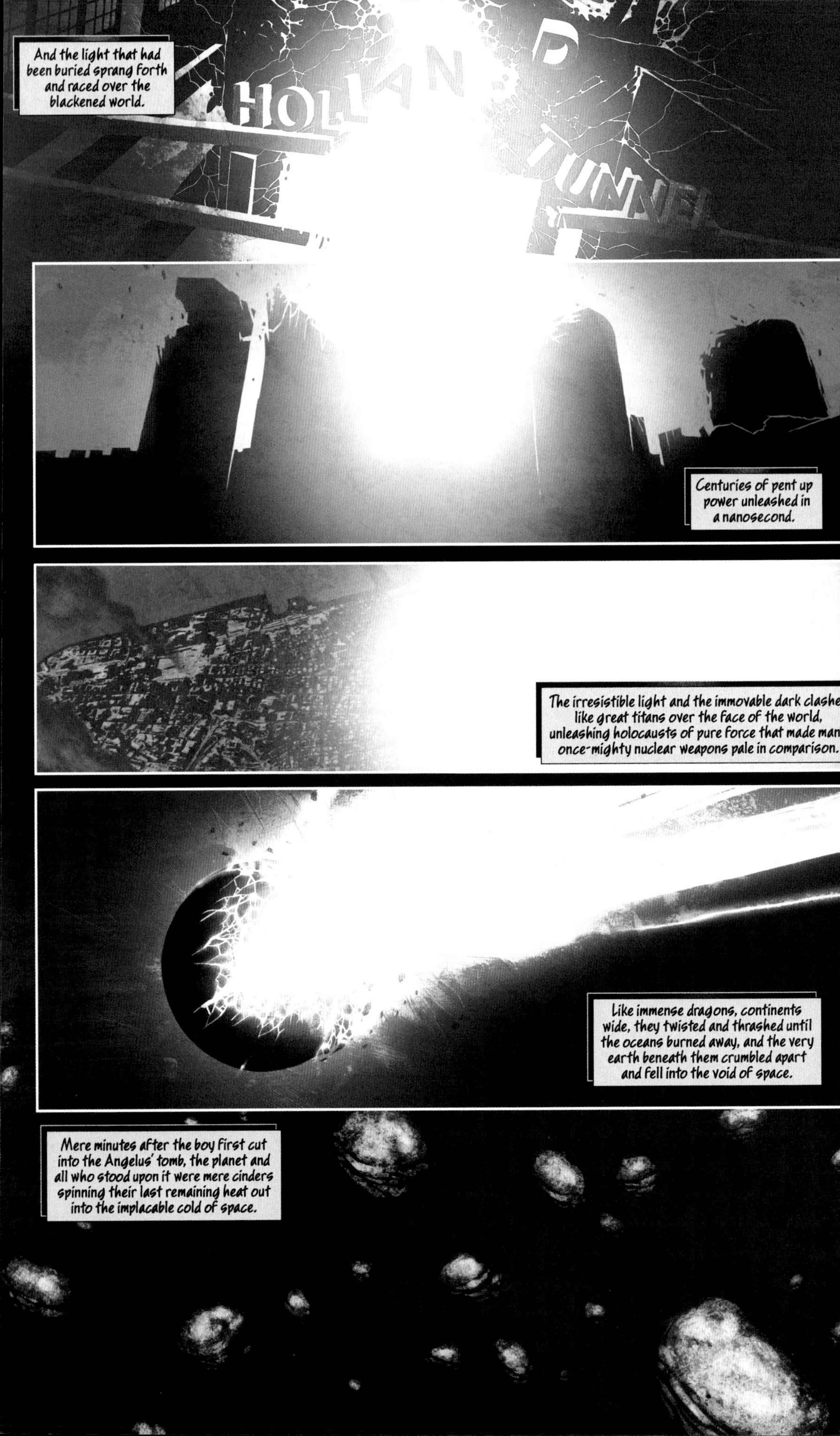
And the light that had been buried sprang forth and raced over the blackened world.
Centuries of pent up power unleashed in a nanosecond.
The irresistible light and the immovable dark clashe like great titans over the face of the world, unleashing holocausts of pure force that made man once-mighty nuclear weapons pale in comparison.
Like immense dragons, continents wide, they twisted and thrashed until the oceans burned away, and the very earth beneath them crumbled apart and fell into the void of space.
Mere minutes after the boy first cut into the Angelus' tomb, the planet and all who stood upon it were mere cinders spinning their last remaining heat out into the implacable cold of space.

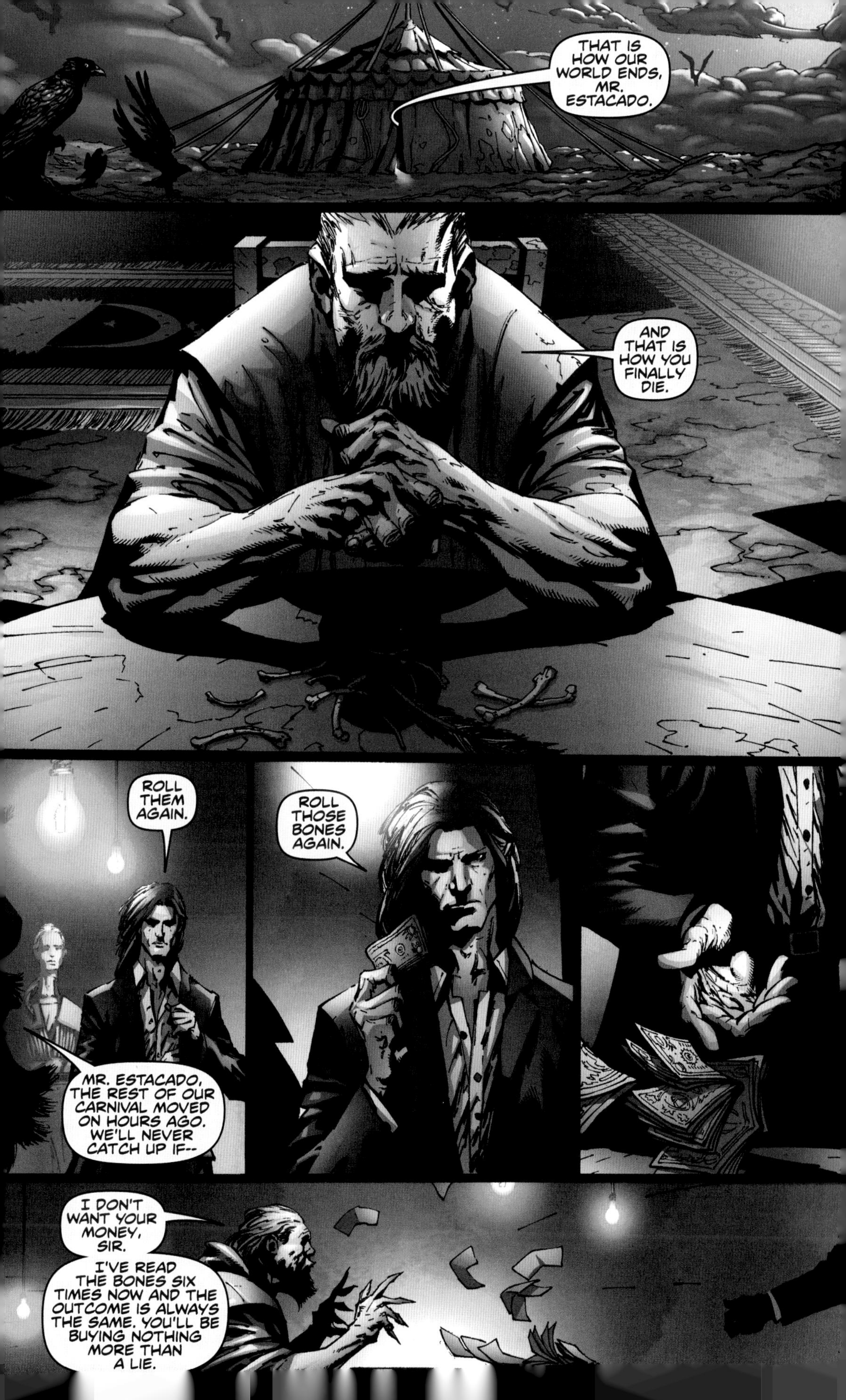
THAT IS HOW OUR WORLD ENDS, MR. ESTACADO.
AND THAT IS HOW YOU FINALLY DIE.
ROLL THEM AGAIN.
MR. ESTACADO, THE REST OF OUR CARNIVAL MOVED ON HOURS AGO. WE'LL NEVER CATCH UP IF--
ROLL THOSE BONES AGAIN.
I DON'T WANT YOUR MONEY, SIR.
I'VE READ THE BONES SIX TIMES NOW AND THE OUTCOME IS ALWAYS THE SAME. YOU'LL BE BUYING NOTHING MORE THAN A LIE.

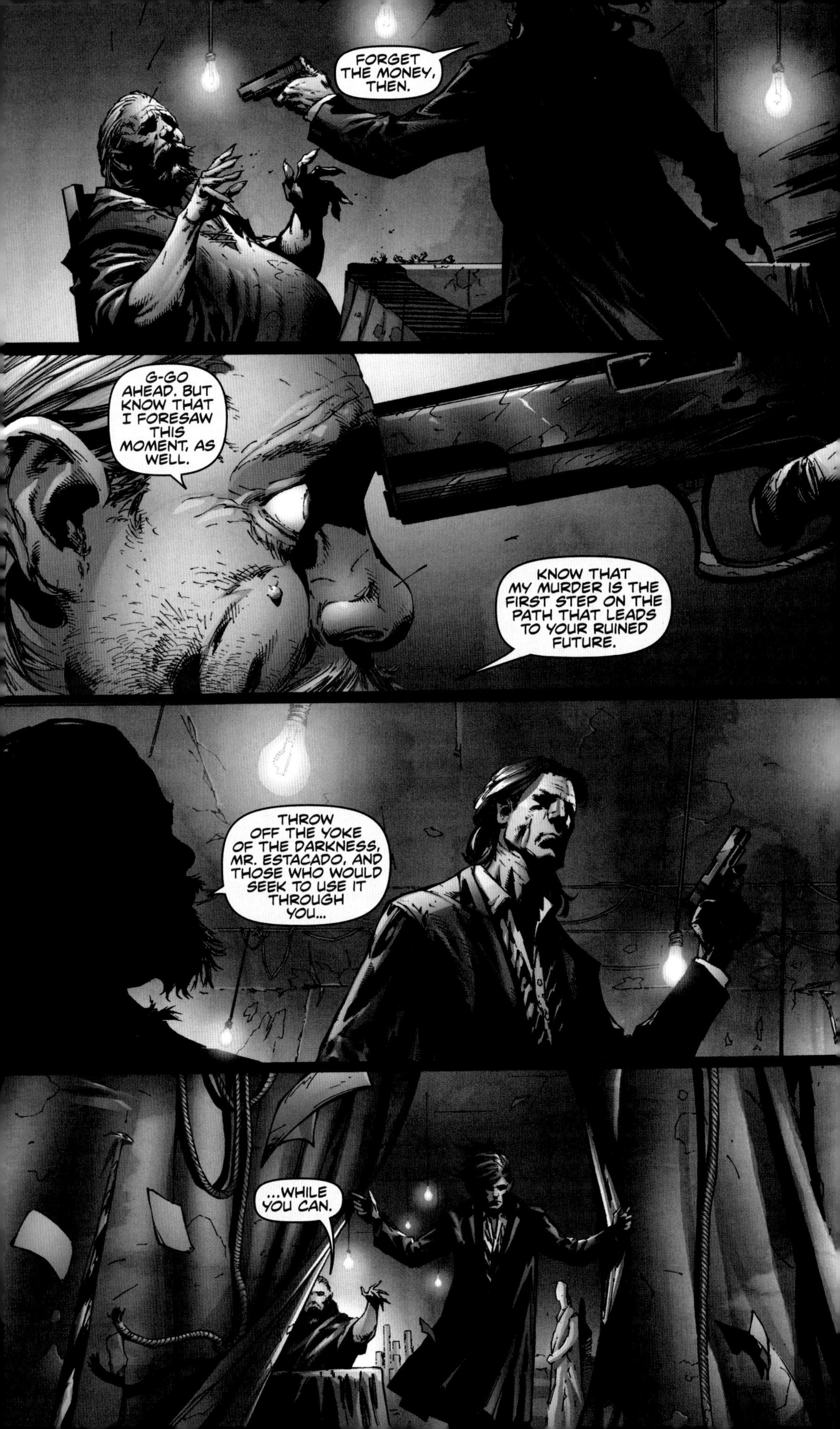
FORGET THE MONEY, THEN.
G-GO AHEAD. BUT KNOW THAT I FORESAW THIS MOMENT, AS WELL.
KNOW THAT MY MURDER IS THE FIRST STEP ON THE PATH THAT LEADS TO YOUR RUINED FUTURE.
THROW OFF THE YOKE OF THE DARKNESS, MR. ESTACADO, AND THOSE WHO WOULD SEEK TO USE IT THROUGH YOU...
...WHILE YOU CAN.

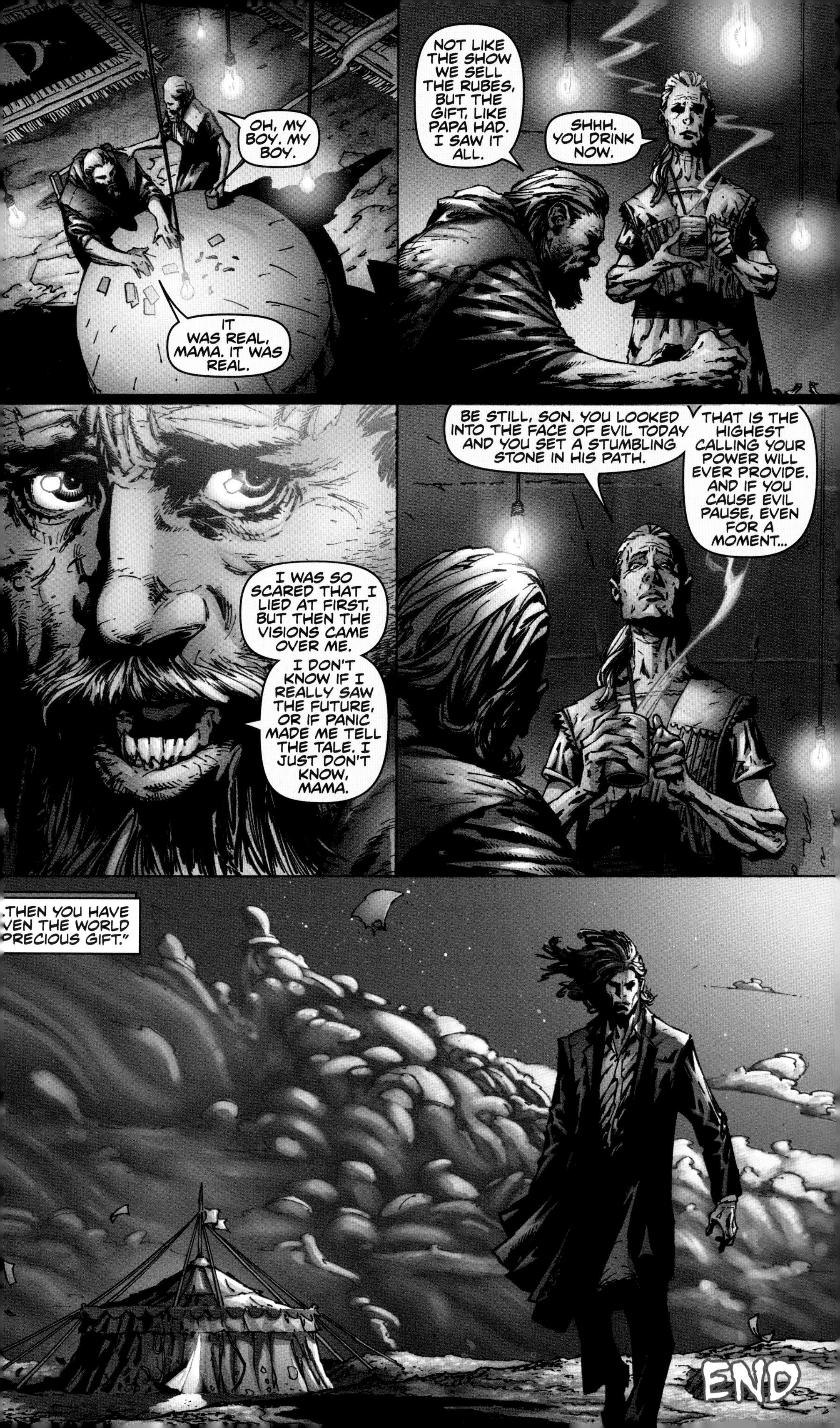
OH, MY BOY. MY BOY.
IT WAS REAL, MAMA. IT WAS REAL.
NOT LIKE THE SHOW WE SELL THE RUBES, BUT THE GIFT, LIKE PAPA HAD. I SAW IT ALL.
SHHH. YOU DRINK NOW.
I WAS SO SCARED THAT I LIED AT FIRST, BUT THEN THE VISIONS CAME OVER ME.
I DON'T KNOW IF I REALLY SAW THE FUTURE, OR IF PANIC MADE ME TELL THE TALE. I JUST DON'T KNOW, MAMA.
BE STILL, SON. YOU LOOKED INTO THE FACE OF EVIL TODAY AND YOU SET A STUMBLING STONE IN HIS PATH.
THAT IS THE HIGHEST CALLING YOUR POWER WILL EVER PROVIDE. AND IF YOU CAUSE EVIL PAUSE, EVEN FOR A MOMENT...
..THEN YOU HAVE GIVEN THE WORLD A PRECIOUS GIFT."
END

THE DARKNESS ACCURSED VOLUME 2

COVER GALLERY

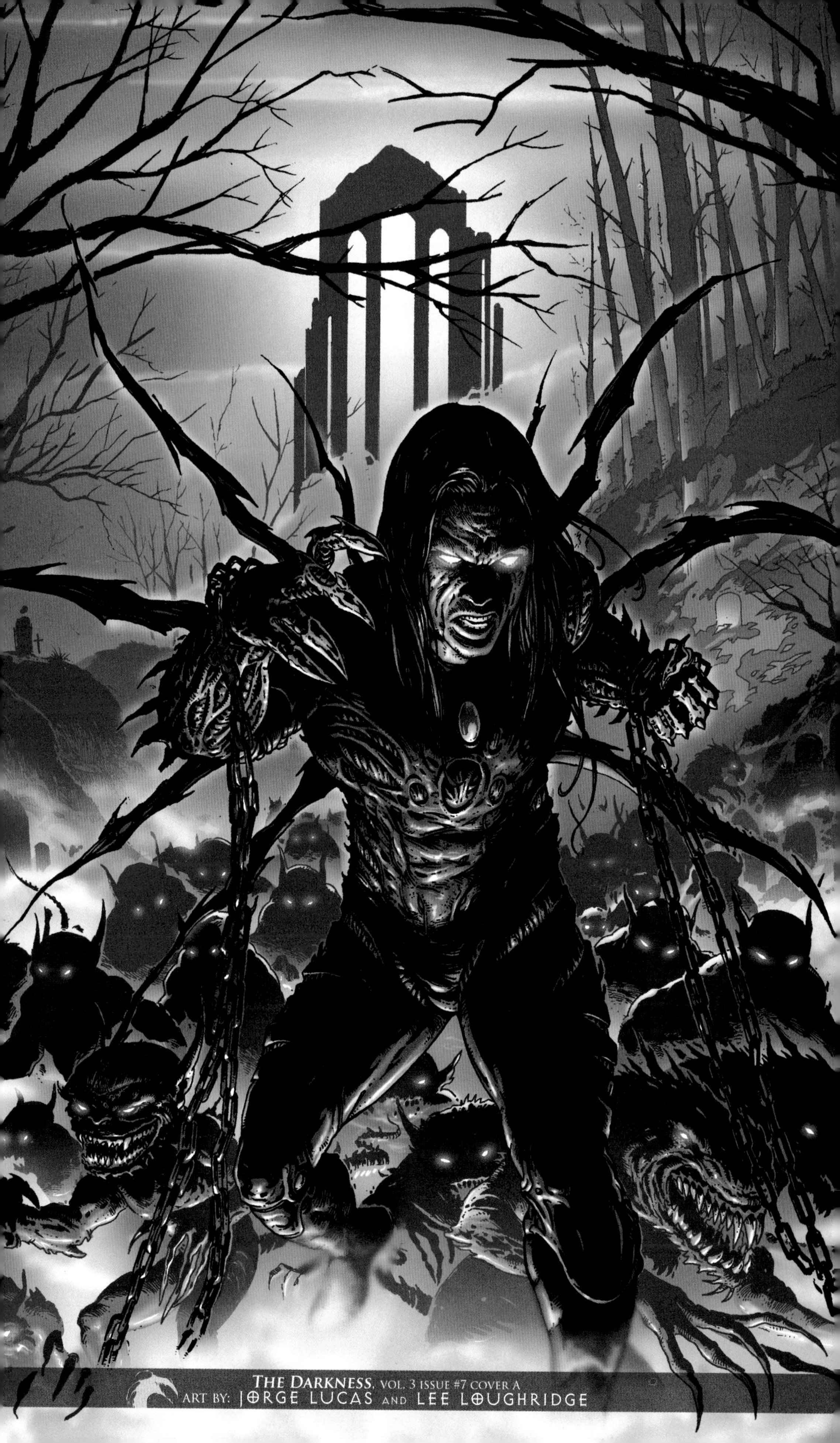

THE DARKNESS, VOL. 3 ISSUE #7 COVER A
ART BY: JORGE LUCAS AND LEE LOUGHRIDGE

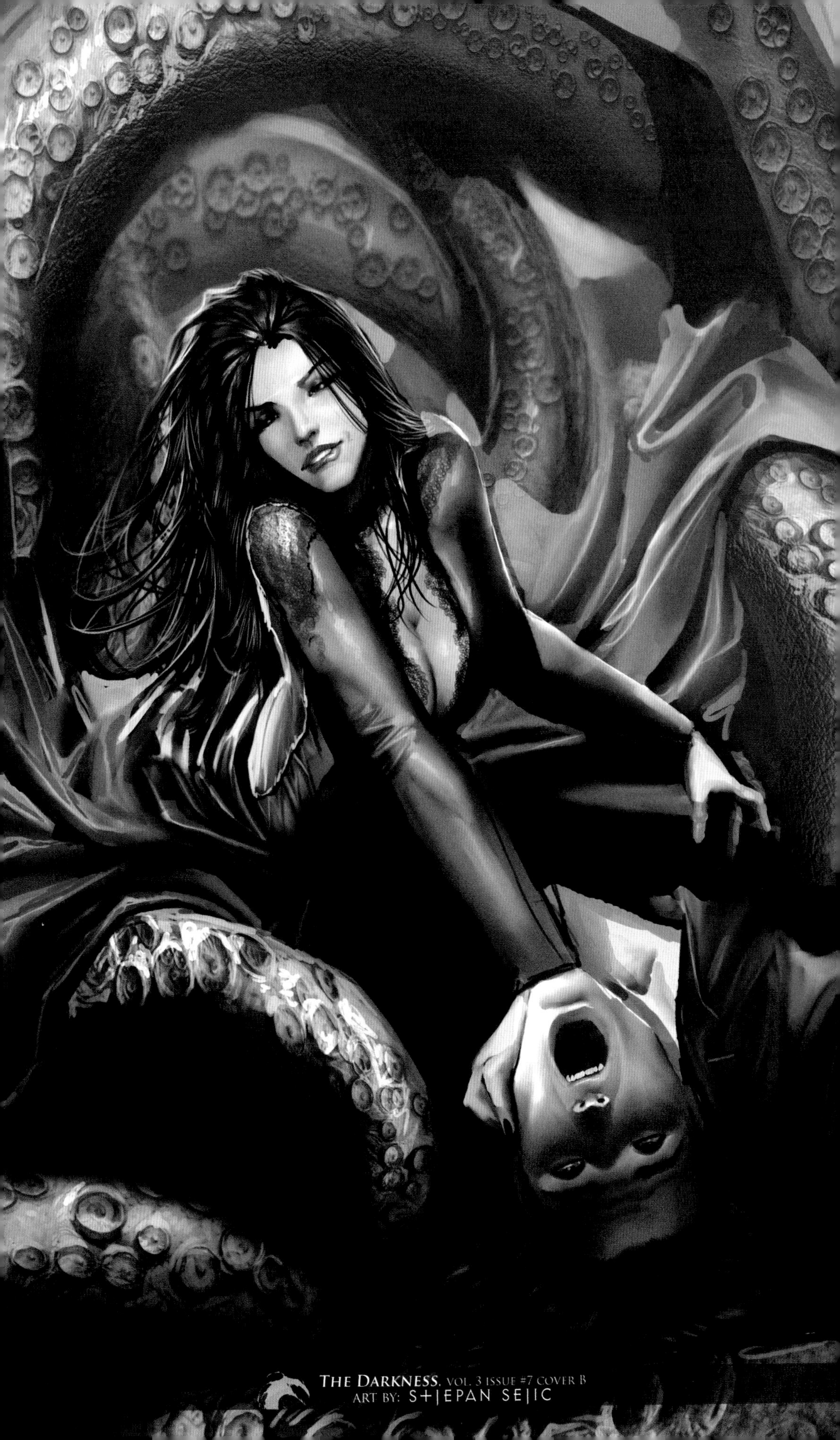

THE DARKNESS, VOL. 3 ISSUE #7 COVER B
ART BY: STJEPAN SEJIC

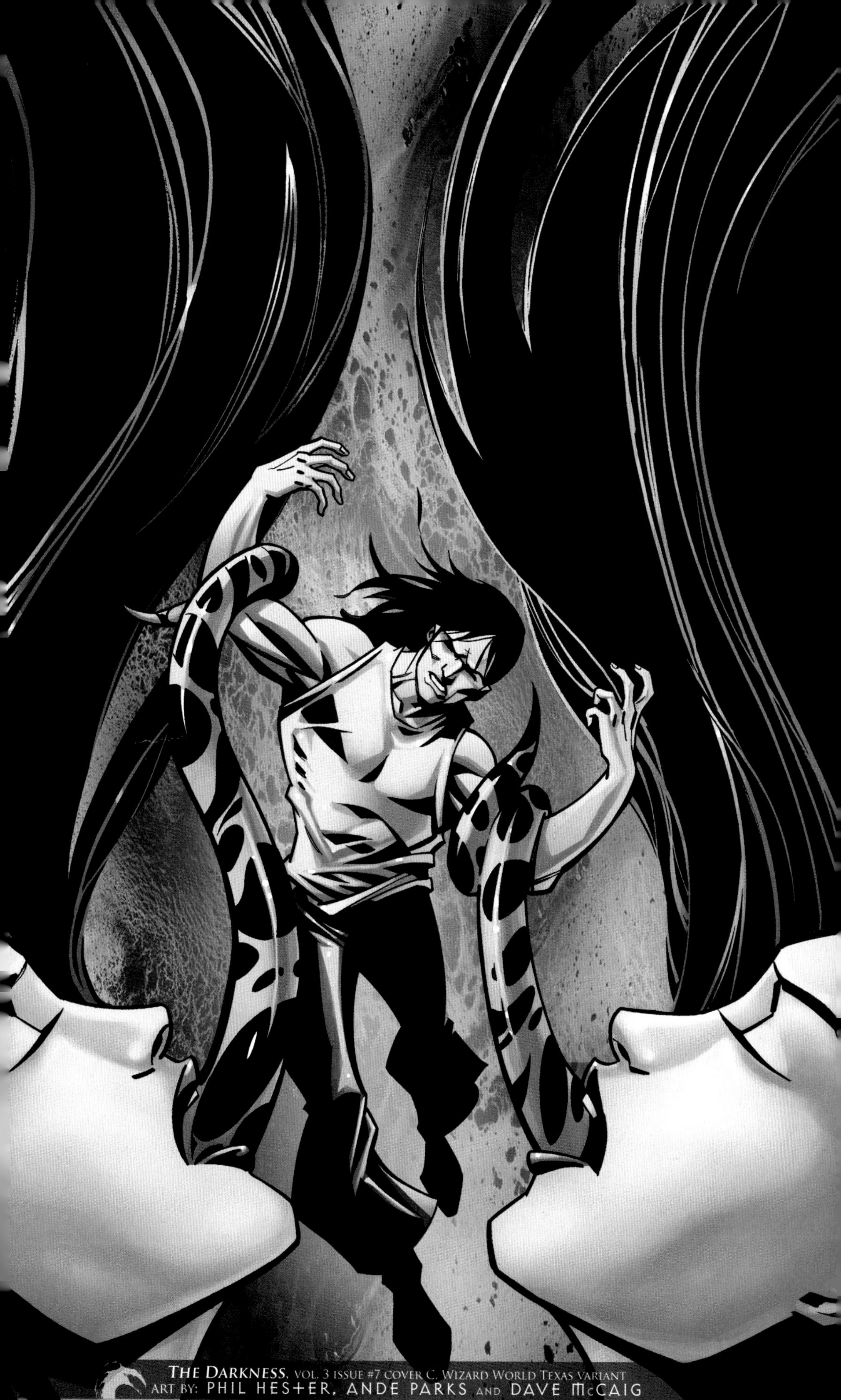

The Darkness, vol. 3 issue #7 cover C. Wizard World Texas variant
Art by: Phil Hester, Ande Parks and Dave McCaig

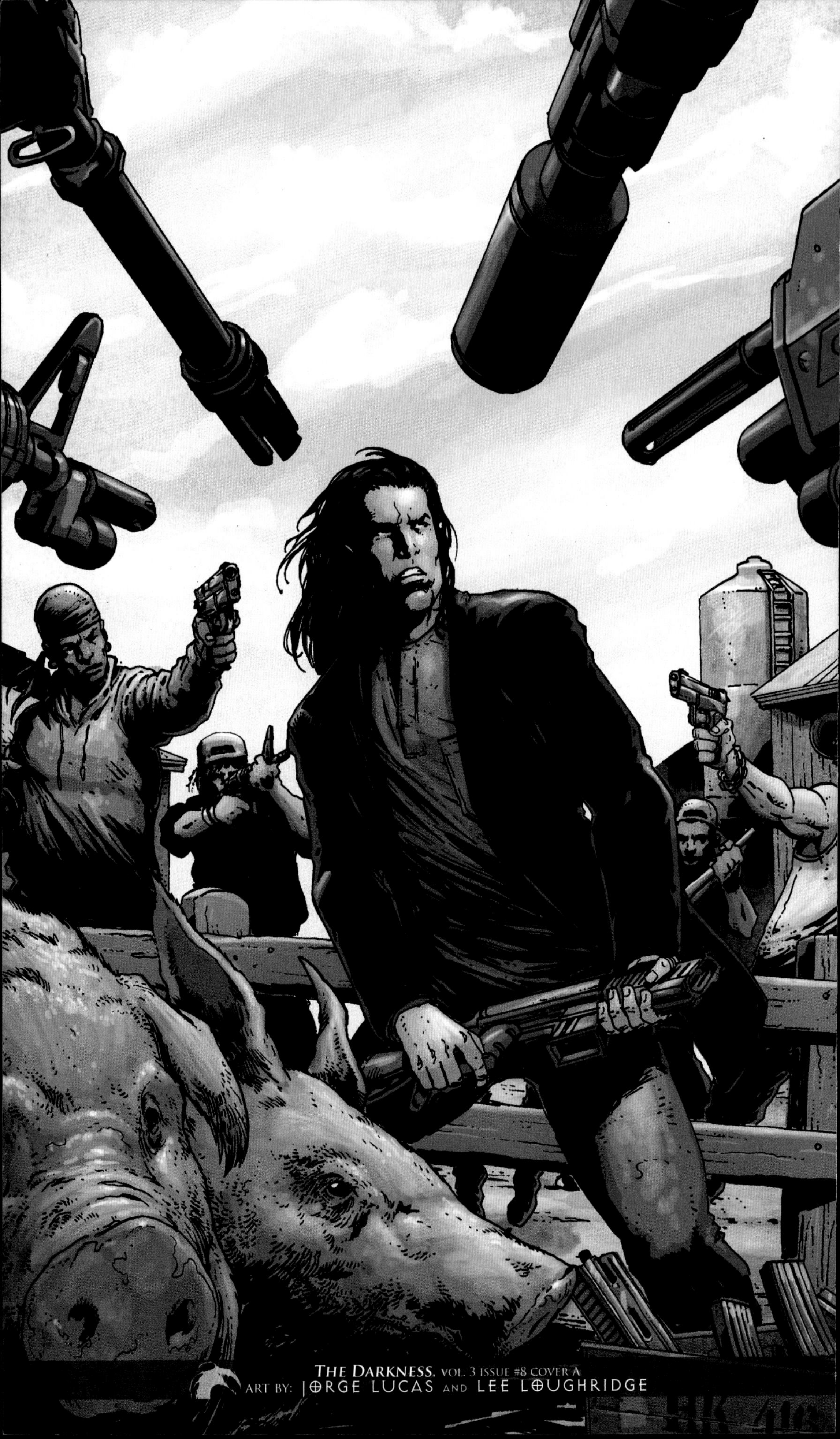

THE DARKNESS, VOL. 3 ISSUE #8 COVER A
ART BY: JORGE LUCAS AND LEE LOUGHRIDGE

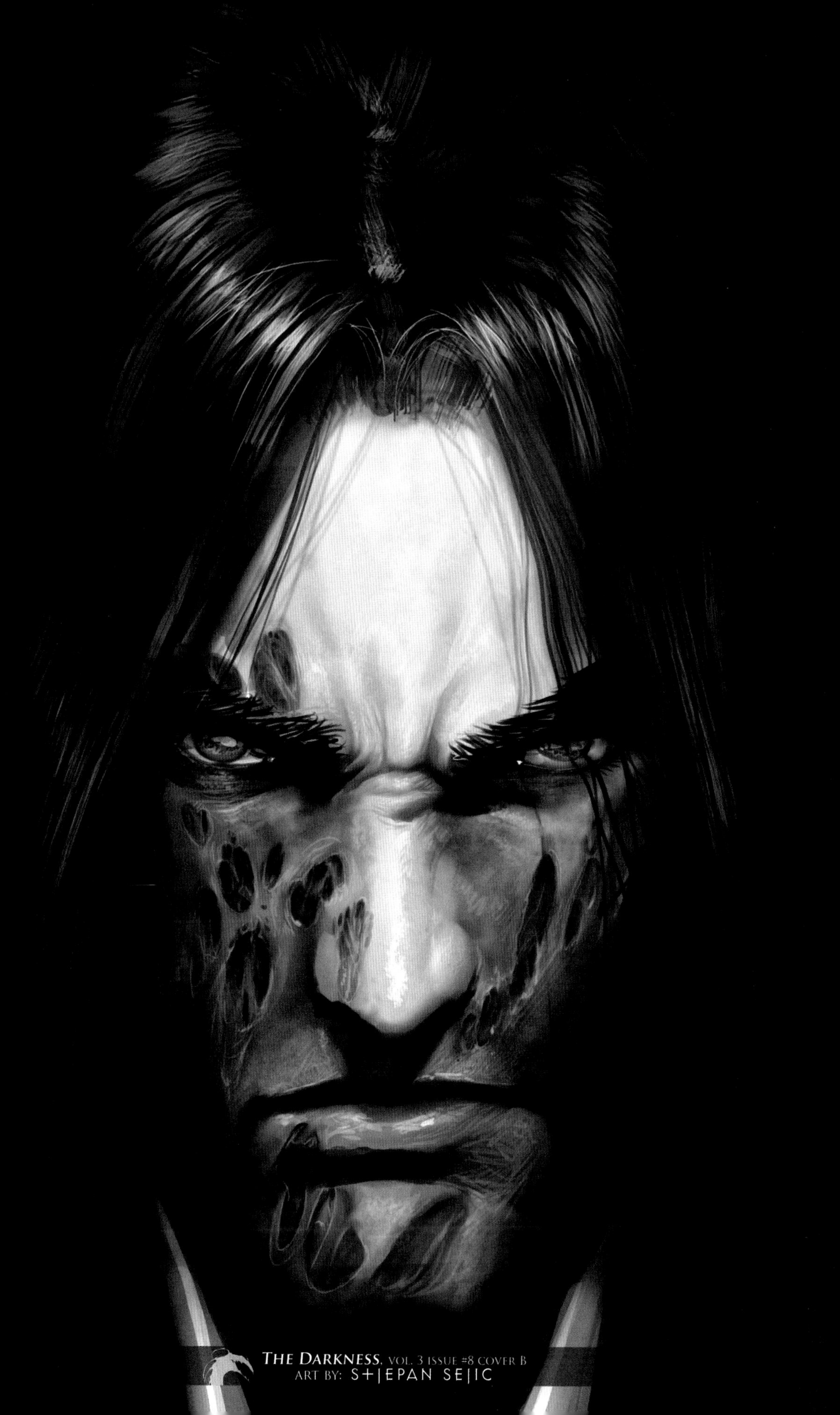

THE DARKNESS, VOL. 3 ISSUE #8 COVER B
ART BY: STJEPAN SEJIC

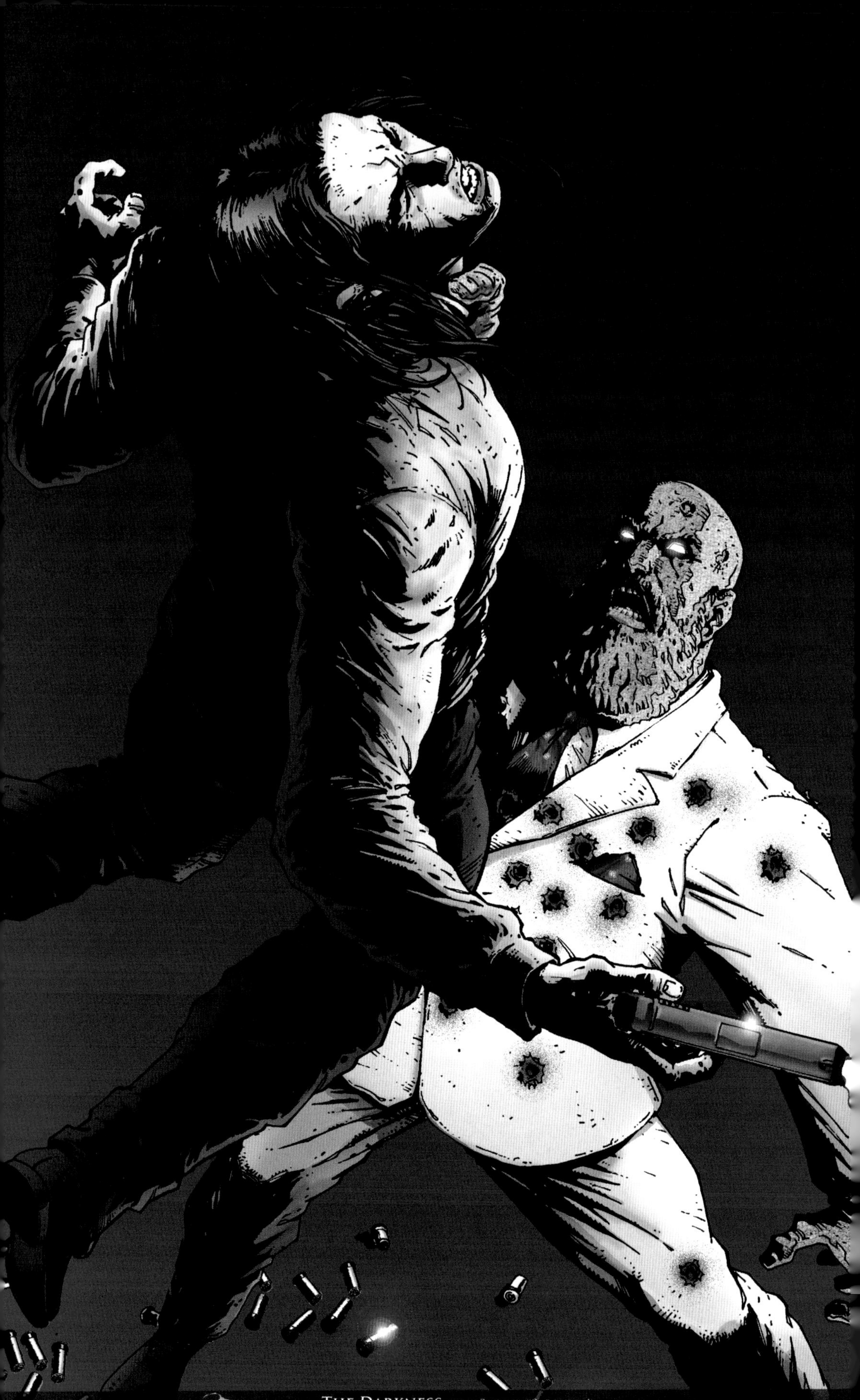

THE DARKNESS, VOL. 3 ISSUE #9 COVER A
ART BY: JORGE LUCAS AND LEE LOUGHRIDGE

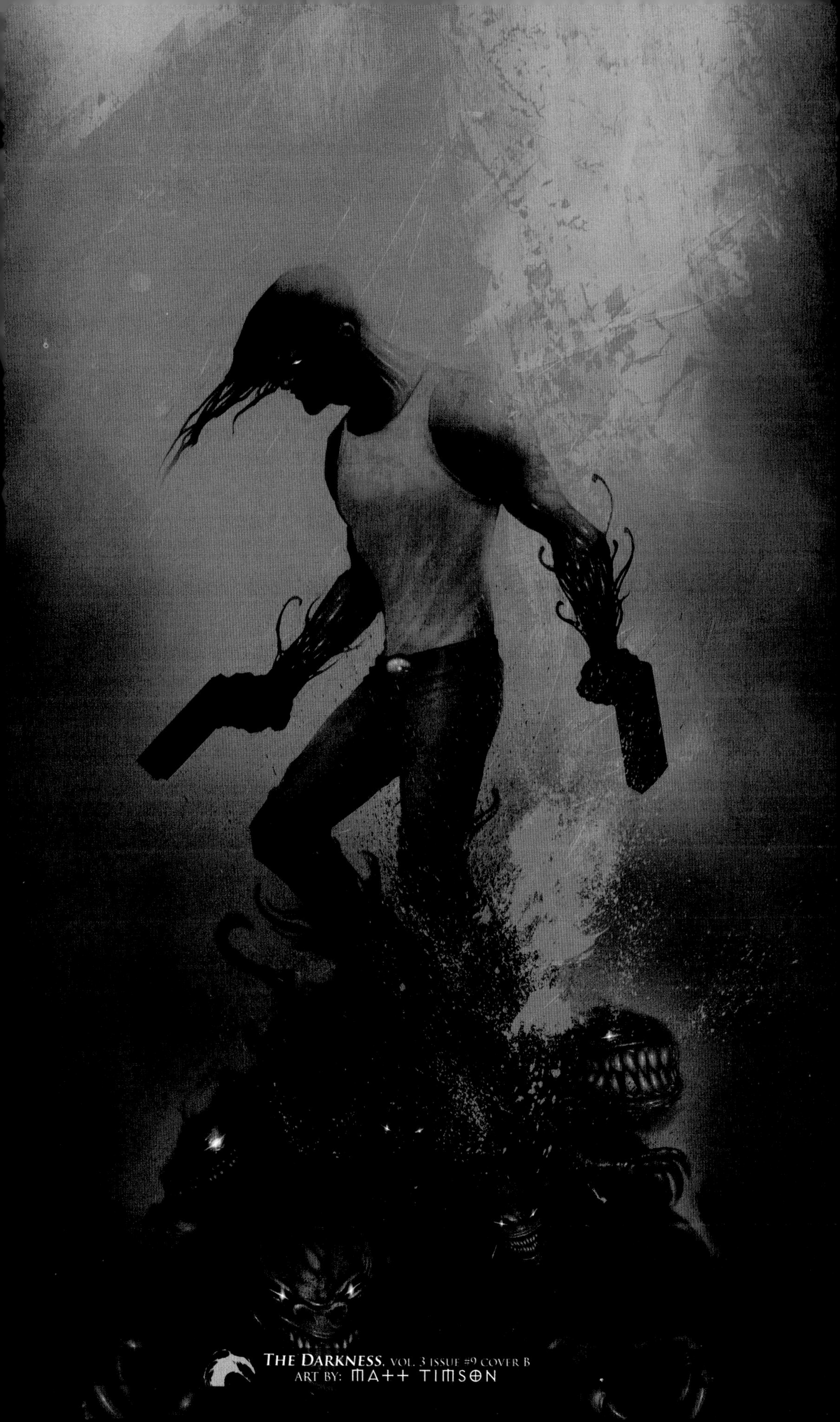

THE DARKNESS, VOL. 3 ISSUE #9 COVER B
ART BY: MATT TIMSON

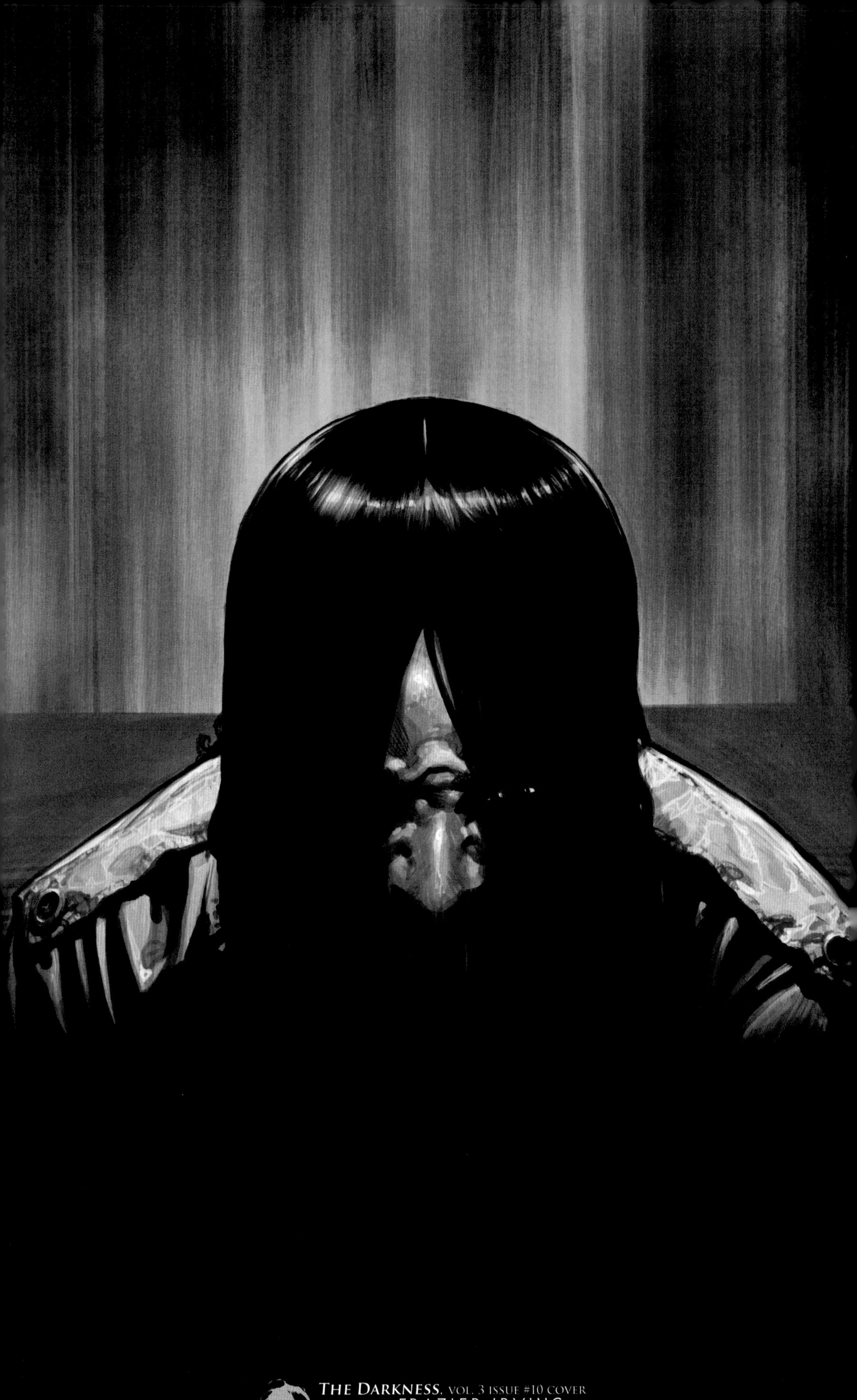

THE DARKNESS, VOL. 3 ISSUE #10 COVER
ART BY: FRAZIER IRVING

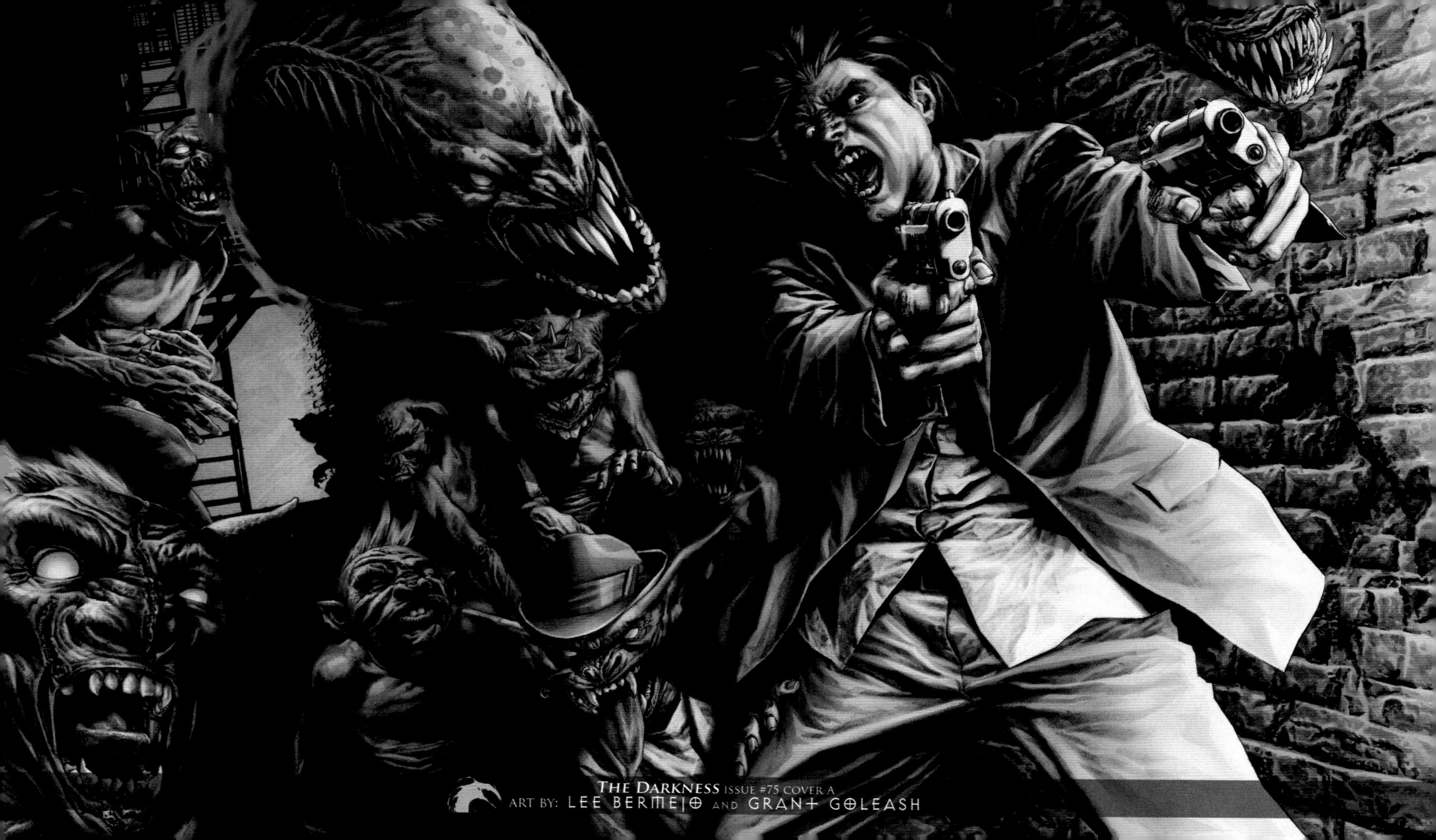

THE DARKNESS ISSUE #75 COVER A
ART BY: LEE BERMEJO AND GRANT GOLEASH

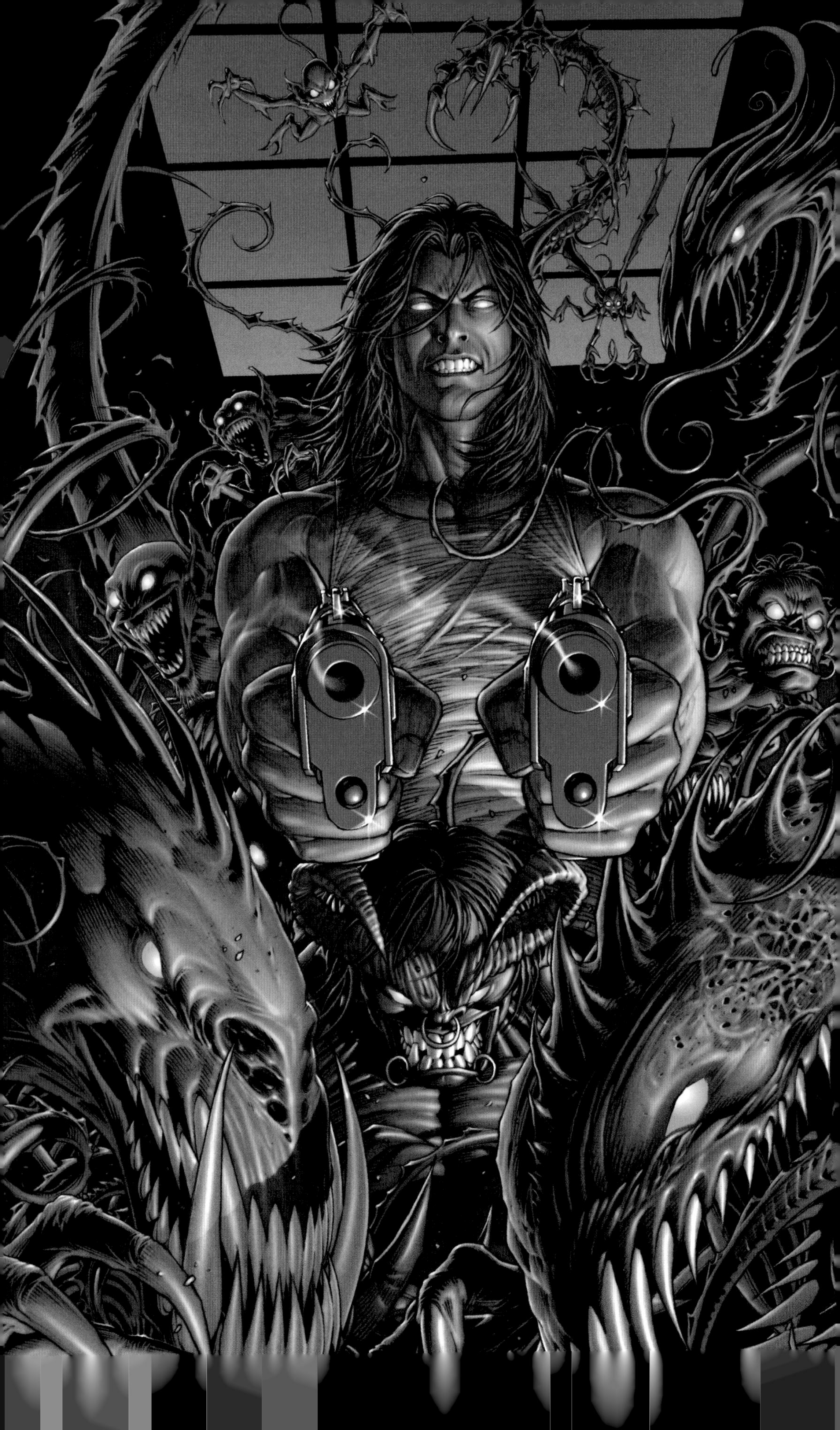

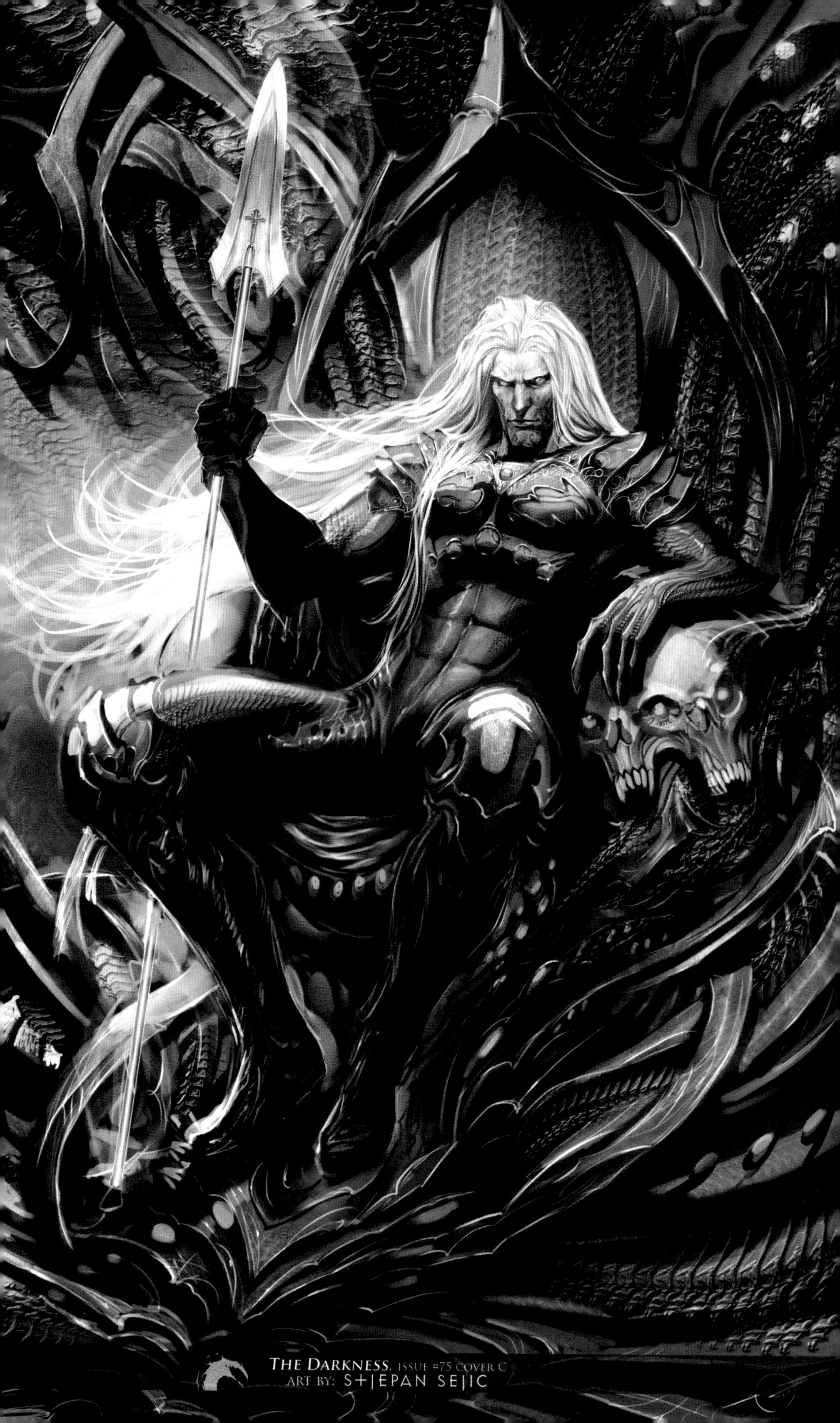

THE DARKNESS, ISSUE #75 COVER C
ART BY: STJEPAN SEJIC

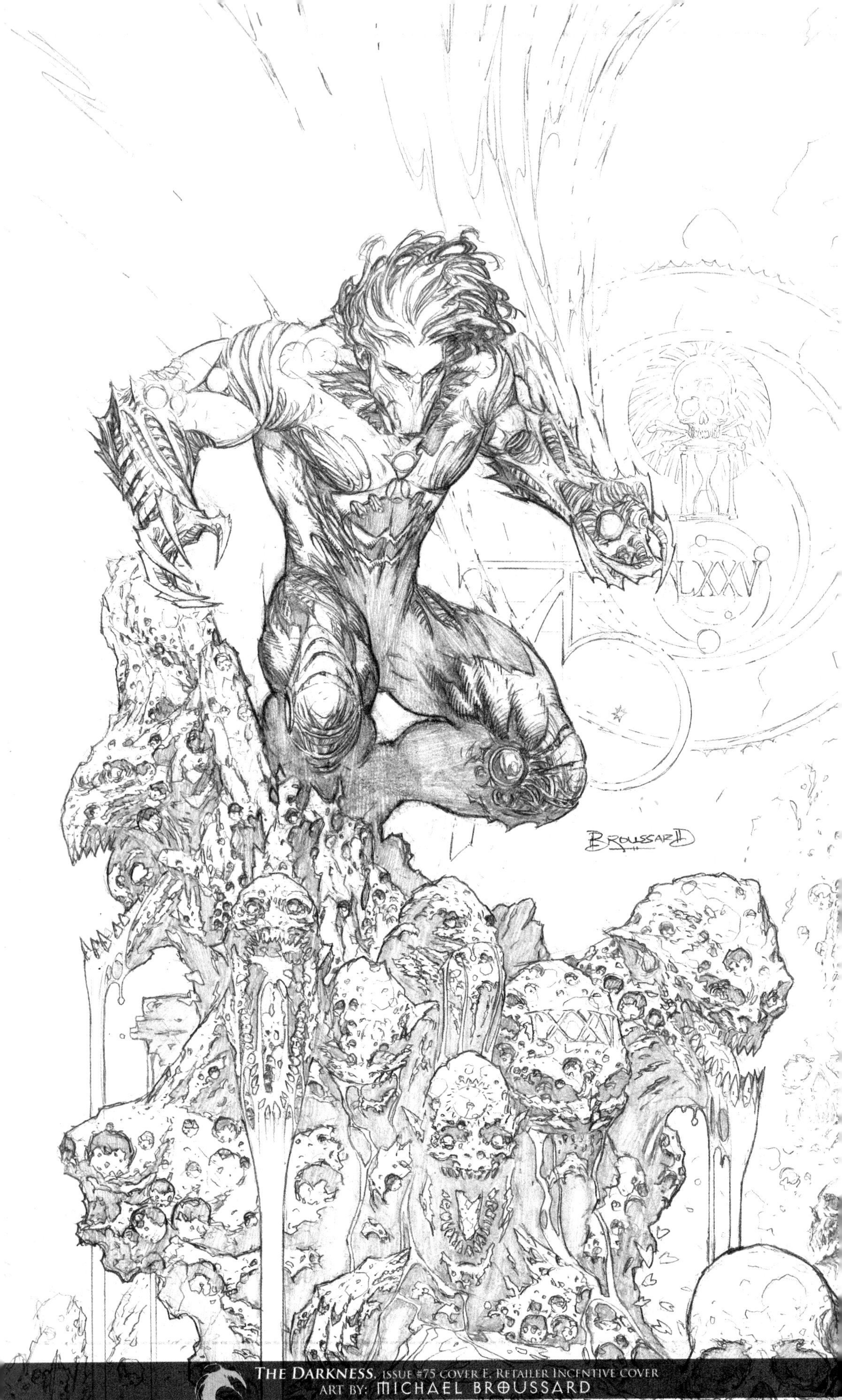
LXXV
BROUSSARD

The Darkness, issue #75 cover E, Retailer Incentive cover
ART BY: MICHAEL BROUSSARD

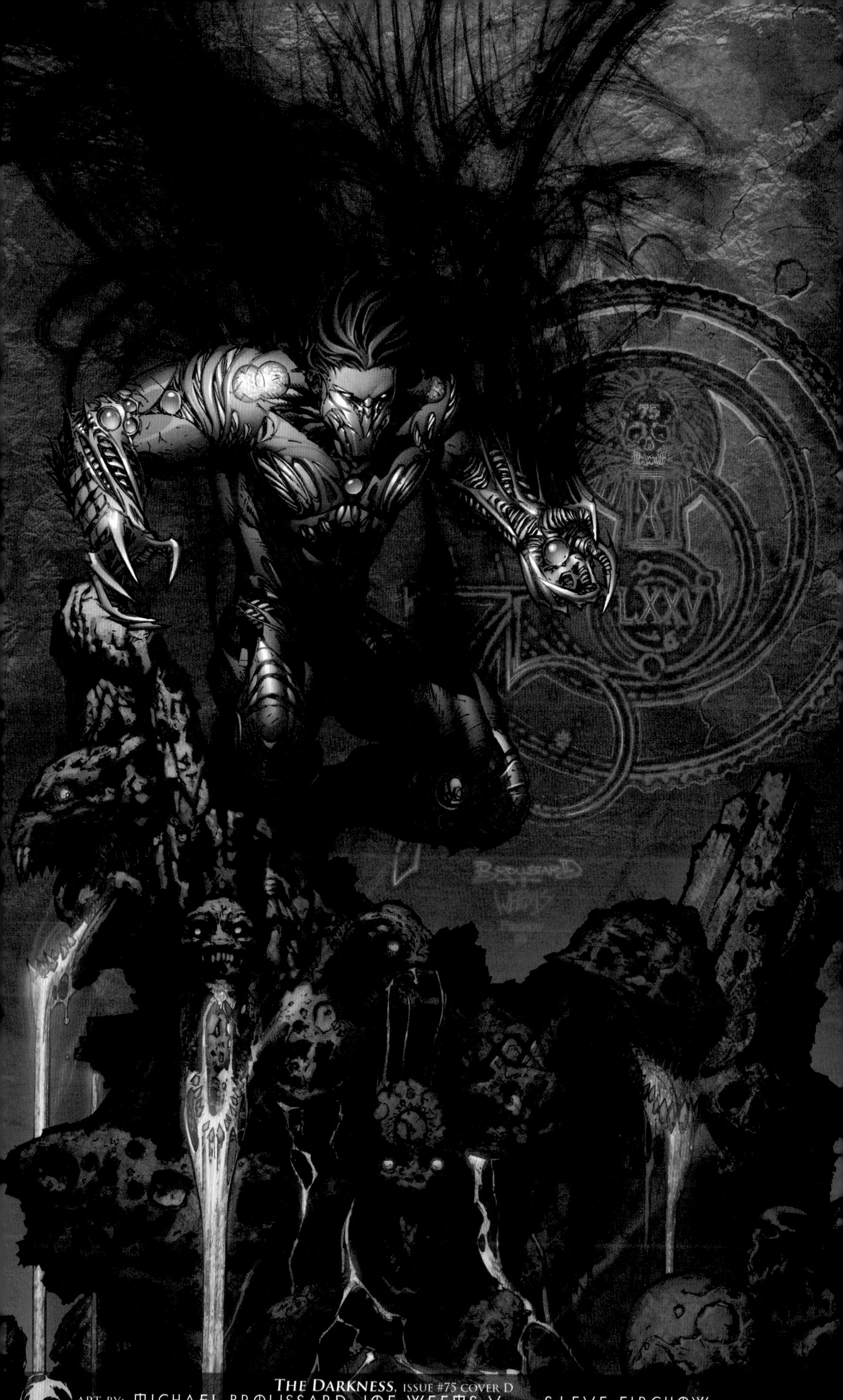
75
LXXV

The Darkness, issue #75 cover D
Art by: MICHAEL BROUSSARD, JOE WEEMS V and STEVE FIRCHOW

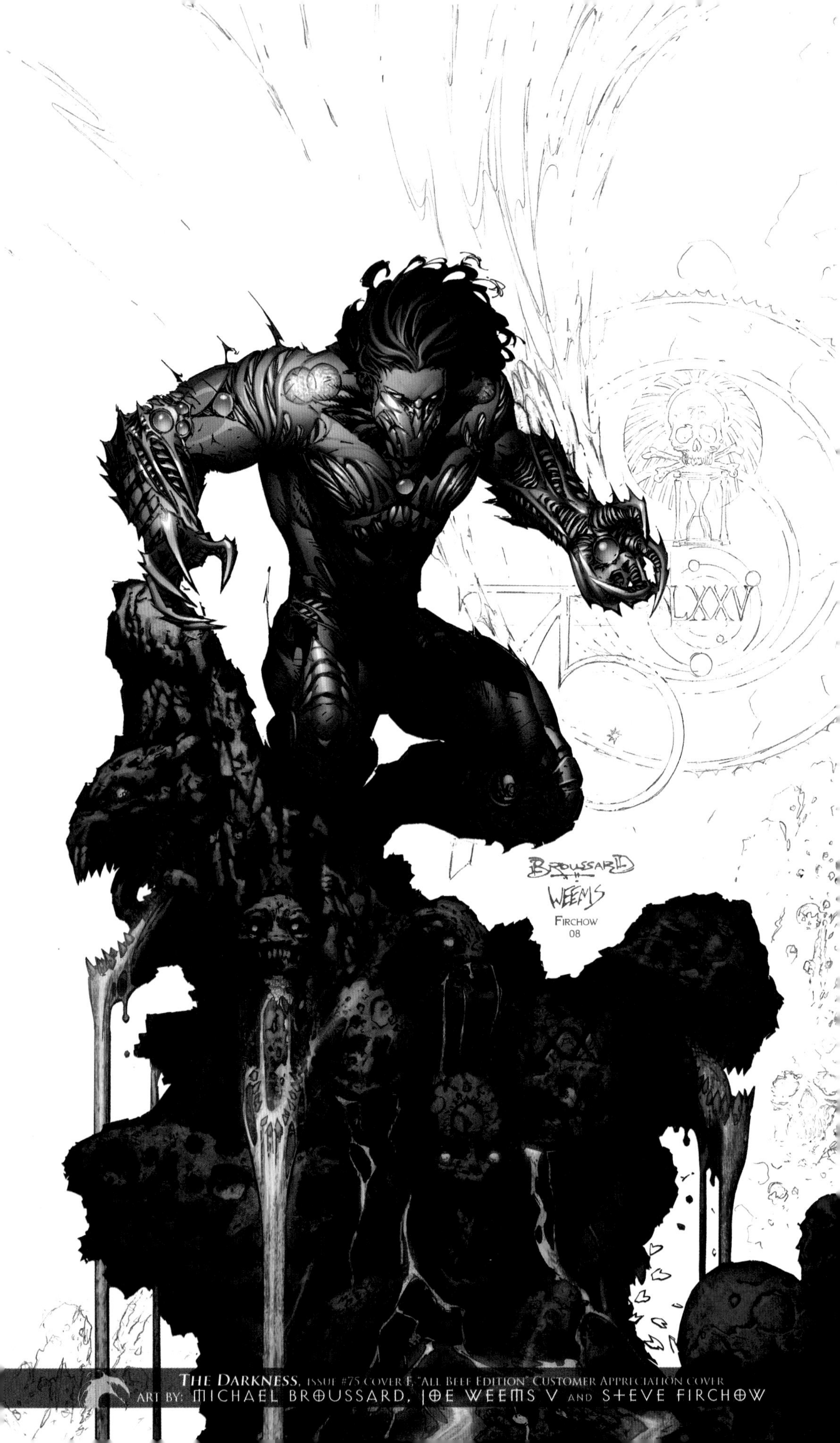
LXXV
BROUSSARD
WEEMS
FIRCHOW
08

THE DARKNESS, ISSUE #75 COVER E, "ALL BEEF EDITION" CUSTOMER APPRECIATION COVER
ART BY: MICHAEL BROUSSARD, JOE WEEMS V AND STEVE FIRCHOW

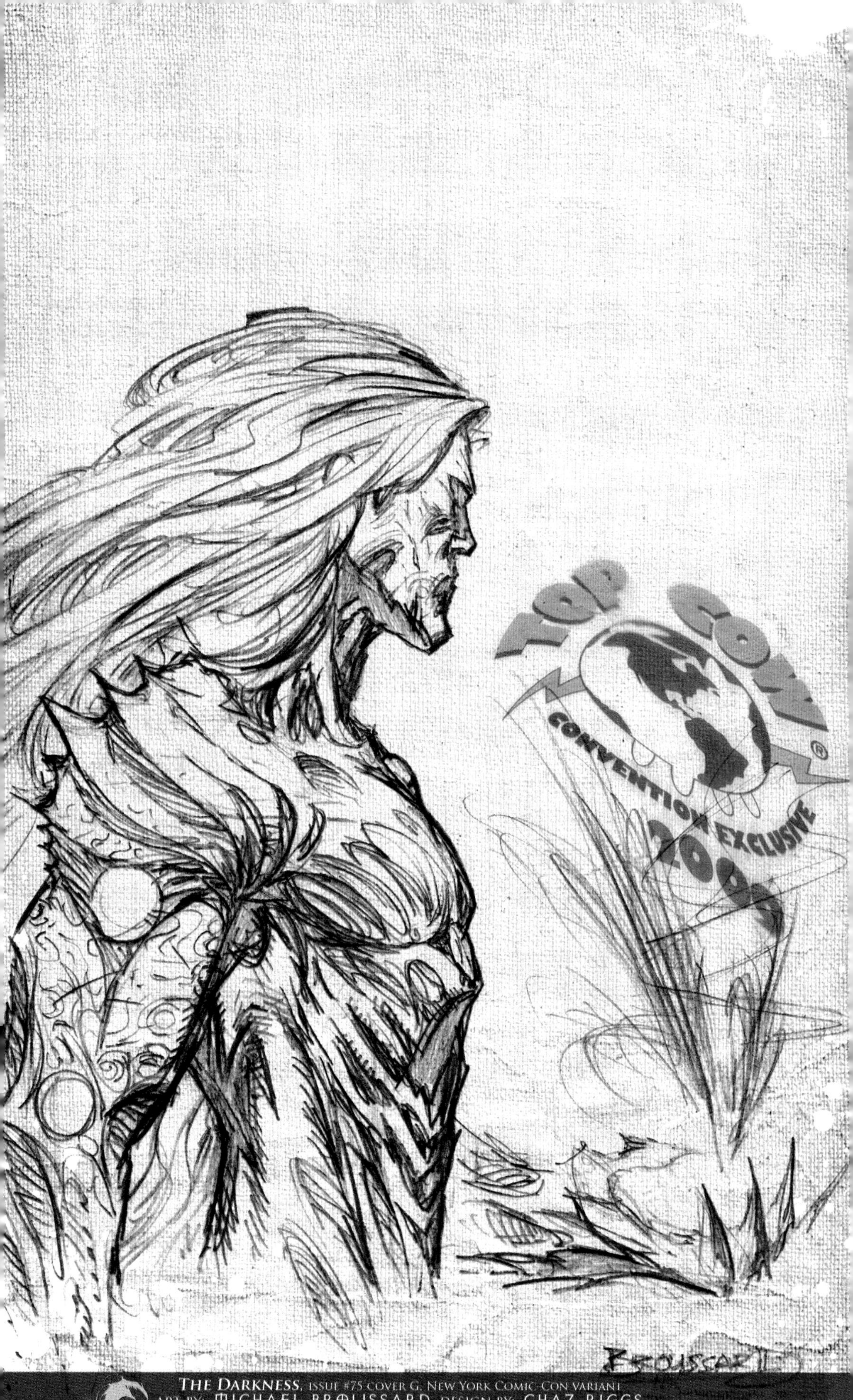
TOP COW
CONVENTION EXCLUSIVE
BROUSSARD

The Darkness, issue #75 cover G, New York Comic-Con variant
Art by: Michael Broussard Design by: Chaz Riggs

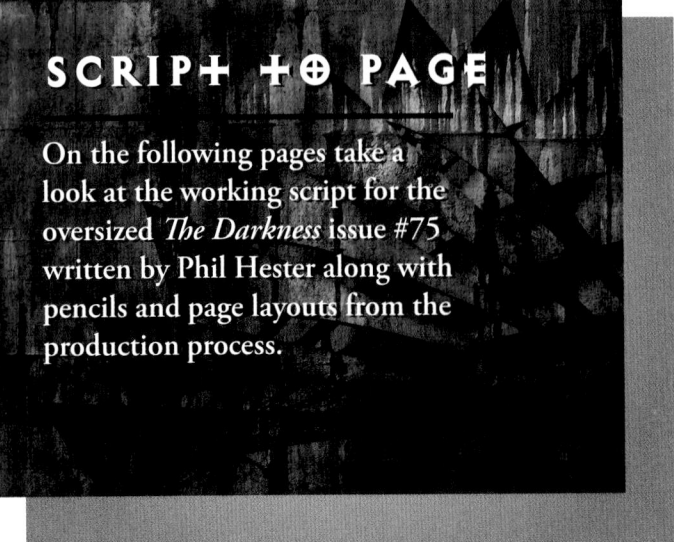

SCRIPT TO PAGE

On the following pages take a look at the working script for the oversized *The Darkness* issue #75 written by Phil Hester along with pencils and page layouts from the production process.

CHARACTERS FOR THIS ISSUE

THE EARTH: Note. This entire story is set in a spooky, Darkness dominated future. It should always be varying degrees of night. The brightest it ever gets looks like twilight or pre-dawn. Also the only functioning things on earth are Darkness factories which pump soot into the air to block out the sun. They should look like Terry Gilliam's wet dreams.

FUTURE JACKIE: Looks just like our current armored up Jackie, but perhaps more slim and his hair should hang down to his lower legs, looking almost cape-like. In the brief moment we see him out of armor his hair will be white and his face will look leathery and cured. Not like a normal human would age, but as if he were unnaturally preserved.

THE ORDER OF THE MAGDALENA: A world wide sect of warrior nuns devoted to surviving Jackie's rule and reviving their lost founder- The Magdalena. They should look like road warrior version of Magdalena, meaning they have the leather armor and capes, but they should look sort of cobbled together with found objects. Their armor pieces should be dull and made from found metal. No gold. They ALL wear night vision goggles, sometimes around neck, and carry spears based on the Spear of Destiny.

SISTER IGNATIUS: A beefy nun of 50. Short, grey hair. A skeptic of the boy's prophecy.

SISTER MARY-KATE: A dead ringer for the current Magdalena.

SISTER ISABEL: Dark haired hispanic nun. Sultry.

SISTER COLLEEN: Red haired and innocent. Young. A true believer.

SISTER FIONA: A black woman of 55 or so, maybe older. Bald and in great shape. Lean fighter. The wise one.

BOY: A ten year old kid from the underbelly of this crappy world. Skinny and pale. Undernourished. Short black hair. Should on some level remind us of young Jackie.

GREY: The rebel Darkling. Just like normal Darklings, but maybe a little fatter.

LYMAN: Jackie's human spy. 60 and fit. Dressed in black, faintly papal robes.

PSYCHIC: An obese, red faced man of 40 with thick glasses. Comic book guy.

MAMA: Psychic's Mom. Looks like an old, white haired holocaust survivor. Wizened.

ARTIST: Someone good with tone. No real figures on this page. maybe someone with an architectural bent. FX heavy. Should be same artist as PAGE THIRTY-THREE.

DARKNESS VOL. 3 #11/75
ABSOLUTE DARKNESS
PAGE ONE

Slow push in from space on the world Jackie has ruined. No features, just grey clouds blanketing the earth. We push past them and see a post apocalyptic earth. Toppled skyscrapers, etc. We see a column of ten or so people scurrying down an otherwise deserted alley. They are too far away to make out any details.

1 NARRATION: I see a ruined world.

2 NARR: The skies are heavy with the smog of great factories devoted solely to the production of more pollution.

3 NARR: Sunlight is strangled by the charred atmosphere, casting the broken cities below in perpetual twilight.

4 NARR: The land is grey and fallow, scoured by harrowing winds.

5 NARR: The sea turns over on itself, a perpetual black bruise heaving sickly yellow foam on every shattered coastline.

6 NARR: The towers of once mighty cities sprawl over the landscape like bleached bones scattered by an unspeakable predator.

7 NARR: And the clever animals that built them - the humans - scurry through the ruins like the vermin they once reviled.

8 NARR: Dying beasts on a dying world.

9 NARR: Whatever made them human spilled out of them and into the cracked earth long ago.

10 NARR: Not so much survivors...

11 NARR: As ghosts.

PAGE THREE

Now we see behind Mary-Kate to the column of people following her from the alley. They are ALL Sisters of the Order of the Magdalena of varying ages. First big shocker of the book. More than one Mags these days! Leading the column is Sister Ignatius. The boy they are transporting is bound and gagged, being pulled along by younger nuns. He shouts out to be freed. The nuns argue about their best course.

1 SISTER IGNATIUS: Be quick about it. True night approaches.

2 BOY: Let me go!

3 SISTER 1: I'm sorry, sisters. He chewed through the gag.

4 SISTER IGNATIUS: Such a troublesome little thing. Do you know how many of our order died to bring you this far?

page 3, pencil detail

ARTIST: Someone good at drawing ladies in action and Darklings.

DARKNESS VOL. 3 #11/75
ABSOLUTE DARKNESS
PAGE TWO

SPLASH. Sister Mary-Kate stands atop a pile of rubble, scanning the blasted city with her night vision goggles. See character description. She should look like a rag-tag, road warrior Magdalena.

1 NARR: For Darkness has fallen over this planet.

2 NARR: Absolute Darkness which will yield no dawn.

3 SISTER MARY-KATE: The way ahead is clear.

4 TITLE:
Absolute Darkness

page 2, pencil detail

PAGE FOUR

As they squabble a patrol of Darklings (including Grey) surrounds them.

1 NARR: And as the humans once hunted the lesser beasts, now they exist only as the prey of another life form.

2 SISTER MARY-KATE: Night falls, Sister Ignatius. Quell your blasphemy before it shines out like a beacon to the dweller in the shadows.

3 NARR: A life form at once more and less than human.

4 SISTER IGNATIUS: You call it blasphemy, I call it--

5 SISTER MARY-KATE: Darklings!

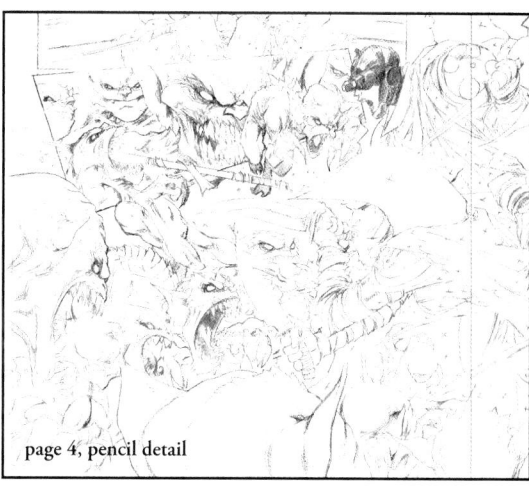
page 4, pencil detail

PAGE FIVE

The Darklings threaten and the nuns form a defensive circle around the boy. The Darklings leap into battle.

1 DARKLING 1: Now what are you silly bitches up to? Sneaking around right here in our boss's back yard?

2 SISTER MARY-KATE: Go ahead, abomination.

3 SISTER MARY-KATE: Call us bitches again.

4 DARKLING 1: Nah, you're right.

5 DARKLING 1: No more talking.

page 5, pencil detail

PAGE SIX

A nice battle page. The sisters actually hold their own against the darklings, who fall back. Mary-Kate knows it's only a temporary reprieve and makes ready to escape when she hears a sinister voice from off panel.

1 SISTER IGNATIUS: They fall back!

2 SISTER MARY-KATE: Sister Ignatius, form a line to cover our retreat.

3 SISTER MARY-KATE: I'll take four sisters and make a break for the emergency route.

4 SISTER MARY-KATE: Magdalena preserve us, perhaps we can reach the temple before-

5 FUTURE JACKIE: Before I find you?

PAGE EIGHT

We stay on the carnage in the alley for a minute, then cut to another alley where Grey leads Boy into a subterranean tunnel.

1 BOY: What- what are you going to do to me?

2 GREY: Nothing. I'm taking you to the sisters.

3 BOY: The sisters are back there.

4 GREY: Ain't nothing back there but a pile of bloody habits by now.

5 GREY: My boss doesn't care much for the Order of Saint Magdalena.

page 8, pencil detail

SCENE THREE- PAGES SEVEN-EIGHT
ARTIST: Someone capable of a sinister looking Jackie.

PAGE SEVEN
Our first look at future Jackie. He's gaunt and somehow more sinister. He tears into Mary-Kate and the darklings jump back into the attack. Grey grabs Boy from the midst of the battle and drags him down an alley.

1 FUTURE JACKIE: How cute, you've actually got the guts to stay in formation.

2 FUTURE JACKIE: Don't mind. Makes things quicker.

3 GREY: C'mon, kid!

page 7, pencil detail

SCENE FOUR- PAGES NINE-ELEVEN
ARTIST: Someone capable of architectural detail. We need a convincing Grand Central and some authentic looking alleys and tunnels.

PAGE NINE
Grey and the boy emerge form their secret path and we see a nice exterior shot of Grand Central still looking more or less intact amidst the rubble of NYC. Money shot of the ruined city.

1 BOY: Your boss? Then why are you taking me to the sisters?

2 GREY: I got my own reasons, boy. You just hang on.

3 GREY: Old Grey's got his reasons.

4 BOY: I want to go home.

5 GREY: Home won't be there, kid. Home ain't there for anyone anymore.

6 GREY: Curtain's coming down on the whole goddamned planet. No sun to grow plants, no food on the shelves, no future.

page 8, pencil detail

Grey and Boy negotiate the ruins around Grand Central and gain entrance through a neglected service tunnel. They come out into the great central lobby of the station which looks surprisingly intact. In fact, the only major difference, and it's a big one, is the fact that every wall is now covered with sheets of scavenged metal that have been polished to a high shine. Gutters run along the sides of every wall and a colossal brazier sits in the center of the lobby. Clear oil fills it. We see some nuns doing battle drills on the floor while some raggedy looking workmen nail some metal on the walls.

BOY: Why do you care? You belong to the Dark Army.

GREY: You realize how boring it is to belong to an army with no enemies?

GREY: This handful of whacked-out nuns is the closest thing my boss has got to opposition these days, and he couldn't really give a shit.

GREY: Seems he's happy to just draw the blinds and let the planet go cold- starve out the few remaining humans who defied him.

GREY: Boss conjured me up nearly a hundred and fifty years ago. Been killing his name ever since.

GREY: This perpetual darkness means I hang around even when I got nothing to kill. Problem is, down time is thinking time, and when I think about the things we did to toss this world--

BOY: You feel sorry? Sometimes when I'm eating something I stole I feel bad for the person I stole it from.

BOY: When I sleep I feel their hunger even though my belly's full. Like that?

GREY: No. Not like that.

GREY: I don't feel regret. Not sure I'm built to.

GREY: Let's just say it makes me tired. Eager for an ending...

GREY: Happy or not.

The pair look out at the lobby when a spear point jabs at Grey, driving him back. A troop of Magdalenas, including Sister Isabel, capture Grey and the boy.

1 BOY: What is this place?

2 GREY: A little sliver of the old world, kid. And maybe a door into the next one.

3 OP SISTER ISABEL: That's far enough, wretch.

4 GREY: Whoa, hey. Hey, settle down. I'm on your side, honey.

5 GREY: This here's the package Sister Ignatius was meant to deliv--

6 SISTER ISABEL: Don't speak her name.

7 GREY: Gkkk!

8 BOY: He didn't hurt me.

9 SISTER ISABEL: Silence, boy.

10 BOY: He saved me!

11 SISTER ISABEL: Bind them both.

SCENE FIVE- PAGES TWELVE, could also extend to page fifteen.
ARTIST: An important Darkness artist- Marc?

Silent page. Jackie stands at the outdoor monument/grave site he had constructed to the memory of Jenny Romano. It sits in what was once Central Park, now just a barren stretch of dead trees in the middle of this ruined city. Jackie stands in front of her grave and a rare sliver of sunlight strikes the headstone and slides down and across Jackie. As the sliver of light moves up Jackie's body we see the armor dissipate and the mummified Jackie beneath, including a bleeding wound in his side. The light passes and Jackie is normal again.

[Troy, you may need to add lettering to the grave/monument.]

page 12, pencil detail

SCENE SIX- PAGES THIRTEEN-FIFTEEN
ARTIST: Someone good at detailed gore and Darkness Jackie.

Lyman addresses Jackie from behind with what he thinks is good news only to find his boss in an exceptionally shitty mood.

1 LYMAN: Master Estacado, our spies report that Grey has accomplished his task.

2 LYMAN: He now stands in the heart of the Order's last remaining sanctuary.

3 FUTURE JACKIE: How long have you been in my service, Lyman?

4 LYMAN: Forty years, Lord.

5 FUTURE JACKIE: Forty years as my eyes and ears among your fellow man, and what have you learned?

6 LYMAN: Learned?

7 FUTURE JACKIE: Grey accomplished his task because he never knew he had one.

8 FUTURE JACKIE: I planted his doubt, fanned his spark of rebellion. He thought he turned away from me, but in truth he never left my service.

9 FUTURE JACKIE: He ran right into the heart of the witches' lair, as I knew he would. His eyes are my eyes, Lyman. They always were.

10 LYMAN: Of course.

11 LYMAN: I- I will take my leave, Lord. Your old wound pains you, it seems.

12 FUTURE JACKIE: Tonight my army will fall on their little coven and soak this island to the bedrock with their blood.

13 FUTURE JACKIE: And I will have no more enemies.

PAGE FOURTEEN

Lyman tries to slink away, but Jackie makes him stick out his tongue for some polluted soot to fall upon, a kind of perverted communion.

1 LYMAN: A holiday, Lord. I will make plans for--

2 FUTURE JACKIE: Hold out your hands.

3 LYMAN: My hands?

4 FUTURE JACKIE: That's it, palms up.

5 FUTURE JACKIE: What fills them, Lyman?

6 LYMAN: I- I don't know. Soot, my Lord.

7 LYMAN: Soot from the clouds above.

8 FUTURE JACKIE: That soot is the fruit of my labor, my finest handiwork.

9 FUTURE JACKIE: Stick out your tongue, Lyman.

10 LYMAN: Stick…?

11 FUTURE JACKIE: You heard me.

12 FUTURE JACKIE: Nothing happens on this miserable world without my consent.

13 FUTURE JACKIE: Grey's eyes are mine, the stone under your feet is mine...

14 FUTURE JACKIE: The soot in your mouth is mine.

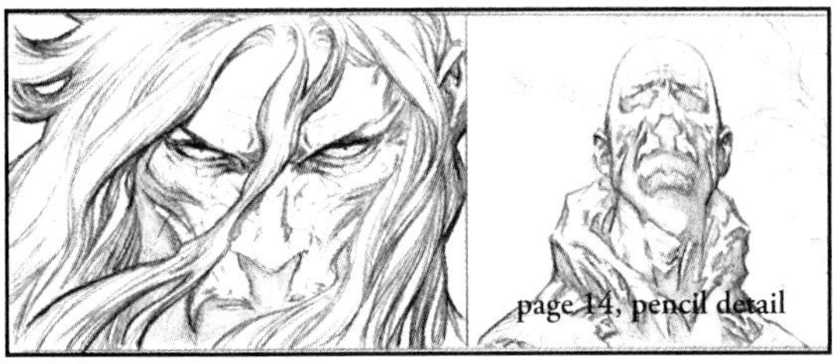

page 14, pencil detail

SCENE SEVEN- PAGES SIXTEEN-SEVENTEEN

ARTIST: Again someone good at different body types of women. Lots of nuns here.

PAGE SIXTEEN

Back to Grand Central. The nuns have gathered around the Boy, and the still bound Grey. Isabel argues that the boy is a fraud. Fiona thinks he's the real deal and opens a big treasure chest in front of him full of shards of polished metal (broken spearheads), beckoning him to chose which once belonged to Magdalena. He hesitates.

1 SISTER ISABEL: But he's a boy! He can never become one of the order.

2 SISTER ISABEL: He's fit to scavenge and burnish metal for the Dawnbreakers. Nothing more.

3 SISTER FIONA: The Magdalena's prophecy is clear.

4 SISTER FIONA: In her final epistle she wrote the herald of her resurrection and of the Darkness' fall would be born two hundred years to the day of her earthly demise. That herald would be an orphan and a thief.

5 SISTER ISABEL: As are most children these days, Sister Fiona.

6 SISTER FIONA: And the herald would recognize the one true shard of the Spear of Destiny, shattered on the night of our dear Magdalena's fall into slumber.

7 SISTER FIONA: Choose carefully, boy.

8 GREY: You can do it, kid.

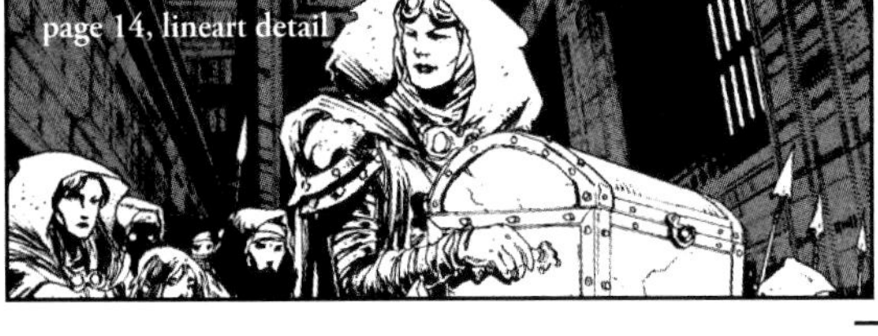

page 14, lineart detail

PAGE FIFTEEN

The soot twists away in Lyman's insides, killing him for interrupting Jackie's reverie, leaving a nasty pile of chewed gore where he once stood.

1 FUTURE JACKIE: Feel it turning, Lyman? Churning?

2 FUTURE JACKIE: Chewing a pathway through your throat, sawing through your veins? Your bones?

3 FUTURE JACKIE: Forty years and you've learned nothing.

4 FUTURE JACKIE: A king with no enemies needs no spies.

5 FUTURE JACKIE: And most importantly, Lyman.

6 FUTURE JACKIE: I am never to be disturbed while at her grave.

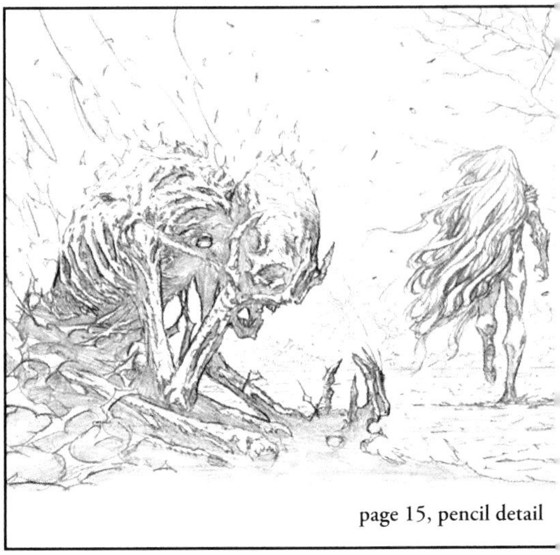

page 15, pencil detail

PAGE SEVENTEEN

The Boy grabs a shard which cuts him. He falls to the ground in a trance, and the nuns gather around.

1 BOY: This one!

2 BOY: Ungh!

3 SISTER ISABEL: It strikes him down! He's failed!

4 SISTER FIONA: Nonsense! Stay back, sisters.

5 SISTER FIONA: The spirit is upon him

6 BOY: I see...

7 SISTER FIONA: What, boy? What do you see?

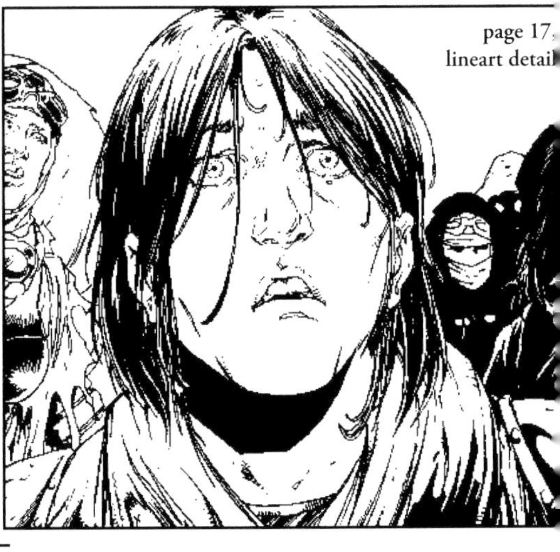

page 17, lineart detail

ARTIST: I'd like to see something painterly here. This should look like a tableau from times past, so something painted would be great here.

PAGE EIGHTEEN-NINETEEN

Double page splash- Flashback to Patience, our current Mags, in battle with modern day Jackie on the ledge of the Empire State building. She is stabbing him in the side while he is reaching out to strangle her. This should look mythic and larger than life. A weird light pours from Jackie's wound. Mags is screaming in pain as the light passes over her.

BOY NARRATION: I see a battle in the sky. A man who wears the night like a coat fights a girl with hair like burnished bronze.

BOY NARR: She strikes at him with her holy weapon and the spearhead bites deep. It sinks into his bone before the evil in his blood shatters the blade.

BOY NARR: The girl's body is destroyed in the cataclysm, but not her spirit. In death she sows the seeds of his demise.

BOY NARR: The man's wound never heals.

SCENE NINE- PAGES TWENTY

ARTIST- Same cat as scene seven, since it's a continuation.

PAGE TWENTY

The nuns stand around amazed. The kid is the real deal. He stands among them, staring out into space, transcendent. The last panel is a shot of Jackie looking out over the city from his balcony atop the only upright skyscraper.

1 SISTER FIONA: He speaks the secret scripture.

2 GREY: Kid?

3 SISTER ISABEL: Magdalena be with us.

4 BOY: There is a tomb.

5 SISTER 2: Yes, yes!

6 SISTER 3: Lead us to her.

7 BOY: There is a tomb which must be opened.

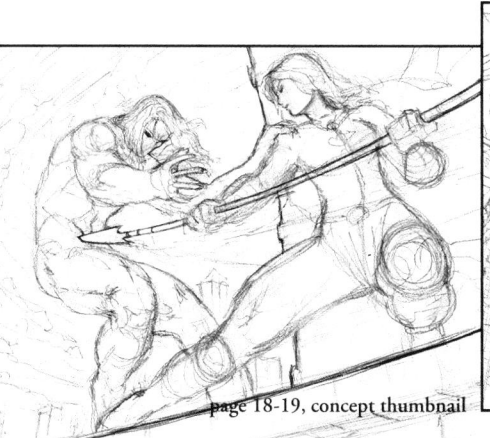

page 18-19, concept thumbnail

page 18-19, concept thumbnail

SCENE TEN- PAGE TWENTY-ONE

ARTIST: Someone with perspective skills to indicate the enormity of the Darklings following Jackie down the building.

PAGE TWENTY-ONE

Jackie steps out over the side of the building and begins to walk down its sheer face. In his wake Darklings spring up and follow him. End with a nice long shot of the building. The entire top half is dark with Darkling bodies descending to follow Jackie into the city.

SCENE ELEVEN- PAGE TWENTY-TWO

ARTIST: Someone capable of realistic backgrounds. We need to see clearly this was once the Holland Tunnel.

PAGE TWENTY-TWO

We see Boy in a male version of the Magdalena warrior outfit for the first time. He leads isabel, Colleen and Grey through the city. They arrive at the shattered, half buried entrance to the Holland Tunnel.

1 SISTER ISABEL: I hate to admit it, but the boy looks good in a battle habit.

2 SISTER COLLEEN: He was born to it. It only took exposure to the holy relic to awaken his power.

3 SISTER COLLEEN: Even now he leads us without hesitation.

4 GREY: Wait up, kid.

5 GREY: We've been on the go for hours now. Some of us could use a break.

6 GREY: I mean, do you even know what this tomb is supposed to look like?

7 BOY: I do now.

8 GREY: You gotta be kidding me.

9 SISTER ISABEL: You heard the child, monster.

10 SISTER ISABEL: Start digging.

page 21, 2nd draft

page 22, detail

SCENE TWELVE- PAGE TWENTY-THREE-TWENTY-SEVEN

ARTIST: A big, extended battle with a huge light explosion, so someone capable of high contrast, well choreographed battle sequence. Also, a long chapter, so someone fairly quick.

PAGE TWENTY-THREE

A wounded Nun shows up on the doorstep to Grand Central. She is tended to, but is hysterical, warning them of Jackie's army.

1 SISTER 4: Sister!

2 SISTER 5: He--

3 SISTER 4: Don't try to speak. Sister Bernadine, call for the medical team.

4 SISTER 5: T- Too late. He-

5 SISTER 5: He comes.

page 23, pencil detail

PAGE TWENTY-FOUR

Jackie and crew smash through the big window and descend on the nuns who fight back.

1 SFX: SKRASH!
ROB- THIS BALLOON IS NOT IN LAYOUT!

1.1 FUTURE JACKIE: Kill them all.

2 SISTER 4: Hold them off! Give the Dawnbreakers time.

3 FUTURE JACKIE: Haven't been to Grand Central for centuries. Love what you've done with the place.

4 FUTURE JACKIE: Although, to be honest, you could have picked a little les conspicuous hiding place.

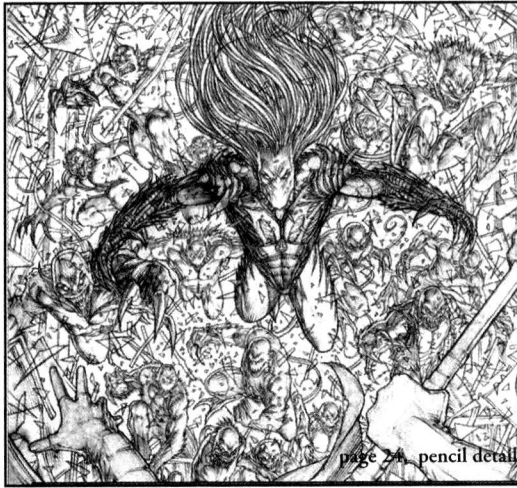

page 24, pencil detail

PAGE TWENTY-FIVE

All out battle. The nuns are falling fast. Fiona fights off Darklings as she argues with Jackie. A troop of sisters with flaming arrows in their bows appears and fires-

1 SISTER FIONA: This is no hiding place, abomination. It's a trap we took great pains to set in your path.

2 FUTURE JACKIE: Okay, so I'm trapped.

3 FUTURE JACKIE: Doesn't seem to be working out so well for you.

4 SISTER FIONA: Dawnbreakers, now!

5 FUTURE JACKIE: You think I can't handle a few birthday candles?

6 FUTURE JACKIE: You're dead women, sister.

7 SISTER FIONA: M- Maybe so. But we die knowing there's one place on this aborted world...

PAGE TWENTY-SIX

The arrows hit the oil in the gutters and braziers and light up the reflective walls. Blinding light. Darklings burn away around Jackie as he struggles to stay armored up.

1 SISTER FIONA: Where the sun yet burns.

2 SFX: FWOOSH!

page 26, pencil detail

page 26, pencil detail

GE TWENTY-SEVEN

:kie struggles to maintain armor in the blinding light as he fights off the maining Magdalenas. It looks like an even match now.

FUTURE JACKIE: Not enough.

FUTURE JACKIE: Not.

FUTURE JACKIE: Nearly.

FUTURE JACKIE: Enough.

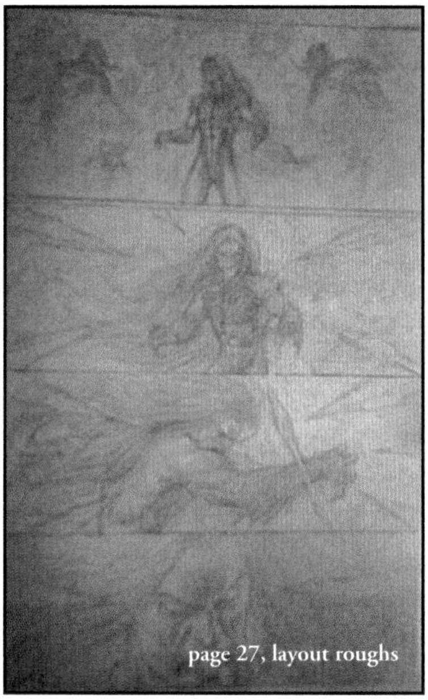

page 27, layout roughs

PAGE TWENTY-EIGHT

From inside a chamber in the buried tunnel. A stone is pushed away from the wall and then tumbles down with Grey. The troop stumbles through the hole to see the weird, HR Gieger-like tomb of what they believe to be the Magdalena. It looks like a big cocoon of dull, black plastic with a bas relief sarcophagus lid featuring a beautiful woman.

1 SFX: Skkkkrt-

2 SFX: Chonk!

3 SFX: Rrrmmmmbl!

4 GREY: D'oh!

5 GREY: Well...

6 GREY: It's a tomb alright.

7 SISTER ISABEL: I pictured something...

8 GREY: Less grotesque?

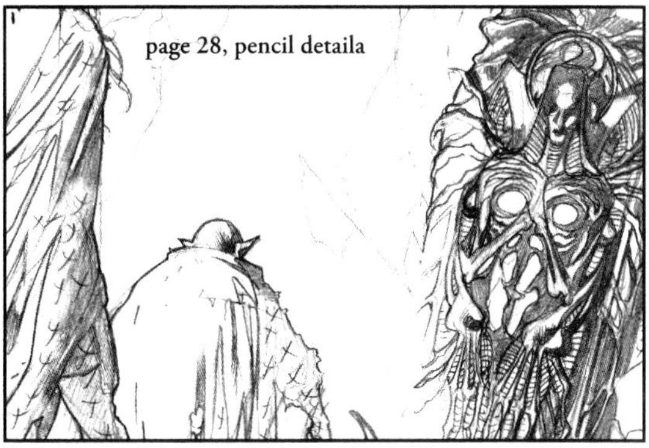

page 28, pencil detaila

GE TWENTY-NINE

e boy walks forward with the shard of the Spear and cuts the top layers en. They peel back like layers of plastic garbage bags. A voice calls out to em from behind. It's Jackie.

SISTER COLLEEN: This is it. It has to be.

3OY: The tomb must be opened.

SISTER ISABEL: Let him. He knows the way.

OP FUTURE JACKIE: Stop!

FUTURE JACKIE: You don't know what you're doing!

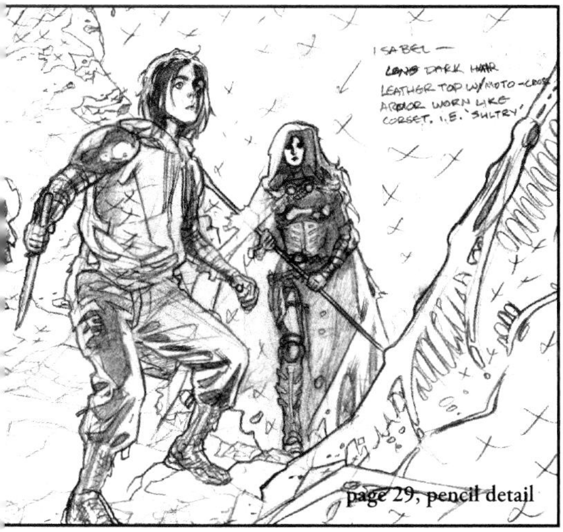
ISABEL —
LONG DARK HAIR
LEATHER TOP W/MOTO-CROSS
ARMOR WORN LIKE
CORSET. I.E. 'SULTRY'

page 29, pencil detail

PAGE THIRTY

Jackie is looking pretty beat-up. He's maintaining his armor, but his skin is bare in some places and open wounds are visible. Isabel and Colleen cross spears in front of Jackie to bar his way. Boy keeps cutting. Grey looks uncomfortable.

1 SISTER ISABEL: It's him!

2 FUTURE JACKIE: You idiots are going to kill us all! This isn't the tomb of the Magdalena!

3 SISTER ISABEL: Liar! You try to undermine our faith even at the moment of our greatest triumph.

4 FUTURE JACKIE: You don't understand. There was another adversary, before the Magdalena, a being of angelic force. My opposite--

5 SISTER ISABEL: Don't listen to him boy. Keep cutting.

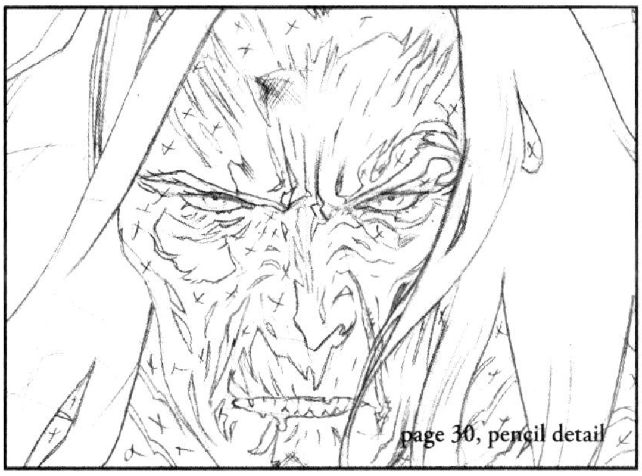

page 30, pencil detail

PAGE THIRTY-ONE

The kid is getting deeper as Jackie commands Grey to stop him. Grey ignores Jackie.

1 FUTURE JACKIE: We fought for centuries. Killing one another from generation to generation in a futile cycle until I trapped her here.

2 FUTURE JACKIE: This isn't her tomb…

3 FUTURE JACKIE: It's her prison.

4 GREY: Don't stop, kid!

5 FUTURE JACKIE: I buried her power, but I could never extinguish it.

6 FUTURE JACKIE: You see it now? Decades of backed up power seeking release!

7 BOY: The tomb must be opened.

PAGE THIRTY-TWO

Jackie rants now as Grey ignores him. Light begins to pour from the torn sarcophagus. The sisters are transfixed.

1 FUTURE JACKIE: Stop him, Grey! I order you!

2 GREY: I don't think so, boss.

3 FUTURE JACKIE: You must obey! You're a part of me!

4 GREY: Maybe that's why I can't. I'm the part of you that you tried to leave behind.

5 GREY: The part that wants all of this to end at last.

6 BOY: The tomb--

7 SISTER ISABEL: It's beautiful. It's beautiful!

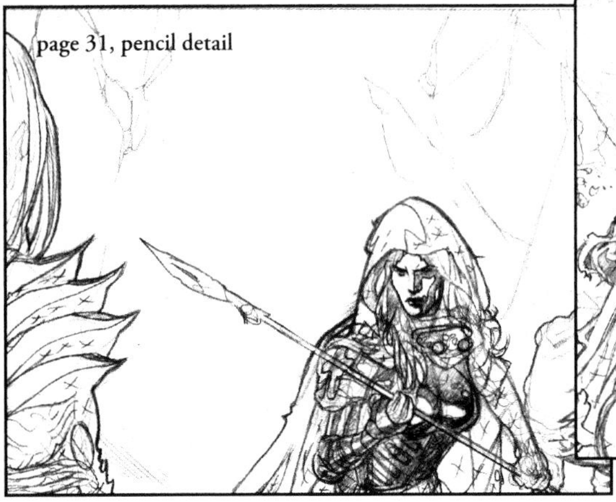
page 31, pencil detail

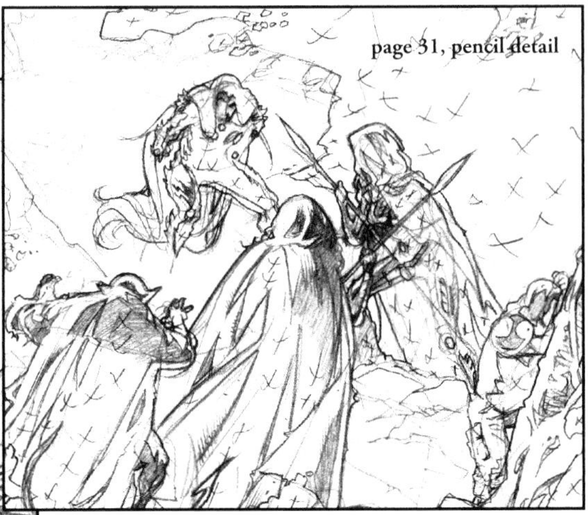
page 31, pencil detail

SCENE FOURTEEN- PAGE THIRTY-THREE

ARTIST: Someone that can do a killer "frozen in time moment". Maybe something painterly.

PAGE THIRTY-THREE

Splash- This should be a straight on shot of the sarcophagus now ripped open from top to bottom. Blinding light pours out, disintegrating any Sisters or Darklings we see in foreground. In the center of the light we see a ghostly after image of The Angelus letting the energy pour out of her, Phoenix-like. Richard Corben? I can dream.

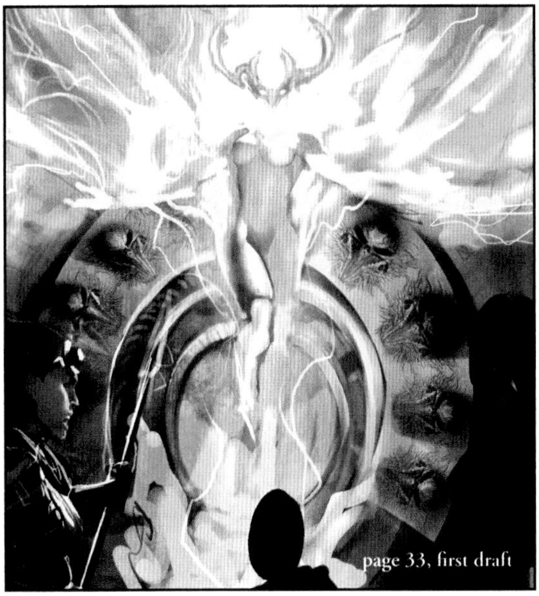
page 33, first draft

SCENE FIFTEEN PAGE THIRTY-FOUR

ARTIST: Same as page one.

PAGE THIRTY-FOUR

The white light rushes out over NYC shattering everything in its path, Akira-style. The wave of destruction sweeps over the earth, cracking it and leaving only smoldering chunks afloat in open space.

1 NARR: And the light that had been buried sprang forth and raced over the blackened world.

2 NARR: Centuries of pent up power unleashed in a nanosecond.

3 NARR: The irresistible light and the immovable dark clashed like great titan over the face of the world, unleashing holocausts of pure force that made man' once-mighty nuclear weapons pale in comparison.

4 NARR: Like immense dragons, continents wide, they twisted and thrashed until the oceans burned away, and the very earth beneath them crumbled apar and fell into the void of space.

5 NARR: Mere minutes after the boy first cut into the Angelus' tomb, the plan and all who stood upon it, were mere cinders spinning their last remaining hea out into the implacable cold of space.

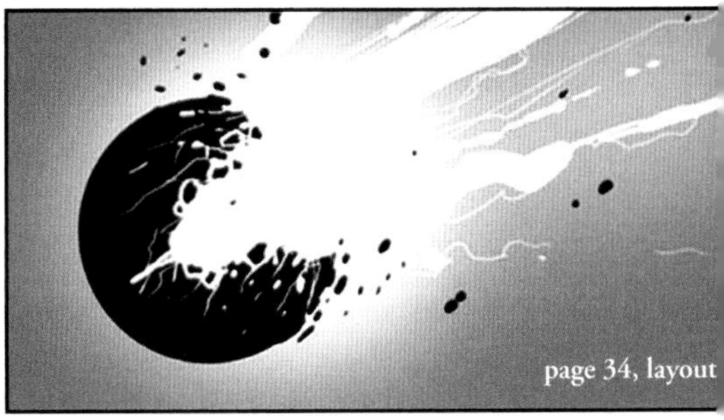
page 34, layout

ᴀGE THIRTY-FIVE

ut to an abandoned fairgrounds in the Meadowlands. A lone carnival tent ands in the moonlight. It is lit from within. It is the fortune teller tent om the midway. Inside Jackie stands enraged before a psychic dude who ares down at a set of bones cast on a small table in front of him. Jackie rows down a wad of hundreds for another reading. The psychic refuses.

PSYCHIC: That is how our world ends, Mr. Estacado.

PSYCHIC: And that is how you finally die.

JACKIE: Roll them again.

PSYCHIC: Mr. Estacado, the rest of our carnival moved on hours ago. e'll never catch up if--

ACKIE: Roll those bones again.

PSYCHIC: I don't want your money, sir.

PSYCHIC: I've read the bones six times now and the outcome is always e same. You'll be buying nothing more than a lie.

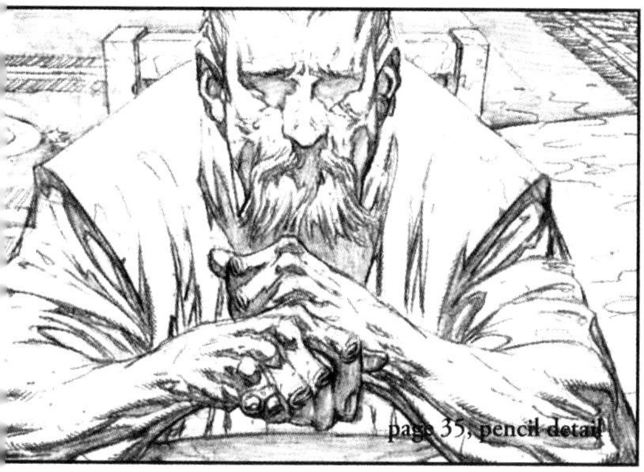

page 35, pencil detail

GE THIRTY-SEVEN

ıma rushes to psychic's side to comfort him. He's just been through an or- al. He can't believe the visions he just relayed. Were they really the future? ıma tells him he did good either way. her last line is over a shot of Jackie lking away from the tent and into the darkness.

MAMA: Oh, my boy. My boy.

'SYCHIC: It was real, Mama. It was real.

'SYCHIC: Not like the show we sell the rubes, but the gift, like Papa had. ıw it all.

ʌAMA: Shhh. You drink now.

'SYCHIC: I was so scared that I lied at first, but then the visions came ɛr me.

'SYCHIC: I don't know if I really saw the future, or if panic made me tell tale. I just don't know, Mama.

ʌAMA: Be still, son. You looked into the face of evil today and you set a mbling stone in his path.

ʌAMA: That is the highest calling your power will ever provide. And if ı cause evil pause, even for a moment...

:AP MAMA: Then you have given the world a precious gift.

CAP: Next: RED RIBBON!

PAGE THIRTY-SIX

Jackie instead pulls a gun and levels it at the psychic, demanding a new outcome. Psychic talks Jackie out of it. Jackie staggers from the tent, truly afraid and stunned.

1 JACKIE: Forget the money, then.

2 PSYCHIC: G- Go ahead. But know that I foresaw this moment, as well.

3 PSYCHIC: Know that my murder is the first step on the path that leads to your ruined future.

4 PSYCHIC: Throw off the yoke of The Darkness, Mr. Estacdo, and those who would seek to use it through you...

5 PSYCHIC: While you can.

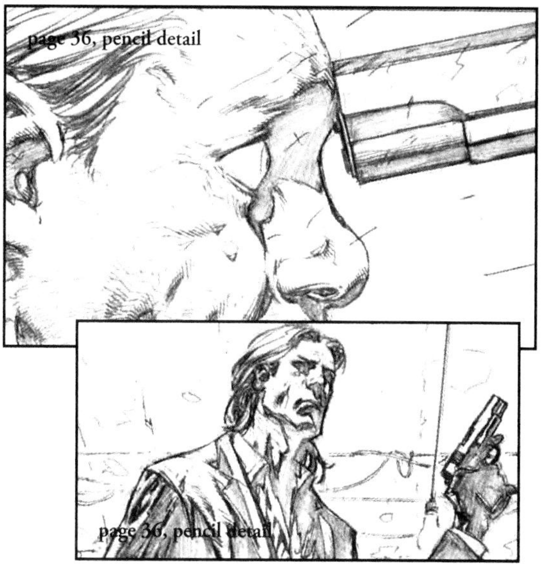

page 36, pencil detail

page 36, pencil detail

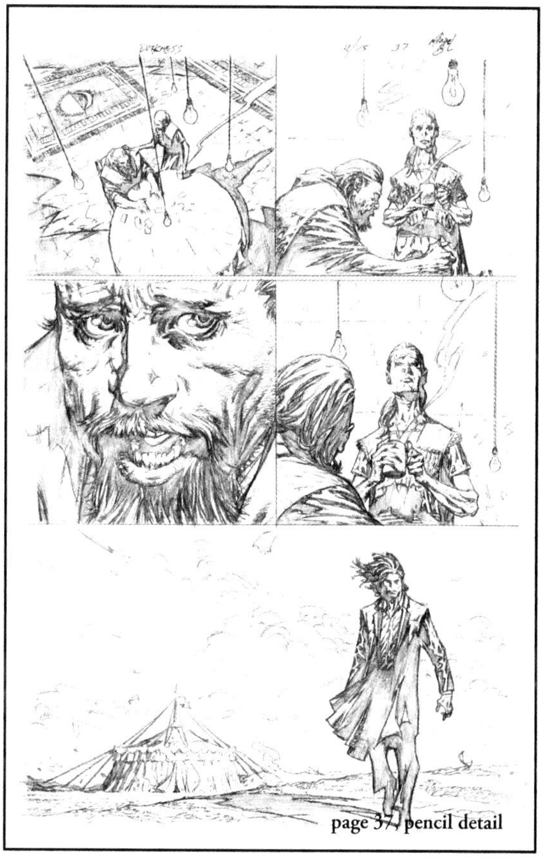

page 37, pencil detail

Jump into the Top Cow Universe with The Darkness!

PHIL HESTER • MICHAEL BROUSSARD
ACCURSED
VOLUME 1

The Darkness
Accursed vol.1

written by:
Phil Hester

pencils by:
Michael Broussard

Mafia hitman Jackie Estacado was bot blessed and cursed on his 21st birthday whe he became the bearer of The Darkness, a elemental force that allows those who wiel it access to an otherwordly dimension an control over the demons who dwell ther Forces for good in the world rise up to fac Jackie and the evil his gift represents, bu there is one small problem. In this story...the are the bad guys.

Now's your chance to read "Empire the first storyline by the new creative tea of **Phil Hester** (*Firebreather, Green Arrov*) and **Michael Broussard** (*Unholy Union*) tha marked the shocking return of *The Darknes* to the Top Cow Universe!

Book Market Edtion
(ISBN 13: 978-1-58240-958-0) $9.99

ENNIS • WOHL • CONEY • LOBDELL • JENKINS
SILVESTRI • BENITEZ • LANSANG • TAN • FINCH • KEOWN
COMPENDIUM
VOLUME 1

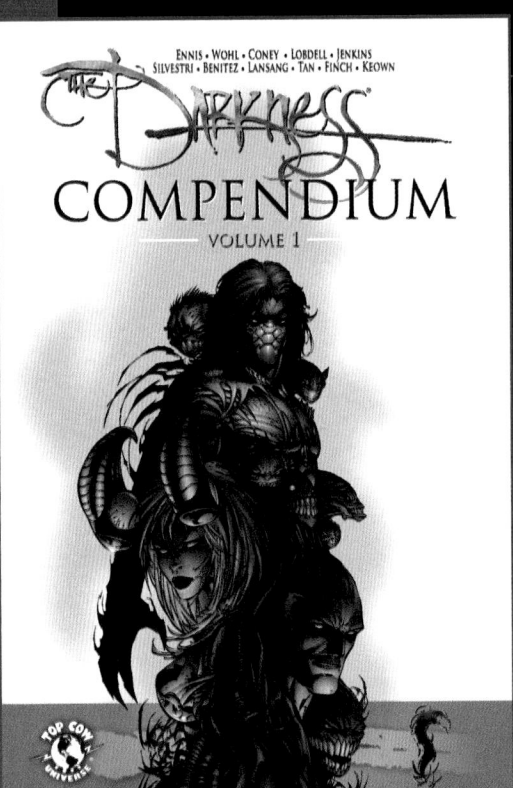

The Darkness
Compendium vol.1

written by:
Garth Ennis, Paul Jenkins, Scott Lobdell
pencils by:
Marc Silvestri, Joe Benitez and more!

On his 21st birthday, the awesom and terrible powers of the Darkness awake within Jackie Estacado, a mafia hitman fo the Franchetti crime family. There's nothin like going back to the beginning and readin it all over again-- issues #1-40, plus th complete run of the *Tales of the Darknes* series collected into one trade paperbac See how the Darkness first appeared an threw Jackie into the chaotic world of th supernatural. Get the first appearances The Magdalena and more!

SC (ISBN 13: 978-1-58240-643-5) $59.9
HC (ISBN 13: 978-1-58240-992-7) $99.9

Read more *Witchblade* in these trade paperback collections.

Witchblade
volume 1 - volume 5

written by:
Ron Marz
pencils by:
Mike Choi, Stephen Sadowski,
Keu Cha, Chris Bachalo,
Stjepan Sejic and more!

Get in on the ground floor of Top Cow's flagship title with these affordable trade paperback collections from Ron Marz's series-redefining run on Witchblade! Each volume collects a key story arc in the continuing adventures of Sara Pezzini and the Witchblade.

volume 1
collects issues #80-#85
(ISBN: 978-1-58240-906-1) $9.99

volume 2
collects issues #86-#92
(ISBN: 978-1-58240-886-6)
U.S.D. $14.99

volume 3
collects issues #93-#100
(ISBN: 978-1-58240-887-3)
U.S.D. $14.99

volume 4
collects issues #101-109
(ISBN: 978-1-58240-898-9)
U.S.D. $17.99

volume 5
collects issues #110-115:
First Born issues #1-3
(ISBN: 978-1-58240-899-6)
U.S.D. $17.99

volume 6
collects issues #116-120
(ISBN: 978-1-60706-041-3)
U.S.D. $14.99

New York City Police Detective Sara Pezzini is the bearer of the Witchblade, a mysterious artifact that takes the form of a deadly and powerful gauntlet. Now Sara must try to control the Witchblade and learn its secrets, even as she investigates the city's strangest, most supernatural crimes.

Premium collected editions

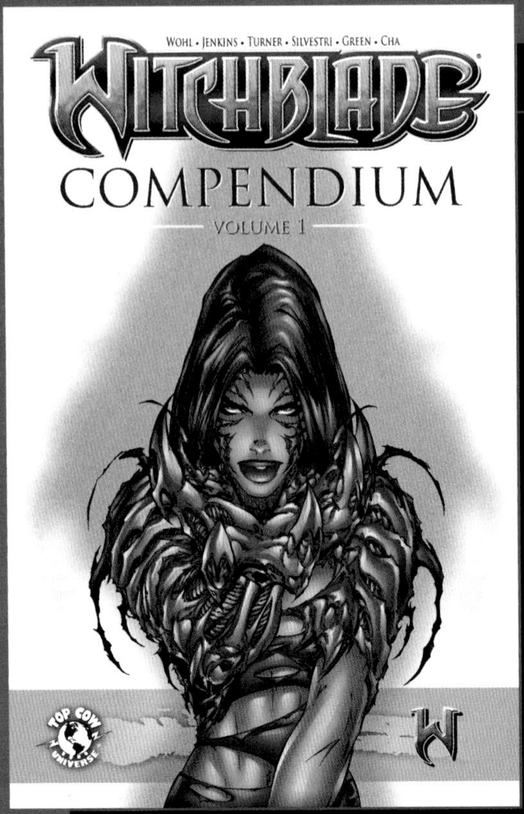

WOHL • JENKINS • TURNER • SILVESTRI • GREEN • CHA
WITCHBLADE
COMPENDIUM
VOLUME 1

Witchblade
Compendium vol.1

written by:
David Wohl, Christina Z.,
Paul Jenkins
pencils by:
Michael Turner, Randy Green
Keu Cha and more!

From the hit live-action television series to the current Japanese anime, *Witchblade* has been Top Cow's flagship title for over a decade. There's nothing like going back to the beginning and reading it all over again. This massive collection houses issues #1-50 in a single edition for the first time. See how the Witchblade chose Sara and threw her into the chaotic world of the supernatural. Get the first appearances of Sara Pezzini, Ian Nottingham, Kenneth Irons and Jackie Estacado in one handy tome!

SC (ISBN 13: 978-1-58240-634-3) $59.99
HC (ISBN 13: 978-1-58240-798-2) $99.99

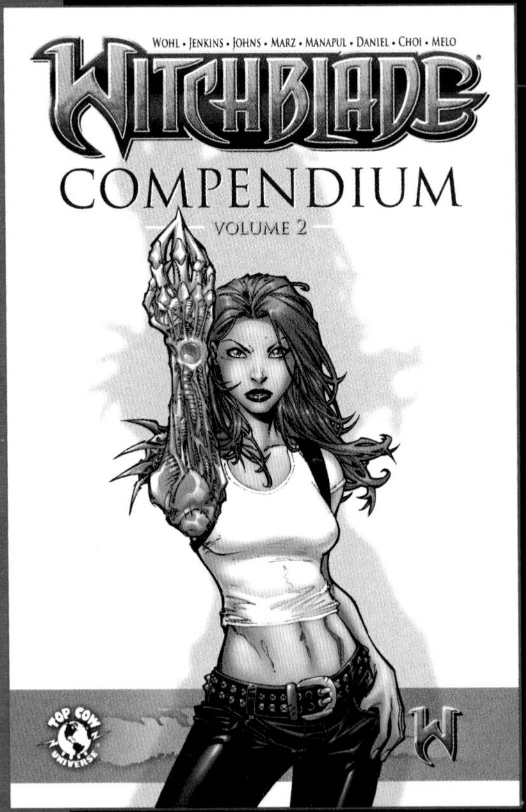

WOHL • JENKINS • JOHNS • MARZ • MANAPUL • DANIEL • CHOI • MELO
WITCHBLADE
COMPENDIUM
VOLUME 2

Witchblade
Compendium vol.2

written by:
David Wohl, Christina Z.,
Paul Jenkins and Ron Marz
pencils by:
Michael Turner, Randy Green
Keu Cha, Mike Choi and more!

From the "Death Pool" story arc featurin the death of a major Witchblade character heading up the NYPD's Special Cases Uni Witchblade bearer Sara Pezzini and her ne partner Patrick Gleason find themselve with more questions than answers as the investigations lead them from haunte museums, dark alleys and forgotten tunne beneath New York City. Meanwhile, th enigmatic Curator leaves a trails of clues f Sara, ultimately leading her to the explosi origin of the Witchblade itself!

Collects Witchblade issues #51-100

SC (ISBN 13: 978-1-58240-731-9) $59.9
HC (ISBN 13: 978-1-58240-960-3) $99.9